G000075113

INDIA THROUGH THE AGES

INDIA THROUGH THE AGES

BHARAT BHUSHAN GUPTA

NIYOGI
BOOKS

Published by:

NIYOGI BOOKS

D-78, Okhla Industrial Area, Phase-1
New Delhi-110 020, India
Tel: 91-11-26816301, 49327000
Fax: 91-11-26810483, 26813830
email: niyogibooks@gmail.com
website: www.niyogibooks.com

© Bharat Bhushan Gupta

ISBN:978-81-89738-00-6
Year of Publication-2006
2nd Impression-2009
3rd Impression-2012

All rights reserved. No part of the publication may be reproduced,
stored in a retrieval system or transmitted, in any form or by any means,
electronic, mechanical or otherwise, without prior permission.

Printed at
Niyogi Offset Pvt. Ltd., New Delhi, India

Acknowledgement

A book is a creative inning!
All my family members
were a tower of inspiration,
chiming my inner clock...

How do I thank
Mr. Nirmal Kanti Bhattacharjee of
Sahitya Akademi!
His consummate editorial touches
gave the final mould to my clay.

I deeply appreciate
the publication strategy of
Mr. Bikash De Niyogi of
Niyogi Books, New Delhi.
He was all ready to sail at a short notice.

Dr. S.S. Bhattacharjee was a special reader,
who had a foretaste of the work,
offering valuable suggestions
at every stage.

*In memory of innocent
inhabitants of the subcontinent
who lost their lives and their homes
in a year of mad fury.*

Contents

Contents

Contents

Contents

Contents

Introduction

The great drama of life has been revolving on Earth since infinity. Time sets a new stage after each Ice Age, when life freezes underneath to redefine geographical boundaries, only to reappear afresh. It is beleived there have been at least four major Ice Ages in the Earth's past. What were once seas and oceans become mountains, fertile plains turn into deserts. Man starts his journey all over again. In time, mobility and curiosity sets fresh stages and standards. Born from the womb of Mother Nature, each participant expresses beauty and grandeur in a variety of moods and colours. After playing their allotted role they leave the stage. This cycle of change goes on endlessly. Civilizations in this cycle are only brief interludes in time and space. The world keeps evolving and dissolving, growing and decaying, through cycle after cycle.

Eons ago, in the pre-dawn of history, Indian sages made a tryst with destiny. They earnestly said, "There is no pleasure in the mundane, there is delight in greatness." They dared to chant:

> Lead me from the unreal to the real,
> From darkness to light,
> From death to immortality!

It is this striving for truth, perfection and universal oneness that has lent an immortal flame to the Indian civilization. During the high and the low moments of achievements, the vast Indian masses might have been illiterate, but never ignorant.

What is civilization?

Civilization is a cultural entity involving values, ideals, artistic expressions and moral qualities shared by individual members of society. The promotion of civilization requires absence of fear and existence of social order. Does the competitiveness of modern times produce fellowship amongst its members? Do the little comforts that make our life easy and pleasant, the only requisites of civilization? Is controlling Nature in all its manifestations a sign of growth?

Civilization ensures fearlessness and the rule of law for freedom of mind and body. It is unrestricted development of personality. According to individual capacities, law in civilized societies offers equal opportunities to all for giving self-expression to whatever is within. Civilization, therefore, is not mere material growth, bound to the place of birth. It is a cultural creation of art, knowledge, conscious awareness, realization and wisdom gathered from experiences of the past. Civilization always seeks new homes where agreeable conditions exist. When people are free from fear and insecurity, curiosity, the mother of all pursuits is created. Man is then on the road to civilization. Contrarily, it begins to decline when impulses to creativity are no more growing; when laws of land are not enforced; when social cohesiveness in population becomes an instrument for the state to play with.

It is in homogeneity and togetherness that the seeds of civilization are sown. The first man did not show his prowess just for himself. It was for him and his woman. They created the first fire, the first home, the first village, the first song and dance. Along the bonfire were the dazzling creations of the new born, the tiny humanity. Facing the capricious fury of nature, they left their homes to migrate to better and safer places.

With the element of intellect growing in each generation, humans are not destined to be the vanishing dinosaurs.

As long as a society preserves the great gift called dharma (righteousness), barbarism remains at bay. Cultural creation, its maintenance, preservation and adaptation are perennially required for its nourishment.

Movement of civilization

Through centuries, streams of invaders came; time blended them to the mother culture of the soil. With tolerance, acceptance and assimilation as the abiding qualities, they consigned to history all bitterness, misery and massacre, accepting happiness and sorrow with yogic indifference as mere turns of fate. *Ahimsa* and peaceful co-existence has been their *raison d'etre*. History has taught them how to handle diversity of race, culture, religion and life. They assimilated this complex maze into a healthy unified whole. Any community in India, today, can walk with the crowd without losing its identity. Out of this amalgam of cultures, history has begotten a new Indian race.

When a region grows arid, it is not able to support life. People then move to other, more fertile regions. They carry with them their skills, knowledge and memories. They take along with them their animals, with which their lives have remained closely connected. Ancient Indian civilization developed when the Aryans from Central Asia and northern Europe sought a new life on the borders of the river Indus. Thus grew the present Indian civilization, built and enriched by generations of new forces. The wheel of change keeps moving at its own leisurely pace. Life ceaselessly keeps seeking fulfillment. It is then that imagination roams in the skies, observing the play of nature. Long observation and experience produces conclusions. These keep flowing on to the coming generations, in the form of experience.

Man is then truly on the road to civilization.

Permanence of change

The cycle of evolution and dissolution can be explained by a story from Indian mythology. It is from an incident in the marriage party of Lord Shiva, the earliest God of the Hindus. The marriage party consisted of a conglomeration of men and animals. There was a variety of men, animals and other strange faces representing different constituents of society. When the crowd reached the residence of his consort goddess Parvati, one of the bride's curious relatives was anxious to know the details of the family to which the bridegroom belonged!

She inquired from the bridegroom, "What is the name of your father?"
"Brahma (God of Creation)," Shiva replied.
"Who is your grand father?" The woman still not satisfied, further asked.
"Vishnu (God of Sustenance)," Shiva again answered.

Perplexed with the two replies and still not able to comprehend the earthly lineage, the old woman again asked,

"Please tell me who is your great-grandfather?"
"That I am," humbly replied Shiva, bowing his head in reverence.

So runs the cycle of creation and dissolution and again creation. It also explains the idea amongst the Hindus about transmigration of the soul.

The barbarian, seeking food, shelter and his primary needs, is at once set on this road. Focussed on survival, life in him develops an impulse to achieve. He becomes strong and sturdy for the game. The physical strength so acquired pays rich dividends in the chase for food. Gradually fear is gone. Instead, there is a dynamic spirit of adventure. New vistas are opened with boundless opportunities for a better life.

In the next cycle, the barbarian-turned-adventurer becomes a story of success. Constituents of happiness are now in his grasp. There is freedom from want and drudgery. There is another precious element at his disposal that was so far denied to him. It is leisure, the time to wonder. Man can now wonder and imagine about the mysteries of nature. There is time for feelings and emotions to be expressed in art, literature and poetry. Listening to the ecstasy of birds, noise and thunder of clouds, the roaring of seas and oceans, rhythmic music of waterfalls and streams, he can now make his own music. Conscious awareness becomes free and provides limitless scope for creative functions.

Soon after, the ego in man wakes up. Human tendencies of greed and competition for survival are born. Man often falls prey to temptation of material comfort engaging himself in strife and exploitation. The two negative tendencies consume his vigour. He now exists without his earlier strength for curiosity and imagination, leading himself to self-destruction.

This is the story of all— individuals and groups; societies and nations.

When civilizations so destroy themselves by self-destruction or neglect or both, there are always others waiting to take over. For one, the cycle has taken a full circle, for the other, it starts again.

Fig. I Cycle of Change

The area of darkness

The cycle of change (**Figure I**) has a dark zone of exploitation, and internal or external strife. This area lies between civilization and barbarism. It refers to exploitation in human relationship between the clever and the ignorant. When in civilized societies, compassion and fairness are ignored, one enters the area of darkness. When material growth is pursued without regard to morals and values are manipulated or when established laws are trampled, the way to barbarism lies wide open.

The tenure of man on earth therefore becomes a pilgrimage from ignorance to learning. When life awakens in him, he starts moving through the cycle of change; when confined to bread alone, it turns inert.

Four pillars of civilization

Four broad factors influence the march of culture and civilization. They are:

1. Geography

Movement of civilizations and cultures bear an over-powering influence of geography in moulding the mental and physical spirit. Societies surrounded by seas take to sailing the high seas. They discover new lands, find new routes to different countries and in time rule the seas. Those in mountainous regions are tough people, negotiating rocks and hills. Full of strength and energy, they are always looking for adventure. This makes them strong, daring and willing to take risks.

Hot and humid climate has its own influence. It is generally able to provide essentials for survival with comparative ease, promoting settled habits. This develops softness towards life, and lethargy towards action. There is penchant for contemplation, imagination likes to fly lofty heights. Story telling, conversation and debate occupy the leisure that is available in plenty. From a study of change in different societies, it has emerged that geography has had a dominant role in enforcing changes that ultimately direct lives of individuals. Inspite of political and social circumstances, geography counters all other kinds of pressures. If ever due to political or economic reasons, changes are enforced against geography of the country, geopolitics interferes to neutralize that change. Geography does not therefore care even for economic or political expedience. Geographical environment shapes the physical constitution of people and the political constitution of states.

2. Economics: Pursuit for survival

Life is linked to economics. For a long time hunting animals was the earliest economic pursuit to satisfy hunger. Thereafter, perhaps a homemaker with nothing to eat found some seeds from the soil that satisfied hunger. Thus may have started the process of obtaining food from the soil. As agriculture appeared a more stable source, it gradually replaced hunting. With agriculture arose other problems that were absent in hunting. Now the soil satisfied hunger. The uncertainties of weather taught storage of food. As needs multiplied, so did the complexities. Cultivation of soil required a settled life. This encouraged establishment of villages. Several hands were required to assist different functions of sowing, cutting and cleaning, etc. The family emerged, as a joint venture. After a hard day's toil, men would sit around to converse and exchange views on weather that vitally affected them. Thus began the value of experience that offered solutions to intricate problems from past experience.

With security of food, possession, competitiveness, cruelty and greed found a fertile soil. The thought for tomorrow bred anxieties for tomorrow. Agriculture helped emergence of modern civilization. It could now provide time without worries. Leisure, the great gift of nature was now available. Man could think and imagine about the wonders in the universe. While it brought in certain positive impacts, it also brought slavery and bonded labour. This arrangement would continue for thousands of years until industrialization. This change refers to the safety and security accruing from a growing agricultural system or the crippling effect of slavery and would introduce new challenges, bringing the present age of information. During the Industrial era, the principle of possession, competition and greed yielded results for some and misery to many. The machines saved labour, bringing riches and leisure. Some of the great works in art, science and literature developed in pockets of such civilized societies.

Information science in recent years has dissolved these negative tendencies bringing the world closer. Co-operation, not competition, is the modern *mantra* for success. The world has shrunk in time and distance so that action in one part has an immediate effect on others. Economic activity can no longer be pursued in isolation. The entire globe is getting to be one family. If one prospers others can not be ignored.

3. Political organization

It is a strange contradiction that human beings by nature are social but by instinct anti-social. They fear society more and are less fond of it. Co-operation under the circumstances becomes a compulsion for existence; it does not emerge naturally. When a hunter accepts the rules of the chase, he joins his fellows for the kill. Left to himself, he would have liked freedom to act as he pleased. Tribes and clans may have been the first to be united in barter and trade. Thereafter, there, may have appeared village communities as local administrative organizations framing and enforcing laws. Gradually, the integration of larger areas resulted in the formation of the state. They combined the power of the people and coordinated the interests of different communities. The nation-states came into existence to control internal conflicts and wage external wars.

To this day, a king, a prime minister, a dictator or an army-general rules so long as either people willingly or through deceit, continue to extend their support.

4. Morals and values

Of the three pillars discussed above, morals and values are the strongest elements to sustain a civilization. Persuasive forces are employed by the wielders of power to enforce morals and values. One of the strongest amongst them is religion. How did religion come into existence? The element of fear created gods. Primitive life in the beginning was full of danger, violence and hunger. When the 'savage' in man was not able to understand the cause of a particular phenomenon, he attributed it to some spirit inside the object. His hope of divine help in misfortune and gratitude in good fortune made him believe in gods.

The wise and clever amongst them took charge to convert belief into faith to which a name was given to enforce morals and values. Myths and taboos helped the religious leaders strengthen their hold. In due course, when knowledge grew and earlier mystic phenomena began to be explained with logic and reason, a natural change set in. The more advanced societies began enforcing the moral values, and became less dependent on religion.

India Through The Ages introduces readers to a panoramic view of her history and civilization. The book brings the saga of her sages and scientists, warriors and vagabonds, poets and philosophers, who, at various periods scripted the destiny of the Indian subcontinent. It enables conscious and sentimental men and women, to understand the national philosophy that has made Indians a curious mixture of extremes. What conditions and circumstances led Indian society to be passive and reflective rather than acquisitive and combative? The reader may be able to find answers to the enigma that makes Indian society one of the happiest on earth, although her majority of people remains poor!

Chapter I
The Indian Story

The Indian story begins with immigration of pastoral tribes from Europe and West Asia. Tranquillity and a salubrious climate in the foothills of the Himalayas nourished a life of thought. Imagination under the scenic beauty of nature, produced the Vedas. As imagination flowered, new ideas, reasoning and the spirit of self-communion gave birth to the metaphysics of the Puranas and Upanishads. With each coming generation, the philosophy of existence produced an intensity of faith. *Sanatan Dharma,* the religion of the Hindus, brought the people of the land together.

As time passed, personal stakes created insensitivity towards change. The weeds that had grown over centuries, were thwarting forward movement. They required pruning. This brought the Age of Enlightenment which gave India great souls like Mahavira Jain, Gautama and Kapila. They stirred human consciousness back to nobleness. Abandoning a life of luxury, they voluntarily went into the wilderness to preach the values of life. The country was blessed with wise men like Chanakya, a compassionate king like Ashoka, an intellectual king like Vikramaditya, a synthesizer of cultures like Kanishka and a magnanimous king like Harsha Vardhana. The rule of such kings and their predecessors brought about a Golden Age in the land of Bharata. For a thousand years the adventure loving sailed to distant lands for trade and commerce, the strong defended the frontiers and men of intellect produced works of arts, science, poetry, astronomy, mathematics and yoga.

Again, leisure that produces works of value was consumed in petty in-fighting, inter-caste quarrels and wealth accumulation. To destroy man-made distortions, nature has her own immutable laws. Waves of invaders arrived to fill the vacuum. Inspired by a new religion, born in the sands of Arabia, Islam had transformed the infighting Arab tribes into an organized and disciplined force. They would conquer the country to make it their home.

After the initial turbulence of conquest and plunder, the Mother Culture of the land resumed the process of integration and blending. While warrior-kings lived lavishly in the country, scholars and refugees from Arabia, Turkey and Iran, came to India seeking better opportunities to lead a new life in the land of promise. Amongst the many whose genius helped elevate arts, literature and culture of the newly adopted country, were Al Beiruni and Amir Khusrau. Within a few centuries, the culture of the soil became the culture of their soul. With time the new amalgam was blessed further with the gift of saints like Guru Nanak and Kabir.

What was happening in the West when India was being drowned in petty religious feuds?

After centuries of similar religious struggles, science was compelling religion to yield her dominant position. Having captured the imagination of the people, mythological fantasies interested them no more. As new knowledge based on rationality discouraged fear of the unknown, natural phenomena began to be clearly understood. Men would rather accept reason than obey what their priests asked them to believe.

This new-found self-confidence, provided by science, created an urge for adventure and achievement. The sea-faring nations sent their sailors and traders for commerce and to discover sea routes to new lands. Courage and confidence rewarded them with the discovery of new continents and shorter routes to rich centres of trade. Amongst several European nations, Britain was superior by far.

> Colombus found a world, and had no chart,
> Save one that faith deciphered in the skies.

In India, the warrior-Sultans, after centuries of ease and licentiousness life had become enervated. Having lost their earlier martial qualities, they had turned complacent. There were others waiting in the wings to replace them. Charged with the fresh zeal of conquest, they started their invasions. In the green valley of Farghana, a brave prince Babar as fascinating as Alexander, won the crown of Delhi. Babar founded the Mughal Empire. His grandson, Akbar, laid the foundations of the first Indian nation state where people of all religions could live on equal terms. First to ban cow slaughter, the greatest horseman, the best swordsman, and one of the greatest architects, Akbar had a passion for metaphysics and patronized wise men like Birbal, Faizi, Tansen and Rahim. Poet Tulsi Das, authored the great epic, Ramayana, in his times.

Within a century, the Mughal Empire disintegrated. The cruelty of Jahangir, wastefulness of Shahjehan and the intolerance of Aurengzeb, converted a strong nation state into scores of independent regions, with each fighting against the other. In the last several centuries, Hindus and Muslims had managed to pool their spiritual resources to build one of the greatest civilizations known to the world. It was all lost within two decades of Aurengzeb's death.

Like individuals, the destiny of nations also depends on the ancient theory of Karma. Sea-faring traders from a small island of Europe, were soon destined to meet and provide the perquisites of extraordinary progress made by science and political freedom. When Britain became master of India, East truly met West. Indian intellectuals, exposed to achievements in science, philosophy, literature, morals and manners, prospered. The two cultures, wrapped in an intimate relationship, redefined Indian culture. Quality of administration, pioneering local self government works and above all the gift of technology, so far missing in the country, began to enrich the soil. These achievements, spanning over two centuries, established a permanent remembrance in all hearts. The discipline, dignity and devotion to duty and the rule of law, shown by British administrators, army and business persons, was to become a model for the coming generations.

It all started with social reforms introduced by Ram Mohan Roy. English language opened the works of Greeks, Germans and French philosophers and scientists. Nationalism and an urge for knowledge again grew amongst people. Suddenly a spate of genius appeared on the Indian horizon. The ignited souls of Vivekananda, Rabindranath Tagore and Mohammed Iqbal revolutionized intellectual environment.

In politics, the *Magna Carta* of Britain, Garibaldi of Italy, Rousseau and Voltaire in France, and George Washington of North America, provided inspiration for liberty. Soon after, Badruddin Tyabji, Gangadhar Tilak, Banerji, Surendra Nath Banerji and Gopal Krishna Gokhale, the first line of intellectuals, appeared on the Indian scene to spearhead the cause of nationalism. The task to awaken the masses, living in the numerous Indian villages was colossal. It required someone who could translate the misery and pain of millions, living and speaking different, languages.

An apostle of truth and non-violence arrived on the Indian scene. He had practised in South Africa, how to bend the law-loving and powerful Britain with non co-operation and non-violence. Not since Gautama Buddha, had such a one walked on the dusty roads of India. Mohandas Karamchand Gandhi would speak softly and act boldly. His quiet nature and body language would fire men into action. At a time when defying British Law was unthinkable, he meticulously prepared a plan to awaken the entire country.

In the Indian freedom struggle, the Dandi March to break the Salt Law, would go down as a watershed. It showed to the masses that a determined and disciplined people could non-violently break even the British might. India, after the Dandi March was in political turmoil. So far, what intellectuals in large cities like Mumbai, Kolkata and Karachi were finding impossible, was achieved after the Dandi March.

Britain began the mechanism of self-government in order to meet the new challenge. This was to continue and expand until the end of World War II in 1945. After the war, having exhausted both the victors and the vanquished, dissolution of one of the greatest Empire began. A member of the royal family of Britain was entrusted with the complex problem of 'departure with dignity'. With his charming personality, Lord Mountbatten remained focussed to the target assigned to him by his Prime Minister. A naval officer, trained in the traditions of the navy and always in a hurry, he completed his assignment to grant independence to India and Pakistan, months early. During negotiations, the last governor-general of India was required to negotiate with Mahatma Gandhi, the philosopher-saint and the architect of Indian freedom movement; democrats like Jawaharlal Nehru and Sardar Patel and an autocrat like Mohammed Ali Jinnah.

Indian society, immediately after independence, faced the stupendous challenge of sudden change. Again, the Mother Culture of the land that has encouraged pluralism, secularism and non-violence prevailed over communalism. The civilized approach of men at the helm of affairs, including Mountbatten, made them act without being terrified or silenced. They crushed the voice of unreason and hatred with firmness. Within a short period, there was food and shelter for all, a strong army was defending the newly created frontiers; and different people followed their faiths without any hindrance.

The people of New India now had faith in the future!

It is this striving for truth, perfection and universal oneness, that has lent an immortal flame to the Indian civilization. During the high and the low notes of achievements, vast Indian masses might have been illiterate but never ignorant. Through centuries, streams of invaders came and stayed; passage of time blended them to the Mother Culture of the soil. With tolerance, acceptance and assimilation as the abiding qualities, they consigned to history all bitterness, misery and massacre. They accepted both happiness and sorrow with yogic indifference as mere turns of fate. Faith in universal acceptance taught them how to handle the myriad diversities. The Indian nation is truly a bewildering and enchanting medley of people!

Continuity of civilizations

Growth of civilization is a slow process. Like geographical changes, it takes its own slow time. When causes of growth in one country fades away, it appears in another. After a period of rapid growth in the western civilization, it was the turn of the civilization on the banks of the Indus and Ganges to showcase its talents. Ved Vyas wrote the Mahabharata; and Valmiki, the Ramayana. Compiling events that had occurred centuries earlier, these men of literary genius edited earlier ballads into fascinating works. They became the Homers of Indian literature. In the same way. Ashoka and Akbar matched the glory of Alexander and Julius Caesar. Time keeps showing that for nature, everyone fulfils his assigned task and then quietly decays. When the time for something to happen arrives, all other elements fall into their places; the missing link suddenly appears to complete the chain.

Through different steps of economic, moral and political elements the earliest 'savage' moved towards becoming a 'saint'. Hunting and fishing, herding and tilling, building and transport, industry and commerce grew with the development of political structure, starting with the family and ending with the state.

Each successive generation imparts its genius to the next through speech and writing. All great civilizations in the past have developed on the above four pillars. Be it the civilizations of Mohen-jo-daro, Dravidian, Egyptian, Babylonian, Greek, Chinese, Persians or Romans—they all flowered in their time and then perished leaving behind memories. They remind us that nothing exists but atoms; and the law of laws is that of evolution and dissolution everywhere, endlessly repeating itself:

> No single thing abides, but all things flow.
> Fragment to fragment clings; the things thus grow.
> Until we know and name them by degrees
> They melt, and are no more the things we know.
>
> Thou too O earth—thine empires, lands and seas—
> Least, with thy stars of all the galaxies,
> Gloved from the drift like these, like these thou too
> Shall go, Thou art going, hour by hour, like these.

—Lucretius

Chapter II
India Before The Aryans

I saw eternity the other night,
Like a great ring of pure and endless light,
All calm as it was bright;
And round beneath it, Time in hours, days, years,
Driven by spheres.
Like a vast shadow moved, in which the world,
And all her train was hurled.

—Vaugham

India: on planet Earth

The United Nations' flag crest has a map of the world. It is like a globe with the North Pole at the centre. We are used to seeing maps on flat charts. This tends to create inaccuracies. Comparative distances between countries appear unduly longer. A far more accurate perception is obtained on the globe when we observe the globe a little keenly: India is suddenly seen at the centre. Our relationship with countries at once becomes more close and accurate. The Himalayan range in the north and north-east appears as a natural boundary; the oceans surrounding the other three sides complete the picture of a continent.

This makes India, Pakistan, China, Indonesia, Malaya and Indo-China countries quite close. We comprehend far better the ease with which Indians traded with South-Eastern countries, thousands of years ago, how our messengers of religion and culture were winning the hearts of people without armies with only reason and love as their instruments.

Looking north, it is different. The ancient route for enterprising merchants, adventurers, and seekers of knowledge was the famous 'Silk Route'. This extended from China to the borders of Europe touching the northern fringe of the Indian subcontinent. In spite of her strategic position on this vital route, the Indians cared little for the only ancient highway. They had reasons to feel so with almost everything of need amply met. The subcontinent remained a world in itself.

A picture of self-sufficiency

Why did the Indians not move out to seek territories and wealth? Was this due to compulsions of terrain or internal self-sufficiency alone?

Terrain and climate does make men strong and active. This quality was therefore not lacking in them. What conquered the propensity of the people was the environment of peace and contentment where mundane desires were fulfilled with little effort. Fresh water streams and rivers, rivulets and lakes spread all over the country. Productive soil and changing seasons made plenty availability of food and water. Temperate weather induced the mind towards contemplation. Hot and humid climate, the monsoon clouds— all combined to discourage physical action. Elements that give birth to art, religion and a contemplative culture were all available in abundance. All these factors combined to make people of the land contented. The only nourishment that was available was from the internal social system, from within.

This lack of interest in countries outside the national boundaries was to cost her people again and again, dearly.

Influence of geography over history

Geography and chronology are the two eyes of history; it is crucial in formation of national boundaries and culture of countries. On India its influence has been overwhelming. The physical map of the subcontinent shows the high Himalayas in the north, Hindukush mountains in the north-west, Vindhyas and Aravallis in the middle and Western Ghats in the south. The great rivers: Ganges, Indus, Brahmaputra, Narmada, Krishna, Cauveri, and their several tributaries are scattered through the entire land mass. Seas on all three sides, engulf the subcontinent the monsoons provide life-giving water, except in some pockets of Rajasthan, which is a desert zone. All the year round, there is plenty of sunshine; temperate climate and rains in winter provide abundant food supply. This makes the entire environment conducive to the life of thought, imagination and thought activate senses. Thus is born art, theology, metaphysics, poetry, philosophy and literature. The Indian mind being ever so close to nature, developed the philosophy of 'oneness' in thought.

This is not so only with India. Be it the Nile valley in Egypt, Tigris and Euphrates in Mesopotamia (present Iraq) in the Middle East, the small islands around Greece, Indo-Gangetic and Cauveri basins in the Indian subcontinent–the story of all ancient civilizations is the same. Political attitudes and warrior kings may change boundaries, but it is geography that commands movement in societies. Politics is capable of creating only temporary change, only to be forced into submission by natural powers of geographical factors. Similarly science may reduce distances, making flow of people easy, even necessary; the sense of identity developed by geography of the homeland are the real roots. Long after compulsions of economics and adventure mellow, the genes ultimately look for their roots. Their influence is a lasting one.

Physical features

1. The Great Himalayan range

During one of the great convulsions of nature the entire landmass of the Indian subcontinent moved towards Asia. This massive collision produced the Great Himalayas. From shallow depressions to high mountain peaks there is no mountain range anywhere on Earth which has so directly influenced in moulding lives and thoughts of her people. In ancient literature, India is described as 'Himachala setu parayantam'–from Himalayas to Rameshwaram. There are sacred Hindu shrines in Amarnath, Jawalamukhi, Kedarnath, Badrinath, Gangotri, Jamunotri, Pashupatinath (Nepal) and Kailasa.

To Indians of yore, the world ended beyond the Himalayas.

2. The Hindukush range

Since the partition of India, a large part of the Hindukush now forms a boundary of Pakistan. There are porous openings at Khyber in the north, and Bolan and Gomal in mid-western regions. The waves of Aryan immigrants from Caspian Sea and Central Steppes entered this country through these passes. Thereafter Persians followed the Aryans and Alexander followed the Persians–all from these routes. As a national boundary, Hindukush only partially served the purpose of a natural boundary.

3. The Gangetic valley and the Bengal delta

The Ganges and its several tributaries flow from west to east. In a country which stretches from north to south this flow has created 'horizontal areas'. Divided into different geographical regions, the areas from north to south have less connection between themselves than if the rivers had flowed from north to south. In the Gangetic valley, this eastward flow has led to integration of population in a closed area of Uttar Pradesh, Bihar and Bengal, converting it into a dominant force called Aryavarta.

4. The Great Indian desert

The vast desert area lying to the south of Punjab has always been an area of refuge for communities displaced by invasion. It is an extension of the desert girdle, a geographical intrusion into India of Middle East. This area is dissected by the Aravallis. To the west of this range lie the lowlands of Marwar and Gujarat and to the east lies the Malwa plateau. The area, being not very productive, was a refuge to those who could not be assimilated in the fertile land. Described as tribals, they sought shelter in areas generally difficult to reach; they preferred to live in hardship than dishonour.

5. The Vindhyas, Deccan and the Ghats

The tableland below the Vindhyas including the Cauveri delta offer the complete entity of south India similar to the Northern Gangetic Plains. The Deccan is geographically a plateau. It has been a rampart of south India, where northern invaders have never been able to establish their cultural or political authority. Even when dynastic changes frequently occurred in the north, the south maintained its integrity. It never followed the course of events of the north.

The southern region therefore remained controlled by its peculiar character. Its people felt more at home with the adjoining countries. Connected by sea the inhabitants of the coastal south were sea faring. They freely moved to as far as Babylon and Sumeria in the West, and Malaya, Indonesia and other South-Eastern countries on ships. The message of the Vedas and Buddha was propagated by such sea-loving people.

It is the Indo-Gangetic and Cauveri deltas that offered people the luxury of settled habits of life with ever-increasing techniques of agriculture. When recorded history begins from round about BC 3000 these regions contain, as they do even today, the majority of the tribals.

Religious scenario around BC 3000

Religious texts mention snow-capped Himalayas throughout the year. Cold blasts blow over the lands as far as the Vindhyas. Everyone is disturbed. Fear and danger is seen on all the faces. Were the gods of the Universe, Shiva and His escort Parvati annoyed? Was nature planning a *Tandava*-dance? Perhaps she is in deep distress herself? Anything that occurred and generated fear was attributed to Lord Shiva.

Floods or drought, earthquakes or thunder, hot winds or cold; it was His pleasure or annoyance that reached the people from the Lord of Kailasa.

People inhabiting the fertile lands during those days were dark-complexioned. The races from the West were yet to arrive! Besides hunting, agriculture and rearing domestic animals provided them with their means of existence. Some contact with distant regions introduced them to invent tools helpful in reducing their toil. One force that united them across different regions of the subcontinent, was their devotion to Lord Shiva. His abode was in the Himalayas. All life-giving elements like river water and rains came through His blessings. This was the belief they lived on; it was a binding force that kept the fear of the unknown at bay.

Early evidence left behind as the relics of past, give an impression of vast natural wealth with forests, rivers and innumerable ponds and lakes, around which people resided. There were no compulsions of boundaries. Between forest lands, fertile areas were cultivated for food; hunting was mostly for pleasure and rarely as a necessity. There always lurked the danger of wild animals. Humans and animals often confronted each other either as hunter or the hunted. The one, who was able to kill the other, won his life.

During these early days it was a wonder how the subcontinent, with a meagre population and little contact with outside could, would be so inviting to immigrants. The mystery was unveiled in the early 20th century. Excavations brought out two highly organized societies: one in the north, around river Indus and the other in the south around river Cauveri. These regions were among the first in the march of civilization. They had established business contacts by land and sea. Perfume and spices, cotton and silk, shawls and muslin, pearls and rubies, ebony and precious stones, brocades of silver and gold were transported by enterprising merchants in caravans. They fetched fabulous wealth. Tales would begin to be spun around their riches. This, in time, grew into a mystical image of India, an image that still clings to her.

Ancient cultures of the subcontinent

1. Dravidian culture

With the modern methods of excavations and interpretation of sign language, we now know that a great Neolithic culture flourished on the banks of river Cauveri by 4000 BC. The life there was on a much higher level of development. The land was occupied by dark skinned people who were called the Dravidians. They were already a civilized people when the Aryan immigration commenced. From earlier times, gold was mined, pepper cultivated and pearls cultured. These goods were traded in distant lands, mostly by sea-routes. Merchants would go to Sumeria and Babylon with these goods and bring back information and ideas prevalent in those countries. In the subcontinent, the more enterprising would occasionally cross the Vindhyas. It was from them that later Aryans would learn the art of village communities, land tennure and taxation systems. Even to this day, the Deccan is essentially Dravidian in stock and customs, in language, literature and arts. They travelled to reach the north as far as the Himalayas and brought Shiva and Parvati from their permanent residing abode on the Kailasa to south India.

Even to this day, the devotees from South India consider pligrimage to Viswanath temple at Varanasi as one of the most pious and fulfilling acts.

2. Mohen-jo-daro

When Cheops (Khufu) was building his first pyramid in BC 2500 in Egypt, the Indus Valley civilization had well-built houses with sanitary systems. There were household utensils used for cooking, toilet outfits, plain and painted pottery, hand-turned and turned-on-wheels earthen wares, terracotta, and copper coins, etc. The gold and silver jewellery, excavated from these sites from the ancient ruins appear as bright as if they have only been bought recently for a modern wedding.

Until the discovery of Harappa (in west Punjab) and Mohen-jo-daro (in Sindh) Indian civilization was supposed to derive largely from the Vedic Aryans and to a lesser extent from their Dravidian roots. After excavation in Sindh and Punjab, it became evident that an advanced civilization existed here from even earlier times than the Egyptian and Babylonian civilizations. The material of tools excavated from the sites were copper, stone and even bronze. This confirmed that the region possessed sufficient skills in metallurgy and craftsmanship to be able to produce such artistic works. At Mohen-jo-daro, the entire city is well-planned, built with burnt bricks, with separate granary, bathrooms, kitchens and living rooms. Due care seems to have been taken for proper ventilation, sweating and mildew. That navigation on the river Indus was used to carry goods to distant places, is evident from the fact that there were found raised platforms for loading and unloading.

The more opulent people used ivory combs. The women of that period, like those of the present, wore jewellery, bangles and rings. The remains left by time silently convey life. If men went out to produce wealth, the women cared to look beautiful and attractive. If the old played board games with dice, children played with toys like bird-whistles, animals moving on wheels, monkeys dancing from strings, toy-carts drawn by bulls or buffaloes.

A closer acquaintance of life reveals a capacity for assimilation and synthesis which gave her people an integrated view. Herein lies the essential individuality of the Indian way of life. As Sri Aurobindo said of the Indian way of living, "In pre-historic India, we see it take a peculiar and unique turn. This determined the whole future trend of society, making Indian civilization a thing apart and of its own kind in the history of the human race."

Even after more than four millennium, going to a typical Indian village, we visualize the same continuity in life, as was found in those times.

Chapter III
The Great Immigration

After walking, walking
An endless journey, there he stands—
Finds relief, and sets off again
On the unending sands...

The nomads of West Asia, around the Caspian Sea had been living by rearing their pastures on the grasslands of Central Asia. The hard life of having to go around difficult terrains in search of food and shelter had made them sturdy, adventurous and bold. During successive failures of weather and infertility of soil, or both, the yield grew insufficient for them and the survival of their pasture. These Nordic people were to play an important part in the history of world civilization. They were a people of the parklands and the forest clearings; they possessed cattles and burned their dead, putting ashes in urns. These Aryans raised crops of wheat and barley. They had an aristocratic social order rather than a divine and regal order. They designated certain families as regal. They cared little for the art of writing. The memories of their bards were their living literature. Every Aryan family had its legendary history in epics and sagas. Compelled to look around for subsistence, they sought space that would promise uninterrupted supply of food for them as well as their cows and enable them to lead a more secure and settled life.

During their usual ramblings with their herds, they may have come across travellers and merchants from the East. In casual conversation, they would talk of a country with vast spaces of forests and fertile soil, fresh water rivers and plenty of regular rainfall. Hearing their tales, the youth would get interested. They would confer with their seniors. At first, the older amongst them, would brush aside the stories and so dampen their curiosity. After some time, when shortages reappeared again due to failed rainfall, they would fondly recollect the tales travellers had told them. The young men would tell their elders.

"In our land, we are suffering for want that is in abundance in that land in the East. Why should we not go and start a new life instead of wasting ourselves?" Chastened with experience, the elders would now listen to the pleadings of the young more seriously. They would discuss among themselves after the day's toil had yielded but little. Gradually, the routine conversation amongst elders became an active decision for the youth. They decided to move to the land of their future destiny.

In a period when only personal communications provided information, the stories of riches in the land, narrated by merchants and traders, would start an exodus of sorts. As these stories inspired the young to adventure, the uncertainties of food for both themselves and their cattle, may have compelled the first immigrants to travel eastwards. This, during the course of time, changed the face of the subcontinent, its culture, its gods, in fact, everything that goes to make societies.

Early batches of such vigorous young men took to travelling on the dusty path for reconnaissance. In time, the movement developed into immigration. Soon, larger batches of these dynamic, resolute and hardy, adventure-loving men travelled through the porous passes of Hindukush. They carried their cows and sheep, horses and bulls, weapons of war and agricultural implements, determined to stay and make a new home.

Life and religion of people

What was the subcontinent like before the arrival of the Aryans as they called themselves? We have read earlier about two developed societies; one in the valley of Indus in the north, and another in the valley of Cauveri in South India. In both parts, people lived in small villages by the side of rivers or ponds engaged in growing wheat and barley. Punctuated with dense forests, the land lacked links to join numerous settlements, scattered all over the country. Isolated from each other, they spoke different languages, had different food habits, but held identical beliefs derived from nature. They had gradually settled to agriculture; hunting being reduced to a sport or resorted to only in emergent needs.

Inspite of a wide diversity in living, they all worshipped Lord Shiva and His consort Parvati, who bestowed them with good crops year after year. Shiva, the bull, elephants and tigers, and the pipal tree *(Asvattha)* were all pre-Aryan introductions.

Because of agreeable climate and soil, agriculture and animal husbandry was the main source of survival. Long distances, difficulties of terrain and a culture of the entire family having to work jointly grew up under the compulsions of agriculture. Living became a routine existence. Rooted in the family or tribe, these small groups had no political organization to serve as a bond between them. Due to long distances and insecurity from wild animals, life remained confined to small groups. There was nothing to bind them to others; everything was centred in and round the family and the cottages near their fields.

There were classes who still pursued hunting for food. Used to regular movement, they did not inherit the peculiarities of an agricultural society like accumulation of surplus for a rainy day and indifference beyond the family. They were fond of a free life of regular movement. They confined themselves to the hills and forests, away from the reach of agriculturists, leading a settled life. They hunted during the day; and made merry after dusk.

The routine of groups following agriculture was different. Abundant food supply and security had made life a routine affair. This in time would lead to complacency. In the process, they forgot the art of resistance. This was to cost them dearly in the future.

Beginning of immigration

Inspired by the stories of travellers, the early batches of these sturdy and adventurous people started coming down the plains of Indus from about BC 1600. They were mostly Eurasians from around Central Asia. Tall, fair complexioned and with aqualine noses, they were a vigorous people full of adventure and dynamism. As nomads, they led a pastoral life, rearing cows and sheep; growing food wherever soil and rains were kind. In their long march eastward, besides animals, they brought their own ideas of gods like Indra and Varuna. While some amongst the stock were pressing south of Spain, their other close relatives, the Italians were making their way in the wild and wooded peninsula. At the other extremity, the Sanskrit-speaking people entered north India. There they came in contact with a primordial Dravidian civilization, from which they learnt much.

The earliest resistance they met was from settled communities in the valley of Indus. The vigour and determination of the Aryans always succeeded against the docility of the local groups and chieftains. Slowly, the Aryans were in absolute control of the entire Indus basin. They were now eyeing the Ganges and land beyond the Vindhyas. Being better fighters, they gradually won over the entire country in a few centuries.

The immigrants, who called themselves Aryans, having settled, sent good tidings back home. They would attract their men with a superb description about their new homes. Fertile soil, vast stretches of grasslands for pastures, forests, fresh water rivers and above all—not-too-hostile inhabitants! This encouraged new waves to follow. The new batches armed with prior information of the geography of the country and travelled the same routes. Now, besides cows, sheep and tools of domestic needs, they arrived in chariots driven by bulls. They also brought spears, battle-axes and armoured vehicles, preparing themselves, if need be, for bigger battles.

Fighting their way against odds, the progeny of the Nordic race, fond of adventure and action, gradually took possession of the entire basin of river Indus. Once the process of consolidation was complete, they moved eastward towards the Great Basin of river Ganges. Here too, the opposition faced from local inhabitants ended soon. After conquest of both the Indus and Gangetic plains in north India, they became masters of the heart of Hindustan. Thereafter, it was a matter of time to be able to command the entire sub continent.

The political history of India has been following this pattern. The victors of plains of the two great rivers, landed up as the masters of the country.

Once the conflict for supremacy ended, the process of assimilation commenced. Both races settled into a life of harmonious living together. Agriculture remained the chief occupation providing sustenance. Growing wheat and barley from the soil, having milk from cows, remedial medicines from plants, wool from sheep during winter and contemplation in the solitude of forests and rivers, as nourishment to the soul, became a part and parcel of thier lives. These became the focal point for the two to integrate. They tilled their adjoining soil, learning from each other. Having common interest in weather and unforeseen calamities, they shared their experiences benefiting each other.

Initial contact of these immigrants was with the inhabitants of the Indus valley, where once flourished the rich civilization of Harappa and Mohen-jo-daro in Sindh and West Punjab (now in Pakistan) . The incoming wave of these immigrants easily overwhelmed their weaker adversaries whose will and strength for resistance, time had sapped. Once, great builders and lovers of good living, they had now grown stagnant. The race that confronted them had superior vigour and weapons. The struggle in the beginning would not have been sharp enough to deter further immigration. It was indeed an adjustment of sorts; the stronger taking possession of the more fertile land, leaving the weaker to clear the virgin forests to start cultivating the new.

This, however, was not to last long. As pressure on fertile lands increased due to greater influx of immigrants, quarrels for land became frequent. The productive land began to be eyed by both. The stronger fought and won. Soon such quarrels may have become frequent. A little later, they turned into group clashes developing later into full-fledged wars.

Armoured Aryans, warriors and chariots driven by bulls and equipped with battle-axes and spears were introduced freely. Being superior in physical endurance and weapons, the Aryans would win the struggle. The contrast between the newcomers and the older Indus people is much in evidence. The

Aryans were destroyers of cities, not their builders. They were the creators of magnificent literature that remained unnoticed for centuries. If the secular preoccupations of the Indus people left their gods in the lurch, the Vedic Aryans spiritualized every detail of their life. This continuity, of which India remains so proud, exists even to this day.

In the Sanskrit version of Ramayana by Valmiki, the inspiration of such wars between the Dravidians and the Aryans is obliquely reflected in the story. It incorporates the Vedantic philosophy and highlights the idealism of the age when it was compiled centuries later. In this respect both the Ramayana and the Mahabharata unfold to a discerning reader the social structure and internal struggles within society.

The tribal

While most of the population accepted the superiority of the Aryan immigrants, some others did not. Fearing absorption, they preferred to move to less fertile lands around the periphery of forests or hills, rather than be swallowed by the new wave. Identity to them was more precious than an easy life. Even to this day, their progeny exists all over the subcontinent. We find their presence in almost every part of India. They are virile and disciplined, often a great deal more democratic than most others. They are a race of people who sing, dance, and try to enjoy life. Tribal folks even today are seen wandering in remote hills, in difficult terrain of jungles and forests. Descendants of a proud people, they were indeed the first 'revolutionaries', who prized their culture and way of life and were prepared for sacrifices to preserve their identity and believed fondly that:

> Happy the man whom bounteous gods allow
> With his own hands Paternal grounds to plough!
> Like the first Golden Mortals, happy he
> From Business and the cares of Money free!
> From all the cheats of law he lives secure,
> Nor does th' affronts of Palaces endure.

Aboriginal, tribal, *adivasi*, call them what you may, as a part of Indian civilization they are a living symbol of its continuity. From the beginning of early encounters with the migrating Aryans, tolerance and co-existence has been a way of life to them. It may be hard to find another community as tolerant as the one in this part of the globe. The Red Indians of America, the Aboriginals of Australia and several other countries have since been wiped out; the tribal and aboriginals of India lead a noble and free life even today. There is no instance, in the long history of the subcontinent, when these people have been forced to flee or have been discriminated against by rulers or the people. The national psyche, developed during a long stretch of practice, was to make India a home of diverse cultures, yet maintaining unity in diversity.

Its strength is revealed from the following incident in China.

Once the famous philosopher and teacher, Confucius was passing through a forest in China with his students. On the way, he heard the wailing of a woman. Confucius asked his students to go and find out the cause of bereavement. They returned and informed him that a lion had killed the son of the woman. "She was in deep agony and in spite of our persuasion, would not be consoled," the disciples told their master.

Confucius decided to go himself. Reaching the woman, he used all his wise counsel to comfort her. However, she continued sobbing.

"What can we do to mitigate your suffering?" asked Confucius.

Between sobs, she muttered, "First my father, then my husband and now my son have been killed by the forest lions; there is now no one left in the family for my support."

"In that case, why don't you leave the forest and settle down elsewhere?" Confucius suggested.

The woman, with her eyes moist, looked at Confucius and said in a soft voice, "The leader of our tribe is an upholder of law; he is just and kind towards us. With all the risk around, I wouldn't leave this place." Such has remained the guiding principle of a simple and proud people who cared little for the so-called luxuries of modern civilization.

Assimilation of races—a nation in the making

We have read how the Nordic race, with their superior strength and weapons won over the local inhabitants. Long struggle and the effort of reconciliation on both sides calmed conditions. As victors, they used their privilege to lay down laws of social cohesion. They defined moral values and laid down rules of governance. Always conscious of their separate identity, desperate to maintain its exclusiveness, they only compromised whenever absolutely necessary and inevitable.

The presiding deity of nomadic Aryans who were often required to fight for survival, was the war god, Indra. For the Dravidians, the presiding god was Shiva. With commonality of interests, both accepted each other's gods. The local inhabitants accepted Indra as the war god; Aryans accepted Shiva as Rudra, Hanuman became Maruti (Vedic Vayu). In time, dark skinned Krishna and the blue eyed Aryan, Rama, heralded a joint pantheon of gods, accepted by both the races.

The Aryans who crossed to the subcontinent, were very particular to marry within their own clan. As however contact with local inhabitants increased, they began to inter-marry with the locals. Even then, in one thing the Aryans would not compromise. This was the colour of the skin. To maintain a distinction between themselves and others, they would only marry fair complexioned girls. This distinction, followed in one form or the other, remains a prejudice even today. Whenever a boy becomes too naughty for the mother to control, she would threaten him with a unique punishment that reflects bias for the colour of the skin, saying:

"If you do not mend your ways, I will marry you to a dark complexioned girl."

How little India has changed since!

Distribution of work

Preservation of identity, from the beginning, has remained important to the Aryans. Differentiation began on the basis of colour, but was extended to division on the basis of work. Agriculture, which was the main source of survival, required production and distribution. This needed people for different operations. Manual workers were required to till the soil; merchants were needed to buy and sell; warriors to provide protection and owners to guide and govern.

The Aryans, being arbiters, divided duties between the four classes. They kept the three functions of commerce, protection and guidance to themselves, creating a class quite different from the three for manual labour. As time passed, this arrangement got corrupted. Instead of dissolving with the passage of time, it became rigid, exploitative and eventually developed into casteism. Practised for a long period, it became a grave social evil that grievously hurt the country. The arrangement framed for smoothness became a cause of a great divide. Even after 3000 years, in spite of social and religious reformers repeatedly pleading against it, the system continues to haunt India.

Prelude to Vedas

The worshippers of Shiva, during the prosperous Harrapan era were lovers of material things. Fond of luxury, as understood during that age, they had devised comfortable brick houses and a reasonable sanitary system. They used metal cooking utensils. To enhance their beauty, women used ornaments. They admired personal beauty and expressed it in figures of clay and stones. The climate and soil of the land provided both good food to eat and clean healthy water to drink.

Descendants of the Nordic race, now called Indo-Aryans, were vigorous and action-oriented. During pastoral existence, they were always fighting battles for survival. Later literature provides glimpses of such struggle in their epics. Now, when life had a settled existence, there was tranquillity and peace to watch and wonder. Observation and thought would lift life above mundane existence. The beauty of the Himalayas, the crystal clear water of the rivers, the dark and roaring monsoon clouds, and the glory of changing seasons, all encouraged a life of contemplation. Thus, the whole universe became their laboratory. Such wise men would faithfully record all their observations; they would express and dutifully record their ecstasy, wonder and the mysteries. The phenomena that produced fear, but could not be explained, became gods. They would also watch and record what was life-supporting. No conceivable human emotion would escape their study.

Men of wisdom conceived the Vedas for the coming generations. This in due course would become the foundation of the Indian civilization. Centuries would pass; new religions in the subcontinent would grow from its roots; other religions and cultures would dip into it giving birth to new ideas.

The formation of the Hindu nation commenced afresh with the philosophy of the Vedas.

Life of Thought

Let me win glory, Agni, in our battles:
Enlightening thee, may we support our bodies.
May the four corners bend and bow before me:
With thee as saviour, we may win in battles.
May all the gods be on our side in battles.
The Maruti, led by Indra, Vishnu and Agni.

—The Rig Veda

Chapter IV
The Vedas

The atmosphere of suspicion and hostility had gradually given place to accommodation and assimilation. The peaceful and tranquil environment offered opportunity for imagination and wonder. The mind, free from exigencies of existence, could now roam unfettered looking for answers to the mysteries of nature. The environment was offering new opportunities for the flights of imagination in the realm of natural beauty. The new race never had it so good when there was abundance of leisure to ponder over the countless mysteries around them. Finer thoughts that lay dormant during the period of struggle and uncertainty started to emerge. Curiosity desperately sought answers to the innumerable wonders of 'Hows' and 'Whys'. On clear Septembers, in the long starry nights, men with imagination watched the moon and stars. They would wonder how it waxed and waned; see the sun set in the west, they wondered why it did not drop down? It surprised them how red cows could give white milk.

Curiosity, the mother of thought, was gradually prodding in them to seek rational answers to their questions! Thus started early thoughts in the minds of those who were to discover the greatest ideas in metaphysics. The timeless philosophy on life, arts and sciences, during this great search, would enrich the world.

The Vedas had started to take shape.

What are Vedas?

Vedas literally mean knowledge. They are a system of higher understanding, which explain how best to utilize the present situation. Vedas are also an expression of the fear of the unknown; they contain prayers to the sun, moon, sky, stars, wind, fire and rain. They express a desire for more cattle, better crops and larger families—a prayer for survival and continuity of race. The study of the Vedas reveal the ecstasy of a child after witnessing the wonderful and fascinating play of nature. Vedas, as composite literature, are a record of infant prodigy, a shocked silence of creation and destruction as observed by early men. As the mysterious began dissolving in the crucible of understanding, they induced appreciation for nature that helps sustain life. It simultaneously developed fear of what is destructive to life.

According to the Vedas, the Lord created the material world. His transcendental energy prevails everywhere. This spiritual energy is scattered as pure vibration manifested in one *mantra* 'AUM' ('OM') that produces the pure sound, vibrating in the universe.

Classification of Vedas

Vedas are a record of observations by the early Aryans. They are compilations of experience drawn by intellectuals to explain the mysterious. Treating different situations and subjects, they continued to expand with time. During the process, they were at times modified and even contradicted. The intellectuals of the new generation kept enriching them with new knowledge that came their way during the course of their work. Out of the many branches, the following four are the broad classification of the Vedas. They are:

1. The Rig Veda
2. The Sama Veda
3. The Yajur Veda
4. The Atharva Veda

Each of these is divided into four sections depending upon the subjects they deal with:

a) The mantras and hymns.
b) The Brahmanas or manual of rituals, prayers and incantation of priests.
c) The Aranyakas or forest texts for hermits and saints.
d) The Upanishads or Vedas after critical conferencing of philosophers.

Vedic literature

The entire Vedic literature is devoted to the study of self-realization and attainment of freedom from suffering. It explores the external world in all its manifestations. After centuries of observation and research appeared *Ayurveda,* the science of medicine; *Gandharva Veda,* which provides knowledge in the field of music, dance and drama; *Arthashashtra,* that explains the art of governance and *Manu Samhita,* the Vedic law book that serves as a guidance of morals and manners of the Hindus. Derived from Vedic literature is the *Shulbha Shashtra,* that describes the Vedic system of mathematics.

The unique collection, often preserved on tree leaves, provided hints of knowledge as it appeared to thinkers of earlier periods. Each generation, with a new perception of the core philosophy, helped supplement this knowledge. This helped enrich literature. For this reason, the Vedas often lack chronology, composition and authorship. The Hindu concept of time and space as derived from Vedic literature has been cyclic. It starts in a circle with the creator and ends with the creator from any point on the circumference.

The Rig Veda (Knowledge of the hymns of praise)

In the modern world of liberalization and globalization, some pages in Rig Veda seem to have been composed for the present time. We claim technology to be transforming the world into a global village. But there is no talk of who will trigger the change. Heraclites, the Greek philosopher very long ago answered what Rig Veda suggests for its achievement. He had said that "man is the measuring rod of all things." If this is so, who is the deity we shall adore with our oblation? *Rig Veda* in one of the verses has answered:

> Meet together, talk together;
> May your minds comprehend alike.
> Common be your actions and achievements,
> No single thing abides, but all things flow.
> Common be your thoughts and actions,
> Common be the wishes of your hearts,
> So that all may live happily together.

Another verse says:

> May we, with common efforts
> And no consciousness of guilt,
> Ascend day by day, higher and higher summits
> Of eternal glory and bliss.

And the message:

"Let noble thoughts come in from all sides."

It is evident that the Rig Veda which happens to be the earliest of the Vedas, directs man not to remain confined, but be global!

The Sama Veda (Knowledge of the melodies)

Sama Veda contains hymns of worship with introduction of melodies. They lend charm both to the singer and the listener. Progress of music, drama and dance owe their expansion to verses in the Sama Veda. Sanskrit mantras and verses of the Mahabharata and Ramayana when sung in their rhythms, create an eclectic environment.

The entire Hindu literature of ancient India derives inspiration from its melodies. The verses of Shankara, bhajans of Mirabai and Chaitanya Mahaprabhu, owe their inspiration to its notes.

May these songs of praise exalt thee, Lord, who hast

Abundant wealth! Men skilled in holy hymns, pure, with

The hues of fire, have sung them with their lauds to thee.

These songs of ours exceeding sweet, these hymns

Of praise ascend to thee, like ever conquering chariots

That display their strength, gain wealth and give unfailing strength.

The Yajur Veda (Knowledge of sacrificial prayers)

Yajur Veda contains the knowledge of various sciences like astronomy, geography and geology. The verses induce the young to gain knowledge, the path of bliss and salvation.

Through Astronomy and Geography

Go to the different lands of the world under the Sun.

May thou attain through good preaching to statesmanship

And artisanship, through medical sciences knowledge of plants etc.

O royal, skilled engineer,

Construct sea boats propelled by water

And airplanes flying upwards.

Be thou prosperous in this world.

Modern religious teachers in their lectures still emphasize the following verse of *Yajur Veda* in their own words:

Find the eternal object of quest within your soul.

Enough have you wondered during the long period of your quest.

Dark and weary must have been the ages,

Of your searching in ignorance and groping in helplessness.

At last when you turn your gaze inwards,

Suddenly you realize the bright light of faith

In lasting truth was shining around you.

With rapturous joy, you find

The soul of the universe—the eternal object of your quest.

Your searching mind at last

Finds the object of your search within your own heart.

Your inner vision is illuminated by this realization.

In this verse, the teacher advises his disciple thus:

O disciple! know God, the creator through Vedas,

Control breath through Yoga,

Through Astronomy, know the functions of day and night,

Know all the Vedas by means of their constituent parts.

The Atharva Veda (Knowledge of magic)

Atharva Veda is a collection of hymns dealing in subjects beyond easy comprehension. It explains the charms of the unexplainable. The verses appear to contain an air of knowledge by a few to impress the many, they are often mystical with an air of vagueness. It appears that a difference of understanding has appeared between the priest and the people. The knowledge in *Atharva Veda* therefore delivered protection from evil powers.

> O Mankind! I bind you together,
>
> Towards one objective, the welfare of man.
>
> May you share the comforts of life equally.
>
> May you accomplish your work with musical accord and
>
> May you, in the pursuit of your ambition at all times,
>
> Engage in work together with goodwill.

Another verse in Atharva Veda exhorts love and devotion to the country respecting other faiths. This verse could not be more modern:

> Work for the glory of your country
>
> And countrymen speaking different dialects.
>
> Give due respects to the faiths
>
> And aspirations of the people.

The song of the Vedas

The Hindu religion has drawn its philosophy and attitude to life from the Vedas. Earlier gods were identical to the Greek gods of sun, fire, water and earth. They were the foundation of its culture and civilization. Reading the Vedas, one is introduced to the names and powers that dominate the Hindu mind. The flow chart in **Figure II** on the next page indicates how curiosity led the earliest thinkers to bring out the message of the Vedas. Hindu religion has drawn its culture and attitude towards life from them. They are the foundations of Hindu culture and its civilization.

As can be observed from **Figure II** curiosity starts thought. How imaginations invite fear and submission to phenomenon, that is a mystery. How did the fear of the unknown create gods? This would compel submission, developing dogmatism and theology. How deeper was the understanding that evolved in religion and philosophy to bring peace and harmony in life!

Reaching this stage it takes two courses—right understanding of nature and its study that leads to development of sciences; its wise application to life, search for human welfare bringing happiness to Man. When religion is hijacked by vested interests; when it is used for selfish motives, both religion and philosophy get corrupted by rituals and intolerance. Barbaric actions and misery soon follow. History of different civilizations reveal that in most cases, rulers and priests used philosophy and religion for their selfish use. When they grew excessive and damaging, reforms and education put them back on track.

Reforms and education therefore have remained and continue to be vital factors to be introduced at different stages in all societies to achieve happiness.

Fig. II Movement of thought towards human welfare

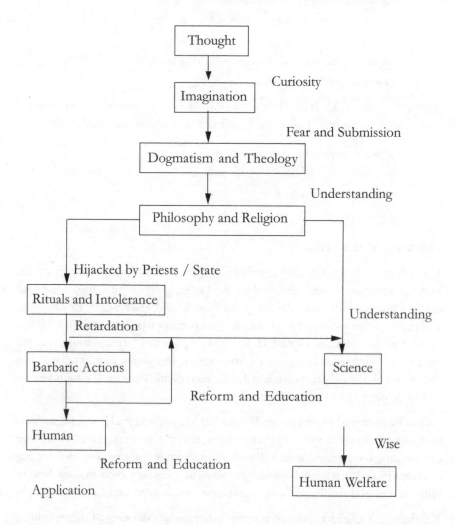

Chapter V
The Ideal of a Perfect Life
The Ramayana

Ye king to be, of Earth! With bended head
Doth Rama pray to you, again and again,
With painful labour have I built this bridge
Of righteousness, leading from earth to heaven;
With the same labour may you guard it well,
And keep it firm in full repair and guide,
Our father Manu's children on it,
And see them safe across, from age to age.

—Valmiki Ramayana

Valmiki, the author of Ramayana, is said to have asked sage Narada, the roving ambassador of gods, "Please tell me, whether there is a perfect man in this world, who is at once virtuous, dutiful, truthful, noble, steadfast and kind to all beings?"

Narada replied, "There is such a one. He loves his subjects; is a protector of dharma, steadfast, liberal, an obedient son, an ideal king, a merciful enemy, and a lover of all beings. All people adore him."

Inspired by Narada, Valmiki initiated his work on the Ramayana.

If the Vedas are observations and prayers of early Aryans, the epic of Ramayana provides glimpses of the life and times of that period. Valmiki may have compiled the epic in Sanskrit from ballads and songs of heroes that fought battles of survival. It contains the history of wars fought long ago. The epic describes the geography of the subcontinent while describing myths, morals and the early struggle between the Aryans and the local chieftains. It describes the beauty of ancient India, her forests, the majesty of her rivers, the ideals of her people and the glamour of her wealth.

It may be a coincidence of history that around BC 700 Homer in Greece was compiling a similar great work, *Odyssey*. The two great epics, one in the East and the other in the West, have almost similar themes and methods of compilation. Following traditions, the book has been read by each generation. Others, who could not read, enjoyed hearing it sung at congregations. Valmiki Ramayana was originally written in Sanskrit. So long as it was the language of the people, it continued to be popular. When Pali replaced Sanskrit as the language of the masses, the Ramayana virtually moved into oblivion.

In the sixteenth century, Tulsi Das, taking events from Valmiki Ramayana as a base, wrote *Ramcharita Manas* in Hindi. The new version of Ramayana became popular at once. To the present day, every village in India, particularly North India, reverentially responds to the devotion of the perfect incarnation. The influence of Ramayana was so deep that it gradually permeated into the psyche of her people. Hindu religion, during the times of Tulsidas, had slipped into fatalism. It desperately needed hope. Besides, Sufism in Islam and Bhakti in the Hindu religion, preached devotion. Tulsidas moulded each character of the Ramayana with devotion (bhakti) as their guiding quality. He revived the broad frame of the epic by highlighting the philosophy of life through devotion yet retaining the moral values enshrined by Valmiki.

Morals of perfection—the ideals

In Valmiki Ramayana, the noblest emotions in human beings have been given practical expression by the 'perfect being', Rama. Other individual characters according to their roles, perform their functions to the same ideals. Yet, like in all great literatures, at crucial moments, the same perfection is compromised. This does not diminish the status of the individual trying for perfection; it only shows the puzzle that this world is. Ramayana often tends to give a dual image of some of its characters. This lends the epic popularity amongst humans who themselves suffer such frailties in everyday life.

Rama, the perfect one, plays the game of life on the canvas of the world with human frailties like jealousy, pride, possessiveness, compassion, sacrifice and devotion—all of which exist side by side. With perfection as an ideal, each character so conducts themselves as to establish long term values.

This great drama contains all these passions and emotions. There is tender narration of innocent childhood, heroic accounts of irrepressible adventures of youth, learned discourses of preachers in boyhood, wisdom of sages at appropriate moments, sacrifices of the young for the sake of elders. An ideal relationship exists between all characters, binding them with different episodes.

Preparations for perfection

Rama gets his spiritual lessons from sage Vashishta. At the age of sixteen, tired of palace life, Rama seeks permission from his father to go around his kingdom. After coming back to the palace from his wanderings, Rama becomes unhappy and disinterested in state affairs. For a young intellect, such an effect is natural. In the early life of Gautama Buddha, we come across a similar situation when he loses interest in worldly affairs.

The worried father Dashratha sends his son Rama to Vashishta to help get over his melancholy. Rama dutifully goes to the sage and tells his plight.

"Why is man confronted with such suffering and paralysing emotions and inclination? Is there any better existence? How should one live in such an inconsistent world? How shall we be saved from pain that follows our likes and dislikes? Shall we be liberated through action or inaction?"

Vashishta gave his discourses to Rama in answer to the questions raised by Rama. The collected discourses form part of yet another great treatise *Yoga Vashishta*. The sage explains how to get over the perplexities of life that cause suffering to sensitive young minds. The substance of his preachings are as relevant today as they were then.

The sage advises Rama in *Yoga Vashista* that "One's own efforts are the only way to end misery. Not through absurd beliefs of destiny but through efforts alone do the wise come out of difficult situations. Everyone is his own friend and foe. If he does not make effort to save himself, there is none other to save him. Present efforts can rectify the errors of past, because present is stronger than the past."

Rama learnt his lessons well to become Valmiki's 'perfect human being'.

Valmiki, in his text, has painted the beauty of Indian forests and the natural beauty of India. Through the passages, he describes the gently nodding green trees in the red and golden autumn horizon, the tall, towering, snow-clad mountains and life-giving rivers.

Valmiki has beautifully described Chitrakoot, where Rama, after his exile, lived for sometime. He paints the canvas of imagination in the months of early summer with a fascinating description:

> The flame of flowers had burst into bloom dotting the trees with orange
> clouds. The Bilva trees had bowed down. The fruit trees were laden.
> Verily, no man could have touched the virgin beauty of the forests.
> Creepers and lianas clung sweetly to the trees. The beauty of flowers
> made the birds sing songs; here kokila (cuckoo), there at the other end
> a peacock; on the bows of trees were bee-hives dripping with honey;
> animals roamed freely.

Such was the valley of Chitrakoot where Rama spent his days after being exiled from Ayodhya.

Relationship between king and subjects

An example of ruler-subject relationship can be glimpsed from an incident in the forest. King Dasharatha, while hunting in the forests of his kingdom, mistakenly kills Shravana, the son of a blind couple. Realizing his grave error, Dasharatha comes to the blind couple, with folded hands. The king says, "Holy father! Holy Mother! Please forgive me. I am not your son; I am Dasharatha, an unfortunate Kshatriya. By the will of fate, my arrow accidentally hit your son while I was hunting. He now lies on the riverbank. He asked me to bring water for you. Do with me now as you please."

This is a supreme expression of humility and fairness by a king. Accepting his mistake before a citizen, the king offers himself for punishment in the court of his subject! Ayodhya, during the rule of king Dasharatha, became a Utopia. Ramayana depicts the kingdom of Dasharatha as a model society. So, when the king rules properly, the subjects also behave properly. This implies that the primary responsibility for proper function is of the ruler. If he fulfils his duties and responsibilities justly, others will do likewise.

Virtue and idealism

The noblest emotions of virtue find expression through the words of Rama. Other characters perform their roles as expected from them. When Sita is wedded to Rama, her father, Janaka, says:

> This is Sita, child of Janaka, dearer unto him than life,
>
> Henceforth sharer of thy virtue; be she, prince, thy faithful wife.
>
> As the shadow to substance, to her lord a faithful wife,
>
> And my Sita best of woman follow thee in death or life.

The decisive moment does not take long. Dasharatha sends Rama to a life in the forests for fourteen years. Janaka's words were no idle advice to his daughter. Sita insists on accompanying Rama to live a life of hermitage. She says:

> Chariots, horses and gilded palace, vain are those to woman's life
>
> Dearer is her husband's shadow, to the loved and the loving wife.
>
> For my mother often taught me, and my father often spoke,
>
> That her home, the wedded woman, doth besides her husband make.
>
> As the shadow to the substance, to her is the faithful wife,
>
> And she parts not from her consort, till she parts with fleeting life.
>
> Therefore bid me seek the jungle and in pathless forests roam,
>
> Where the wild deer freely roams and the tiger makes his home.

Bridge over the ocean

During the war with Ravana, crossing the ocean to reach Lanka was virtually impossible. The Sea advises Rama that impossible tasks require forethought and action, not just dreaming and praying. The dialogue between the ocean and Rama is the poet's exhortation for action *(Karma)*. On Rama's request to provide space for his monkey army, the Sea suggested: "You have in your army, a mighty monkey Nala, son of Vishwakarma, an excellent engineer. Ask him to lead in the construction of a causeway across me to Lanka. I will do my bit by bearing the entire weight upon my chest and holding together, the boulders and trees."

The entire army was thus able to cross the ocean and defeat Ravana.

Model government–*Rama Rajya*

Rama Rajya is described as an ideal government. Qualities of the king and devotion of the subjects, highlighted in the epic, is not mere idealism. They are attainable attributes of good administration in every age. Medical and healthcare, social laws and customs, law and order, honesty and harmony are the fundamentals of good administration. Valmiki, in Ramayana, describes *Rama Rajya* thus:

> Death untimely, dire diseases, came not to his subject men;
>
> Robbers, cheats and gay deceivers, tempted not with lying word,
>
> Neighbour loved his righteous neighbour, and the people loved their lord.
>
> Trees their ample produce yielded, as returning seasons went,
>
> And the earth in grateful gladness never-failing harvest lent.
>
> Rains descended in their season, never came the blighting gale,
>
> Rich in crop and rich in pasture was each soft and smiling vale….

The land was rid of untimely death and disease. Being a widow was not unbearable. There were hardly any child deaths for mothers to weep, robbers and cheats were rare, there was truthfulness. Neighbours loved each other. People were God-loving (not god-fearing). The trees were laden with ample fruits and flowers. Mother Earth always yielded abundant harvest with little effort. Rains always arrived in time. There were no destructive storms, hurricanes or typhoons. Gifts of nature were always timely. The soil was fertile and yield was in abundance. With liberal gifts of nature, so forthcoming, the nation was happy and prosperous in its professions.

Tulsi Ramayana

Tulsi Das wrote Ramayana in the sixteenth century, when Sanskrit had slipped into oblivion. India was passing through a religious catharsis. Guru Nanak,

Ramanuja, Kabir and Sufi saints were all advocating devotion. He therefore wrote his version in Hindi, the language of the people, with bhakti at the core of all characters of the work. Valmiki covers morality, creation of wealth, pleasure and liberation. Tulsi Das, in the same characters, subordinates all the four to a fifth dimension—devotion (*bhakti*). Each character of Tulsi Ramayana exhibits this characteristic in his/her conduct. Vedic philosophy in Ramayana is admirably studded with similes and metaphors that are in common use. For the village folks, Tulsi Ramayana is a wise companion. We may go to any part of North India, Tulsi Ramayana is quoted and sung by men and women of all ages. During the festive season, scenes from the Ramayana are enacted and its composition repeated by performing actors in the village squares. Time may have changed the style, make-up of actors may be rich or poor, but enthusiasm and devotion for it remains unaltered. Tulsi Ramayana helps bind people of the country with a common faith.

Valmiki Ramayana places emphasis on fusion of races—the need of the 16th century. India was passing through a religious catharsis. Guru Nanak, Kabir, and Ramanuja, all were advocating devotion for a happy life. There was complete change in the social and religious life of the people. The Sufi saints of Islam, along with their Indian counterpart, all advised devotion as the route to salvation. Tulsi Das, in his later version of the Ramayana, provided a new found pride in a god with super human powers. He himself acknowledges this when he says:

> Worshipping Rama is matter all,
> Means of worship matter not.
> Without index, it is zero all,
> A figure lends value all.

Tulsi Ramayana exhibits Rama's complete devotion towards his parents, Bharats towards his brothers and Hanuman's devotion to Rama. Each character is a model of devotion. Amongst others, devotion of Mareech towards Ravana and Jatayu's to Rama are naturally portrayed by Tulsi Das more emphatically than by Valmiki.

Indians are often considered to be complex characters—capable of reaching for the highest ideals and falling to lowest degradation at another time. The influence of the Ramayana and the Mahabharata, is visible on their character even today. There are some who greedily amass wealth all their lives, while others who happily give everything away; there are some who feed ants and others who commit the cruellest crimes. The Ramayana, in happiness and adversity, has always been a source of strength to the Hindu mind. During festive seasons, its recitation and performance sets traditions for the young. In old age, its recitation helps practice the philosophy of peaceful living as enunciated in the Upanishads.

Chapter VI
"Triumph doth on virtue wait"
The Mahabharata

The Mahabharata is the greatest work of imagination in poetry consisting of the history, culture, religious morals and spiritual heritage of ancient India. Presenting a portrait-gallery of heroes and heroines, it conveys both their ideals as well as depths of degradation. The mystical poet Vyasa, is credited with collecting the numerous bards and poetic descriptions of ancient India, into a garland of nearly 100,000 verses. Vyasa, literally means the 'arranger'. He was the last to have abridged and arranged the Mahabharata with the help of centuries of work. It is often said that what is not in Mahabharata cannot happen. Like the Ramayana, the Mahabharata is based on historical facts of bygone centuries. The narrative system of Mahabharata is highly complex. Repeatedly, as we move with the story of ancient India, we notice that history appears as a record of social, religious and political incidents. Convinced that Time and Space are a fabrication of human mind, morals and culture take precedence over history. The gigantic poetry assimilates the work of scores of writers before it was complied in the present form.

Construction and compilation

When Vyasa took to arranging the Mahabharata, the Kshatriyas were the warrior class who had enabled the Aryans to dominate the native inhabitants. The basis for the epic was such wars, tales of violence, gambling and deceit. The metaphysics of the Upanishads, duties of a king, righteousness, truth, beauty, the philosophy of Kapila and Gautama Buddha—all have been magnificently studded in its construction. Since it was customary in those days to transfer such poems into songs, the singers also may have contributed a flavour of their own. The reader occasionally comes across a sudden change. This confirms editing of centuries of work in a smooth flow of ideas. Origin of the race in Bharatavarsha (India), starts with King Dushyanta and Shakuntala, getting a son. He was named Bharata, whose descendants were the Kuru race.

The great war in the field of Kurukshetra highlights both the righteousness and degradation, bravery and cowardice to which men can rise or fall. It provides a platform for presentation of the high philosophy man is capable of.

In delivery and subject, the Mahabharata resembles Homer's *Iliad* and *Odyssey* that describe the wars in which the Greek heroes and gods fight injustice.

At the time the Mahabharata war began, social organizations had begun to emerge. This had made life more orderly. The most far reaching of the moral laws so framed, were the division into *Varnas* (castes). It was a classification of men according to the occupation they followed. Henceforth, they, their elders, and the coming generations had to follow the same occupation. This was to grow into watertight compartments that subsequently developed rigidity and division within society. The Mahabharata combines the religious codes of Kapila and the moral and social laws of Manu, transfixed at appropriate intervals to blend Indian philosophy and social manners in the mainstream.

The conflict between the Kauravas—Pandavas and the Gita are widely read, the stories of Shakuntala and Satyavan-Savitri, Nala-Damayanti which also form a part of Mahabharata, are comparatively less known. Poet Kalidas, who lived in the age of Vikramaditya, has dramatized the story in *Shakuntalam*. His life and work profoundly influenced Sanskrit literature. A chapter ahead has been exclusively devoted to his contribution.

Satyavan and Savitri

Love is a fundamental facet of the human element. In Mahabharata, it tends to triumph over death. In the story of Satyavan and Savitri, which forms a part of the epic, Savitri is able to convince Yama, the god of death, not to take away her love.

Savitri says to Yama when the god comes to take Satyavan away:

> Without my husband, I am dead, as it were
>
> I want no happiness if I am deprived of my husband.
>
> I do not want heaven, if I am deprived of my husband.
>
> I want no beauty, if I am deprived of my husband.
>
> I have decided I will not live without my husband.

And the intensity and force of that love defeated Yama, Death. Savitri has been potrayed as an ideal character in this episode. The poet describes her charm to the reader in the following verse:

> Come with youth its lovelier graces, as the buds their leaves unfold,
>
> Slender waist and rounded bosom, image as of burnished gold,
>
> Deva Kanya born a goddess, so they said in all the land,
>
> Princely suitors, struck with splendour, ventured not to seek her hand.

Savitri was in love with Satyavan. He, as ill luck would have it, was destined to die in the next twelve months as predicted by the good old sage Narada to her father. So, when his father implores Savitri to change her mind, she says:

> I have heard thy ordered mandate, holy Narada counsels well;
>
> Pardon witless maiden's fancy, but beneath the eye of Heaven.
>
> Only once a maiden chooseth twice her troth may not be given,
>
> Long his life or be it narrow, or his virtues great or none,
>
> Satyavan is still my husband, he my heart and troth hath won,
>
> What a maiden's heart hath chosen that a maiden's lips confess,
>
> True to him thy poor Savitri goes into wilderness.

As ordained, when the messenger of death Yama comes to take Satyavan away from Savitri, she argues, like Nachiketa in *Katho Upanishad*. Yama is so impressed with her arguments that he lets her husband remain alive.

Interpretations of dharma

There are three different interpretations of dharma in Mahabharata—one by Sri Krishna, the other by Yudhisthira and the third by Duryodhana. All the three represent the moral dilemma based on a single definition.

Sri Krishna discusses the nature of dharma and points out that dharma sustains the world and it is based on truth. But it is always difficult to follow the path of truth. At times truth appears like untruth and vice versa. Therefore if a person does not know the essence of dharma, he is bound to be confused. Krishna maintains that the true nature of dharma could not be understood with Vedas alone. One has to use logic and intelligence to understand the right course of action. Understanding dharma is of universal benifience and welfare to all.

The Rajdharma of king as explained by Bhishma to Yudhisthira says that the duty of a king at the time of adversity is different. It does not at that time accord to his normal functions. It is difficult to understand dharma during such periods. Discussions, customs, practices and one's own conscience as to what is right for the kingdom, becomes the deciding factor. Bhishma finally advocates application of intelligence rather than violence for the right course. He states that in an emergency, dharma is based on *artha* (material values). It is with *artha* that a king could overcome calamities.

The third concept was of Duryodhana. He argues that action is the basis of dharma as the world belonged to the powerful. They should therefore both enjoy and protect the cause of dharma. Amoral hedonism was not considered seriously by the interpreters of the Mahabharata.

With definition of dharma changing, the moral dilemma of politics becomes obvious. Any immoral action by the king, howsoever justified, could not escape criticism by the people. It is always difficult to draw a line between the self- aggrandisement of the king and the interests of the state. Any king who tries to use power for his personal glory, could turn into a tyrant. Bhishma advised Yudhisthira to always take people into confidence before deciding the course of action.

Applied to modern times, how little have principles of dharma changed!

The battle of Kurukshetra

The battlefield of Kurukshetra was the scene of war between the two Kshatriya cousins. Vyasa gives an idea of the carnage where millions were killed in eighteen days; Bhishma alone killed thousands of soldiers. We may have read descriptions of wars in different languages, of different countries, at different periods. Never a bloodier battle was fought as at Kurukshetra in ancient India!

The genius in Vyasa must have wanted to convey a message for future India! What was that he wished to convey? To seek an answer we may revert back in time to the existing social and political conditions. There had been a succession of great religious and moral preachers. The messages of Mahavira and Gautama had driven the cream of Indian society towards contemplation in monasteries as a route for salvation. Consequently, the young stock of the nation had grown complacent and indifferent to the world around them. Leading a life of peace and tranquillity in monasteries was their interpretation of practising religion.

Vyasa, as a great visionary must have felt intensely agonized. He may have decided to inspire the youth to understand that violence for righteousness and vigilance for compassion is essential for the survival of a country. He could not have focused better than the dialogue between Arjuna and Sri Krishna to portay Arjuna's unwillingness to fight his family. Even Krishna, who always commanded non-violence and compassion as the highest virtues in man, asks Arjuna to take up the fight even if it involves one's own kith and kin! Right in the midst of the armies of the Kauravas and the Pandavas, Arjuna requests Krishna, his charioteer, to let him have a glimpse of those he has to fight. Watching his nearest and dearest as 'enemies' he surrenders his arms and prays to Krishna:

> As I behold—come here to shed
> Their common blood—you concourse of our kin,
> My members fail, my tongue dries in my mouth,
> It is not good, O Keshava! Naught of good

Can spring from mutual slaughter! Lo, I hate

Triumph and dominion, wealth and ease

Thus sadly won! Alas what victory

Can bring delight Govind, what rich spoils

Could profit, what rule recompense, what span

Of life itself seem sweet, brought with such blood?

Krishna, as a divine incarnation, commands Arjuna to fight wrong even if committed by one's own relatives:

Yield not to impotence Partha

It befits thee not,

Shake off this wretched faint heartedness,

Stand up, Oh harasser of foes.

To encourage struggle, Vyasa even glorifies lamentation of death. The wife of Duryodhana proudly faces the death of her husband and sons:

Mark again, Duryodhana's widow, how she hugs his gory head,

How with gentle hands softly does she hold him on his bed;

How from her dear departed husband turns she to her dearest son,

And the teardrops of the mother choke the widow's bitter groan;

Like the fibre of lotus, tender, golden is her frame.

Oh my lotus, Oh my daughter, Bharat's pride and Kuru's fame!

If the truth resides in Vedas, brave Duryodhana dwells above;

Wherefore higher we in sadness severed from his cherished loves?

If the truth resides in Shashtras, dwells in sky my hero son;

Wherefore higher we in sorrow since their earthly task is done?

Theme and symbolism in Mahabharata

The theme of Mahabharata is the drama of the struggle between good and evil. Sage Vyasa transmutes the human conflict to a divine plane. On the symbolic level, we can say that the Pandavas represent the nobility (davia sampat) and Kauravas, the wicked tendencies (asura). While Arjuna represents the human, the other four Pandavas represent different kinds of endeavour in a human being. Yudhisthira represents the ethical values (dharma), Bhima represents material values (artha), Nakula the social values (kama), and Sehdev, the spiritual values (moksha). Draupadi symbolizes intellect, depending upon nothing in the world but the supreme Self. They are led by the divine self of Krishna to the ultimate goal. Evils represented by Duryodhana, as the embodiment of the mind filled with impurities. Karna is the embodiment of exaggerated egoism; Shakuna, that of falsehood. Dushashana is the embodiment of evil servitude.

A significant symbolism is indicated when both Arjun and Duryodhana reach to seek Sri Krishna's help for their respective causes. The incident shows that even when the choice for redemption is available, the evil mind opts for lower material benefits. Before the war, Lord Krishna offers either himself without any army, or his army without him. Arjun chooses the unarmed Krishna, while Duryodhana feels happy with the Dwarka army. Having chosen Krishna, Arjuna puts the chariot of life in his hands.

Bhishma, the uncle and Vidur, the stepbrother and minister of the blind King Dhritarashtra, are personification of wisdom and virtue. In all matters of state, they always advised the king righteously. Vyasa epitomizes righteousness and firmness as the foundations of ruling a country.

In the Mahabharata, at critical moments, both Vidur and Bhisma miserably fail to exercise their high position. If men of virtue ignore their responsibility towards the state and do not advice the king what is right, they fall down from their high pedestal. Two instances in the epic make the turning point. Once, while gambling in the court of Dhritarashtra, the Pandavas lose the game of dice to Duryodhana who orders the humiliation of Draupadi. The two pillars of righteousness and truth sit mutely when their daughter-in-law is dishonoured, both being frozen to inaction. It took Krishna to rescue the queen in the court.

After it was decided that there would be a war, Krishna comes to the court of Dhritarashtra as an ambassador of peace. He places a compromise proposal seeking only five villages for the Pandavas. Bhishma, Dronacharya, Vidur and other men of virtue sat idly listening. Duryodhana contemptuously rejected the proposal. The two elder statesmen, Bhishma and Dhritarashtra did not lift a finger to stop the destruction of the race.

In the Mahabharata, Vyasa clearly conveys that for dharma to prevail, struggle against evil must be waged at the appropriate time. For the sake of peace, a nation must be prepared for war. Noticing complacency in society of that period, Vyasa must have had foreboding of future events that were to cast their ugly shadow on a country wedded to non-violence by her religious thinkers.

Bhagwad Gita

The Bhagwad Gita is the brightest jewel studded in the Mahabharata at a later stage. There is hardly a man of distinction in India who has not written his commentary on its celestial texts. *Swamis* and saints, presidents and prime ministers, *acharyas* and administrators, all have drawn their interpretations of perhaps the greatest work of philosophy ever produced in the world. Gita is not just a textbook of knowledge; it is about the art of living in an ever-changing world. As a flowing stream, its waters are ever fresh. The interpretation of thoughts may change with time, but never its message. The learned of every age keep finding new light in its philosophy in an evolving world.

Studying the Gita, the precious possession of humanity, provides answer to myriad problems faced by men in the world. The Kaurava mind, represented by Duryodhana, is full of *Rajasik* (kingly) and *Tamasik* (sensual) qualities; the Pandavas possess *Sattvic* (virtuous) qualities. Gita explains the difference between the two forces. Each human being possesses both positive and negative thoughts. This creates duality in his action. Gita provides inspiration and method to lift the mind above duality. In the Kauravas, representing negative tendencies, sinful motives are born to blind Dhritarashtra. He is wedded to Gandhari, an intellect that is voluntarily blinded. In Dhritarashtra, the mind is born blind to truth. Gandhari, having deliberately blinded herself to truth, refuses to recognize it.

"To be or to do! That is the question!" becomes a perpetual dilemma for both the king and the queen.

Resistance to evil is the essence of growth. If one does note resist evil at the right time, one becomes worse than wood. Resistance to non-self is the first step towards growth of a man's personality. This incessant development is simply the process of 'being' one's self more and more. This 'becoming' is a fuller 'being'.

The greatness of a man is not what he does, but what he was and has since become through his effort. To 'be' then is infinitely higher than to 'do'.

Some of the thoughts in the celestial song are meant for regular contemplation:

> The Yogi is higher than the ascetic;
> He soars above the seers, who know,
> Higher than those who work, too, is he,
> Therefore, Arjuna, be thou a Yogi.

We only need to substitute 'Arjuna' with the 'youth' and the poet's message becomes true for every age.

Modern man seeks achievement without corresponding inner growth. They therefore miss the meaning of 'becoming'. Consequently, they remain ever restless, always seeking achievement. Poet Vyasa portrays the pathetic picture of such people in the Gita thus:

In quenchless longing lost,

By fraud, conceit and lust inspired, they strive.

On satisfying their desires, such men are bent,

Believing, that alone is truth,

Enmeshed by a hundred hands of hope,

Steeped in lust and wrath,

Amassing wealth by lawless means,

They strive to get their heart's desire.

Such a person as this thinks that:

'I alone will offer sacrifice,

Scatter gifts and rejoice,

As none before me ever did'.

Truth that is unity

Modern mind has confounded knowledge with personality. Therefore, he does not feel humiliated at his mind being divorced from speech, his speech from action. This two-fold diversion is accepted as inevitable, often as a sign of modernity. To be able to live in truth, poet Vyasa says in the Gita:

Better one's own thankless dharma,

Than alien task tho' well performed.

Better to die, doing one's own task;

Another's task is fraught with danger.

What is true of men is true of a country. A country has its own *swadharma,* pre-destined by its history, its culture and its inner strength. Any attempt, to achieve a result, inconsistent with its *swadharma,* unsupported by a unified control of its thought, words and deed, lands it into danger.

"See what I have secured today!" they say.

"On this my mind is now set, next.

This wealth is mine; this much more,

Shall be mine again."

"This enemy have I slain today;

Those others I will slay anon,

I am the Lord; I enjoy, as I like;

Successful, happy and strong am I,

Who can rival my wealth, my birth?"

Enveloped in ignorance, these,

> Maddened by countless thoughts,
>
> Caught fast in illusion,
>
> Held in thrall by sensual pleasures
>
> Rush headlong into Hell.

Gita provides strength of character through understanding the significance of devotion. Once this strength is achieved it becomes real personal power; not the worldly power of domination or the glitter of wealth. One gets a silent satisfaction when the play of life is understood. This understanding is the contentment of body and spirit.

The Indian mind is essentially a philosophical mind. We may go to any part of India, an average villager will surprise us with his rudiments of thoughts. Gita is a true companion in times of crisis. During the period of darkness, it lends invaluable support to the soul and spirit.

The knowledge contained in the Gita has kept alive the freedom of spirit, faith and culture of the Hindus amidst intervals of turbulence. If contemplation of Truth is the last preoccupation of wisdom, the text of the Mahabharata must be read and understood by both the young and old. Not only does it contain the wisdom of action in every situation, it is full of stories within stories that are as true today as they were in ancient times. Vyasa himself is said to have summarized his teachings in the verse:

> I am shouting at the top of my voice with upraised arms! But alas, no one listens to me: It is by way of dharma that one can achieve *artha* as well as *kama*. And why don't you pursue it wholeheartedly? The way of wisdom is that the demands of the passionate desire and craze for selfish possessions must be regulated by the norms of ehtical conduct. It is that which ensures *loksanghra* (welfare of all) such that it is the broadest and the most enlightened goal that humanity can ever have; it is a goal that even God cannot treat lightly.

> This implies the good of universal humanity, the perfect co-existence of one and all in this world, without worry or rancour. It is a dream that can only become a reality when there is keen awareness of the universal moral law. When this becomes a reality our actions get attuned to the demands made by that Eternal Law of life viz. dharma.

Chapter VII
Metaphysics of the Hindus
The Upanishads

Centuries of observation and thought produced the wonder that is the Vedas. They recorded the happenings and hopes of that period as history; the incomprehensible, as transcendental philosophy; the relationship between living beings as sociology; and interdependence of men with nature, as the moral laws.

The Upanishads emerged from the Vedas when the wise of successive generations through knowledge obtained from the world explained the physical as well as metaphysical phenomena. It was not the work of individuals or of a lifetime; this was a continuous process of seekers of truth. They would sit together by the fireside in winter or a shady tree during summer. They would meditate over the enigmas of nature, completely absorbed until they themselves became a part of the universal, all embracing oneness.

The Upanishads are a result of intense debates and exchange of views and deep contemplation. The wise were thus able to isolate history, sociology, mythology and philosophy from the Vedas. As footprints on the sands of time, they provided material for the great epics of the Ramayana and the Mahabharata. Indeed the entire ancient literature of India in some form or the other is studded with the philosophy of the Upanishads.

This study may have may have continued for nearly three hundred years. During this period more than two hundred Upanishads were produced. Their working began like the research of modern scientists. Starting with observation, they would sit together, discuss different subjects with a vision for the future in the light of past experiences. Never in a hurry, they would apply their findings to life experiences, observe their effects and reason out their conclusions.

Such men lived a detached life. This would enable their senses to concentrate, and transmit direct signals to their intellect. The faculty of intuition thus illuminated, their individual consciousness could experience universal reality. The secret of prosperity of ancient India in the spiritual and material world was because of this direction to thought and action during this period. In thought, it expands and lifts consciousness to cosmic dimensions; in practice it is the art and science of living!

Indian society sustained and grew with the benefits derived from the knowledge of such men. It has since constantly nourished it's culture

Of the two hundred Upanishads originally known, the passage of time has only retained the following twelve:

1. Isavasya Upanishad
2. Keno Upanishad
3. Katho Upanishad
4. Prasna Upanishad
5. Mundakya Upanishad
6. Sevetaseratra Upanishad
7. Taitriya Upanishad
8. Aitreya Upanishad
9. Chandigya Upanishad
10. Brihadaranyaka Upanishad
11. Brahma Upanishad
12. Bindu Upanishad

What are Upanishads?

Upanishad are opinions and conclusions about the mysteries of life and death. They do not represent any consistent system of philosophy. To prove the point, characters are made to ask questions. Their answers provide the clue. The reader is able to delve deep to arrive at his own conclusions. As records of research at different levels, they contain both the simple as well as the most profound thoughts that ever crossed the mind of man. Upanishads have compared the path of knowledge and actions. According to them, action may be a preparation for salvation or liberation, but can never deliver. They are emphatic to conclude that only through knowledge can liberation be achieved.

Isa Upanishad

Isa Upanishad insists on attainment of the Knowledge of Reality when it says "doing work in this world, one should wish to live for 100 years". It perceives that action is not an obstacle. It says that " action cleaves not a man; it reconciles knowledge of the one and of multiplicity," praising creation and its relationship with the Self. The text contains eighty verses out of which a few are given:

1. "All habitation is given by the Lord. Whatever is in the universe is in perpetual movement. Though renunciation, live and enjoy this universe for a hundred years. Lust not after any man's possession."

2. "One who sees everywhere the self in all existence and all existence in the self, feels no hatred after this realization."

3.   "The face of Truth is covered by a golden veil. O, Sun! remove the
      covering so that it can be held by me so that I can perform my duties
      rightfully."

4.   "Oh God Agni, knowing all things that are manifest, lead us by the
      good path to the felicity; remove from us the devious attractions of sin
      so that I can reach you. Also free me from reaction to my past sins so
      that there is no hindrance to my progress."

Prasna Upanishad

Prasna Upanishad is a philosophical treatise that explains the relationship
between Atma (soul) and the world of objects. Like all other Upanishads,
it starts with enquiries by six disciples. The Master gives answers to the
questions put by his disciples.

One of the questions asked is about the relationship of the *Atma* with the
objects of the world experienced through the five senses: the eyes, ears,
nose, tongue and skin. Pipilada explains that energy and matter are products
of the Total Mind. By asking the source from which this energy comes, the
corollary to the question is raised.

Pipilada answers that it rises from the Self, the pure conscious centre in us
which is the life spark of each individual. To say that something is born out of
a spiritual centre would be a false philosophical statement. This is because in
the theory of cause and effect, the cause must die away to become effect. It is
further explained that *Prana* (life consciousness) is to *Atma* (soul), what shadow
is to the physical body. Shadow is caused by the physical body, illumined by
Prana (consciousness). In the process, the object which is the body, is not
reduced or tempered with if the shadow has emerged out of it.

Pipilada sums up the philosophy of Prasna Upanishads, explaining that beneath
the flux of things, "existence has supreme unity and immutable stability".

The message that emerges from Prasna Upanishad is:

> The one God hidden in all living beings
> The living witness biding in all hearts-
> The wise who seek and find Him in themselves,
> To them alone belongs eternal joy.

Just as rivers, when they reach the sea, disappear and get their names and
forms liquidate into oneness with the sea and all is called the ocean, so also
these qualities that go to make the *Purusha* (personality), disappear and their
names and forms, destroyed. He becomes one without past, immortal.

Katho Upanishad

Katho Upanishad contains, in question and answers, an inquiry about death.
Young Nachiketa is cursed by his father in a moment of anger to go and meet

death. He goes to the God of death to find out what is so strange about death. Yama, pleased with his obedient conduct, tells him that he is yet a boy and should forget the question. Instead, Yama is prepared to grant him any worldly boon. The clever boy however refuses to be allured. He insists on seeking an answer to his question on 'what lies beyond death'. Katho Upanishad is a dialogue to explain and answer the question of young Nachiketa.

"The one who keeps the company of the wise will rejoice after he has understood the nature of pleasures in damsels, songs and dance. He would choose the path of knowledge concerning the soul."

"The ignorant who lives in the midst of ignorance but fancy themselves as wise, go round and round without reaching anywhere. They are like blind men being guided by blind."

"The wise man who is meditating on the self, who has entered into the dark, who is seated in a cave, who dwells in the abyss just as God, who has left both joys and sorrow, friends and foe behind, has already known what lies beyond death."

Keno Upanishad

Keno Upanishad sings the glory of Brahman, the all pervading, the source of all sense organs.

"Brahman is not an object. He is all pervading, mysterious, incomprehensible, pure consciousness. He is known from intuition or self-recognition. Those who are endowed with pure and subtle intellect can easily grasp the subtle ideas of the Upanishads."

"Knowledge of Brahman arises in those persons who have purified their minds by austerities, self restraint and works either in this birth or in several other births."

"Austerities, self restraint and Karma, the Vedas with all their members are its foundation and Truth is its abode."

Aitreya Upanishad

The entire Aitreya Upanishad is devoted to the praise of wisdom. Beginning with creation, wisdom is the basis of protecting all.

"Fire becoming the speech entered the mouth; air becoming smell entered the nostrils; sun becoming sight entered the eyes; the deity becoming sound entered the ear; the herbs and trees becoming hair, entered the skin; the moon becoming mind, entered the heart; death becoming Apnea, entered the navel; water becoming semen, entered the generative organs."

"Wisdom is the basis of it all."

Roots of Hindu Religion (Sanatan Dharma)

A study of the different Upanishads broadly concludes that Truth has infinite hues. A seeker is able to see only one colour the others, see another. All colours are illuminating. What is important is to understand and admire the rainbow. This is what brings unity and tolerance in all living beings.

A brief introduction would indicate that the Upanishads are the roots of Hindu religion. Rituals, pilgrimages and congregations are nourishment that keep it vibrant. From time to time the enlightened of different ages add small streams that ultimately join the main river. The sacred river keeps majestically flowing, illuminating the minds of generations.

A set pattern of life, from ancient times, dominated the Hindu psyche. The son of man is born with three great social debts upon him. First, to God who has created the world of objects and given senses to him to witness nature. Second, to his ancestors who have given him body wherewith he knows life. Third, to the learned who stored knowledge, age after age, to enlighten his mind.

He repays his debts during the course of his conduct in life. The first debt is paid by doing good to society, through improvement of the environment around him. The second is repaid by bringing up his family and children, educating them and making them capable citizens. The third debt is repaid by handing over knowledge to the younger generation, so that the wheel of life keeps revolving.

Life has been following this pattern on the subcontinent for centuries. India has remained unchanged even amongst great changes. The rise and fall of empires; the brutalities and philanthropies of kings have not been able to change her psyche developed by the Upanishads. Its philosophy contains the secret of continued contentment both in adversity and prosperity of successive generations.

The great German philosopher of the eighteenth century, Schopenheur, says about the Upanishads:

"In the whole world there is no study so beneficial and elevating as that of the Upanishads. It contains the oldest philosophy and psychology of the human race. It is the first attempt to understand the mind and its relationship to the world."

It may be mentioned that the social history of India has been somewhat different from her philosophical approach. While oneness and unity was advocated by our wise men, the establishment did not accept it. They divided Indian society on the basis of birth and not worth. This ruined her progress particularly after the middle ages when its need was felt more intensely. In its hour of trial the political unity of India was found wanting.

In modern terminology, the message of the Upanishads is given in a condensed form in **Figure III.**

Vedic Sanatan Dharma: Hinduism

The philosophy of the Vedas and the Upanishads are the roots of Hindu religion. This has to be practically followed in everyday life. There are four distinct stages. All human beings pass through the prescribed stages. In life, they have certain duties and responsibilities towards the world they are born in. These four stages have been coded in the following extract from the Hitopadesha (guidelines for welfare). A Hindu is expected to follow them during his journey of life.

1. *Brahmacharya:* Age for acquisition of knowledge
2. *Garhasthya:* Work for bringing up the family
3. *Sanyasa:* Detachment and self sacrifice
4. *Vairagya:* Self realization

The Hitopadesha says. "If in the first part of life thou did not gather precious knowledge virtuously, nor cherish spouse and child nor earned by fair means; in the next quarter, nor perform good deeds of self denial, charity, sacrifice; in the third portion of thy mundane life how in the fourth stage when feeble and old, can thou find thyself and God?".

As a code, it provides the foundations of Hinduism in practice. Devoid of rituals and mystics, they were good then, are good now and shall remain so as long as there is life on the planet. It is said that in change, India remains unchanged. A keen observer does not fail to notice the average life of an Indian, which is unconsciously so guided.

Fig. III Upanishads: Human Personality

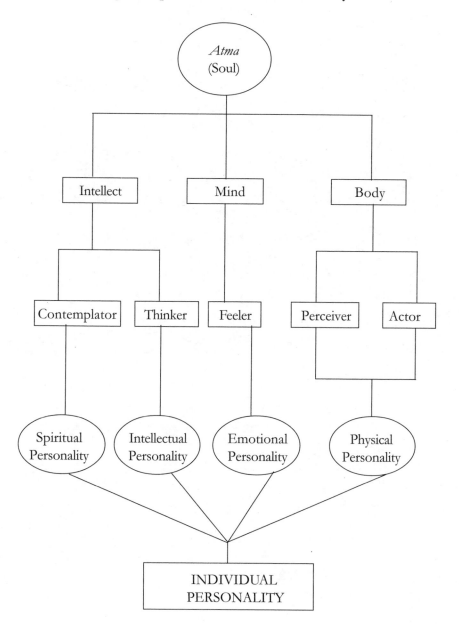

Chapter VIII
'Reformed' Vedanta
The Puranas

During one of his usual rounds, Narada, the representative of the gods, was passing over planet Earth. He was surprised to see Vyasa (author of the Mahabharata), leading a rather depressed life. Reporting the strange spectacle to Lord Vishnu, he reverentially inquired its cause. The Lord said, "Vyasa has delivered my message in the Mahabharata to the intellectuals; he has yet to serve the cause of *bhakti* (devotion) for the common man. His work is still incomplete, hence his restlessness."

Narada promptly conveyed this to Vyasa, advising him to write devotional poetry so that the common man could better understand the philosophy of the scriptures. Vyasa, like several others, got busy working on the Puranas. Amongst the many such volumes generating popular interest, the following eighteen are common.

1. Brahma Purana
2. Padma Purana
3. Vishnu Purana
4. Vayu Purana
5. Bhagwad Purana
6. Naradiya Purana
7. Markandya Purana
8. Varaha Purana
9. Agni Purana
10. Bhavishya Purana
11. Kaivarta Purana
12. Linga Purana
13. Skanda Purana
14. Vamana Purana
15. Kurma Purana
16. Matsya Purana
17. Garuda Purana
18. Brahmananda Purana

What are the Puranas?

The Puranas begin by describing how the world was created. They contain roles of different gods and kings who performed great deeds. While describing them, different writers at successive periods, incorporated the superstitions, myths, love stories and beliefs prevalent during their time. They all, however, never lost sight of the main message, beautifully tucked in absorbing tales. They contain spicy descriptions to excite and enchant both the readers and listeners. When time made them stale, they would be rewritten, containing new ideas without losing their original appeal.

The Puranas mean 'an old description'. With the decline of Sanskrit, the metaphysics of Upanishads became increasingly difficult for common understanding. The wise men of the age devised the medium of the Puranas to convey the philosophical messages for easy understanding. This was to condense philosophy into exciting and interesting stories within easy comprehension of the common people. All ingredients that make a description absorbing have been used to narrate them. Besides helping to develop curiosity and devotion, they carry morals and develop the art of living with hope even under adverse circumstances.

As we find from the numbers, the Puranas were developed over a long span of several centuries. Most of them were written during the period when Buddhism and Jainism ruled Indian minds. The writers, having understood the Indian mind, revived the Hindu spirit through interesting stories of the gods. This was largely responsible for the re-emergence of Hinduism after its decline during the period Buddhism reigned supreme. Even though the Puranas contain about 400,000 couplets, one way or the other, the central Hindu theme that all life in universe is one, is never lost. Having been read or listened over a long time, it serves as a grand repository of Hindu superstition in myths as well as its deep philosophy.

The stories generally convey the two extremes, leaving people to follow the middle path. The numerous gods and rituals that had emerged during this period, were all absorbed within its fold. Like so many rivers falling in the sea to become an ocean, Hindu religion enfolded them all. The Puranas, at a crucial time of Hindu history, were able to lend strength and pave the way for the spirit of revivalism. As we proceed with our story, we would notice how it appeared to lend continuity and strength to Hindu civilization.

Philosophy of the Puranas

Puranas describe the world as a perpetually evolving and dissolving phenomenon, whose creator is Brahma, sustainer is Vishnu and destroyer is Shiva. On the purpose of creation, the Puranas inform there is no final purpose of creation. The concept of progress is merely notional. It is a cycle of endless repetition.

An individual is not just a person; he is a link in the chain of life. They consider, both animals and humans, interconnected. Life in plants may find a field to act in an animal. Similarly, life in an animal may be born in a human. Life thus keeps ascending in the process of evolution, finally merging in the Divine. For an understanding of life, the Puranas propound that each existence bears the penalty or enjoys the fruits of an earlier life. Bradh-Vishnu Purana says:

> The mineral and the vegetable worlds,
> Unmoving, count b'tween them two million forms;
> Nine hundred thousands, the aquatics then;
> Reptiles as many; birds a million;
> Then comes the mammal world, three millions;
> Four hundred thousand kinds of anthropoids;
> Two hundred thousand human species, last.

The Puranas emphasize that an individual is not really an individual; he is a link in the chain of life; a species is not really a separate species. All life on the planet is one; it is interchangeable; an animal can become a man and a man, an animal. Many incarnations of the soul are like years and days of life. The soul in this manner passes through countless incarnations until it attains *moksha* (salvation).

Theory of Karma—reward and punishment

The Puranas convey the Vedic philosophy of dharma for easy understanding of people at all times. The core message remains the same; only the method is modified to suit the altered situation. The Puranas advise that rewards and punishment operate on the laws of Karma. This makes man the custodian of his destiny both for good and bad conduct. They emphasize karma, not fate, to be the real custodian of human destiny. It clarifies that in fate, there is an element of helplessness; karma is inspiration for moral upliftment. For immoral actions, one has to go to hell; heaven awaits those who lead a beneficent life. To keep faith with the wicked and the vigilant, there is a limit of residence at the two places. Fresh opportunity is offered to live life on earth again in accordance to the laws of Karma.

A Hindu assumes that each life is bearing the penalty or enjoying the reward of an earlier birth. In order to keep the spirit of hope alive, it says that Karma cannot be without its effect; if not in one life, it will appear in the next. The cycle keeps revolving when good and bad deeds are compounded as rewards and punishments.

Modern biology and sciences support this theory. We are children of our ancestors and fathers to our children. Defects of quality, of fathers to some acts, pass through genes in us just as they are transmitted from us to our children. The theory of Karma was an excellent way to teach people to resist violence. It imparted the Hindus a moral unity and obligation to all life on the planet. In this manner, the Puranas succeeded in installing in the Hindu mind, love for all creatures and to shun violence of any kind. The theory of Karma proved so flexible that it could explain away even unjust actions haunting the mind. A Hindu, with the help of this theory was able to explain and feel satisfied even with harshest injustices on himself or the man next door. All ups and down that life offers, in any shape or manner, were at once accepted. It is often accepted that a Hindu mind is essentially a contented mind. Karma has been able to explain the ever-existing inequalities amongst men with a philosophic indifference. It is able to justify all ignoble deeds and sufferings that otherwise torture the mind of a logician. The *Garuda Purana* says:

> Sorrow or joy, none other gives to us;
>
> False is the thought that others give us these;
>
> Our own deeds bring us their own just fruits—
>
> Body of mine! Repay by suffering!

To explain evil and to find for common people a scheme that may atone and enable them to accept life with good cheer, has been the job of all religions. The Puranas are one in the same chain whereby people could mitigate their undeserved suffering with hope and consolation.

Impact on Indian mind

The theory of Karma propagated by the Puranas proved most effective and logical. They have been accepted as an effective instrument for good moral conduct. In spite of several animal instincts in man that are injurious to humanity, it has perennially kept him on the track for civilized conduct.

The moment this philosophy is accepted, the inequalities and injustices of man to man; their quarrels, their miseries, wealth, poverty and intelligence, become the result of past existence. The apparent injustice one feels in life is explained away. Man is more at peace with himself and his environment. Instead of feeling frustrated, he tends to look forward for improvement through Karma.

One of the central beliefs, on which the belief of the Hindus rests, is the theory of Karma. It has steered its followers through vicissitudes of time. This, after all, is what almost all religions in the world have tried to explain; not the cause of suffering, but undeserved suffering. They try to explain evil and show alternatives for a more pleasant life, accepting suffering with grace and peace.

The philosophy of Karma has enabled India to be peaceful, contented and non-aggressive even when faced with barbarous provocation!

Shrimad Bhagwad Purana

Amongst the Puranas, the *Bhagwad Purana* is the most popular. Its stories are so enchanting and full of worldly wisdom that almost everything done in good faith is permissible. The interesting and absorbing stories of gods performing everyday deeds like human beings, make the *Bhagwad* the beloved scripture of the Hindus. No wonder it eliminated all other Puranas. It became one work that is widely read by all classes in North India. The modern *Bhagwad Purana* is again a revised version of the original. The text is entirely devoted to the life and message of Shri Krishna as an incarnation of Maha Vishnu. After reading the entire Purana, we find it to be entirely devoted to the glory, glamour and greatness of Shri Krishna. Right in the beginning it says:

"The Lord of the Universe, for his pleasure and play and for the salvation of mankind, assumes different forms in different ages. The Lord, though without form and attributes and beyond all *gunas*, projected this Universe out of his Divine powers."

The Puranas have mainly concentrated on Karma and incarnation. In *Bhagwad*, Vyasa focusses on developing devotion for Shri Krishna; right from his childhood to the time he leaves his mortal body.

"When Krishna went away from the World, taking along with him *dharma* and *jnana,* there arose the sun of *Bhagwad Purana*." So popular did *Bhagwad Purana* become, that successive generations accepted its message as the fifth objective of life; the other four being—

(1)   Morality (*dharma*)
(2)   Wealth (*artha*)
(3)   Pleasure (*kama*)
(4)   Liberation (*moksha*).

Some passages from Bhagwad Purana

To modern India the *Bhagwad* is a condensed and simplified version of ancient knowledge narrated through interesting stories. It has been a symbol of solace to the readers, as would appear from some of its selected passages.

"Man experiences suffering, misery and death, all caused by ignorance, until he wakes up and seeks the divine Truth."

"When the moon is reflected in the ocean, the waves in the ocean make it appear restless, but in reality, the moon is steady and calm. It is the water that is restless. Similarly the attributes of the non-self are superimposed on the Self and it is the ignorant man, who through maya, identifies the attributes of finitude and bondage with himself; but this bondage is never in the true Self."

On wealth

"Most men are engaged seeking wealth and material comforts. They are spending all their energy in providing such things for themselves or their families. Life, like wind, is short. It is therefore entirely on us to be ever seeking the temporal or the permanent!"

On wisdom

" Truly wise is he who is unstirred by praise or blame, by love or hatred. He is not moved by the opposites. The wise man who looks upon himself as the unchangeable reality, though his senses move in material objects, knows himself to be not the doer but witness of the senses responding to their objects."

"The most ignorant man is similarly happy like the most wise, each in his own way. Those who are in the middle, neither completely ignorant nor completely wise are worst. They have understood the apparent, but are devoid of bliss of God."

"If anyone does harm you, do not return the injury caused by him. Think good of him, because love conquers all. When the Lord of the universe is loved, the whole world is filled with rejoicing".

The study of the *Bhagwad* shows that its basic thoughts have been derived from the Gita. Yet, to meet the needs of all, *Bhagwad* explains the metaphysical with examples that were later revealed by science.

The *Bhagwad* salutes the one engaged in service with the following:

"Blessed indeed is that one; glorious indeed is that action; true indeed is that life; enlightened indeed is that mind; fruitful indeed is that word which is devoted in the loving service of all living beings, which also is the Self of the Universe."

Deliverance (*moksha*—salvation)

The ultimate objective of an average Indian is deliverance. In life, he aspires for release from the chain of endless desires. When dead, his ideal is to escape rebirth. The Puranas maintain their vibrancy by absorbing various practices that kept emerging in society. To promote larger existence, different practices like yoga, penance, charity, renunciation and the usual acts of sacrifice were emphasized. Such acts of sacrifice, consciously or unconsciously, improved the life of Indians.

The two great Hindu epics, Ramayana and Mahabharata glorify *moksha*, (freedom from rebirth). In answer to a question as to what is the most wonderful thing in the world, Yudhisthira replies, "Man after man dies; even after seeing this, men still move about as if they were immortal." Similarly, in Ramayana, Sita asks her reward for fidelity through every redemption from temptation and trial, by death:

> If in truth unto my husband I have proved a faithful wife,
>
> Mother earth relieve thy Sita from the burden of this life.

Without undue worry for the final purpose towards which the whole creation moves, it emphasizes the fallacy of 'progress' and the permanency of change. First the Upanishads, four thousand years ago, then Gautam Buddha, two thousands years later and again after two thousand and five hundred years, in modern times, Mahatma Gandhi sought not to be reborn.

Chapter IX
Origin of Caste System
Its Causes and Effects

When the Aryans arrived in India they met a new race. The earliest reference to the caste system is traceable from the *Rig Veda* with reference to division of work. These were written after the initial suspicion and conflicts were over. Interpreted in the light of the Vedantic psychology, it was in its origin a scheme for social organization, linked with four stages of life, viz. educational organization consisting of the learned or Brahman class and the student or the *Brhmachari*; a defence (executive or political) organization consisting of the chivalrous or the Kshatriya class; an economic organization, consisting of the commercial or Vaishya class and the householder *(Grihastha)* order; and an industrial or labour organization, consisting of *Shudras* or workman class as servants and the *Sanyasi*, as a spiritual person.

The new arrangement was devised as a great broad mould into which could be poured the multitudinous tribes of the entire land. It is observed from the detailed description of the Laws of Manu, the formulator and arranger of these laws, that these included local customs, tribal customs, long standing family customs. The biological principle incorporated with the system are the two laws–(1) law of heredity and (2) law of spontaneous variation or mutation–gradual shifting from occupation to heredity succession. The four castes names were indicative of their respective occupations. The system of occupational guilds was prevalent even in the West. There were the Smiths, working with hot iron; Butlers, connected with food services; and Priests, performing duties alike that of Brahmins. Then there were King Log and King Stork, who were autocratic despots and dictatorial monarchs in the West.

Adverse effects of the Laws of Manu

In time, western societies, under economic compulsions and social changes, moderated the extremes. In India, not only did they continue but got corrupted with passage of time, deeply damaging the social structure. Sanskrit scriptures say, "Laws and customs have to change with time, place and circumstances." There is no code of human action (code of Manu being no exception), which indefinitely continues to benefit all equally and produces only good results. In fact, when it has lived its utility, it must change and be replaced with a new code suiting the circumstances of the age. It must be remembered that here is no uniformity, no finality and no permanence, in man-made laws of any kind.

Manu himself declares that dharma (laws), rights and duties change with the age of humanity. The laws are different in every age—be it *Satyayuga,* the age of virtue; *Treta,* (where virtue fall by a fourth); *Dwapar* and *Kalyuga,* the age of misery. All the four ages together make a Mahayuga. Of this, we are supposed to have passed 3,888,888 years out of a total life of a *Kalpa* which is 4,320,000,000 years.

Manu had framed the laws at a time when the *Sanatan dharma* was the accepted creed of Indian society. Social conditions changed with time, the laws of Manu remained collecting new aberrations. Earlier classifications made one class permanently attached to their professions denying opportunities to members of the other class. This, being against the laws of Nature, could only prevail for a short time. In due course the system turned into a disaster, alienating a large population of the country from the mainstream. Whatever the benefits of enforcement of caste endogamy to other conditions, it proved to be an excess; it fractured the entire social system.

New forces of change

Thinkers of later period were no mute witnesses to the damage inflicted by the caste system to the entire social system. Gautam Buddha and Mahavira were the first to shift the basis of the social organization that was ruining society. Both wanted and largely succeeded in shifting back, the basis of the Indian social organization, from crass artificialized heredity to elastic, rational, natural and spontaneous variation. A whole chapter of the Buddhist *Dharampada* named 'Brahmana-Yaggo' is devoted to the exposition of the nature of the true Brahmin:

> Not matted locks, no birth in any clan,
> Or family, or from some mother's womb,
> Can make a man a real Brahmana.
> He who is true, pure, dutiful; sins not
> In deed, words, thought; gathers not worldly goods;
> Bears patiently hard words, bonds beatings too
> And lets not anger rise within his mind,
> Strong with the strength of all forgiveness;
> Him do I call a real Brahmana.
>
> Mere birth makes not a real Brahmana;
> Nor makes a Shudra; deeds and ways of living,
> Appropriate, make either one or the other.

> The sun doth make the day; the night the moon;
>
> Courageous chivalry, the Kshatriya;
>
> Wisdom and thoughtfulness, the Brahmana.

Buddha, while supporting the classification, was against its imposition by birth. It clearly indicates that the virus of caste system had entered Indian system, causing the wise to worry.

Jainism during the same period was even more vocal and blunt:

> The human race is one, though it's made up
>
> Of many tribes with many names. But four
>
> Broad classes may be plainly seen therein,
>
> The men of studious vows are Brahmanas;
>
> Who practice use of arms are Kshatriyas;
>
> Who gather wealth by lawful merchantry
>
> Are Vaishyas; those who live by service- wage
>
> Are Shudras. By their occupations only
>
> Are the four thus marked off; no otherwise.
>
> The birth of anyone cannot be seen
>
> Upon his face; his actions can be seen.

The attempt made during ancient India was in a manner befitting the era. It was an age when India rivalled the great Empires of the Romans, the Macadonians, the Persians and the Chinese. As social changes put greater pressure for change in system, its rigidity proportionately increased. Excessive selfishness by custodians and trustees, deriving unearned privileges, would not let the system be reformed. On the contrary, their resistance stiffened, bringing new restrictions, until we reach the age of medieval India.

When man does not hear the voice of reason, Nature, through its immutable laws, interferes. The caste system having weakened society, was divided into different compartments, each at war with the other. Even the *Bhagwad Purana* was equally rigid on the caste system when it said:

> Better one's thankless dharma
>
> Than alien task though well performed
>
> Better to die, doing ones own task;
>
> Another's task is fraught with danger.

Sceptics may interpret it in a manner suiting their convictions, but truth from the verse, shows the unholy unity of the privileged custodians and consequences accruing from it. The adverse effect of the system weakened the nation socially and politically. It became tempting for others to take advantage of India's weakness. New forces soon arrived to fill the vacuum. Islam, in medieval

India, demonstrated the fallacy of the ancient arrangement by showing how individuals, performing different functions, were treated equally as fellow human beings. How at the social level, they dined and prayed together and demonstrated brotherhood amongst men! During this period, Hinduism grew weaker. First Buddhism and later Islam, with a forceful influence of goodwill, exposed the shortcomings of the caste system.

Acharya Shankara responded to the call for change in the *Sanatan Dharma*. With tremendous energy and deep knowledge of the Vedanta, he restored. Hinduism to its earlier status that was earlier relegated during royal patronage to Buddhism. With the restoration of priesthood, caste system, got sanction as a social system once again; it was further strengthened by restoring the lost respect of the Brahmins. After few centuries, once again, efforts were made by saints and sages like Ramanuja, Ramananada, Guru Nanak and Kabir. Having realized the damaging effects of the system on polity and social unity, they tried for its eradication. But exploitative tendencies of innocent people proved too strong to be dislodged. As Muslim political domination grew, the Brahmins ceased enjoying special privileges. Being treated like the others, they too were required to pay taxes in the new regime. The attitude of the perpetrators instead of mellowing down, grew more and more rigid. During medieval times, it reached inhuman proportions inflicting poverty and untouchability on its victims; it restricted stimulus to enterprise and creativity. The high class 'trustees', to consolidate their hold, further multiplied castes into sub-castes. It was considered that greater the number of sub-castes, more secure and indispensable their position.

A review of the system

We have discussed the evolution of the social arrangement nearly four thousand years ago when social relationship was in its formative stage. The ancient Indian civilization recognized, enunciated and essayed to apply, the principles consciously and deliberately. History of other societies confirm that similar arrangements existed for identical reasons. The challenges faced by the caste system during its infancy were too great to bear. It was a miracle; inspite of lack of royal support, the system survived. The strength of survival perhaps lay in the philosophy of Oneness amongst all human beings as laid down in the *Sanatan Dharma*. It is ironical but true that philosophy, in practice, contradicted the social system. The learned may argue, quoting scriptures but the ugliness of the system cannot be denied.

We must not forget that on the long road to civilization, social order and cultural creation accelerate progress. History and geography may determine the direction of society, but evolutionary laws are made by the wise of the age. In India, the element of 'heredity' has been grossly exaggerated and made rigid; in the West, blind competition is too much in the fore. As in politico-economical life of nations, 'trustees' make themselves beneficiaries, leaders become exploiters; protectors turn into oppressors; feeders become the devourers; public servants change into public master; and thereby perennially cause instability. In the span of life of the human race, the present times with their characteristic cultures based on physical sciences and machinist intellectuality, require a democratic and socialist polity. It is not enough to merely pray and hope that god's will will be done; it is necessary to know what that will is. It is not enough to be willing to do one's duty; we ought to be aware of what that duty in a particular situation is.

The Age of Enlightenment

It is only the man with a most perfect divine moral nature
who is able to combine in himself
quickness of apprehension, intelligence and understanding—
qualities necessary to exercise
command, imagination magnanimity,
generosity, benignity and gentleness—
qualities necessary for exercise of patience,
originality, energy, strength of character and determination—
qualities necessary for the exercise of
endurance, piety, nobility, seriousness, order and regularity—
qualities necessary for exercise of
dignity, grace, method, subtlety and penetration—
qualities necessary for critical judgement.

—*Confucius*

Chapter X
Vardhaman Mahavira

We join the story during the period when the philosophy of the Upanishads had ignited the imagination of the intellectuals. India was producing unparalleled wealth. Excessive religion had created a leisurely class, which loved pleasure and power. Imagination, devoid of action, continued to fly to lofty heights. If there were characters like Charavaka denouncing metaphysics, there were saints preaching abstinence.

New stars were rising in the horizon. They were Mahavira and Gautama Buddha. Both represented reactions to excessive religiosity and rituals. This was particularly apparent amongst the rich who were fond of leisure and pleasure.

In the middle of the sixth century BC, a boy was born in a wealthy family at Vaishali in Bihar. When the boy reached the age of 31 years, his parents, according to prevailing customs of the clan, duly starved themselves to death.

Such an acts was utterly shocking to the young man.

To seek understanding of such dreadful practices, Vardhaman, as he was named, stepped out from his home in search of truth as an ascetic. For thirteen years, he would wander all over the country, without accepting any practice already in vogue. Instead, he sought rational explanation to what went around him. Mahavira, like a modern scientist, would go about experimenting, observing, analysing and arriving at conclusions.

After another thirteen years, he was for the first time, acknowledged by a small group of people as a conqueror– 'jina'. They called themselves Jains and gave the title of 'Mahavira' to their leader.

Teachings of Mahavira

Vardhaman Mahavira (BC 599-527) initiated thought by suggesting that nothing is true except from one point of view; from the other, it may probably be false. The concept of absolute truth during those days held sway over the Indian minds. This was shattered when Mahavira stated that the Universe had existed from eternity and that its infinite changes and revolutions were due to the inherent nature of the universe rather than the intervention of a deity. Starting on such a note, subsequent disciples provided a variety of changes to the old theories handed down from the Vedic age.

Mahavira lived and preached in an age when free thought dominated the minds of men. Belief in many gods had grown during a long period of stagnancy. This was now challenged by him. Priests had so far been suggesting that for a happy next life one had to undergo penance during the present. Yet man was more concerned with happiness in the present life than what lay beyond! Promises that penance in this life will yield luxuries in the next now appeared unconvincing to them. The need of the age therefore demanded deviation from old practices. If it was necessary to discriminate between right and wrong, peace and penance; it had to be now, in this life.

People had enough of metaphysics! Destiny had sent to India men like Mahavira and Gautama Buddha almost at the same time to fight old, worn out beliefs. Both of them would focus away from the Vedas and the Upanishads. Their philosophy would centre not on gods or incarnation and similar other practices preached by priests. They would talk of peace of mind and happiness in this life.

As a seeker, the core of Mahavira's philosophy was duality. Nothing in the world was true except from one point of view. Logic and reasoning was the instrument to discover what was right; one developed theories and opinions within the framework of his surroundings. What was right earlier was no more relevant. According to Mahavira, absolute reality is too vast to be comprehensible. It is like blind men probing an elephant. One who is able to reach and feel the ears, considers the world to be a colossal fan; the one who is able to reach the foot, considers it to be a huge pillar. All judgements are therefore essentially in a frame, unable to encompass the entire reality.

As we move further, we will find that other religions, born in different environment with different social structure, reached the same conclusion.

The Vedas and Upanishads were the guiding stars of that age. Anyone could interpret them to suit his ways. Suddenly there was a new religion that not only did not seek any inspiration from the Vedas but dared to contradict its sayings.

About creation, Mahavira and his followers taught that God was not necessary to create the world. It has existed from eternity and will remain till eternity. Changes that keep occurring in the universe are due to inherent powers in the nature of the universe rather than because of action by a deity.

This question remains unanswered even after three milleniums. Modern world's greatest scientist, Stephen Hawkins has this to say about absolute reality:

"The God! I view God as a metaphor of philosophy."

" If we do discover a complete theory, it should be understandable by everyone, not by just few scientists. Then, we shall as philosophers, scientists and just ordinary people be able to take part in the discussions of this question that why it is that the universe and we exist. If we find the answer to that, it will be the ultimate triumph for the human reason, for then we shall know the mind of God."

Influence of new over old

As Jainism spread through in the country, its overpowering influence over society began changing the thinking of people. Followers started idolizing successive saints of Jainism. In time, they began to be worshipped as men who had reached Godhood. As the number of such saints increased, the religious pattern of other religions and Jainism began to grow indistinguishable.

Mahavira had rejected the Vedic theory of reincarnation. When later saints began to be worshipped as Gods, acceptance of rebirth was only the next step. This appeared in the form of transmigration. Jains believed that their extraordinary sayings, after their deaths, lived in some shadowy realm, unaffected by the world of censor. They were above any chance of rebirth for sometime but the spirit would appear in a fresh form later.

This was as near to incarnation as could be in the light of Mahavira's declaration.

An ideal Jain ascetic

An ideal Jain ascetic is required to take five vows :

1. not to kill anything,
2. not to lie,
3. not to take what is not given,
4. to preserve chastity,
5. to renounce pleasure in all external things.

Since pleasure has been considered base, the idea was to be indifferent to both pleasure and pain with freedom from the objects of the outer world. This was exactly what the Vedas and Upanishads taught!

Starting with doubt, the mother of reason, the Jain religion, enriched and moulded by environment, became a prominent faith. India was taking its initial steps towards a pluralistic society where thousand flowers shall bloom simultaneously with each offering its unique pleasant smell.

It was indeed a glorious age that gave India three of it's greatest thinkers one after another—Mahavira, Gautama Buddha and Maharishi Kapila.

They were all wealthy and could have lived a life of luxury. Yet they preferred penance and asceticism at a time when India was full of riches; when it had no threat of invaders; these great men voluntarily chose an ascetic life. Future kings who would rule India during her golden period largely followed their example; they avoided craving; when old, they would voluntarily hand the reigns of power to the new generation. Mahavira's contribution to spiritual life helped develop non-violence and abstainence from greed in all manner.

Chapter XI
Gautama Buddha

When good grows weak
When evil increases,
I make myself a body;
To every age I come back
To deliver the holy,
To destroy the sin of the sinner,
To establish righteousness.

—Bhagwad Gita

The earliest Aryans had produced the Vedas and the Upanishads. During the sixth and fifth centuries BC, India were blessed with Mahavira, Buddha and Kapila. They found that the old scriptures needed reforms. They discovered that the bliss they looked for was still a delusion. Truth that may free man from misery had still to be realized! Enquiry about such questions, during this period, was a quest, not only in India; similar thoughts were also being explored in Greece and China. Amongst the uncertainties of physical nature, the wise were seeking truth for a blissful life.

Buddha was born in BC 563 in the Himalayan town of Kapilvastu. As a prince, he had every material comfort. He was delicately nurtured, had different palaces for different seasons of the year. Surrounded by luxuries of a prosperous kingdom, he grew up in abundant material comfort. Yet, at the age of 21 when affairs of state could no longer confine his movements indoor, he was inadvertently exposed to disease, misery and old age. He pondered over the meaning of life and suffered the ennui and anguish most of us suffer in our late teens.

He had two alternatives—either to enjoy the pleasures and luxuries of life or to try the tools offered by religion and spirituality. Being born a prince, he had already enjoyed the first; so he decided to go in for the second.

He left his wife and son behind one night in search of the cause for all the miseries of human life and its solution.

His wanderings

During the decade of his wanderings in search of emancipation, he travelled from place to place searching for teachers. He would approach the masters of his time for knowledge. He learnt whatever they could teach; but remained unfulfilled. He would fast; lead an ascetic life of a yogi and perform penance to achieve his goal but without results. He even started living on just a few morsels of rice until he was reduced to a moving corpse. Many years of self torture only poisoned any holiness that may have developed as a result of self-denial. He rejected it all and turned to his Will within to seek an answer.

The turning point

Suddenly one day, Buddha remembered an experience of his childhood. Once, while waiting for his father, under the shade of a *jambu* tree, he had enjoyed a state of consciousness, characterized by a sense of freedom, bodily well being and mental happiness.

He left fasting and similar acts of self-torture. Soon he was again in robust health. Sitting under the Bodhi tree, he resolved to leave only after he got the answer to the miseries of life. The pillars of Buddha's teachings emerged from that deep contemplation. There is *'dukha'* or discontentment and it's cause is craving. Discontentment can be got rid of through the eight skills called 'Eight Fold Path'.

While most of us experience discontentment, few understand the cause. According to Buddha, we live constantly in a state of craving. We crave what we find pleasurable physically, emotionally and psychologically and reject what we do not. This constant craving, grasping and rejecting is our restlessness, our state of discontentment and is caused by lack of understanding of three key truths: that everything including us, exist interdependently; that everything is constantly in change; and the way out of *dukha* is neither in increasing consumption nor abstaining from it.

Suddenly, one day he had visions of birth and death in the endless stream of life. He saw every death frustrated with a new birth; every peace and joy balanced with new desires and consequent discontent; new disappointments, new grieves and new pains!

When he rose from the seat under the Bodhi tree, he was transformed. In his own words, "Thus with mind concentrated, purified, cleaned, I saw Beings passing away and then being reborn; low and high; in happy or miserable existence according to their Karma–the Universal law of reward and punishment." He reached to the conclusion that:

"Happiness is possible neither here or hereafter. Only peace is possible—only if the cool quietude of craving ended."

His pilgrimage to preach

Buddha set out to preach his gospel in accordance with the then social life of the community. India lived in villages, punctuated with towns, generally located by the sides of rivers. Agriculture thrived. Population was sparse. There was plenty of everything for human needs. There was time for debates, declamations and dialogues and other spiritual pursuits. In such an environment people were only too willing to listen to what Gautama would preach.

Buddha, throughout his life invariably insisted upon knowing the world, to live in awareness. This was in direct contradiction of earlier teachings that gave preference to the non-material, unknown and unknowable. The new knowledge that Budhha gave was revolutionary in thought. It made people conscious of the material world. The Hindu religion created out of the Vedas and Upanishads, was at once challenged. People could now understand and assimilate what Buddha advised. It appeared more practical following after Buddha's, preachings.

A silent revolution started that would engulf not only India but entire Asia. Buddha's teachings would remain and stand the test of time.

Buddha as a teacher

Gautama started preaching from Sarnath in modern Varanasi. He would walk from place to place accompanied by his favourite disciples. Not caring for tomorrow, he would feel contented to be fed by local admirers. He would typically hold discourses in gardens or woods by the side of a river. The afternoons were devoted to meditation, evenings to instruction. His discourses contained questions, moral parables and courteous controversies. He would gently put his message before the audience. The callous indifference to writing continued even during his period. Buddha and his disciples followed the same practice. He would empower his messages in *Sutras*. These were memorized, propagated and quoted by his disciples.

This use of the mind for memorizing was to pay India rich dividends in the field of mathematics and later, in information technology.

Preaching of Buddha

Buddha preached the reformed version of the Upanishads in easy-to-understand dialogues. Reason governed his speech. During debates with intellectuals, he would avoid talking about eternity, immortality and God. About infinity, he would just smile! He never entertained questions about the beginning or the end of the world; whether the soul is the same as the body or different from it. Buddha was opposed to the caste system. He told his disciples thus:

"Go into all lands and preach our gospel: the rich and the poor, and the high and the lowly are all one and that all castes unite in this religion, as do the rivers in sea."

His most popular message to the masses was: "Saintliness and contentment lie not in the knowledge of the Universe and God, but simply in selfless and beneficent living."

Buddha preached at a time when Hindu religion was tilting towards theology. He offered a reformed version of religion and social evils that had crept in society. Buddha defined enlightenment "to be the direct perception of the past, present and the future. It enables intuition to give its findings without the channel of mind."

The Eight-Fold Path

To get rid of misery, Buddha advised an eight-fold route to peace.

(a)   Death carries away the man who seeks only the flowers of sensual pleasure, just as torrential floods, carries away a sleeping village.

(b)   Do not criticize others for what they do, or have not done. Beware of what you yourself do or have not done.

(c)   Just as a beautiful flower is radiant, yet lacks fragrance, so are the beautiful words of one who does not act accordingly.

(d)   The fragrance of flowers even that of sandalwood or of essence, even that of jasmine or of incense, cannot go against the wind. But the sweet fragrance of intelligence spreads the fragrance of its virtue in all directions.

(e)   As long as evil action has not borne its fruit, the fool imagines that it is as sweet as honey. But when the action bears its fruits, he reaps only suffering.

(f)   Those who amass nothing, who eat moderately, who have perceived the emptiness of all things and those who have attained unconditional liberation, their path is as difficult to trace as that of a bird in the air.

(g)   To one who is respectful to his elders, four things increase: Long life, Beauty, Happiness and Strength.

(h)   Moderation in speech, control of mind, abstention from evil actions – these three modes of action are to be practised first of all to attain the path shown by the sages.

Buddha declared that the above laws of reflection are immutable within the flux of change. His sermons remained the same from the first day to the last. Once he set in motion the 'wheel of truth', it used to be almost a repetition with difference only in emphasis.

Realism and uniqueness

In the history of religions, nothing is stranger than the fact that the preacher never talked of God, immortality, eternity and supernatural powers. Buddha would say that infinity is a myth and that an atom can never fully understand the cosmos. Inspite of all our knowledge, it will always remain very small. For forty years, he ceaselessly delivered his message as one man to another man. The serenity and modesty we find in his numerous statutes all over the world, reflect the modesty and love that flowed in his heart.

More than all enemies, an undisciplined mind is your worst enemy. More than your father, mother and family, a well-disciplined mind does greater good.

As a bee takes the essence of the flower and flies away without destroying its beauty or perfume, so let the sage wander in the world.

To his disciples, he advised them to go into different lands to preach the gospel they had learnt. In due course of time, it began resounding all over India and countries beyond. Without shedding blood or using cohesive power of the state, with goodwill, as the instrument, his disciples created a unique awareness in the masses. It helped India to prosper both materially and spiritually. Buddhism that travelled to Tibet, Mongolia, China and Japan was influenced by Vedic philosophy, adopting itself to practices and myths that prevailed in those countries. While it was useful for the time being, the change brought about by the coming generation started deviating from the original thought. The life of thought that guided the destiny of the subcontinent helped India to enter the Golden Age. This period was to last for nearly a thousand years. The strength his philosophy provided made people go to distant countries for propagation of spiritual knowledge.

All religions in course of time develop theological overtones. After the Prophet has passed away, his disciples, unable to maintain the same level of realization, modified and reinterpreted the meaning. Soon the original essence was gone, only its upper crust remained in the form of rituals. This also happened with Buddhism. Faced with the simple and clear policy of the Eight-Fold Path, people flocked towards Buddhism. Vedanta in course of time had slipped into dogmatism and theology. It needed a shock treatment. Buddhism provided this shock by pointing out the shortcomings that time and misinterpretation had rendered to the original philosophy.

The well-known twentieth century philosopher Bertrand Russell says: "Of all the religions which prevail in the World, I am attracted by Buddhism."

Soon after Buddha was gone, another great thinker, Kapila, appeared on the Indian horizon. He revolutionized Vedantic philosophy as practised in that age. Great thoughts and prosperity often compliment each other. The glorious days of India had begun with the impetus and the meaning added to life by Mahavira, Buddha and Kapila.

Let us now understand Kapila's graphic ideas about the Creator and the created.

Chapter XII
Kapila–'The Perfect Being'

The Vedas describe the sky, sun, earth, fire, light, wind and water–the elements of nature as their earliest gods. These natural causes were subsequently personified and made into deities: sky, was called father Varuna; mother earth as Prithvi; the rain god being Paranjaya; fire was agni; the wind, vayu; the storms, Indra; the furrow in fields, Sita.

By fifth century BC this mysticism gradually developed into the metaphysical. The Vedas had started with divinity and concept of several gods. Centuries of observation and understanding brought new knowledge to modify the original thoughts. Nature was no longer a stranger; the wise had begun understanding its rythm. Gautama and Mahavira, who preached Buddhism and Jainism during this period completely neglected to mention gods in their sermons. Logic and reason appeared more authentic and convincing guides.

Restless deep blue seas, a single continent, brownish rocks glittering here and there with particles of bright minerals, then a continuous process of volcanic eruptions, dust and vapours, with lava flowering in hot crimson rivers. A never ending sound of sea waves, explosions, changes in temperature with cycles of day and night. Such may have been the perceived picture of the planet in the imagination of the earliest thinkers! These were now being understood more and more.

In an age of high intellectual activity, there appeared a great, perhaps the greatest ancient philosopher of India. He methodically and in precise terms, explained evolution of life from matter. He described human life with its happiness and pain, without the existence of a creator. This perfect human being was Rishi Kapila, who gave the world the Sankhya system of philosophy. This enabled, albeit only partially, removal of fear out of which gods were created during the earliest periods. With the vagaries of time, his fame remained largely confined amongst intellectuals. Lord Krishna, in the Bhagwad Gita, Chapter X, *Shloka* 26 pays the highest tribute to Kapila when he says:

"Of all trees, I am Aswastha, (Peepal Tree); of Devarishis, I am Narada; of the Siddhas (perfect ones), I am Muni Kapila."

Lord Krishna himself has singled out Kapila for this great status as the most perfect amongst all thinkers. The Gita, it may be pointed out, mainly follows the Sankhya system. Kapila perceived the play of nature, drawing conclusions from direct perception. So far, the unexplainable was drowned in mysticism or attributed to the Creator; not so in Sankhya system. For the first time a thinker clearly perceived complete independence of the human mind with full confidence in its powers.

Sankhya system

Developed by philosopher Kapila around BC 500, it is perhaps the oldest philosophy of the world. "There is no mystic Being who controls our destinies; no redeemer; no bestower of salvation. Instead, there is complete independence and freedom. We are responsible for our pleasures and pains according to the level of understanding of individual." The philosopy of Kapila starts with the assumption that the goal of all human beings is to eradicate suffering.

Kapila examines this complex system of evaluation with precision. He postulates how consciousness (*Purusha*) triggers the evolutionary powers (*Gunas*) of matter (*Prakriti*) in the ever revolving cycle of birth, death and birth again. He makes no distinction between matter, plants, animal and human life. According to his philosophy, they are all part of an infinite chain acting according to their inherent qualities.

Two thousand years later, Charles Darwin arrived at a similar conclusion, about the unity of evolution on earth.

Kapila deals with human suffering on an intellectual plane by stating that suffering, during man's journey, is neither created nor cured by any creator; it can only be cured by understanding. Effort by shedding pain and increasing pleasure by physical means is of no avail. This logical, step by step, perception is the philosophy of Sankhya, which literally means enumeration. Kapila proceeds to name 25 realities (*Tattwas*) which make up the world. He arranges these realities in a relationship which may be indicated as follows:

> *Prakriti* (producer) is a physical principle. Through its powers of evolution (*Gunas*) it produces intellect *(Buddhi)*, the power of perception, which through its evolutionary powers *(Gunas)*, produces:

(a) The five elements of sensory powers of the internal world:

    (i)   Sight
    (ii) Hearing
    (iii) Smell
    (iv) Taste and
    (v)   Touch

(b) Mind (*Manas*), the power of conception.

(c) The five sense organs {corresponding to five sensory powers of (a)}:
  (i)   Eyes
  (ii)   Ears
  (iii) Nose
  (iv)   Tongue and
  (v)   Skin

(d) The five organs of action:
  (i)   Larynx
  (ii)   Hands
  (iii) Feet
  (iv)   Excretory organs and
  (v)   Generating organs

(e) The five gross elements of the external world:
  (i)   Ether
  (ii)   Air
  (iii) Fire and Light
  (iv)   Water, and
  (v)   Earth

Purusha (spirit, consciousness), a universal psychical principle which, though unable to do anything by itself, animates and vitalizes *Prakriti* and stirs its evolutionary powers to all their activities.

Role of a creator

Kapila, like Mahavira and Buddha, did not require any one to create *Prakriti* (matter) or *Purusha* (spirit). He argues that something cannot be created out of nothing; hence the creator and the created are the same. This is perhaps the reason why the self-realized feel the presence of the creator in the created which is the world of objects!

The Sankhya system explains that everything in *Prakriti* is either bound or free. If God is free, he had no need to create a world. If bound, he is imperfect and not God. If God is good and has divine powers, He would not have perhaps created such an imperfect world, with so much suffering; with such certainty of death!

This must have been a challenging idea about God, particularly when, fear and uncertainty dominated life. After being bold and contradictory to the concept of God held by priests and people of that age, Kapila wisely avoids offending those who had fixed their minds on the Vedas by tickling their vanity and saying, "Vedas are an authority, since the authors knew the truth."

Evolution and dissolution–a chain in continuity

Kapila says, "*Prakriti* (producer, substance) never develops the *Gunas* (evolutionary powers); never act by themselves; they do so only through the inspiration of *Purusha* (spirit, consciousness). The physical world is animated, vitalized and stimulated to evolve by the psychical principle everywhere." The relationship between *Prakriti* and spirit is like that of magnet and iron; it attracts iron (*Prakriti*) which with the evolutionary powers (*Tattwas*), moves the cycle of evolution and dissolution. The *Purusha* (spirit) does not however undergo any change; it acts like a catalyst, starting the reaction, but not undergoing change in itself.

Explaining the *Purusha,* he says: "The spirit has the ruling influence over *Prakriti*, the evolving world caused by their proximity. This impels Prakriti to go for steps of production; the attraction between the two leads to creation. In no other way is spirit the agent or concerned with creation."

The spirit is therefore the same in all organism; it does not share any individuality which is essentially physical. We are what we are, not because of our spirit, but because of our origin, evolution and experiences of our bodies and minds. While mind is a part of the body like other organs; the spirit is secluded.

The spirit is free within us all; mind and body are bound by the laws of evolutionary powers (*Gunas*): Spirit therefore does not act; what acts is a combination of body and mind.

Evolution of self

Evolution of the Self has been explained by Kapila as a process. It is the Self that generates the functions of sight, hearing, smell, taste and touch. These, functions then produce the organs of eyes, ears, nose, tongue and skin. When religious scriptures preach understanding of Self, they only mean awareness about all our sense organs. Modern religious philosophers like J. Krishnamurthi and Acharya Rajneesh have always placed greatest emphasis on awareness.

Mind, body and suffering

Kapila treats the world of mind and body as substance. They are a result of evolution by natural process, bound by the cycle of growth, decay and growth again. The mind is perishable but not the spirit. Only the individual self, bound up with matter and body, is born, dies and born again. Says Kapila:

"Suffering results because individual self is bound with mind and body. Bondage is caused by not discriminating between the self and the turbulence of ever striving egos." When *Maya,* the unsubstantial show of life and time, becomes the all important part of existence, suffering is inevitable. "The escape from suffering is in understanding and realization that the essence of all, is the spirit; it is safe beyond good or evil, joy and pain, birth and death." When this is accepted as a fact, difficulties of life do not really have any effect. A person, who has understood and realized this truth, becomes merely a witness of happenings. He is aware; but not affected.

Kapila advised that, "the only knowledge of twenty five realities is that neither I am, nor is ought mine, nor do I exist." In other words, he means to say, that personal separateness is an illusion. All that exists is the vast evolving and dissolving froth of matter and mind, of bodies and selves and the quiet eternity of immutable soul. This thought irrespective of religious inclinations has entered the psyche of India. Repeatedly it has been expressed by coming generations in different languages. It arrived at the harmony of the spiritual mind and intuitive reason. This is the secret of happiness of the Indian people. It is the source of continuity of her culture and civilization.

Kapila has ruled over the Hindu minds ever since he initiated the Sankhya philosophy 2500 years ago. It reigned supreme for a thousand years, side by side with Buddhism. Both had a common base to start with—denial of a God. Buddha and Kapila had thus completely reformed the philosophy of the Vedas and the Upanishads, taking everything that was rich in them.

But in India things perhaps never change:

A missionary from Kerala appeared to revive the Vedas and its attending priests. He brought back not only God, but all the gods. Shankaracharya, the genius debater convinced the learned of the age with his new philosophy. He would rather accept several gods than go along with the Sankhya of Kapila. He would defend all the gods; bring Buddha within the fold of Hinduism and revive priesthood and the caste system that were to fall on evil days. There is a chapter on Shankara and his works here. The reader may find it of interest to identify the differences in the ideas of Kapila and Shankara. Science has since considerably widened the vision of evolution; modern philosopher–scientists like Darwin and Kant have provided their versions. The enlightened can draw their own reasonable conclusions.

Today, after nearly 3000 years, if Narada, the eternally roving ambassador of the gods, was to pass through a typical Indian village by the side of river Ganga, he would not miss the use of words like *Prakriti, Purusha, Manas* and *Gunas,* certainty of death, birth and death again. The villagers, having had their dinner would talk of the indestructibility of the soul. They may not be able to explain Sankhya's philosophy; but Narada as the ageless communicator of

Indian mythology, would connect and understand that the village folks are really referring to Kapila's Sankhya. Vedanta and Shankara may have later influenced the Hindu mind, but an old Indian saying rescinds that "There is no knowledge equal to Sankhya; and no power equal to yoga."

Kapila on yoga

Yoga is as old as the Vedas. When Kapila placed emphasis on physical and mental wellbeing, yoga began to be considered from another dimension. This was the need for self control; developing control of the senses being the most vital amongst them.

What is yoga?

It is the yoke of discipline consciously imposed for achievement of supernatural power and intelligence. According to Kapila, "matter in any form is the root of ignorance and suffering." Yoga seeks to free the soul from all sense phenomena; it is an attempt for enlightenment and understanding through physical control of the senses. Kapila's yoga does not seek union with God; he does not believe in a creator or a giver of rewards and punishments. Instead, it is one of the objects on which the soul may meditate as a means of achieving concentration and enlightenment. The aim is to disassociate the mind from the body.

We often notice, during festivals by the riverside at holy places, some ash covered, tangled hair, oddly postured figures. They represent the old time yogis. They claim to be engaged in self-mortification, developing insensitivity to pain and hallucinations through fasting and countless other acts that attract common folks. Some of these may however be merely means of making a living!.

A true yogi is said to have met Alexander during his travels in India. The person who could bear pain so silently attracted Alexander. He invited the yogi to come and be with him so that he could study his technique. He would in return, concede all his needs.

The yogi refused; saying that he wanted nothing from Alexander, "being content with the nothing that he had".

Chapter XIII
The Rise of Indian Civilization

In the evolution of civilization, history and geography emphasize their close relationship. Our story starts with the Aryans making India their home. Physical features and climate made agriculture a natural choice to get food for survival. Periods of good rains blessed the earth with good crops. Want and scarcity became the lot of farmers when weather failed them. The changing mood of seasons completely transformed the environment. The dull yellow leaves began to appear thirsty during summer. When the dark monsoon clouds thundered, there would be greenery all around. The multiple tunes of birds, the tenderness and ferocity of wild animals; the emotions and sentiments of men and women, changed with seasons. The vast expanse of forests, large rivers flowing majestically down to the plains from the high Himalayas encouraged men to contemplate on diversities of nature. Searching the cause for existence, their minds would wander into metaphysics. They discovered that the universe follows a perfect rhythm, thereby concluding that a Force must be guiding this vast and complex universe.

The first step towards civilization was born as this Force began to be identified as God. Within the framework so drawn, the process of creating social order and cultural creation commenced.

Ever since the Indian mind set on this track, it has never looked back. The early Indian thought produced the Vedas and the Upanishads. They describe Reality (*Sat*) as Being but also spoke of Non Being (*Asat*). *Asat* (untruth) is the error, a self-deceit, confined only to the material world. It considers 'I am' as only the physical body, separate from others, hiding truth by ascertaining separateness from the Universal, 'I am'. In reality, that 'something' is beyond positive comprehension. It is the Infinite Self; the super terrestrial view that admits reality of the material cosmos and accepts a temporary duration of life on earth.

Thus it is that God and Satan, angel or devil is man.

> Thus Nature of the universal self;
> This Universal Nature doth all:
> Yet Man deluded by false egoism
> Believes 'I am the actor' not that Self.

Following this thought at the early stage, the Hindu life on the subcontinent accepted three essentials:

1.   Belief in the immortality of the soul.

2.   Life on earth as a temporary sojourn for development of spirit with heaven as the permanent abode.

3.   Development of the spirit to be the aim during life on earth for attainment of salvation.

After centuries of life dominating the above belief, the appearance of Mahavira, Buddha and Kapila introduced a new approach to the subject. The metaphysical concept shifted to logic and reason rather than to the super terrestrial. The elements of Buddha's teachings which influenced people of that age were Love, Truth, and Righteousness. Kapila, like a modern scientist, started with logic. He reasoned out first the evolution of the human body and thereafter the system. The theories propounded by Kapila more than 3000 years ago, were eventually confirmed by modern science during the nineteenth and twentieth centuries.

The preachings of Buddha soon ushered in a silent revolution that reformed the earlier practices. Instead of the extremism of the past, both in thought and social behaviour, the new philosophy expanded and brought into focus, the realities of existence. It advised the middle path. This found favour and acceptance with the rulers for building harmonious relationship. Buddhism soon became not only popular in India, its message reached other Asian countries too.

Thought in the West

During the same period in the West, Greece led in the study of nature and its phenomena. Thinkers like Anaxagoras had the courage to deny that the sun and the moon were not gods. He declared that they were only stones. There was Pythagoras, who worked on mathematics to come out with an ingenious method of calculating distances. Another philosopher, Heraclitus said, "Men do not know what is at variance, and what agrees with itself." And, "to God all things are fair and right, but men hold something wrong and something right." Thus he showed a relationship between the opposites. We are all aware of the story of Socrates. For running a school, he gladly accepted the punishment of death.

Who taught?

All great thinkers tried to inculcate in young minds, the basic ingredient of civilization like honesty and truth! The approach to communicate this knowledge however differed. In India, it was passed on to the next generation through *Guru-Shishya Parampara*, by word of mouth in which the demonstrative effect was often lacking. In Greece, it was taught to the youth in schools and practised at homes. Socrates ran one such school, in defiance of the authorities. This cost Socrates his life. He was executed because he dared to challenge powers against the truth. Once again, in the fifteenth century when knowledge of science was rising, its propagators faced a similar wrath from religious powers. Galileo, an Italian scientist, faced persecution for speaking what he practically saw and was prepared to show to others. Reason and observation proved the writings in the scriptures false! The result was:

The Indian approach led to metaphysical development; the western method, to growth of science.

Monastic life and life of action

We have seen that people are generally more vigorous in cooler climates; they tend to get comparatively docile in tropics. The early signals of such a propensity appeared on the western borders of India. First, the Aryans and thereafter the Macedonian, Alexander, the disciple of Greek philosopher Aristotle, crossed the Hindukush mountains. He had reached the borders of India chasing his old foes, the Persians. Having reached the banks of River Indus, the army of the Indian king Porus, calmly waited for Alexander to attack. Continuous rains however would not let him attack Porus. Exasperated of waiting, he planned a surprise attack. One night when it was dark and heavily raining, he silently marched with his crack soldiers some fifteen miles upstream under extremely difficult conditions. While, he himself, was crossing, his feet got stuck in the marshes of the swollen river. Facing severe odds, overcoming difficult hurdles, he would frequently get exasperated. During those moments of struggle, he remembered only his fellow citizens of Athens bemoaning, "Oh you Athenians, will you ever believe what risks I am running to earn your praise!"

One of the greatest warriors of the world was running every risk, facing every hardship, to earn the applause of his fellow citizens! On the other side of the river, was Porus, the product of the Indian environment holding all the advantages– home ground for a battlefield; a much larger and superior force, full of confidence and courage. But he would not attack; he would merely wait for weeks for an attack from the enemy. What stopped him to take the initiative to attack? Heat not only induces leisure but also produces reasoning for inaction. It is not cowardice; it is disgust for violent action! As we move on, we will find a repetition of this tendency.

Indifference towards writing history and not drawing lessons from the past has always cost the country and her people, some sufferance!

Effect of Alexander's raids

Alexander's raids had exposed the weakness and strength of the two distant lands. It was a wake-up call to Indian potentates who were used to fighting amongst themselves rather than jointly meeting the challenge from across the borders. The ignominy of their defeat however inspired an old Brahmin, Vishnugupta and a youth, Chandragupta to fight the foreign invaders. Chanakya, as he is known to history, trained the youth, Chandragupta in the art of war and diplomacy. The two belonged to the kingdom of Nanda in Patliputra. Both being victims of the king Dhanananda's wrath, they sought revenge. At Taxila near the north-western borders, Chandragupta collected some local princes and defeated the Greek garrison.

The rest is history. Chandragupta Maurya established the first Indian Empire.

Change in religious thinking

Like everything that detoriates with time, Hindu religion was now no more able to satisfy the changing needs of a new social order. The teachings of Gautama Buddha on the other hand were deeply influencing the minds of the masses. Successive kings therefore embraced the new philosophy. They encouraged its propagation in other Asian countries. The dynamism and foresight exhibited by Chanakya and Chandragupta, ushered an era of prosperity and strength that was to last for a thousand years.

Indian civilization at the peak of her glory followed the reason and logic of Mahavira, Buddha and Kapila. They combined the metaphysics of the Vedas and the Upanishads to physical sciences developed during centuries of prosperity. This provided greater exchange of ideas, trade and commerce with other countries, blending in the cultures of the east and the west.

The Golden Age of India
(BC 325-AD 648)

The world's great age begins anew,
The golden years return.
The earth doth like a snake renew,
Her weeds outworn;
Heaven smiles, faiths and empires gleam,
Like wrecks of a dissolving dream.

—*Percy Bysshe Shelley*

Chapter XIV
An Era of Ideal Governance

In himself the ruler combines the glories of all the great gods. By tender fostering of peoples, he manifests his 'Vishnu'—nature. Attracting and delighting the hearts of his people by the mild grandeur and nobility of thoughts, words and deeds, he is the very king of gentleness and beauty, beyond even the Moon of the autumn time. Like the sun, he warms the earth and draws from it, only to give back again in purer streams. Like fire, in splendour; like Indra, unconquerable; like earth in patient forgiveness. In gratifying the yearnings of men, he is like Heaven; raining ever all nourishing things. Like the god of the clouds unfathomable; like ocean, in Sattva in unshakeable grandness, the king of the mountains; like the Lord of Dharma in the spread of education; like Himalayas, abode of eternal snow.

In the science of social organization, Manu, has thus defined an ideal ruler. Centuries after Manu appeared on the Indian horizon, another genius, Vishnugupta, known to history as Kautilya, worked on the duties and responsibilities of a king. As a master of good and firm governance, he outlined the qualities of a successful ruler. When Alexander, in his youthful fancy entered India, chasing his old foes, the Persians, he had underrated the capacity of the Indian spirit and culture. Surprised to find a highly developed society, the young Greek saw things happening in practice, what his teacher, Aristotle had taught him. He saw that what his teacher taught him was actually practised in India. When Porus surrendered after his defeat, Alexander asked him what treatment did he expect?

"Treat me in a kingly way," Porus answered.

Alexander again asked. "For my own sake, thou shall be so treated, for thy own sake do thou demand what is pleasing to thee?"

Porus replied that, what he had said also included the reply for the second question.

In his reply, Porus was only spiritually expressing the impermanence of victory and irrelevance of defeat.

Effects of Alexander's raids

The victories of Alexander had revealed the grave weaknesses in the defenses of the subcontinent. It was a warning for the country. Lack of co-ordination between numerous principalities, neglect in updating the art of war, poor planning and an inadequate spy-system for information were some of the reasons responsible for the Indian defeat. Temporary occupation of the Greeks over India had a positive effect. It sounded a wake-up call! The wise felt for the first time that besides intellectual and spiritual pursuits, defense of borders was an urgent need. The situation desperately needed a man of the moment. Nature answered the call by presenting India with Chanakya or Vishnugupta, also popularly known as Kautilya.

India's pathfinder—Kautilya

From childhood, Kautilya was a gifted planner and administrator. For his brilliant qualities of mind, inventiveness and imagination, he rose to be a minister in the powerful kingdom of Nanda at Patliputra. With his diligence and foresightedness, he brought success and prosperity to the kingdom. Soon, he was the king's most trusted advisor. This created enmity amongst other court officials. They began spreading canards against him. Succumbing to them, the king in his wrath, threw Chanakya out of Pataliputra.

Incensed with the wholly undeserved punishment, Chanakya or Kautilya was filled with rage. While leaving the kingdom, he vowed not to return to Pataliputra until he had destroyed King Nanda of Magadha. The king possessed a huge army. Kautilya was gifted with a mind that could plan and advise. Execution required an extraordinary soldier with military talents to be able to defeat a large army. He found a relative of the king who, had been similarly disgraced by the king. He too nursed similar contempt and hatred. In Chandragupta Maurya, Kautilya found what he sought. Henceforth, both of them would work together to seek revenge for their dishonour. In the process, they would help raise the fortune of the subcontinent.

With the rule of Chandragupta Maurya, the first Indian Empire was established. As the first minister of the king, Kautilya would start an era of good governance, that lasted a thousand years.

The call of the country

Kautilya sensed an opportunity in the establishment of the Greek forces, on the banks of Indus. The wise Brahmin was the first whose ears picked the call reaching him from the stationed garrisons of Alexander under Selucius. Destiny had associated him with a distinguished disciple who could faithfully carry out his vision of the future. He now set to bring his plan into action through Chandragupta. Collecting nearby princes, Chandragupta attacked the Greek garrison under Selucius, whom he defeated the Joint efforts of the man of extraordinary keen intellect and an ambitious young warrior, succeeded in clearing the way to Pataliputra and challenging King Nanda. The tottering regime of Nanda was shattered and Chandragupta Maurya was declared king of Pataliputra. Next, he set out to bring princes of the adjoining kingdoms together. Those who dared to defy, Chandragupta won them in battle. In a short time, the entire north India, from Afghanistan to Bengal and from Kashmir to the Vindhyas, was united under the illustrious king Chandragupta Maurya and his mentor and minister, Kautilya.

Change in political supremacy brought about a change in supremacy of religion. The message of Gautama and Kapila began influencing, first the intellectuals, followed closely by masses. This heralded the rise of Buddhism in India that was to dominate the country for several centuries until a young genius from Kerala absorbed it within Hinduism.

Arthashastra

Arthashastra is a document of diplomacy and state administration written by Kautilya for guidance of kings and ministers. Deriving inspiration from Manu, the law maker on adminstrative, political, economic and religious components, *Arthashastra* is its reformed version. *Arthashastra* is a work of keen observation and diligent study of human nature. It contains details of the strength and weaknesses of heads of states, inclination of state officers to use power for personal ends, the psychology of war, peace, and general administration. It is of guidance in every age and can never go out of date. It is a book of value for all times, because its conclusions and remedies are derived from human nature that hardly changes even even in centuries. Some of its extracts will go to show how true they are even today.

1. "Beware of your neighbours. They may be your friends today, but are sure to deceive you one day."

(The tragedy of Chinese aggression in 1962 would not have occurred, had India taken serious note of her military advisers to prepare a defense belt on the mountains. India refused to accept that a friendly neighbour would contemplate attacking her best friend!)

2. "Truth often does not escape from palaces. This is because back-biting is the most prevailing weapon around the centres of power."

3. "It is possible to know the path of birds flying in the sky, but not the way of state officers, moving with their intentions concealed."

4. "For victory in war, one must employ all means: intrigue, spies, winning over enemy's people, siege and assault."

5. "If against several charges, only one is proved, against an officer of state, he is liable for punishment against all. This maintains the highest integrity amongst state functionaries."

Arthashastra has linked forty different types of embezzlements in various departments. They are based on procedural irregularities, wrong reporting, suppression of facts, deliberate delay in crediting the amounts into the state treasury and discrepancies in receipt and payments. To prevent the scope of misuse of power and misappropriation, *Arthashastra* advocates the non-permanency of tenure of officers. Frequent transfers are to be used as a means of eliminating the chance of officers developing vested interest in the place and position of posting. Kautilya was the greatest statesman-administrator of ancient India. He was the leading light, a man of real-politick, a wise counsellor and one of the key figures responsible in ushering in the Golden Era. With his broad vision, astute diplomatic sense, strong administration and sincere advice, he welded together scattered principalities within the country. All through the Golden Age of India, successive kings would follow *Arthashastra* in their royal duties. Those who failed to follow its instructions faced sufferance.

Qualities of a king

The qualities of a king/head of state, as defined by Kautilya, are:

"Inquiry, listening, a clear perception, retention in memory, reflection, deliberation, drawing conclusions and firm adhesion to conclusions arrived at."

The king, in his personal characteristics must be:

"Free from passion, anger, greed, obstinacy, fickleness, haste, back-biting habits and possess a smiling face."

Chandragupta Maurya, following policies of his mentor, went ahead to build the foundations of the greatest empire of his period.

Chandragupta Maurya–liberator and unifier

Kautilya had assessed the damage Alexander's raid had done to the country. His priority was to drive out all traces of Greek armies left in India after Alexander's departure. He worked hard to accomplish this objective. When achieved, this gave the new regime considerable moral strength. Weaker kings gradually came within his fold. Chandragupta Maurya ruled from Pataliputra with Kautilya as his first minister.

When Chandragupta ruled northern India, Selucius, a General of Alexander, inherited his eastern empire from Asia minor to Indus. He dared to cross his borders and attack Chandragupta. But the star of Mauryas was on the rise; Selucius was duly defeated. This cost him dear. He had to surrender the greater part of his eastern possessions of Gandahar in Afganistan. The Mauryan Empire now extended from Afghanistan to Bengal and from Kashmir to the Vindhyas.

Democracy in Indian monarchy

In the ancient world, the king ruled his subjects with divine authority. India, with her intense spiritual training had a different idea. It considered service to people as the chief responsibility of a king. When crowned, the king would take this oath before the people. This again is a modification of the oath laid down by Manu for kings at their coronations—"May I be deprived of heaven, of life, and of offspring, if I oppress you." The routine of the king was fixed. He had to be always ready for immediate work. Public work could not wait for his pleasure. If a king is energetic, his subjects would be equally energetic. "In the happiness and welfare of his subjects, lies his happiness; whatever pleases himself, he shall consider as no good."

On such high ideals was the first empire of India established.

Rule of Chandragupta

In course of time, Chandragupta depended more and more for advice on his mentor and minister. To save time and inconvenience, he invited him to stay in the royal palace. Chanakya refused, saying:

"I would rather be with the people. This would keep my hands on their pulse."

Kautilya continued to live in his modest cottage amongst the people.

Chandragupta followed a strict daily routine. He would rise and start with meditation; next he would look over the reports of his agents, issuing such instructions as necessary; then he would meet his counsellors; followed by attending finance and defence matters. He heard the suits and petitions of his subjects. At the end of the day, he would dine and read religious texts. The capital of the Empire, Pataliputra, was efficiently administered. The number of departments of administration, planning of cities, extent of trade and commerce in distant lands, amazed the visitors of foreign countries. With hard work, wisdom and statesmanship of both Kautilya and Chandragupta, life in India took a turn towards evolution of politics, trade and commerce, freedom of worship, and development of science and arts. It was a period when the famous centres of education at Taxila and Nalanda were growing. Students from neighbouring countries were coming to the two great universities for education and knowledge. Kautilya planned; Chandragupta, executed. One was of extraordinary intellect; the other an outstanding and ambitious soldier. One, a great political thinker, the other possessed inexhaustible inventiveness, practical wisdom and diplomatic skill; fortitude and determination...

The genius of Chandragupta Maurya and Kautilya commenced an era of prosperity and good governance,

Outlines of administration

In the *Arthashastra,* we find rules for efficient administration. One of the most important criterions was the selection of officers and men required in different departments of administration. The recruitment to public services was only through competitive examinations. The village headman administered law with five members (panchayat). The department of navigation, city administration, buildings and roads, forests, military training, almost every department which goes to make administration efficient, existed in the kingdom. It was a period of intense activity when the foundations of modern working institutions were laid. The vicissitudes of time have changed boundaries of the subcontinent. Afghanistan, Pakistan and Bangladesh are no more part of the great unit that India was during that period. The rules of decision making in tribes, panchayats and *jirghaz* however still remain the same as envisaged by Kautilya for Indian administration.

Chandragupta ruled for twenty-five years. He achieved almost everything set by Kautilya. As trade and commerce brought wealth, India was counted amongst the richest countries of the world. All this was possible through ruthlessness, violence, even justified and lawful cruelty. He applied every method prescribed in the *Arthashastra* to hold and strengthen the empire. But violence breeds fear. Unpalatable decisions made Chandragupta suspicious and weak. After the vigour of youth had ebbed, Chandragupta lived in mortal fear and uncertainty. Each night he would change his sleeping chamber fearing assassination.

Violence of any kind goes against the Indian temperament!

The great famine

Then, Mother Nature unfolded her own plans. A country that had not known famine was faced by its ravages. A prolonged famine engulfed the empire. In spite of his best efforts, the king found himself utterly helpless. Nothing could mitigate the suffering of the people. When efforts fail, only prayers remain. Chandragupta abdicated in favour of his son to lead a life of a Jain recluse and pray. Twelve years passed, but mental peace eluded him. He would consult all scriptures, seek advice of saints and sages; there was no solace for his soul. Obsessed by asceticism, he ultimately starved himself to death, giving the throne to his son, Bindusar. History remembers Chandragupta Maurya as a great soldier-king who unified India. He put the country on the path of unprecedented achievements. He may have used compulsive and cruel methods, but was never unjust. He laid the foundation of civic administration in the country. Yet, he died of a broken heart.

Bindusara—the philosopher son

Chandragupta had passed on his crown to his son so that he could lead an austere life. Bindusara governed the empire on the footsteps of his father. But his heart was in intellectual pursuits. Perhaps, he noticed how, inspite of the best efforts of his father, the cruel famine had destroyed his will power! Inclined to resignation, he surrounded himself with philosophers and intellectuals sages of different religions.

In the reign of his father, India was in business with most of the known world, more particularly with the Middle Eastern countries. Damascus in Syria was famous for making the best swords. India was known to produce the best steel in the world. Bindusara, during his spiritual discussions, had heard of the wise philosophers of Greece. He requested the king of Syria to help him find a philosopher. After due efforts, the king of Syria regretted his inability to find any philosopher for Bindusara who was willing to travel to serve the king. There is an orthodox belief that if a wish is sought earnestly, it is definitely granted. Soon after, Nature herself fulfilled Bindusara's keen desire. The king was blessed with a son, to be later called, Ashoka, the Great.

Ashoka—the Great

Ashoka took over the reigns of his dynasty in royal style. The guiding light remained the rules and policies laid down by Kautilya. One of the key policy being: "To be just and kind to the law abiding; harsh and cruel to criminals." Mothers used to scare their children with stories of Ashoka's cell! What was so terrifying in the prison? The dreaded prison had a strange rule. Whoever entered the prison was not to return alive.

Once, a Buddhist monk was sent to this prison. As per orders of the king, he was thrown into the boiling water. To the surprise of prison officials, he is said to have come out unhurt. The process was repeated but the result was the same. The monk remained alive. This wonder was conveyed to the king. Not believing the story, Ashoka personally came to the prison to see for himself the strange phenomenon. Witnessing the sight, he too was puzzled at the strange sight. While Ashoka was leaving the prison, the jailer respectfully reminded the king of his orders that no one must leave the prison alive. The king was outraged at the arrogance of the jailer. He promptly ordered him to be put in the boiling pot instead of the monk.

Ashoka's spiritual journey towards Buddhism had started.

Conscience awakens

The prison incidence made Ashoka contemplate the fallacy of his order. He abolished the prison.

Another great upheaval would alter his entire concept of crown and commitment to his subjects. The war in Kalinga had to be fought. There was mass massacre of more than one hundred thousand men; nearly one hundred and fifty thousand were taken prisoners, This was followed by pestilence in which many thousand more died of disease. The two tragedies filled Ashoka with remorse. His conscience would not let him rest. He vowed never to go to war again. History records several great kings and generals who won wars. Alexander and Julius Caesar won successive wars, but their thirst for greater achievements would refuse to die. There was Genghis Khan who won every war that he fought. When the enemy was defeated, he used to give a call to his soldiers:

"The grass is mowed; now feed your horses"– a signal to loot and plunder the helpless population.

Ashoka is remembered as the greatest king ever; Genghis Khan is considered a barbarian. The works of ancient Indian philosophers like Manu did not go in vain. They helped build a civilization so strong at the roots that no storm could weaken its continuity. Ashoka, having witnessed the cruelties of war, vowed never to fight. This unique act of compassion made history.

Advancement of Buddhism

During the reign of Ashoka, Buddhism became the dominant faith of the people. After all, the message of compassion, non-violence and renunciation were similar to the teachings of the Vedanta. More and more people subscribed to the commonly accepted styles of life. They did not like the ugliness that had started to show up in the Aryan arrangement of classifying people in different categories from birth. Buddha, too, had denounced this arrangement. Ashoka, respecting the will of his people and led by his own inclination towards Buddhism, actively worked to promote a homogeneous social arrangement.

During his reign, messengers went to Ceylon, Burma, China, Japan and even to Syria and Egypt, to propagate Buddhism. While doing so, he was always conscious of other faiths, sowing seeds of religious secularism. To every religion, he gave equal respect. Conveying this to the people, he desired his message to be inscribed on the stones for present and future generations. These edicts, some destroyed by the ravages of time, convey a vivid picture of life during his period. They confirm that his endeavour was to fuse and bring Vedanta and Buddhism, nearer. He had understood that after many centuries, the Aryan arrangement on *Varnas* was only a working arrangement to suit the times. If it grew later into an evil, it was because of its selfish interpretation.

Ashoka, while encouraging Buddhism, made efforts to remove distortions in the functioning of the Vedanta.

Some edicts of Emperor Ashoka

Ashoka's edicts reflect the progress society was making towards secularism.

1. "The king does reverence to all men of all sects, whether ascetic or householders, by gifts and other forms. The essence is restraint of speech; reverence, not only to one's own faith but all faiths; and avoidance of undeserved depreciation of others."

2. "The king announces that all his subjects are his beloved children and that he will not discriminate against any of them because of their diverse creed."

3. "The law of piety is excellent. But what does it consist of if not compassion, liberality, truthfulness and purity?" (The hint is towards piety reduced to mere rituals during that period.)

4. To improve the impact of his edicts on the people, the king put one as an outcome of his efforts. It says, "Now by reasons of practicing piety there is no slaughter of living creatures. There is better behaviour between men and their parents and elders. This will further increase with practice. It will continue to be followed by the king's children and grandchildren."

5. "All human beings should have security, self control, peace of mind and joyousness."

6. "All religious sects should live harmoniously in all parts of his dominion."

Let the edicts be known to people from time to time, were his instruction to the officials of state.

Welfare schemes

Ashoka was ever eager to work for the public good. He initiated schemes to cultivate herbal plants at suitable sites. For patients, he established hospitals throughout his kingdom. In the field of science, special departments were established in universities. The social arrangement, imposed by the Aryans, was showing signs of discontent amongst the depressed in the empire. Ashoka established a separate ministry for the tribal; as an act of supreme service to his people, he desired his ministers to bring him directly all the problems of the people. For them, he was always available; at all times, at all places and at any hour.

Reign in retrospect

With advancing age, Ashoka would devote more of his time propagating and practicing Buddhism. By now, ancient India had developed into a multi-religious society. This created a wedge between the king and the priestly class whose privileges were declining. They secretly grew jealous of Buddhism and began planning schemes to restore their rights.

Ashoka's work to spread Buddhism in distant lands was receiving tremendous response. At home, it was sowing seeds of discontent. While in his youth, he treated all religions with equal respect; later, his inclination towards Buddhism cost him his throne. In old age, his grandson took physical possession of the empire. Ashoka was left to practice austerities in the closing years of his life.

Thus ended the reign of one of the greatest and the most compassionate monarch on earth who listened to his conscience to surrender victory willingly. Ashoka's zealous propagation of one religion became a cause of envy, even anger for the priests of other faiths. The march of Indian civilization would introduce many other rulers, who would, similarly, bite the dust for their overindulgence in religious affairs.

Kanishka—an era of achievements (AD 120)

The Mauryan dynasty ruled India for nearly five centuries. Brihadratha was the last, whose end came when his own commander-in-chief assassinated him. Usurping the throne, he started his own dynasty. This too was shortlived. After Ashoka, the chief patron of the Buddhist religion, jealousy between the two religions, disturbed harmony and social relationship in the land. As governance started to grow weak, religious infighting surfaced. Religious priests started working against each other, causing instability in the country. The empire that Ashoka nourished with such devotion and care, could not, as a result, survive for long. Fresh foreign invaders like Bactrians (Greek), Sakas (Synthians), Palhavas (Persians) and Kushans (Turks) were frequently raiding the borders. The Mauryan rulers, were now found wanting in sagacity and diplomacy. They could no more handle the complexities of a caste-ridden structure.

The foreign invaders were waiting for just such an opportunity. When they noticed that the country had grown weak due to incessant in-fighting, they commenced their raids. The raiders disrupted the instruments of governance so assiduously built during the reign of Ashoka. Possessing no deep cultural or religious roots, the raiders however could not disturb the mainstream of social life. On the contrary, soon after, they were themselves absorbed in the vast cultural and religious environment of the subcontinent. After some struggle, they made India their home.

Religions at crossroads

In the first century AD, Huns from Central Asia captured Kabul, extending their victory further to northwestern India. It appeared that the country would keep on facing wars and slavery. However, the star of India was shining bright and clear. Another great warrior from amongst the Kushans appeared on the Indian scene. Kanishka was able to successfully drive out the intruders. Normal life was resumed, social and religious equations showed signs of change. The king revived development schemes that had floundered during the brief interval. Art, literature and health schemes again started receiving royal patronage.

The inner strength of Indian civilization duly assimilated the changes that had occurred during the interim period. The Kushans, from across the borders, infatuated by India's tropical climate and a rational religion in Buddhism, gradually settled in the country, making it their home. In the past as well as in future, this uniqueness of Indian soil and culture would continue to attract different races and cultures. They would come as warriors but in due course, fall in love with the country, lending her unity in diversity.

Kanishka would provide India and her people, a rule that would allow freedom to all religions to flourish and regain their earlier impetus. After he ended such conflicts, the road was cleared for unprecedented progress in economic and social sectors. Present day Indian culture, by and large, is a gift of the social and religious customs that took shape during this period. Kanishka started his reign with the command, "Let the teachers of every creed be welcome." This had become necessary because of too much emphasis on religions. In the past, it had always been a cause of conflict. Kanishka, as a wise king patronized a synthesis of different cultures. Therefore, the two main religions, Buddhism and Hinduism, both flourished without strife amongst themselves.

Roots of modern Hindu culture

The Hindu religion derives its religious philosophy from the Vedanta. The Aryans, who had migrated to India, had introduced discrimination based on colour of the skin. After conquering the country, they chalked out a system of work distribution. This in time grew, to monstrous proportions. The caste system that followed was to create wide differences in society. Both Buddha and Mahavira, fearing its harmful effects, tried to reform this aspect. As long as Buddhism remained in power, elements enjoying privileges of this arrangement lay low. For a thousand years during which Buddhism enjoyed royal patronage, the Hindu priestly class could not react. Buddhism, having reached its climax, began to decline. Buddhism was laying greater emphasis on renunciation. The intellectuals of the country became soft and peace-loving. Others, particularly of the neglected castes, were already feeling alienated. A large population of the country, unwittingly, drifted from the mainstream of Indian life. This kind of breakup, within the country, encouraged attacks from across the borders. Adventurers collected warriors, infused in them some religious venom and entered the country by force. Greeks, Persians, Scynthians and the Kushans easily descended on the plains of the Indus and the Ganges to settle in the fertile soil of the country. Within a generation or two, they were, like present day Indians in the USA, absorbed in the mainstream of the country. This induction of new talents induced creativity without disturbing our religious or cultural ethos.

Buddhism and Hinduism at crossroads

Buddhism had grown to be popular amongsts the masses because of its emphasis on a casteless society and its practical wisdom for a good, peaceful life on earth. It had become popular amongst intellectuals because of its rationalism and logic. Its philosophy being simple, it needed no priests or interpreters. It advocated:

> Kill not for pity's sake—and lest ye stay
> The meanest thing on its upward way.
> Bear not false witness, slender not, nor lie;
> Truth is the speech of inward purity.
> Give freely and receive, but take from none;
> Clear minds clean bodies, need no *Soma* juice.

Mahayana—synthesis of Vedanta and Buddhism

Under Kanishka there was again a spurt of religious zeal, like in the period of Ashoka, which overflowed Indian frontiers. It was an age in which men's minds were stirred by great thoughts and emotions; it was a time when Indian culture was being enriched with new orientations. Kanishka convened a Buddhist council. Buddhist literature, earlier written in Pali, now appeared in Sanskrit. Like everything that is affected by time, Buddhist religion also could not resist the winds of change. In order to retain its vibrancy amongst the masses, 'Mahayana' the greater vehicle–a synthesized and reformed version, was presented by religious experts. Under instructions from Kanishka, the council which met in the salubrious climate of Kashmir adopted the new version of Buddhism. It incorporated Vedantic mysticism and even copied Hindu rituals in practice. But for its glorification of castes, the new arrangement helped remove religious irritants between the two religions. Mahayana announced the divinity of Buddha, adopted the asceticism of Patanjali and popularized the practice of yoga. Sanskrit again came into prominence replacing Pali. This at once touched the hearts of Hindu scholars. With changes introduced through Mahayana, Buddhism became much like Hinduism. It introduced the practice of using holy water in worship, burning candles and incense before the deity– thus the practices and traits common to the Hindus became prevalent in Buddhism.

The central idea in Buddhist teaching was the gospel of universal salvation based on the idea of fundamental oneness of all beings. Mahayana broadened the field of emphasis and made 'friendliness' and 'compassion', the essential tenets of his teachings. The old creed was not abandoned; it was merely enlarged to absorb ideas from Hinduism. Just as original Buddhist reformation did not completely break with its Vedic faith, so too the Mahayana.

As Hinduism gained strength, Buddhism's synthesis and its gradual absorption in the mother religion began. It was now being realized what monasteries had contributed to encourage intellectual youth and how the country had been deprived of their talents in both defence and economic growth of the country. Even so, religious antagonisms of the past did leave their adverse effect on the unity and integrity of the nation as a whole.

Age of fulfilment–glory of the Guptas

During the fourth century AD, India reverted to small and divided states, governed by petty princes without a responsible central government. In a vast country, interspersed with forests and rivers, with means of communication not sufficiently developed; central authority was no more as strong. Under such conditions, division of the country into small principalities was only natural. The old culture of the Greeks, Kushans and the Mongols only added to its diversity. The earlier vigour of thought diminished. Again, mythology and myths were back in business.

The imaginative genius of the land produced yet another proud son. Not relying on strength of martial qualities, but in modesty and sincerity, he would assemble the scattered principalities of the adjoining states, to achieve collective strength. The diplomatic lessons of Kautilya and his own constructive approach, bestowed on Chandragupta, the central leadership of the country. In the next generation, this work would be consolidated by Samudragupta, to bear fruits in the third generation. If earlier centuries of the Golden Era were a preparation, the zenith of glory was reached during the rule of Guptas. It became a period when Indians followed and practised the teachings of a refreshed and reformed Vedanta.

If Greek civilization reached the pinnacle of glory during the reign of Pericles, ancient India achieved it during the rule of the Guptas.

Chandragupta I (AD 320-330)

Chandragupta had inherited a small kingdom around Magadha. His marriage to the daughter of the ruler, in the adjoining state brought him both influence and luck. Being a ardent soldier, he made good use of his talents. He mobilized his resources to keep extending his territory. But force did not work as much as persuasion could. His own reign was without any outstanding achievement; he spent most of his time in consolidation, expansion and again consolidation.

The reign of Chandragupta provided that continuity of peace and security, essential for peace and harmony amongst the population. This in turn provided leisure to intellectuals for creative activity. In this manner Chandragupta gave the kingdom such momentum that it helped Samudragupta make his rule the most prosperous and memorable. When Samudragupta succeeded him, the Empire was on solid foundations. His son, Vikramaditya, was destined to be remembered as the greatest ruler of India, following the illustrious lineage of Ashoka and Akbar.

Samudragupta–the Wise Ruler (AD 330-380)

The way of wisdom is pursuit of truth with intelligence. Unlike Ashoka, Samudragupta inherited a smaller empire surrounded by the tiny principalities. Each followed its own laws of administration without regard to what was happening in the adjoining territories. In the beginning, he had a few of them under his control. To manage such a delicate relationship required dexterity, diplomacy and a measure of military strength. After the end of Kanishka's rule, there was a virtual vacuum in governance. Samudragupta, with a combination of lessons from Kautilya's *Arthashastra*, succeeded in managing the complexities of royalty with wisdom. He brought together smaller states under one umbrella, making them a cohesive and homogenous unit of his empire. So wisely and intelligently did he manage that when he died after ruling nearly half a century, the empire extended from Assam to Afghanistan and from Himalayas to the Western Ghats.

To manage such a vast empire, with means of communications still in its infancy, Samudragupta shifted his capital from Pataliputra to Ayodhya.

Samudragupta–an ideal Indian king

India attained great heights during the reign of Samudragupta. He laid such strong foundations that after his death, the reign of his son would be recorded in history as a period when Indian civilization reached its zenith. As a wise ruler, he would leave religion alone, encouraging or discouraging none, but being tolerant to all. Even today, if we were to look for a copy book king who would suit the diversity of Indian society, Samudragupta will top all amongst the Indian galaxy of kings. With the knowledge of past history when kings were defeated for getting too involved in religious activities, Samudragupta, had grasped the weakness of religion as a tool for governance. Samudragupta had learnt how kings supporting a particular religion, became unpopular even with people of their own faith. He had realized from the example of Ashoka that pursuing any one religion by the king becomes injurious to peace in the country. He had concluded that religions have a tendency to practice and promote divisive attitudes; they merely help divide people, leading them to endless conflicts.

Samudragupta's policy towards defeated kings was particularly magnanimous. Employing compassion as a policy towards defeated kings, he often restored their wealth and status. Being a man of refinement, he lavishly promoted art, literature, science and music. The money collected from taxes was allocated for the welfare of the entire population. The policy once again revived the pre-Buddhist code of oneness found in the Vedanta. It proved to be a sort of renaissance of Hindu religion and culture, not by its rituals, but by the core philosophy so admired by intellectuals.

This interest in Vedanta helped revive original texts written in Sanskrit. The great Sanskrit grammarian, Panini, improved its grammar, making Sanskrit one of the finest world languages. His work helped a great recovery in Sanskrit. Soon after, some great Indian poets and dramatists appeared on the Indian scene.

Vikramaditya–'Son of power' (AD 380-414)

India now reached a height of development unsurpassed since Gautama Buddha and a political unity achieved only during the reign of Ashoka and Akbar. To be both an intellectual and a great warrior was a rare combination. Vikramaditya was one of those rare few who was at home with poets and philosophers alike and would not hesitate to handle the sword. Always keen in extension and consolidation of his empire, he served his people like a father figure. Being fond of art and literature, he loved being surrounded by poets, dramatists, artists and religious priests.

As communication for effective control of a vastly stretched empire became precarious, Vikramaditya shifted his capital to Ujjaini from Ayodhya.

Rule of Vikramaditya

Vikramaditya governed India treating his subjects like his sons. The glimpses of *Ramrajya*, described so vividly by Valmiki in the Ramanaya, found a practical form during his reign. The Golden Age had, indeed, reached its climax. There was everything that an efficient ruler was expected to provide. There was security, peace and prosperity. Pluralism and secularism practiced in the past, allowed creativity to flourish. All religions enjoyed equal rights and privileges. The king invited the learned of different religions from time to time for intellectual discussions. This would enable each side to understand and appreciate the other. The court was studded with nine 'jewels', each a genius in his field. There was the famous poet Kalidas, a master of similes; poets, Magha and Bhavabhuti; Bharavi for wealth of meaning; and renowned astronomers Aryabhatta, Varahmahira and Bramagupta; and the lexicographer Amara. They were the nine jewels who adorned the court of Vikramaditya.

Sanskrit, revived in the earlier century, developed into a language of the people. Vikramaditya himself being intellectually inclined, occasionally wrote poetry and was a keen scholar. New towns and cities during his reign grew fast. Educational institutions were multiplying. Trade and commerce increased, not only within the country, but also beyond the borders, filling the state coffers with wealth.

What was so extraordinary in Vikramaditya's personality that placed him above other rulers?

His virtue and strength lay in not patronizing any of the half-a-dozen religions, the people of the country followed. Although he personally was interested in Buddhism, he gave equal regard to all religions. Instead of patronizing any religion like his predecessors, he would keep the state aloof from it.

The administration of the empire was developed to such efficiency that wealth from all corners reached the capital Ujjaini without undue pressure. Trade and commerce in silk, pearls, condiments and other refined metals brought riches from West Asia, Italy, Korea and China. Maintenance of peace and prosperity encouraged the young to develop their talents in arts and music. The atmosphere created by Samudragupta and Vikramaditya enabled development of the sciences centuries ahead of other countries. It is an enigma that in spite of such solid foundations, the momentum of growth could not be sustained. We will get an opportunity to analyse the reasons in some details ahead.

After Vikramaditya died, his son Kumaragupta became the emperor. His undistinguished rule lasted for forty years. During his period religious conflicts between Buddhism and Brahmanical Hinduism came out in the open. The religious conflicts so started generated hatred amongst fellow citizens. From then on, the process of weakening of the country's roots began. With the central authority getting weakened, the rulers of distant territories within the empire, began itching for independence. With disunity amongst different communities sapping the vital energy of the nation, the process of disintegration commenced. The momentum of India's strength and pride began slowing down. Monarchies became weak–if a competent king is succeeded by a relatively less mature, the enemies of the state get active.

In the sixth century, Huns from Upper Mongolia were regularly threatening the entire civilized world. China, India, West Asia and parts of Europe, were on their hit list. Raiding frequently, they assessed the defence of the country. Soon, the adventurous and bolder amongst them would terrorize and invade, win and stay on in the country.

The terror of the Huns

The nomads from Central Asia, even earlier, had been striking terror at intervals. It was Hannibal, who centuries earlier, had surprised Romans crossing the Alps mountain with an army of elephants. This time it was Atilla. He was out to destroy the last remnants of the Roman empire. Related to these tribes were the Huns who had been harassing the Indian kings. They had tested India's weakness and kept striking until they succeeded. After ceaseless struggle, Toromana established himself as king of Malwa in Rajasthan. He ruled cruelly, but was no match to his son Mihiragula in cruelty. He had a passion for killing and destruction. One of his pet amusement was to throw elephants from hilltops into the valley below and watch them die.

Such acts of vandalism roused the Gupta kings, who were still ruling most of north India. Mihiragula was defeated and captured. Indian kings, like their people, have always been magnanimous in victory. They do not like killing prisoners. Following the tradition, they merely threw the wicked beast beyond the borders.

The unusual compassion and kindness of Indian kings towards their enemies was to be repeated time and again resulting in injury to themselves. India, in glory and strength, has always been magnanimous. It is noteworthy that those amongst the tribe, who preferred to stay, were not disturbed. They lived on in the country. Gradually, they were absorbed in the mainstream, adopting Indian customs and culture. The distinguished breed still adorn parts of Rajasthan. Huns however remained in ascendancy in India for almost a century until another distinguished son of the Gupta dynasty, Harsha Vardhana, appeared as the redeemer.

Harsha Vardhana (AD 606-648)

During the brief interlude of a century, the Huns continued to disturb peace in India. Then Harsha Vardhana, a prince of the Gupta dynasty, captured the entire north India and established his rule. Although the country felt safe from north, danger continued to lurk from the northwest and the south. He therefore changed his capital from Ujjaini to Kannauj. From Kannauj he ruled for forty years bringing peace to the realm and prosperity to his people. Harsha Vardhana was an expert military general and a man with personal charm. Like his predecessors, he too was good at music and poetry. Some of his compositions have been preserved for posterity. They are found in several rural areas of Uttar Pradesh and Madhya Pradesh even today.

Rule of Harsha Vardhana

No civilization on earth so far had such a long period of greatness and glory as enjoyed by India during the last thousand years. The spiritual growth, attained by Indian sages, had left an indelible mark on the minds of their kings and courtiers. It was however a mixed blessing. Guided by the morals of religious scriptures, these illustrious kings discharged their sacred duty of providing peace and protection against external danger. The lessons of good governance, outlined by Kautilya in his *Arthashastra,* were not fully practised. Creation of sustainable institutions for long term governance was a crucial area often neglected by great kings!

The reign of Harsha Vardhana was remarkable for outstanding work in construction of roads and other public utilities. He had a passion to serve his people. To this end, he devoted all his extraordinary energy. Like Vikramaditya, he never allowed personal hobbies of art and music to interfere with his responsibilities. His devotion to the needs of people, his competence and prowess to work for their welfare became a byword. Kings of distant territories would revere his wishes and obey his commands. His subjects could approach him at any hour of the day and night, such were his orders to his courtiers.

Devotion to religion

As a king, Harsha Vardhana was also religious. Starting as a worshipper of Shiva, he too would espouse Buddhism in later years. Like Ashoka, he devoted considerable time and energy in propagating Buddhism. Unlike Ashoka, he never allowed his personal preference for Buddhism to come in the way of respecting and encouraging other religions. Every five years, he would hold a colossal religious festival, inviting thousands of monks and priests professing different religions to join him. Jain and Buddhist monks, Hindu priests and men of arts and sciences were fed along with the poor and orphans. Harsha, in this respect, remains famous for his magnanimous ways of giving charity and respect. History merely informs how wealth was employed by kings to build monuments of glory; they display their magnificence of power through such monuments. It was not so with Harsha Vardhana. He would distribute the surplus of the royal treasury to the poor in charity every five years. The distribution of this wealth would continue until the treasury was completely empty. At the end of the festivities, the king would part even with his personal jewellery.

When Harsha died, court intrigues started. Fights between religious interests surfaced. Discontent and jealousies had been brewing since the Mauryan kings patronized Buddhism. During the Gupta period, both were given opportunity to prosper. The unrest brewing between the two major religions now came in the open. Like the people of a country, each nation develops a national psyche, which inspires her people to contribute their skills for the coming generations. What inspired them and how did it find expression? Were any lessons learnt and remedial measures taken or advised by her thinkers? Answers to these questions are available from the socio-religious reforms, literature and poetry, research and development in the field of sciences. In the next three chapters we shall analyse the achievements for the good of Indian people and humanity at large.

Chapter XV
Zenith of Sanskrit & Hindu Heritage

Researchers claim that Sanskrit first came to Persia from the south of Russia. When the Persians crossed Afganistan, they called themselves Aryans. Their religion and language showed a close relationship with those Aryans who had reached and settled in north-west India. Darius, the king of Persia, in one of the inscriptions, describes himself 'a Persian of Aryan descent'. Sanskrit, the language of the Indo-Aryans, is perhaps the oldest 'mother language' to which several European languages belong. It is the surest sign of the cultural unity of the entire human race defined by all the religions of the world. Sanskrit literally means 'pure', 'perfect', 'sacred'. Prose writing being not too prevalent, it was mostly in verses that it expressed human feelings and emotions of early times. In the fourth century BC, the language was perfected and brought to its present form by the two greats; one a grammarian and the other a master of *Shastras*–Panini and Patanjali. They are credited to have laid the foundation of verbal genetics that rediscovered the beauty and gave new life to Sanskrit. In time, it became one of the sweetest, rhythmic and most expressive languages. Their genius is evident from a study of the language before and after.

Language for expression and cultural development

Culture is the way of life of the people living at one place. It is an aggregate of customs, institutions, manners, standard tastes and moral beliefs. Culture is transmitted by the family than by schools. When family life fails to play its part, culture detoriates. Right from the beginning, agriculture has remained a source of livelihood for Indians. This has encouraged passivity of the mind. After the soil has been tilled, it is ready for sowing. The farmer, thereafter, is required to depend on the weather. Agriculture, in this respect, has dominated and moulded life on the subcontinent. It has taught the farmer a passive way of life, encouraging daily duties, largely confined to family and the village. Besides efforts to get a good crop in each season, much depends on the vagaries of nature. Effort, therefore, does not become a habit; it appears only as an emergency that needs attention because it is inevitable. In normal times, after the day's work is done, members of the community relax and gossip. During the summers, enverated by the heat, they take rest under a tree. When it is winter, they kindle fires to keep themselves cosy. As the monsoon clouds gather, they welcome the rains, singing ancient lores. Fond of leisure and conversation with their fellow farmers, they would talk and argue, exchange notes on the weather, seek and generally accept advice of their elders. Drawing inspiration from the environment, they release their emotions in singing tales of valour and myths coming down from the distant past. Contemplative by nature, they ponder over the mysteries of the universe, writing verses in praise of their gods. Watching the vastness of the sky, their minds would turn towards metaphysics and sciences.

Another habit, inculcated through agriculture, is that of saving. An Indian is by nature frugal because of uncertainties. Surplus food, during good weather conditions, was saved for the 'rainy' day. As and when rains failed, there was shortage. The habit of saving would then come in handy. Religion, poetry, songs of perfection, the stories of villainy and heroism, gossip, serious conversation—all combined to make the entire nation spiritual in outlook. It was a complete world of their own in which they lived and prospered. It never occurred to them that there were others in the world beyond their borders, who, when hungry, would look elsewhere for food!

Such being the national psyche, the language of communication would continue to reflect this approach in national literature, poetry and idealism. In the initial stages of growth in the Vedic era, the thoughts of *Acharyas* and philosophers used to be recorded in Sanskrit on the bark of trees and leaves. These writings were preserved in libraries to be written again on more secure sheets. The works being mostly in verses, could easily be passed on to the coming generations through oral communication.

Rise of Pali and decline of Sanskrit

During the Golden Era when successive Indian kings followed Buddhism, Pali, instead of Sanskrit, became the spoken language of the people. During this period, the philosophic and other literature continued to be written in Sanskrit that was no more the language of the people. It is significant that during this period, having lost popularity amongst the common people, it was confined amongst scholars and the priests. Like Latin and Greek in Europe, it became merely a language of refinement and scholarship. The lack of touch with people robbed that fertility which, during its regular use, is enriched by the people. As Pali grew in popularity and Sanskrit declined, the Vedic hymns began to be chanted in the same manner as in modern times. They were read with reverence by the Brahmin priest with the people repeating them without understanding their meaning or significance.

Rise of Sanskrit–advancement of civilization

After five hundreds years of rule by Mauryan kings, Buddhism and along with it the language Pali, reached their zenith. The Gupta kings, having learnt from the past, decided not to encourage any particular religion. Instead, they gave equal respect to all. This enabled Sanskrit to come to its own. The past glory of the language was not only revived with the efforts of Pannini and Patanjali, Sanskrit was also made an improved language. By fifth century AD, essential elements that give rise to civilizations were in place. Earlier Sanskrit scriptures and works, like the Ramayana and the Mahabharata were given a new flavour. Social security and peace were provided to people against external dangers and internal conflicts.

Of all conditions, peace and social security are most important for talents to a free expression. The responsibility of the ruler to provide security from external and internal aggression and strengthen political organization is most crucial. When this element exists, pursuit of knowledge and moral traditions grows from within. Philosophers and men of imagination add knowledge in the grand chain of discoveries. People by themselves usually follow morals and traditions. Thus does the quality of life of future generations improve. Relics built by kings in mortar and stone decay with time. Cultures and civilization rise or fall. But knowledge and morals become permanent preserves of human civilization that last as long men can recognize their worth.

Political organization and social security

Successive kings of the Golden Era, except Chandragupta Maurya, cared only for administration and immediate security. There was little effort to strengthen political organization as emphasized by Kautilya in *Arthashastra*. To keep their hold on people and meet day to day challenges, the rulers preferred to shift their capitals. If Chandragupta Maurya ruled from Pataliputra, the other Chandragupta shifted to Ayodhya. Vikramaditya felt safer in Ujjaini, which was the capital of his empire. Harsha Vardhana considered Kannauj a better capital. Such changes did keep peace but it was a weak edifice. As we shall find out, it crumbled at the slightest shock. The length and breadth of the country demanded construction of roads and other public utilities to provide better communication in times of emergency. In the absence of such a network, defending borders and interaction between people was found wanting. Governance had followed a set pattern. Cyclic in nature, it might start with the monarchy; thereafter came the aristocracy, followed by democracy and ending with dictatorship. A rule of thousands of years could not proceed beyond monarchy!

The kings of the Golden Era maintained peace but neglected political and administrative organizations for solidarity of the country. The empire always remained prone to sudden attacks from outside and insurgency from within. Even so, personal dynamism of the kings kept peace in the land and encouraged knowledge to flourish. The pursuit of knowledge in various branches of literature, arts and physical sciences received tremendous impetus. Indian genius truly flowered during these centuries when men excelled in their field of activity, leaving their indelible mark.

Kalidasa–the poet laureate

Sanskrit reached its zenith during the rule of Vikramaditya, which had all the pomp and pleasantry of a prosperous reign. Trade, commerce, intellectual and trading interaction between the learned and the businessmen of other countries, was frequent. It provided the realm with riches and glory. Time has washed away all but the fragrance of literature of that period has spread beyond the frontiers of time. Chinese, Persians, Arabs, Turks and Greeks came to India with different objectives. Some came for business; others for knowledge; some others to rule. If riches attracted warriors, educational institutions attracted scholars to learn medicine, mathematics, logic, grammar, law, military sciences, surgery, astronomy and philosophy. India was a shining star. The kings governed with the sensitivity which parents show towards the care of their children.

When elements of progress are thus available, nature rewards the environment with her gifts. Kalidasa, the great Sanskrit dramatist, poet and a master of similes, was one such prize.

Kalidasa's works

Kalidasa was one of the greatest exponents of drama, literature and poetry in Sanskrit. He represented the consummate expression of poetic art and sublimity in imagination. His Sanskrit lyrical drama–*Meghadoota*, describes the emotions of a *Yaksha,* belonging to the hills in the north, and exiled in Ujjaini, the capital city of the king. Nonchalantly watching clouds sail over his prison cell, he fondly remembers his beloved. In a fit of deep emotion, he asks the floating rain clouds to take his message to his beloved residing in the foothills of the Himalayas. He even provides a clue to his 'messenger' clouds so as to enable them not to lose their way through Ujjaini. Kalidasa, in this manner, describes the king's palace and gardens:

"Smell the most fragrant earth in the burnt woodlands, and as you release your raindrops, the deer dancing in the gardens, will show you the way." Also,

"When you have reached the foothills of the Himalayas, tell my beloved":

> I see her body in the sinuous creepers,
> Your gaze in the startled eyes of the deer;
> Your cheek in the moon,
> Your hair in the plumage of peacocks
> And in the tiny ripples of the river,
> I see your sidelong glances;
> But alas my dearest,
> Nowhere do I find your whole likeness!

Kalidasa wrote his works during the reign of Vikramaditya. As an observant courtier, he recorded what he witnessed for posterity. He depicts in his dramas the aristocracy of the rich, the purity and simplicity of the poor and the sagacity of the saints. Reading *Meghadoota*, one discovers that Shakuntala's son Bharata, was the first amongst the kings of Hastinapur in the Mahabharata.

The story of *Meghadoota*

Kalidasa was fond of describing natural surroundings through the geography of the country. He takes the reader over the Vindhyas while on the way to the Himalayas, describing their forest wealth and innumerable rivulets. The scenic beauty described in the drama is like a running commentary of a modern cricket match! Instead of the pavilion for the commentator, the poet is on the aerial chariots of clouds. Thus is he able to comprehend the vastness of the forests, the grandeur of the valleys and its simple, honest and pure inhabitants.

The drama starts with a king chasing a deer in the forest retreat. This, to the forest dwellers, is *Sharanagum Sarvabhootani*—an abode where all creatures find protection and love. The forest dwellers plead with the king to spare the life of the innocent animal, running helplessly for its life. The plot is at once lifted to the highest nobility, providing a glimpse how men during ancient times treated animals.

"Never, Oh! Never is the arrow meant to pierce the tender body of a deer, even as the fire is not for the burning of flowers," say the people to the king, pleading for the animal's life.

Sentiments such as these were responsible in moulding the minds of the people in India even when they enjoyed the highest level of prosperity and peace! Thus was influenced by the cultural life of the Indian people when their great works of literature eulogized non-violence even towards animals.

Moving on, there is a village dweller, living in the beautiful surroundings of the forest with ponds where lotuses of exotic colours bloom. The dweller has a foster daughter, Shakuntala, who is living with him. One day, king Dushyanta happens to pass through in his chariot. He glances at the beautiful girl and is bewitched by her beauty. Kalidasa describes the thoughts thus:

> She seems a flower whose fragrance none has tasted;
>
> A branch no describing hand has wasted.
>
> Fresh honey, beautifully cool.
>
> No man deserves to taste her beauty,
>
> Her blameless loveliness and worth,
>
> Unless he has fulfilled man's perfect duty–
>
> And is there such a one on earth?

The king seeks permission of the sage to marry Shakuntala. The consent is given and both are married.

Shortly after, Dushyanta is required to go back to his kingdom. He promises to return soon and take her to his kingdom. When the king does not return even after prolonged waiting, Shakuntala consults an astrologer, who says that the king does remember her. He also says that Dushyanta will continue to remember her as long as the ring given by him is on her fingers.

One day, while taking a bath, the ring slips into the pond. By chance, a fish swallows it. Deprived of the ring, both the sage and Shakuntala reach the palace. They narrate the entire past to the king. Dushyanta however is not able to recollect anything. Shakuntala, dejected and frustrated returns. The sage advises Shakuntala not to despair:

> Yet much reflection dearest makes one strong,
>
> Strong with an inner strength nor should thou feel,
>
> Despair at what has come to us of wrong.
>
> Who has unending woes and lasting weak,
>
> Our fates move up and down like a circling wheel.

She starts living in another forest, where she bears her child, Bharata, from king Dushyanta.

Meanwhile, a fisherman catches the fish that had swallowed the ring, which bears the seal of the king. The fisherman dutifully gives back the ring to king Dushyanta, who after getting the ring, at once remembers everything again. He decides to go and meet his wife in the forest. Travelling in his flying chariot, he alights with dramatic providence at the very hermitage where his son and wife are living. There, Bharata is playing in front of the cottage. Dushyanta feels the emotions of a father. Shortly afterwards, Shakuntala arrives at the place looking for the boy. Both Dushyanta and Shakuntala meet. Dushyanta seeks forgiveness for his loss of memory. Both return to the kingdom with son Bharata.

Meghadoota (the messenger of rain) as a Sanskrit drama, expresses human emotions, the morals, manners and relationship between the king and his subjects. Its dramatic description creates a unique familiarity between generations to recognize their past. In it, Kalidasa sings about the beauty of India's hills and rivers and fertile plains and mountains. It describes the grandeur of prosperity of her great cities. All this is done through the pictorial narration of spring and monsoon clouds, roaring past central India towards the Himalayas. In another composition, *Ritusambhara*, Kalidasa describes the cycle of the seasons. The picture so drawn reflects the life and foliage of forests so abundant in ancient India. Here is how he describes the arrival of spring:

> Their blossom-burden weighs the trees,
> The winds in fragrance move;
> The lakes are bright with lotuses,
> The women bright with love;
> The days are soft, the evenings clear
> And charming everything.

> The groves are beautifully bright
> For many and many a mile
> With Jasmine flowers that are as white,
> As loving woman's smile;
> The resolution of saint
> Might well be tried by this;
> Far more, young hearts that fancies paint
> With gleams of loving bliss.

Kalidasa paints a graphic picture of the monsoons in the drama. Everything around may have changed since Kalidasa wrote this drama, but the scenic beauty of nature still remains unaltered; only the time and inclination to observe and appreciate is perhaps missing:

> The rain advances like a king
> In awful majesty;
> Hear, dearest how his thunders ring
> Like royal drums and see
> His lightening banners, wave; a cloud
> For elephants he rides.
> And finds his welcome from the crowd.

In *Kumarsambhava*, Kalidasa paints his divine *yogi* in silent meditation:

> Calm as a full moon resting on a hill,
> A waveless lake when every breeze is still,
> Like a torch burning in a sheltered spot,
> So still was He, unmoving, breathing not!

Kalidasa was one of the nine gems in the court of Vikramaditya. A distinguishing fact of his writings is the absence of philosophical introduction in describing life of those times. He concentrates on the beauty and vivacity of description, rather than delving in the realm of philosophy. In *Yaksha*, Kalidasa excels his own works. His works provide glimpses of life during those happy and prosperous days when life in India was at its zenith of glory.

Mavamitra is another of Kalidasa's lesser known Sanskrit dramas depicting the morals and culture of ancient India. It describes the sensual pleasures available for a king. Starting the drama with an invocation to impress the need of restrain in sensual pleasure, it enlightens the present generation of relationship between man and woman.

"Let God illumine for us the path of Truth; sweep away our passions bred out of darkness."

He describes the orgies of sense pleasures indulged by kings. Along with it, the drama shows the ugliness of treachery and cruelty, which are the natural outcome of such uncontrolled passions exhibited in ambition. It describes that ambition does generate unrestricted material goods; but along with it, also produces uncontrollable passions for their possession.

The hero of the drama, Agnimitra, as the name suggests, is full of uncontrolled desires. The heroine, Dhairini, again as the name suggests, is an embodiment of patience. Kalidasa, with artistic deftness, combines the role of the heroine with infinite dignity possessing a clear conscience. She rises above all belligerence, betrayal and insults showered on her. During the play, she remains steadfast in performing the duties of Indian womanhood as immortalized in the play.

After Kalidasa, Sudraka is another literary genius of the period. As a contemporary of Kalidasa, his most famous play is *Mrichchakatika (The Little Clay Cart)*. It is full of realistic descriptions of the life and times of the age. It contains different ingredients like human pathos and political intrigue—revealing human frailties at different levels. The story briefly describes the love of a poor Brahmin, Charudatta, for a virtuous courtesan, Vasantsena. It manages to bring about the downfall of the wicked king Palaka. The trial scene, like all other trial scenes, is able to save the hero at the last moment. The play paints a picture of the era with such depth that the reader finds himself emotionally placed in the life and times of that period.

Sanskrit literature is particularly rich in fables. The world owes the advent of the now popular fairy tales in English language to the writings in *Hitopadesha* and *Panchatantra*, the two most popular fables first produced by India. The two great Indian epics, the Ramayana and the Mahabharata, were recast in the present form, during the rule of Vikramaditya.

Chapter XVI
Socio-Religious Reformation

Indian thought, from ancient times, has been deeply influenced by metaphysics. Be it geography of the country or a regular flow of cultures, it has always helped improve the quality of intellectual life. This life was often at the expense of action. This was because people were able to obtain food, as the necessity for life, from the soil rather than the more adventurous method of hunting. So long as the monarchs managed to keep the country's boundaries safe, all was well. Kings followed religion as an easier way to instill moral values amongst the people. But India had always had several religions. The rulers of the Golden Era, with combination of military strength, benevolence and fear, kept peace.

Now, what is metaphysics?

" Metaphysics is an attempt to think things out to their ultimate significance; to find their substantive essence in the scheme of Reality. It is highest of all generalizations. It is the science of Being and Understanding."

Be it because of the unpredictable nature of Indian climate, or uncertainties of life emphasized in Hindu philosophy, metaphysics has remained an integral part of social, cultural and political life of Indian society. It has always influenced the mind and character of her people. Generations of saints and sages interpreting it found consolation in bad times pursuing the core pleasure of abstract thinking. Indian genius, from ancient times, has excelled in synthesizing the opposites. Even as present day challenges warrant singlemindedness in pursuit of objectives, Indian ethos has never ignored balance and equilibrium. This apparently tends to slow life's forward movement; yet from a larger perspective it helps preserve the continuity of culture and civilization. This continuity is a cause of surprise and wonder for the world; it has been a great gift of wisdom from our earliest thinkers.

Teacher-student relationship

In ancient India, lessons in learning started with elementary education. The teacher would sit under a tree; students squatting on the grass. After the teacher had initiated the subject, it was open for students to exchange views amongst themselves. As the young grew in age, the subject would be elevated to higher levels. Conversation would rise to discussions and debates. By the age of twenty, the imaginative mind had learnt to comprehend and develop rational analysis. The king reflected the people's mood by personal participation, inviting the learned for debates.

Centuries of this routine helped students to learn the age old ideas conveyed by the teacher. Obedience to the teacher demanded acceptance of what he conveyed as truth. Students were to reverentially learn and follow what the teacher taught. Following this principle through generations, a convention was thus established. This was the *Guru-Shishya parampara*. With vicissitudes in fortune, they may deviate in practice, but never in idealism. Today, the rich Indian philosophy has been reduced to rituals. Each one reminds the other of ideals, seldom put to practice. An average Indian, be he a resident of rural or urban India, just loves conversing and idealizing on imaginative issues and is by nature a contended person. Indian society, in good and bad times, has always revolved around this axis.

Scenario in other parts of the world

While India remained drowned in philosophy and thought, pondering over the mysteries of nature, let us see what interested others in distant lands during the same period.

Athens and Rome, during this period, were two prosperous cities representing an advanced western civilization. Where would a visitor find their men after work? Instead of conversation and debates like in India, the men are gathered in a stadium awaiting iron clad gladiators to emerge in the ring. They would appear on horses, clad in shields from head to foot, with spears pointing towards each other. Then, a life and death struggle would start in the stadium watched by an excited audience. Of the two competing warriors, one would be dislodged from the saddle and instantly killed.

"Hurray! Hurray!" The stadium would be wild with cheers for the victorious; but no tears were shed for the dead.

The West had developed the warrior culture, ever ready for physical action. Similarly, the savage tribes of Arabia were always fighting each other for food. Physical action and uncertain supply of food had made them a warrior nation.

India today takes legitimate pride in claiming that she never attacked any country. India honoured her saints and sages, while others were idolizing their warriors. Kindliness and compassion always dominated her thought and action. But this imbalance of human nature was not to the liking of Nature. Man is for both thought and action. There must be a balance, if not at the personal, at least at the social level.

Bhratrihari–the saint of goodness

The life of Bhratrihari is an index of socio-religious morals and customs of his times. It shows sensitivity of soul, standards of character and love for literature. It highlights the Vedantic philosophy, encouraging renunciation that the Indian sub-conscious mind always looks forward to. Indian attention towards space and time being vague, its exact calendar remains shrouded in uncertainty. His writings reveal that Bhratrihari belonged to royal lineage. He devoted his early life to sensuous pleasures, possessing a sharp intellect and a flair for poetry. According to the legend drawn from his poetry, Bhratrihari loved his queen Pingala. One day a yogi came to his court and offered him a fruit in appreciation of his just, fair and prosperous rule. The fruit had the power to defy old age.

The Raja offered the fruit to his beloved queen. But, the queen was in love with someone else. She gave the fruit to him. This man, in turn, was in love with yet another woman; he presented the fruit to her. This woman, who now received the immortal fruit, had always admired Bhratrihari for his fairness and kindness towards his subjects. She considered that the most deserving one of the eternal fruit was the Raja. She came to the court and presented the fruit to Bhratrihari.

When the entire chain of events was revealed, Bhratrihari was utterly shocked. He decided to renounce his kingdom and take to *sanyasa* (renunciation). The event finds mention in his poetry thus:

> She, with whom all my thoughts dwell is averse,
>
> She loves another. He whom she deserves,
>
> Turns to a fairer face. Another worse
>
> For me afflicted with deep fires.
>
> Fie on my love and on me and her!
>
> For most on love, this madness ministers!

Verses of Bhratrihari

Bhratrihari wrote his verses in three different moods. Possessing rare intellect, his writings cover all the three phases of life. They prescribe a schedule for achieving particular goals at different stages of life. There is love of sensuous pleasure in youth, duties connected with creation of wealth and finally spiritual achievement.

Shingara Shatakam are verses on romance and love. They beautifully describe the romance of love and sensuous pleasure, taking the reader to the world of fantasy. The hundred verses, written by Bhratrihari, are absorbing. They contain the opulence of ornaments, restrained dignity in conduct and delights of sensuous love and its sublimation.

Niti Shatakam are the second category of verses which describe the worldly wisdom and morals to be followed for a virtuous conduct during the journey of life. They are rules for successful and happy living. It is accepted that pursuit of pleasure, wealth and prosperity is the noble objective of all living beings. But it is also important that laws of morality and values continue to govern life. At moments of weakness, there is a temptation to dilute these values. This may provide some quick gains; but soon it turns worse.

Vairagya Shatakam are verses describing the path to spiritual achievement. These relate to arranging a life of renunciation and unfettered freedom.

Bhratrihari demonstrated the truth of his verses by leading his life through all the three as mentioned. He enjoyed the sensuous pleasures of youth, including ruling his kingdom justly. Possessing a natural bent of mind for poetry, he produced verses for all times. He renounced the world when the call from his heart came to do so. During the stage of renunciation, in one of his contemplative moods, he says:

> Once upon a time the days seemed long for me. When my heart was sorely wounded, through seeking favours. Yet again life seemed all too short, when I sought to carry out all my worldly desires and ends. But now as a philosopher, I sit on a hard stone in a cave on the mountain side; time and again I laugh when I think of my earlier life.

An insight to his philosophy is revealed from some of his famous verses:

> 1. Learning is verily the highest duty for man. It is a treasure concealed and well protected; it places within his reach enjoyment, honour and happiness; it is an object of reverence even for those who are worthy of reverence. While journeying in strange lands, it is a friend; it is the highest deity. Learning is honoured by kings, but not wealth. One destitute of learning is a beast.

> 2. Who would not adore and revere good men who rise by bending low with humility. They evidence their own merits by extolling those of others; gain their ends by projecting extensive schemes for others; and censor with sweet patience and calm fortitude, the calumniators whose tongues are noisy with harsh syllables of accusations? Such are their marvellous moods, the noble ways, whom men delight to honour and praise.

> 3. The sun causes sun-lotuses to expand without solicitation, the moon, though unasked, causes the moon-lotuses to bloom; the clouds yield water without soliciting; good people direct their efforts towards the good of others, of their own accord.

4. Courtesy is the ornament of the great; temperate speech of the hero, peace and content of the learned, wrathlessness in hermits, noble expanse of the rich, forgiveness of the strong, modesty of the righteous; but good character, which is the root of all these, is the highest ornament of all.

5. Wise people thus describe the character of a true friend; he dissuades you from sin; urges you to good action; keeps your secrets; publishes your merits; does not forsake you in distress; and helps you in time of need.

6. Those are the noblest persons who, giving up self interest, bring about the good of others; those who undertake business for the sake of others, not inconsistent with their own good are men of the middle order; those that stand in the way of the good of others for their own benefits, are demons in a human form; but we know not what to call them that oppose the good of others, without any advantage to themselves.

Bhratrihari places character of a person above all. In his *Niti Shatakam*, he says:

Better if this body falls from the lofty peak of a high mountain against some rugged surface and is shattered to pieces in the midst of rough rocks. Better is the hand thrust into the fangs of a huge serpent or deadly bite. Better falling into the fire; but not the wrecking of one's character.

The life of Bhratrihari provides glimpses of the national mood of those times. The grandeur, virtue and steadfastness of kings and their subjects were now under decline. Nearly a thousand years earlier, a Gautama had left his young wife and child to find the cause of suffering; at this period, another prince was not only abandoning his wife but also his kingdom for unfaithfulness.

Treading the lonely path

Vedanta sums up the purpose of life in the laws of truth and righteousness (*dharma*), wealth and prosperity (*artha*), pursuit of pleasure (*kama*) and finally, unfettered spiritual achievement (*moksha*).

India has preserved her knowledge and wisdom mostly in verses. The Ramayana of Valmiki and the Mahabharata describe everything that happened or could ever happen in this complex world. Her scriptures have always subordinated worldly wealth and power to knowledge and virtue. The message is rapped and is conveyed in poetic myths. The great poets of the period have been direct, brief and absorbing.

There were three great poets of the age. Bhratrihari, Surdas and Chandidas. Surdas, the blind poet, belonged to the region where Krishna was born. He therefore composed his verses narrating the naughtiness of the young lad of Vrindaban (Mathura). Thereafter he dwells on Krishna's youth and the wisdom of his actions, bestowing permanent devotion to the Lord. People get delirious with joy while singing his devotional songs.

Chandidas was a devotee of the goddess Kali. He wrote his verses in Bengali. He influenced entire Bengal spiritually with his devotional songs, which made people dance before her image in ecstasy.

Bhakti towards God is the essence of these poets. Modern India continues to follow with the same enthusiasm and devotion what these poets had offered in their compositions.

That the times had changed, would be confirmed by the happening during the 'Twilight Centuries' ahead. A young sage from South Kerala would soon appear to rectify the damage inflicted by petty religious fueds between Hinduism and Buddhism for supremacy amongst the Indian masses. Let us then study how Adi Shankara was able to revolutionize Hindu religion with his forceful advocacy and indomitable spirit.

Chapter XVII
Shankaracharya–Silent Revolutionary

"Brahma satyam Jagat mithya
Jeevo Brahmaiva naaparah"
(*Brahman*, the Absolute alone is real;
this world is unreal and the individual
soul is no different from *Brahman*.)

—Shankaracharya

Beginning with the Vedas and the Upanishads, religious leaders had elaborated the spiritual science with reforms. These had become necessary because of changes brought about by time. Mahavira, Gautama and Kapila were the three great thinkers of India who revolutionized thought in the country. They translated their observations into reforms and practised what they preached. Earlier, written in Sanskrit, religion was wrapped in metaphysics; common people needed interlocutors to understand them. With time, the interlocutors became priests. They would add their own self-interest in their explanations. This introduced corrupt practices in religion. In course of time, the substance was lost, only the skeleton remained. Even the priests lost touch with the soul of religion.

Shankara lived just 32 years; taking *sanyasa* while still a boy. During his short life, he achieved what efforts of centuries could not accomplish. With wisdom, kindliness and a broad universal vision, he brought a revolution in Hindu religion. He demolished contradictions between Hinduism and Buddhism. While convincing others, he would not take support from logic. He argued in favour of insight to extract the internal truth from the temporal; the whole out of the part. Thus was he able to convince the most learned scholars and teachers of his age.

Roots of his philosophy

Indian philosophers, from the earliest time of the Upanishads, maintained God (*Brahman*) and Soul (*Atman*), as one. The great thinker Badarayana, as far back as BC 200, preached this as the gist of the Upanishads. Now, almost a thousand years later, Gandapada, revived the idea with emphasis. He, in turn, influenced and taught this to a young lad of fourteen years from Kerala. Armed with this philosophy, Shankara fought the frustrated Hindu mood of that period. In a short time, he converted the most learned of his time to his view. Shankara, the young *sanyasi,* with his 'magical arguments' again established the supremacy of the Vedanta and the dominance of the Brahmins. His pet argument was:

"It is not logic we need; it is insight of understanding the essential out of the irrelevant," advised Shankara. The other important point in this connection was: willingness to observe, inquire and think for understanding's sake; not for wealth, fame or power. Shankara asserted that sensations and intellect are not sufficient to understand Reality. It is the 'insight and intuition' of spirit that reveals Reality.

Early life

Shankara was born in an orthodox Brahmin family in AD 788. At an early age, he started learning from family traditions and his teacher, Gopala. During his early years, he found the environment around him rather hostile. He had acquired strict Brahmanical traditions from the family. A passionate desire burned within him to reform the Hindu religion. To devote himself entirely to this pursuit, Shankara sought renunciation from the world (*sanyasa*). Then, his father died. His mother was now alone. She would not let her son be lost to *sanyasa.*

There is a story on how his mother agreed to his adopting to the path of renunciation.

Once, while taking bath in the river, a crocodile caught Shankara. His mother, standing on the banks was helpless. Even when the son cried, she could do nothing to save him. When death appeared certain, Shankara implored her mother to let him take to renunciation or let the crocodile devour him. Caught between *sanayasa* and death, the mother chose life for her son.

At the age of sixteen, Shankara renounced the world.

Thus started the mission of the greatest revolutionary and reformer of all times. In a short span of fifteen years, he would transform the ancient philosophy of the Vedanta into the vibrant Hindu religion. Intellectual content based on philosophy of the Upanishads along with rituals and beliefs in several gods have flourished in India. His magical capacity could convince the two opposite divergent views to appear logical and be acceptable to the learned priests at Varanasi.

His philosophy of Vedanta

Shankara introduces his philosophy by stating us that knowledge starts from our senses. He says that sensuous adaptations transform reality. It does not permit the 'real' to reach us. Cause and Effect; Time and Space, give reality a different shape. He believed that whatever was perceived was inextricably mingled with the things perceived, thus altering reality. The world exists; but it is Maya; it is delusion. It is a phenomenon, an appearance created by our thoughts. Our limitation is that we perceive only within the frame of Space and Time; or think in terms of Cause and Effect. We may call it ignorance or a defect in our mode of perception; or the handicap of the physical body that we notice a flux of change in the objects of the world.

Shankara prescribes intuition and insight as the only instruments to understand Universal Reality (*Brahman*). When we remove Time and Space from our perception; Cause and Effect, from our consideration; we see our souls (*Atma*) shared by all selves and things. This undivided and omnipresent Self, is the same as God (*Brahman*).

Shankara on God

Shankara starts with ego and *atma*. He considers ego and *atma* to be two selves in beings. Simultaneously, these are two worlds–nominal and phenomenal. There are two deities, Creator and *Brahman* or the Pure Being. Shankara, with this definition, is at once able to justify worship of several gods as well as his philosophy of 'Reality'. He calls it 'Existence'. "It cannot be proved by logic or reason, but is a practical necessity," he says. Reality, therefore, is everything inclusive. It is neuter, indestructible, above gender; beyond good and evil, above all moral distinction, all differences and attributes; all desires and ends.

Brahman is the Cause; *Brahman* is the effect, the timeless and secret essence of the world.

The age required such a philosophy to harmonize opposites. He would accept any combination and defend them vigorously to maintain the unity of Hindu society. In this respect, he was a master debater, producing such arguments in favour of his synthesis that the most learned in the land accepted his ideas. Shankara was convinced that to save Hindu religion from being divided into narrower and narrower sects, this was the only way. Today, if Hindu religion unites the entire country, speaking different languages and following different customs, it is due to the crusade of Shankara, launched at a critical period. It served to save disintegration of Hindu society.

Pilgrimage to the north

After consolidating Hindu religion in the south, Shankara was advised to move to north India. The eternal city of Varanasi was the centre of all learning. It was the seat of intellectual and religious heads. It was here that high priests of the Hindu religion came to test their intellectual knowledge. Shankara had a complex task of defending the worship of several gods as well as the philosophy of universal unity in *Brahman* (consciousness). With his strong and unshakeable insight, he was able to satisfy the learned priests of north India.

Brahmanism and priesthood had declined during the Golden Age when Buddhism was reigning supreme. Shankara wrote his works in Sanskrit that saw a revival, particularly amongst the intellectuals. The necessity of explaining them to people required the services of interlocutors again. The cult was once again revived.

The four seats of transcendental wisdom

To preserve the great wisdom of the Upanishads for posterity, Shankara decided to establish four seats of learning in the four corners of India. He envisaged spiritual wisdom to flow from these centres, establishing a bond of unity among the people for generations to come. The colossal work undertaken by him required incessant travel to all corners of India. During his travels, Shankara gained practical knowledge of various systems and practices followed by innumerable sections of the society. He discovered that countless factions, in the country was quarrelling with each other for supremacy. He met their leaders and brought them under one fold. Soon he was the master and unquestioned leader of Hindu society.

Shankara appointed spiritual heads at each centre giving them names like Saraswati, Puri, Bharati, Teertha, Ashrama and Giri. They were to be within the fold of four seats of wisdom established at:

1.   Jagannath Puri in the east,
2.   Sringeri in the south,
3.   Dwaraka in the west, and
4.   Badrinath in the north.

The arrangement made by *Acharya* Shankara is followed even in present times, almost in the same form.

Collective wisdom of Shankara

Shankara defined the important constituents of his thoughts thus:

1.   *Atma* (Consciousness): Is the source of all life. It gives capacity to the sense organs to perceive, the mind to feel, and the intellect to think.

2.   Virtue and morality: Shankara called virtue and morality the pillars of the Hindu religion. When practised individually, they are a cause of egoism, but are of value when one's own self is identified with the self of others.

3.   God: Shankara considered God as Existence (Consciousness). He makes a distinction between God and personal god. He considers personal god a necessity offering solace to the limits of intelligence and encouragement to morality; God being indescribable, limitless, spaceless, timeless, causeless and changeless.

4.   Being: Is the Reality (Brahman). To be one with God means to rise or sink beneath the separateness and brevity of self; to rise above, forgetting worldly interests, considering different divisions and things to be one; a universe in which there are no differences.

5.   On man: Man is distinguished from plants and animals in that he has not only the growing power of plant world and the moving power of animal world, but also the power of reasoning, determination, discrimination and willing. Men, who use their powers with discrimination and realize their good ambitions, turn into gods.

6.   Blissful state: It is to renounce possessions, consider neither the concept of good nor evil; ignore all personal qualities. There must be no self-interest or pride. He warns that good deeds have no relevance in Maya. Only when Maya is lifted, reincarnation ceases.

Every Hindu household sings *Bhaja Govindam* to elevate his soul. It is the most popular devotional song amongst the Hindus. Translated in English from Sanskrit it says:

> Fool! Give up the thirst for wealth; banish all desires.
> Let your mind be satisfied with what is gained by Karma.
>
> Do not be proud of wealth, of friends or youth; time takes all away.
> Learning all this quickly, world is full of illusion, enter Brahman.
>
> Time is flying, life is waning, yet the hope does not cease.
> The body is wrinkled, the hair has turned grey,
> The mouth has become toothless, the stick in the hand shakes,
> Yet man does not leave hope.
>
> Persevere equanimity always:
> In thee, in me, in others, there dwells Vishnu alone.
> See every self in self, and give up all thought of difference.

It is an unforgettable sight to watch rugged and sweating Indian villagers, walking on dusty path towards their fields. They have this song on their lips;

hope and contentment in heart. Each morning when they gets up, there is the musical tone of *Bhaja Govindam* that helps to elevate his surroundings. Shankara's philosophy gave to India and her people, the gift of joy in poverty, defeat, in misery itself.

Builder of modern Hindu religion

What were the extraordinary qualities of this man who achieved so much in just fifteen years of his working life?

1. In knowledge, he was a perfect *Gyani*.
2. In *Karma*, he was ideal for all.
3. In *Bhakti*, he was the noblest of *Bhaktas*.
4. In teaching, he was a mobile university.
5. In organization, he was a perfect organizer.

Several centuries later western philosopher, Kant, in *Critique of Pure Reason* expressed like Shankara:

"All knowledge comes from senses and reveals not the external reality itself, but our sensory adaptation of reality. By sense then, we can never know the 'real' except in the garb of time, space and cause."

Spinoza, another German philosopher, would say the same thing, like this:

"The greatest good is the knowledge of the union, which the mind has with the entire Nature."

A homage to vision

At a crucial turn of history, Shankara, all by himself, wedded Vedanta to Hinduism. Elements of compromise, reflected his writings, beautifully blend the two. This paved the way for accommodation of new religions that were to follow in the country. Even when Islam held a dominating position in India, future generations of preachers continued to follow the essence of Shankara's thought. Thus, both Sufism and Bhakti movements that followed with the arrival of Islam in medieval India, advocated this similarity of the two religions.

In recent times, the traditions established by Shankara would be faithfully carried by Swami Shivananda, Chinmayananda, and Bhoomananda—all from Kerala, where Shankara was born. They enthrall the soul of their audience with his devotional songs (*bhajans*) and interpretations of vedantic scriptures. While Shankara helped revive *Sanatan Dharma*, it simultaneously encouraged growth of brahmanical hierarchy of the caste system. While both Buddha and Mahavira had preached dissolution of the caste based on social order in Indian society, Shankara, while displacing Buddhism from India, again established the old system. At a time when new forces were knocking at the doors from North-west India, revival of the old social system would damage internal unity that would be required to meet the challenges of coming centuries.

Chapter XVIII
Rise of Sciences in Ancient India

It is one of the curious facts of history that some of the world's greatest thinkers were born within a hundred odd years of each other:

Lao Tse (BC 500) and Confucius (BC 550) were two wise men born in China; Kapila (BC 500) gave India the famous philosophy of Sankhya. Gautama Buddha (BC 563) is known the world over as one who has influenced humankind the most. Socrates (BC 469) and Plato (BC 428) were the Greek philosophers who talked of reason and relationships. They preached that knowledge cannot be derived by senses; it is only achieved by using intellect. In earlier chapters we read how geography, economic pursuits, political organization and morals, influenced movement of civilization in different societies all over the world. In India, as in ancient Greece and China, the mind was free to fly to dizzy heights. We saw how saints were also engrossed in subjects like state administration and the sciences of physical and temporal life. Being the country's intellectual brigade, they were responsible not only for the spiritual life but also the temporal. In ancient India, religious priests besides preaching morals also dealt with physical sciences. Christian Europe also followed the Dark Ages. If therefore India excelled in the Life of Thought through her saints and sages, they also provided an impetus for the development of other subjects.

Astronomy

The love of Indians for astrology helped develop the science of astronomy. The first Indian treatise on astronomy was *Siddhantas* in BC 425. Varahamihira was the first Indian astrologer whose work is described in one of the *Siddhantas:* "The Earth, owing to its force of gravity, draws all things to itself." Another significant feature of the *Siddhantas* was the use of the time-cycle of *Mahayugas*. According to it, "A *Mahayuga* starts at an epoch when all planets are in conjunction. During a *Mahayuga*, they will all perform an integral number of revolutions and at the end they are again in conjunction." A *Mahayuga* is made up of 4,320,000 years and is divided into four *yugas: Satya, Treta, Dwapara* and *Kali*.

During the first century AD, Indian mariners were using a fish-shaped iron dipped in oil as a mariners compass. This would always point to the north. Later, Varahamihira and Aryabhatta in the fifth and sixth century AD respectively, expounded their astronomical theories. Aryabhatta assumed all *yugas* of equal duration; while others took it to be in the ratio of 4:3:2:1. In other words, *Kali yuga* (the yuga at present) would be 4,32,000 years. Calculation of planetary orbits led to several developments in mathematics. The decimal system was the climax of the work done by Aryabhatta. This system later reached Europe through the Arabs. They explained eclipses, solstices and equinoxes, stating that the earth was a sphere. This was many centuries earlier than what Galileo was to declare in Italy centuries later.

Brahmagupta systematized the astronomical knowledge of Aryabhatta and Varahamihira. The *Siddhanta* states that the earth, owing to its force of gravity, draws all things to itself. All these observations, based on calculations, helped develop mathematics. Indian astronomers and mathematicians, credited with some very significant works, helped other branches of science in other countries.. Amongst them all, Aryabhatta's contribution to mathematics has been of considerable importance.

Mathematics

Amongst the different sciences in which India led, the decimal system is the most effective and useful. For sometime, it was known as an Arabic invention. the Arabs were the first to translate these works from Sanskrit, acknowledging its origin from India. Formerly, India expressed all numbers by symbols of tens, receiving a value by position and absolute value. Apparently a simple idea, missed by the best of mathematicians, it had a revolutionary effect on future calculations of complex problems. Similarly, Buddhayana first calculated the value of *pi* in the sixth century AD. He explained the concept of what is known as the Pythagorean theorem. Another significant work was discovered by Bakshali–a manuscript discovered in a village of Peshawar (Pakistan) dealing with square roots, progression, income and expenditure, profit and loss, etc. Algebra reached Europe through similar works translated by the Arabs.

Aryabhatta, Brahmagupta, and Bhaskaracharya had invented the signs in algebra. They brought the concept of negative quantity. Without it, algebra could not have served future science. The most interesting part of their work was its preservation through poetry. In this manner, it could be easily memorized. Being in verses, despite mass destruction of valuable literature by barbarians, it could be preserved. Bhaskara anticipated differential calculus and Aryabhatta delved in trigonometry. Both Greece and India, it would be observed, were doing original work in this field. The Arabs, because of their extraordinary mobility, served the cause of knowledge by dissipating information to different parts of the world. Amongst the greatest of such Arab mathematicians, who not only did original work in the field of mathematics, but also translated ideas from India for the world, was Al-Khwarazmi who lived in Baghdad.

Physical sciences

In physical sciences, as in other branches, both Indian and Greek thinkers were discovering the basis of future developments. The founder of Vaisheshika philosophy, wrote that the world was composed of atoms of as many kinds as there are elements. Jaina thinkers taught that all atoms are of the same kind. Kanada was holding the view that heat and light are varieties of the same substance. Udayana taught that all heat came from the sun. Vachaspati interpreted light to be composed of minute particles emitted by substances and striking the eye. They were all original works of research, serving as complimentary to other branches, resulting in products that would become the beacon light of civilization.

Chemistry

Development of chemistry in India is a corollary to the growth of requirements for better living. During the reign of the Guptas, when Rome was the greatest European power, India was exporting the highest quality of chemical products to the Roman Empire. By the sixth century AD, the Romans looked towards India for the best and the most refined luxuries. Therefore chemical industries that depended on processes like calcination, dyeing and tanning, soap making, glass and cement flourished. The products were renowned for superior quality. Nagarjuna devoted a whole volume discussing the properties and uses of mercury. Anatomy and physiology, employed in medical science, are only its offshoots. They being linked to each other, we shall discuss the achievements in chemistry along with medical sciences.

Medical sciences

From the earliest times, next to the passion for religion and thought, elimination of pain has remained a matter of paramount importance for Indians. They were therefore devoted to the knowledge of medicine and health. *Ayurveda* is the earliest source of this knowledge. It became the earliest school of medicine and health care known to humans. Ancient India knew most of the fundamental medical knowledge of today. Understood was the description of ligament, lymphatic, nerves, plexus, fascia, adipose, vascular tissues, the digestive system and various muscles. *Atharvaveda* was the first to indicate this knowledge which was subsequently modified into *Ayurveda* – the science of longevity. It mentions that illness is a result of disorder in one or more of the four humours—air, water, phlegm and blood. Its treatment is recommended with various kinds of herbs. Being a country conducive to growth of plants this was but a natural outcome of geography. This combination enabled India earn the respect of the world in the field of medicine.

Dhanwantari followed by his students Sushruta and Charaka, are three great names in this field. Amongst them Sushruta was a professor of medicine at

Varanasi. Dhanwantari besides medicines, specialized in surgery and Charaka compiled all earlier works in the field of medicine and surgery for use by coming generations.

"Not for self, not for fulfillment of earthly desires of gain, but solely for the good of suffering humanity should you treat your patients, and so excel all."

This was the first code of conduct for doctors. Even to this day, almost the same code of conduct is followed in the medical profession worldwide.

Because of their devotion and proficiency, doctors of ancient India were in great demand in Middle Eastern countries. Kings invited them from Greece and Persia. The great Caliph of Baghdad, Haroon-ul-Rashid, occasionally invited Indian doctors to establish new hospitals.

During the great period of *Ayurveda*, the political situation had begun to detoriate. This had a negative effect. The knowledge that masters of medicine taught at these centres of learning, instead of being taught, began to be cornered by few. They would not divulge this knowledge in written words. Instead, it passed from father to son. This suffocated growth. It gradually started slipping into fewer hands. Those who practiced *Ayurveda* lost the urge for new ideas. Meanwhile, nature was encouraging new sciences to emerge. The vacuum created by *Ayurveda* was filled by Yunani and Allopathic systems.

Metallurgy

The iron pillar standing at Qutub near Delhi has been silently paying tribute to the genius of the ancient metallurgists of India. Its composition has defied modern knowledge. Ancient India manufactured high carbon steel much earlier than any other country. Damascus was then famous for making the best quality swords. To manufacture these swords, steel was exported from India. So famous was Indian steel for making swords that king Porus is said to have presented Alexander with a gift of this special steel. How the ancient Indians mastered the art of extraction of zinc, galvanization and refining of gold and producing corrosion-resistant steel by adding high phosphorus and low sulphur is still an enigma.

A historian of ancient Rome records that during the reign of Julius Caesar, industrial and luxury goods from India were so much in demand that they were draining the economy of Rome. He particularly refers to the import of silk, cotton fabrics, leather and consumer goods like, soap, glass and cutlery.

Essential unity of humanity

The study of growth of material sciences has a message. It reveals how individual ingenuity in one country and in isolation, tends to expand for the greater good. Inspite of physical difficulties of travel, terrains and communications knowledge, like air, flies to all sides. It does so not for 'self' but because of an inner urge for creativity. Leading nations of the ancient world, Greeks, Persians, Indians and Arabs contributed towards the growth of civilization. Each country, at a given time, in small measure or large, contributed towards the growth of material sciences. If the north provided one link, the south added another to make the chain stronger and firmer. When there was a period of darkness in Europe during the Middle Ages, Asia became the torch bearers. The purpose of creativity and the will to achieve a goal keep the cycle of life alive on the planet.

The Twilight Centuries

The vulture fastens on its timid prey,
And stabs with bloody beak, the quivering limbs.
All's well, it seems, for it.
But in a while,
An eagle tears the vulture into shreds.

—Voltaire

Chapter XIX
Price of Freedom–Eternal Vigilance

Signals of divisiveness, mutual acrimony and in-fighting, emanating from within the subcontinent, were heartily picked up by hungry hunters itching for action and a better life. Barbarians and nomads are accustomed to danger and skilled in killing. For them war is another kind of pursuit for food. They have nothing within to stir their conscience. They do not even feel the risk. On the contrary, it is an enjoyment and recreation for them. They were vigorous men, physically arduous, who were motivated to aggression by compulsions of survival. Hordes of Scythians, Huns, Afghans and Turks, had long been waiting for an opportunity to enjoy the leisure that follows abundance. They noticed the speculating, dogmatic, inactive and divided people having the best of both worlds, while they, the hard working, sturdy and ever-on-the-move, suffered from want. It was however still several centuries away when the full impact of one's weaknesses and other's strength, would show results. An incident of ancient England aptly conveys the message.

In ancient England, Vikings from the North Sea countries occasionally raided the coast of England. They looted, plundered and murdered, spreading devastation, bloodshed and terror. The booty they collected from the rich and poor of the country, served them for a time. The campaign was repeated when they required more. Gradually, the need developed into greed; raids became more frequent. With each campaign greed for more grew until it became unbearable.

Success and luxury had made the once robust plunderers over-confident. They did not realize that their earlier vigour had mellowed their will to struggle.

Next time, reaching the coast of England, instead of getting straight into the business of bloodshed and plunder, they sent a message to the English princes: "If you wish to avoid fighting and bloodshed, send us what we have come here for; we will return without harming you all."

The English nobles and squires met to consider the proposal. They all agreed that "fighting is futile; let us send them what they want and be done with it." However, a young prince amongst them stood up against such abject surrender. He said, " It is certain that fighting them, we shall loose. This however would

not end our misery. We must show our grit and stand resolutely against them."
He suggested that, "We may agree to their demand for wealth but seek a fight
all the same. The purse demanded would only be passed on when we have
been defeated."

This was agreed. The invitation to fight was sent. There was a bloody fight.
The English lost. The booty was handed over as agreed. England had seen the
last of the pirates; having seen the tenacity of the enemy, the pirates never
returned. The challenge had weakened their will. When a nation is prepared
for war, the enemy seldom dares.

In medieval India, others from afar, struggling against the forces of nature
and obdurate environment, were envying the rich crops in fields, and the luxury
of leisure on the subcontinent. They dreamt of wealth and abundance while
facing scarcity at their homes. Inspired to acquire, they would unite to become
strong and invade. They would attack, destroy, plunder, murder and if possible
enslave and rule! It is a sordid tale thereafter.

Decline of Buddhism and revival of Hinduism

The Mongols and the Tibetans were the two earliest races to take to Buddhism.
They had understood religion only through myths and rituals. The monks, to
attract their interests, considered this the only way. Meanwhile, Hindu religion
based on the Vedanta as explained by Kapila, also started falling into mythical
hyperbole. Soon both religions fell from their high pedestal. Even preachers,
who were supposed to know and guide, instead of explaining the meaning
and significance of their philosophy, deviated from the real. Masses were left
to interpret according to the levels of their intellect. The in-fighting between
the Hindus and the Buddhists, helped foster disintegration within the country.
Both the rulers and the ruled had accepted Buddhism for its rationalism in the
early wave of its popularity. Now, when like everything else, corrupt practices
had also crept in Buddhism, the moral strength of the country weakened.
Buddhist monks, to meet the challenge, started to copy the myths from Hindus.
While its appeal outside the country increased to an extent, in India it had the
opposite effect. Hindus, who had accepted Buddhism earlier, now found
both religions almost the same. Hindu priests saw their chance. They started
suggesting, "when everything between the two religions is the same, why change
at all?" Masses gradually began drifting back to Hinduism. The process was
accelerated by Kumaila Bhatta and later by Shankaracharya of Kerala.

The people of India began returning to the Vedas and Upanishads. In a brief
span of time, the two religious leaders infused a new enthusiasm, with rituals
recast for the people to follow. In a short time, everything of pre-Buddha
period, along with its class distinctions and rituals, were reverted to.

When Gautama Buddha was born, Indian thought had reached its peak. During the long period of a millenium, successive kings followed and propagated the moral values of Buddhism. To reform old practices, Buddhism tried to change earlier practices. They made efforts to introduce social change necessitated by time. Repeatedly, they would feel frustrated, harming homogeneity amongst people. Personal stakes of priest had penetrated deep into the system. There was resistance to every change. Thinkers like Kapila, Kanada and Bhraspati, who had laid the foundation of *Sanatan Dharma*, were ignored. They were not heeded, when it came to sacrifice of privileges.

Buddhism preached both economic and social equality.. Kings tried to enforce this in several ways. This brought prosperity and harmony in the land. Both spiritual and material life flourished. As soon as the privileged class sensed that the state was weak, they would rise swearing on religion. All earlier efforts would thus be wasted. Society returned to its earlier form of compartmentalization between castes and creeds. To strengthen their position further, Hindu priests reluctantly accepted Buddha as another incarnation of Vishnu. The Hindu pantheon of divinities, already loaded with deities, had one more.

Weakening of India–call for change

In 'The Cycle of Change' Fig. I, there is a common area of darkness between civilization and barbarism. It is significant that there is darkness, both in civilized and barbarous societies. This is because internal strife amongst either creates darkness. The cause of strife could be religious inequality or exploitation of the weak or both. History records that most stable societies, on this account, withered. India allowed its acquired moral and economic strength to be wasted in such petty quarrels. Exploitation of a large section of the population kept some of them away from the mainstream. Divisions widened in time, increasing self-centered activities. Sects created yet more divisions in different religions, each claiming superiority over the other. This led to fragmentation. In a multi-religious, multi-cultural society, division can only lead to disaster. The Indian environment now sought change. Centuries of accumulated wealth in the hands of a few, was seeking worthier claimants. Nature, through its immutable laws, brought it about by creating circumstances and situations.

Fragmented country–divided people

By sixth century AD, the old simplicity and strength of Hindu life had broken. The kings, forgetful of their duties, had become self-seeking epicureans. India was split in tiny states with no central authority. Petty rulers with large egos governed small states. Self-realization, advocated by the Vedanta, was reduced to selfishness. Mahavira and Gautama's non-violence was interpreted as non-resistance to evil. The heritage of Chandragupta Maurya, Ashoka, Samudragupta, Kanishka and Harsha Vardhana was buried in internal fighting. The central government having broken down, defense of borders from external attacks was nobody's business. The numerous religions, having practised and preached non-violence and renunciation, had transformed a brave and bold people, hiding under the camouflage of 'non-violence and spiritualism'. This had turned the entire society placid, passive, introverted and unresponsive to external dangers.

Clashes between society and religion are necessary to keep the population aware of the necessity of the country's defence. In its absence, individuals become indifferent to collective action; mythology and theology start governing the minds of men. In India of those times, the spirit to struggle and oppose injustice had disappeared. Religion was reduced to rituals. Castes and races fought each other for supremacy. A life of imagination, idealism and thought that had made the country rich and prosperous was forgotten or channelled to self-centered activities. The impetus for knowledge was blocked by petty religious and caste struggles. From ancient times, conducive climate and easy availability of food had helped thoughts to flourish. So long as it had this vigour and dynamism, society continued to be dynamic and creative. When the same strength was fettered in internal quarrels and self-centred activities, they paralysed progress. There was less interest in the community and more in activities that promoted greed, envy and hatred.

Every one was suspicious of the other, each thought only for his own survival.

The new shape of religion

During the reign of Buddhist religion in India, the shape of the mother religion was altered. Myths and rituals governed instead of its metaphysics. The earlier emphasis on inner self development lost its track. The heroes of the Mahabharata and the Ramayana became gods with supernatural powers. Keeping faith in those gods and following prescribed rituals became 'true' faith. To be a Hindu, only the following four became the only preconditions:

1.　　Recognition of the caste system.
2.　　Leadership of Brahmins.
3.　　Reverence to cows as a divine symbol.
4.　　Acceptance of the law of Karma and transmigration of the soul.

The great philosophy of the Vedanta, was reduced to blind faith, surviving only in name. Degeneration of society in the north had commenced after invasions of the Huns and Gujjars. Internally, adjusting to new methods, the masses adopted every ploy their 'priests' and 'saints' practised.

The story below, points to the tricks of their trade and gullibility of their followers.

A saint, in order to strengthen people's belief in him, announced that he possessed powers to walk on water. To give a practical demonstration, they fixed a date, time and place when he would perform the miracle. The faithful assembled by the riverside where the demonstration was arranged.

When the saint arrived, he addressed the devotees, "Do you all consider that I have the supernatural powers to actually perform the miracle?" The crowd that included the devotees of the 'inner circle' shouted with one voice, "We entirely believe you could walk on water."

"In that case, I do not need to perform the act," he declared to the gathering and walked away.

Invasions and anarchy

The first raid was by Bin-Qasim in AD 664 on Multan. He did not fail to notice the internal weakness of the country. This encouraged others to conduct such raids at will. It was in AD 997 that Mohammed Ghazni from a small state in Afghanistan, came with an inspired force of dedicated soldiers. He promised them immense wealth in victory. To instill courage and passion, the wily leader and a magnificent thief, called plunder and murder, a 'holy war'. Descending on the plains of the river Indus, he ransacked ancient works of architecture studded with jewels and precious stones. Within days, the wealth accumulated over the centuries was carried away.

Encouraged by his successes, Mohammed Ghazni would attack again; each time, with better results. This went on for nearly seventeen years. Each time he would come with a force more fierce than the earlier one, taking gold and other precious articles in plenty.

The raiders found the country without any organized defence. Instead they were all fighting with each other, ready to align even with the raiding army to make their own brothers bite the dust. The people had developed caste and racial prejudices towards each other; finding fictitious reasons borne out of envy. The numerous religions that flourished on the subcontinent were preaching non-violence and renunciation. This made individuals indifferent to martial qualities required for defending the country both from barbarians and invaders. There was no collective thinking. Hinduism, the dominant religion, preached 'self-realization,' locking up the surplus wealth in temples. The entire philosophy and metaphysics was drowned in ritual and the focus was on selfishness.

Life had narrowed down to individual existence at the expense of society.

Raids of Mohammed Ghazni

Mohammed Ghazni was the ruler of Ghazni in Afghanistan. Finding the treasury empty, the young and ambitious Sultan looked around to seek wealth and feed his army and people. He learnt that his neighbour possessed immense wealth that was locked in their temples. He was informed that his co-religionists were already reaping a good harvest from their newly-won territory in Sindh.

Ghazni made up his mind; but camouflaged his intentions of loot. He collected a band of his soldiers and fired within them both greed and religious passion. He promised a good share of the loot and plunder which was going abegging in the land of the 'infidels'. To stifle his own conscience, as well as that of his men, he called his campaign a 'Holy War'.

During twenty-five years, Ghazni came calling seventeen times. Each time he carried loads of gold, silver and other valuables. The wealth accumulated in temples for centuries, was usurped in a few years. The docility and individuality of the residents must cause wonder! Had the practice of non-violence, during the days of Buddhism, reached ridiculous proportions? Was it envy amongst princes that made them indifferent to law and order? Each raid demoralized the princes, bringing disunity amongst them. In one such raid, a prince after his defeat, is said to have told Ghazni, "I have been conquered by you. I wish you should now not be defeated by others".

Facets of Ghazni

During his seventeen raids in India, Ghazni accumulated enough wealth to make him the richest king of the world. The plundering, slaying, and cruelty used to loot the enormous treasures, haunted him in his old age. While shedding tears of repentance, he had considerable burden on his conscience that needed unburdening. Sufi saint Abu Hasan helped him seek the peace that he longed. In later life, the tyrant would repent and pray:

"Yes, this world is woven in darkness. My years are wasted. I have built but a kingdom of darkness; I cry for the kingdom of light. I realize that to love mercy is to walk the way to peace and joy."

In the words of Ghazni, "after youth has passed, conscience in everyone preserves the gifts of Virtue and Morality."

Success and failure

What was so powerful about Ghazni's raids that he could enter such a vast country seventeen times without losing even once? It was not so much the lack of patriotism of one side and religious fanaticism on the other. It was the strategy and mode of war that determined the results of each raid. Ghazni and his soldiers came on horseback. The Indian princes used elephants, fighting with bows and arrows; Ghazni had with him a secret weapon of war. His soldiers wrapped their arrows with naphtha. They would light them and shoot, not towards the soldiers, but on the elephants. The elephants, seeing fire, would run amock. In the process, they would trample their own soldiers. The Indian weakness was in being indifferent to the art of war and dependence on supernatural powers to help them win without effort, without learning lessons from the past. A society brought up in spiritual and non-violent environment could not reconcile to the extreme violence. Yet it could assemble sufficient moral courage and strength to patiently bear poverty, violence and injustice with yogic indifference.

The Delhi Sultanate

When Islam lost the battle of Tours in France (AD 732), her co-religionists were enriching themselves through loot and plunder, getting plum trophies in India. Social and economic attitudes of people had condemned Indian civilization to a slow torture. Exploitation and religious tenacity had given greed and perversion a free license. The priests were holding sway over temples. The princes exploited their subjects; and merchants in trade cornered wealth for themselves. The people, who created wealth, were themselves embroiled in the envy of castes and creed. Nature, to enforce her law of indestructibility and continuity, inspired the hungrier neighbours, suffering from want, to restore the balance in nature. The sword ultimately deposes those who become kings by the sword. The Ghaznavi dynasty had accumulated wealth that now tempted others. Mohammed Ghori, a non-descrip Turk, fought the successors of Ghazni in Afghanistan, annexing both his wealth and territory. Getting rich and resourceful, he planned to attack Delhi. In Qutubuddin Aibak he had an outstanding general. During this period, several Rajput princes governed a large part of north India. But, instead of offering a united stand, they kept on fighting each other.

Through cunning and diplomacy, Ghori and his able general Aibak, after several battles with the Rajputs, defeated most of them. Prithviraj Chauhan, the prince of Kannauj died fighting Ghori. In a short period, ghori was able to win Delhi (1186). Ghori, unlike other raiders, decided to stay and rule his possessions in India.

After Ghori died, his general Qutubuddin Aibak, took over the reigns of Delhi in 1206. The Delhi Sultanate was, from now on, formally established. In a short period, Aibak was able to defeat several petty princes in north India to consolidate his empire. As a ferocious, merciless and fanatical ruler, he was able to bring some national unity after several centuries of disunity. He was the first after Harsha Vardhana to have laid the foundations of an unitary government. Although his means remained cruel, he also possessed human qualities of charity and creativity. He was named 'Lakh Baksh' (giver of lacs in charity). For one of his victories, he built the famous Qutub Minar at Delhi.

The next to follow was Balban. He terrorized the population with acts that would put even animals to shame. Followed by him was a woman Sultan Razia. A capable administrator, possessing qualities befitting a king, she however belonged to the wrong sex. Her own generals and *qazis* could not accept her extraordinary qualities. She was finally removed from the throne by assassination. Allauddin became the next Sultan (1296-1315). History remembers him as one who would agree to lift the siege of Chittor if only he was allowed to have a glance at the beautiful princess Padmini. He kept the Mongols at bay from India and extended his dominion over a major part of the country. He unshackled himself from the Ulemas saying, "I do not know if this is lawful or unlawful. Whatever I think to be good for the state, or suitable for the emergency, I do".

Brave words at a time when religious sanction to every action was essential for the survival of the king!

The cruelty and injustice unleashed was not to last long. People at large began scathing with revolt. Their masters had betrayed the soldiers who had joined the so-called 'holy war'. They could now see into the game. It was clear that greed of conquest and wealth and not a 'holy war' was what they fought for. Having thus lost the support of not only the local population but even of their own soldiers, their hour of reckoning arrived. This was in the form of Tamerlane who descended on India in 1398. Tamerlane had arrived in the capital with a force full of the now popularly camouflaged slogan of a 'holy war' through which innocent soldiers were sacrificed for greed. It was now the turn of Tamerlane to take away the ill-gotten wealth to his home at Samarkand that was accumulated not only by the sultans but even by the rich in the city. On the people of Delhi, he inflicted suffering, slaughter and humiliation for sustaining a wicked rule so long. After the Turks came the Afghans. The two Pathan sultans, Firoz Shah and Sikander Lodhi made no effort to change the policy of the earlier sultans.

When Ibrahim Lodhi ascended the Delhi throne (1517), he started with all the bad omens. Whatever he did to 'improve' went wrong. The moment had arrived for the cycle of time to take another turn. The Indian climate and easy access to riches had made the sultans and their generals lazy, corrupt and indifferent to the art of war. Those who ruled India were men of fierce courage who suffered from the prejudices of religious bigotry. They did possess the culture and ability to recognize but not to practice. Being always scared of a vast hostile population, they dared show no mercy lest it be taken as a sign of weakness. Let us not forget that it was an age of chivalry. Definition of barbarism was quite different during those times. Culture was defined as one's ability to survive.

Although the rulers extracted tributes inhumanly, they did not carry the wealth outside the country, to either Ghazni or Samarkand. It was consumed in constructions and luxuries that ultimately benefitted the country.

Arrival of Islam

The Turkish Empire of the Tartars, stretching from the Great Wall of China to Iran, in the sixth century AD, occupied Afghanistan. When Turkey converted to Islam and entered Afghanistan, Indian monarchs ruling in different states had grown weak fighting each other. As a sequence to internal struggles, divisions between them continued. During the seventh century AD, the Arab Empire became an absolute monarchy under the Caliph who was the successor of Prophet Mohammed. It was a great period of Arab expansion. Within hundred years, by AD 732, the Islamic Empire extended from Gibraltar and Spain in the West to river Indus in the East. The Arabs had conquered a great part of the world including Syria, Persia, Egypt, Carthage and Spain. Crossing the Pyrexes mountains in Europe, they invaded France. It was at Poitiers that Charles Martal defeated and thus stopped Islamic forces from advancing any further in France.

What was so unique in the religion that infused such ardour in the warriors, who till the other day, were wild tribes fighting amongst themselves?

Arabia before Mohammed

Arabia, before Mohammed, was a land of lawless tribals, surrounded by countries of a more developed civilization. It was isolated and cut off by vast tracks of desert. Traders would carry their merchandise to and from surrounding countries. The Arabs mostly lived on their flocks and herds. Occasionally they would loot caravans not properly protected. They grew coarse food, with primitive tools, wherever water was available.

There was no law, except the law of the strongest. Loot, arson, and murder were common. Against atrocities committed by the strong, no questions were asked. Initially, these conquests began as mere raids. Seeing the weakness of the countries they conquered, it followed by permanent occupation. Gradually as they grew in experience, they dared further. Soon Islam became the dominant religion in some of the richest lands of the world. The culture and luxuries offered by new conquests led them to live and learn from civilized societies.

While sultans were spreading terror in the name of religion, the Caliphs, who represented the head of the clergy, were getting weaker in Baghdad. The Mongols from the East and the Christians from the West, were inflicting on Muslims what the sultans were doing in India. The Islamic empire in the Middle-East began showing signs of disintegration. Basic elements of civilization were rudely shaken. Men of art, poetry and literature were out seeking more congenial environment to express their talents. Violence and terror are inimical for men of creativity. They are not able to find that peace which is the mother of creativity. Under such conditions of fear and uncertainty, the spirit of enterprise in society slackens; the zest for achievement ends. Consequent to stagnation, decline follows.

Islam was now enjoying a period of rise and glory. There were others fired with similar zeal for conquest. The invasions from tribes in Central Asia and Christianity brought instability in the Islamic world. Intellectuals and creative men sought safer surroundings. Amir Khusrau, a Persian, like hundreds of other such men of genius, left his home to come to India where he could live, think and create in peace. The works and contributions of such men to Indian language and culture would introduce far reaching changes in the life of its people. They would turn out to be acts of intellect in different fields of human endeavour.

Chapter XX
Islam & Prophet Mohammed

Bismillah-ir-Rahman-ir-Rahim
Al-hamdu-lillahi Rabbil-alimin
(Lord of compassion! All praise to thee
Creator and Protector of the world.)

—Quran

The Arabs had conquered a great part of the world under the banner of Islam. It inspired the warriors with extraordinary religious zest. In the initial flush of faith, zeal and enthusiasm, warriors conquered the entire Middle-East, African and Indian territories. Islam crossed the Pyrennes mountains in Europe to invade France. Our study of other religions informs that after a prophet is gone, his message takes a few decades to reach the common people. The question arises as to what was a so unique in the religion that infused such ardour in their warriors?

A study of the life of Prophet Mohammed and the Quran will provide the answer!

Life of Prophet Mohammed

Prophet Mohammed was born in AD 576 in a poor family at Mecca. It is a town 45 miles from the Red Sea. The town was then an important centre of trade and commerce. Caravans from the port of Jeddah passed through Mecca. Mohammed grew to be a modest person in an otherwise immodest and cruel society.

After living a greater part of his life in a pure and honest manner, he always felt himself in disharmony with the environment around him. To lessen this, he would occasionally fast to make himself purer and nobler. He would seek spiritual light to remove the darkness that surrounded him.

For forty years, Mohammed lived like an ordinary inhabitant of the land. He pursued a simple, organized and truthful life. Not known for the qualities of diplomacy, preaching or oratory, he never gave any discourses or practiced metaphysics or religion. There was no tinge of oratory in his dialogues. He never mentioned subjects like politics and laws of sociology. He never handled a sword. He was consistent only in being kind, gentle, human and contemplative.

Then, one day he went into a nearby cave for meditation. He was entirely transformed after his return. The whole of Arabia watched in awe and wonder.

Prophet of God

Prophet Mohammed returned from the cave and appeared before the people with a message. It was unique in philosophy and wonderful in reforms. He expounded the complex problems of metaphysics and theology. He delivered inspiring speeches on the decline and fall of empires and nations. The peace loving former trader was now a brave soldier and a great general. In nine years, he conquered the whole of Arabia. Islam was accepted and began to be practised as a religion. After his death, the momentum and inspiration generated by him helped conquest of neighbouring countries.

Mohammed left no instructions as to who his successor would be. After some confusion, the faithful finally decided to choose a Caliph (successor) to the Prophet. He was to act both as a spiritual and political leader of Islam. Abu Bakr was the first to be so chosen. Caliph Omar (AD 634-644) succeeded in unifying the whole of Arabia; in the next seventeen years, the Arabs woulds won Syria, Armenia, Palestine and Egypt.

Mohammed compiled the Quran as delivered by God Almighty.

Teachings of Quran

In the entire creation, only man enjoys real freedom. He is completely free to choose one, two, or more alternatives. His activity is creative and procreative. Man is exhorted to use his intellect to understand himself and the world around him. Every individual is moving towards perfection. In addition, perfection is achieved through self-realization.

According to the Quran, if man employs his immense potentialities for moral and material advancement of humankind, his conduct is good. The divine guidance points out the way to self-realization. This guidance, as mentioned in the Quran, may be summarized as follows:

1. Everything, animate or inanimate, is endowed with the capacity of development; its development being guided by the Supreme.

2. It must be supposed that the guiding power acts upon things from outside. It is inherent in their nature and acts from within.

3. Man, by virtue of possessing an autonomous Self, occupies a privileged position in the Universe. Divine guidance is offered to him in the form suited to a free and rational being. It however does not curtail his choice or freedom of action.

4. For man *Wahi* (revelation) is the vehicle of Divine guidance. God selects a *Nabi* who receives the revelations and faithfully communicates them to his fellow-beings.

5. The *Wahi* is God's words. It transcends human intellect but does not conflict with his Reason; it rather supplements it.

On Reason (*Din*) and Faith (*Iman*)

The Quran expects man to think and use his power of understanding. The path that leads to success can only be followed with the combined help of reason and revelation. It lays stress on correct knowledge. The Quran advises to rid the mind of all preconceived notions, give close and earnest attention to revelations and have full confidence in *Iman*.

On Reason (*Din*) and Passion as a spiritual force

Islamic philosophy of *Din* is the development of human fellowship.

The conflict between reason and passion is as old as history. A balance between them leads to a happy and rich life. Passion says, 'Lead and trust the fate'. Reason says, 'Look before you leap'. Quran says that reason, when clouded with passion, is a hindrance in pursuit of worthy ends. It can guide only when it is functioning properly. We must not therefore allow passion to dominate our reason. Hence, if reason has to have full control, it must be trained and developed like other faculties of the mind. Reason functions according to the role given to it.

In the final analysis, to side entirely with passion is more harmful than to side with reason.

On Reason and Revelation

Reason is a good guide for physical life. But existence constitutes more than physical life. It seeks truth and reality. In this area, reason has its own limitations. Here divine guidance is required to fulfil our destiny. Revelation is therefore a supplement to reason and the guide for metaphysical improvement. The Quran differentiates between body and soul; matter and spirit. It advises to make full use of our intelligence to understand and appreciate the ultimate Truth. Being in the domain of revelation, science cannot provide any guidance.

Quranic view on God

According to the Quran, God is the creator of Time and Space, far beyond the grasp of minds of men. He is supreme over all; nowhere but yet everywhere.

> To God belongs the East and West;
> Wherever you turn, there is the Face of God;
> God is all embracing- all-knowing. (ii.109)

The will of God works in three distinct spheres. In the realm of *amr* it is not subject to any laws. In the Universe, His Will assumes the shape of immutable laws to which all physical beings are subject. These laws of nature are immutable on which the entire scientific edifice stands. As regards man's domain for free will, he has the freedom to feel, judge and choose any course of action open to him. After this discretion, his freedom ends.

The result will ultimately catch up with the laws of the universe.

On laws of requittal

The laws of requittal work unerringly. There is integration between acts and their results. In the sphere of physical actions in the universe, this can be condensed as below:

a. A man's voluntary actions directly influences his personality.
b. Dedication to noble ends results in improvement of personality.
c. Indifference to, and denial of, absolute values, leads to the disintegration of self.
d. Man is responsible for his actions and must accept their consequences.
e. Man cannot shift responsibility to anyone else.

Quran on development of human personality

Modern science has partially explained parts of mystic phenomenon through Laws of Nature. Physics explains the phenomenon of the expanding universe. Biology has opened the entire theory of evolution from protozoa to homo- sapiens, atomic theory has partially explained consciousness. Possessing a free-acting self, he can develop and attain his own ends by free choice and personal efforts. Man cannot be forced to develop; he has to develop himself. Man creates values; values enrich and expand his nature and raise it to the level of pure existence.

The law of 'Aubiyyah' in the Quran says that God carries forward the universe and everything in it from one stage to a higher one. It is therefore natural that there are different stages of growth in man. The process is evident in the outer world. Within, it takes the form of self-development.

On interdependence in Universe

The Quran says that all things in the Universe are interdependent. They need to help each other for growth. The sense of participation in social activities adds a new dimension to the self, provided it does not inadvertently allow the ego to expand. Social service is therefore a means of dissolving the ego and encourages development of self. It must be remembered that the self shrinks and contracts only in solitude; it grows and expands with active participation.

The Quran has very significant 'group activities' directives in this regard. Self-realization is possible for man only in his society. It has to be based on justice and respect for human personality. A society dedicated to higher values will grow and prosper; if it remains stagnant, society will decay. The Quran therefore exhorts:

> And hold fast all of you by the chord of God and be not divided.
> Humanity is advised to work for common goal: The welfare of all.

Quaranic concept of Self (psyche, personality)

The Quran says that Self partakes in Reality and consequently enjoys permanence and stability. The trials and influences it goes through, do not transform it into something different. It starts with potentialities and never ceases to be itself. It is essentially dynamic. Self is like the flame of a candle, which shines for a moment and then is quickly swallowed by the surrounding darkness. Being unreal itself it cannot enter into a meaningful relationship and co-operation with the Real. It retains its identity throughout. The trials and influences do not transform it. Self is a mere witness; it starts its career in under-developed form. Equipped with immense potential, it may or may not actualize this potentiality. Yet, it never ceases to be itself. It is not passive material but actual. The endeavour is to get close to the most perfect Self. To that extent, the journey is towards perfection, tasting the joys of proximity to goodness, truth and beauty.

Self is affected only by the results of its own actions. "Cultivate in yourself the qualities which reflect the divine attitude," says the Quran. Self is a member of the social group. Only in society can man enjoy mutual mental health and function efficiently. Self longs for co-operation; without, it loses zest for life. It is happy when engaged in purposeful activity; happiest, when it has a feeling of participation in the cosmic purpose.

The Quran speaks of relationship between God and Man as a partnership. With the help of Self, he can humbly work with God, in carrying out the divine plan. It speaks of goodness, truth and beauty to be the divine plan on which the cosmos works. He should, therefore, work for the sum total of goodness in the Universe. The Quran calls upon man to co-operate with other men in the pursuit of goodness.

Liberalism: cause of victories

The Quranic form of religion is life-fulfillment; not life denial. The Quran commands to face facts; not to take refuge in myths and fantasy. Asceticism, quietism, monasticism are repugnant to Islam. The body is not considered an impediment to spiritual growth; it is an instrument for spiritual attainment.

It remains a wonder of warfare, how a bunch of tribesmen, under an inspired leadership, overran highly organized societies. There was almost no destruction, except where other religions were deeply entrenched. Life of the local population was generally not disturbed. The conquered population co-operated as 'friends'. They were willing to exchange their experience and knowledge. The Arabs and Turks were thus able to acquire in a short time the collected works and wisdom of centuries. Being inquisitive students of knowledge, they gradually acquired all the refinements of different civilizations. Often, this sudden transformation of abundance and power dazzles the possessor; not so with the Muslims. They were helped by their faith to maintain themselves.

The essence of Quran, mentioned in 172(ii) is:

> It is nor piety that you turn your faces,
> To the east or to the west.
> True piety is this:
> To believe in God and the Last Day,
> The angles, the Book and the Prophet,
> To give of one's substance, however cherished,
> To kinsmen and orphans,
> The needy, the traveller, the beggars,
> And to ransom the slave,
> To perform the prayer *(salat),* to pay the alms *(zakat).*
> And they who fulfil their covenant,
> When they have engaged in a covenant.
> And endure with fortitude
> Misfortune, hardship and peril,
> These are they, who are true to their faith,
> These are the truly god fearing.

The two important teachings of the Prophet that serve as a constant guide are:

1.   Restrain from temptation
2.   Social compatibility

Even when surrounded by abundant luxuries in the acquired territories, they would refrain from indulgence.When they succumbed to them, others, more vigorous, replaced them. They generally governed their domains with justice after the initial hiccups. It was only because of this that a few thousand soldiers could manage large populations. The other factor that made governance smooth, was their identification with the lands they won. After a generation they would become a part of the country; in the next two generations, drawing nourishment from the soil, they would establish their roots in the new land.

Age of Reformation

Life is preserved by purpose;
Because of its goal, its carvan bells tinkles.
Life is latent in seeking,
Its origin is hidden in desire.
Keep desire alive in thy heart,
Lest thy little dust becomes a tomb.
Desire is the soul of this world of hue and scent,
Nature of everything is faithful to desire.

—Mohammed Iqbal

Chapter XXI
Confluence of Faiths

The empire of the Caliph of Baghdad was the most powerful in the world when China and Japan were great powers in Asia. India, during this period offered a divided scenario, governed by small princes with large egos. Hinduism and Islam met in the Indian subcontinent as rulers and the ruled. Europe, at that time, was still struggling to extricate herself from darkness with only occasional light from individuals. We have seen that long after political power is lost, the influence of religious culture continues. Following this maxim, even when political power in India had changed hands, religious culture continued to exert itself. Conflict, as a part of human nature, now found fulfilment in religious conflicts. It was in such a scenario that the young and dynamic religion, born in the sands of Arabia, arrived in the country equipped with its own philosophy and cultural ethos. It brought a new social message that every human being was born equal in the sight of God. It was a strange sight for local inhabitants to find soldiers and their generals praying and dining together!

Sultans from different tribes of Afghanistan, ruled India for nearly 300 years and were outright warriors. They did not pretend to possess experience of running governments or coming from any cultured background. It was no strange matter if they could not understand the complex Indian way of life, their philosophy or religion. They never even tried, or even cared to try in the beginning. Having won the prize by brute force, they retained it by force. In the name of religion, they had conquered a higher civilization. It however required developing a new relationship. The mettle of this work fell on intellectuals, historians and Sufi saints of the ruling community. Men like Al Beruni, Amir Khusrau and Al Gabr were to create a new force of unity for the forward movement of civilized life. Abu Mashar, the famous Arab astronomer of the ninth century learnt astronomy at Varanasi for ten years.

Al Beruni, the first of the learned Arabs, had come with Mohammed Ghazni. He learnt Sanskrit to study Hindu scriptures. Thereafter, he translated them into Arabic. This helped understanding between the two communities. Apart from books on astronomy and medicine, Al Beruni translated nearly twenty other texts. Having done his work, he records:

"I have written on the doctrine of the Hindus when I thought this would help elucidate the subject." He dared to comment on the deeds of his Sultan that "Ghazni utterly ruined the prosperity of the country. This is the reason that Hindu sciences retired far away from those parts of the country conquered by us, and fled to Kashmir and Varanasi, where our hands cannot reach."

Synthesis of two religions

What is religion? What is its scope and limitations? As a dominating force, each society, at one time or the other, is confronted with its scope and limitations. Societies that get over it; move forward; others just get entangled in its cobwebs. They keep struggling, wasting their energy in interline quarrels and imaginary obsessions. Religion is therefore a kind of science that provides answers to the mysteries of nature and immensity of mind and heart. It surpasses all knowledge. The psychological and compulsive effect of religion is purely impulsive. Through positive impulses, religion commands morality; with negative impulses, it arouses brutal tendencies of struggle.

The wise use religion only to provide solace to the soul; the wily use it to acquire political or material power over others!

Gradually, the wise amongst both religions made efforts to start the healing process of synthesis. The one mellowed down its aggressiveness; the other regained its old spirit of imagination and thought. The union fused into humility. Sufism of Islam and Bhakti movement of the Hindus, became the same face of religious devotion. Both began to flourish together. Saints like Khwaja Moinuddin Chisti, Sheikh Nizamuddin Aulia and Chaitanya Mahaprabhu were the products of this age. This union grew to such a strong foundation that even today devotees do not discriminate in religion at such places. Followers of both communities travel long distances to pay their obedience at such places of common devotion.

Blind faith versus reason

As authority of reason grew, answers to question of 'how' and 'why' began to satisfy people. Medieval view that centred around man's earthly existence, as a mere preparation for life after death was replaced with fulfilment in the present life itself! This awareness began growing amongst intellectuals and men of knowledge. It would produce great poets, artists, adventurers, sociologists, biologists and philosophers. It became an age of great achievements, producing reforms and revolutions, inventions and discoveries, wealth and victories all over the world. The seeds of knowledge, sown by great thinkers, now began blooming. When knowledge of science developed in the West, people were curious to know even more. They would go in search of new lands, and discover new routes. Vasco Da Gama from Portugal found the way to Calicut in 1498. Columbus discovered America; Captain Cook, while on a mission to study stars, found New Zealand and Australia. There was David Livingstone, who toiled in the marshes of Africa, to discover the interior of the 'Dark Land'.

The dynamic forces unleashed by curiosity and adventure would spread all over the world. They would fight battles and win new colonies, bringing riches to their homes. The opening up of the world could no longer permit societies to exist in isolation. Relations between nations were not confined to geographical boundaries. So long as rational answers were not available to natural phenomenon, religious beliefs prevailed.

India would still take another 200 years before these vibrant winds reached her coasts. A sea-faring nation, from a small island in Europe, would bring them. United Kingdom would take the initiative to introduce the new discoveries to India in the eighteenth century!

Environment in India

Arabs, Afghans, Turks and Persians had entered India as warriors and conquerors. Those who followed them were warriors, technicians, intellectuals and the clergy. As followers of Islam, they had their own social and spiritual practices. Having won the country in the name of religion, they always looked towards the priests for guidance. The priests, at every stage, would interfere and interpret actions of their co-religionists. It was an arrangement of sharing power during which social and cultural aspects of governance were given little attention. Its effect on the Indian pschye was overwhelming.. The earlier freedom they enjoyed in the religious, cultural and spiritual life, underwent a change. Discussions and debates, which were part of the Hindu ethos, mellowed. They searched for solace in religion; the concept of happiness in the next life gained strength. Pessimism, never felt by people in its long history, crept in all aspects of life. This madness and greed of a few, deadened human sensitivities. The exploiters would enjoy the present; the exploited would be advised to dream for a non-existent future in the next life. The clever would eat and drink on this earth; the innocent was asked to wait for joys in 'paradise'.

Religious culture presented a picture of numerous cults, worshipping several gods with each maintaining its own identity and rituals. The social fabric presented a picture of a society divided into different classes of caste and status. Intellectuals and the leading class within different religions, who followed and recited scriptures, merely did so as a formal affair. They missed both its message and substance. People were left entirely confused and leaderless. Minds of men were dominated by a pessimistic attitude towards life. The wheel of life would keep revolving with both vice and virtue so well mixed that it was impossible to identify either.

Amongst the many Muslims who had now settled in India, there were two classes: one was of the immigrants who had come to the country as warriors, artists, religious priests and intellectuals seeking new opportunities to express their talents. The other class was of those who lived in India and admired its broad social approach. They embraced the new religion to regain their self respect and dignity that had been denied them for ages. This fusion soon provided its rewards. There was a spate of creative activities. The new knowledge that came into the country from Europe and the Middle East, triggered economic activity.

As more immigrants arrived, a common language became an essential requirement for communication. Taking words from Arabic and Persian, and the language spoken around Delhi called 'Hindawi' or 'Brij Bhasha' as base, a new language, understood by both communities, began to blossom. After the conquest of Delhi, this language would be known as Urdu. The immigrant Muslims soon started settling in towns and villages of India, adopting the land as their home. From the first generation, they would toil the fields, giving and learning new techniques from each other. They would even fight their co-religionists to defend the honour of their village, town and country.

During this period, Delhi developed into a literary centre of Persian. But Mongols from the north were threatening the empire where Islamic religion and culture flourished. Bokhara was then a great university centre of learning. Due to pressure from the Mongols, men of refinement left their homes and found refuge in Delhi. Immigrant Muslims who came from different parts of the empire, witnessing the variety of Indian landscape, spontaneously praised the changing seasons, the bountiful and myriad agricultural produce, the flowers and animals. They enriched the country with new knowledge from different parts of the world. The intellectuals amongst them studied afresh the ancient Vedantic philosophy. They found that Islam and Hinduism believed in unity and eternity of God; that knowledge and learning was a common interest amongst people; that even though men speak different languages, their inspirations, emotions and love for beauty are the same.

Amongst several notable Muslims who came from abroad, one was Amir Khusrau. His contribution to language, art, culture and fusion represents the hundreds and thousands of outstanding personalities who came and made India their home. Such men of outstanding ability, translated ancient Indian works and retrieved long-forgotten Indian knowledge for human benefit.

Proficient ambassador–Amir Khusrau

Eight centuries ago, a distinguished family from Turkey came to settle in a small town of Etah in U.P. Soon a boy was born to them. He learnt both Persian and Hindi. Instead of seeking a job in the service of the sultans, he preferred to go into nearby villages and enjoy the countryside. As he grew, his talents in literature, poetry and philosophy attracted the attention of the Delhi sultans. He offered his services to the court, like so many other young men from Turkey, Arabia and Iran. This young boy, Amir Khusrau, reflected the new spirit of assimilation, adoption, tolerance and love for the new home. In this way does creative culture follow political change. Knowledge and genius have never been contained within geographical or political boundaries. Creativity combines to improve and grow. A favourable wind blows and it carries the fragrance to all corners. While the sultans ruled, their job was confined to collect revenue, maintain law and order, keep the clergy in good humour and lead a life of license and luxury. Harmony and synthesis of culture only interested the intellectuals and men of skill. Amir Khusrau was destined to be nature's choice to perform this function.

The ambassadors of culture

Kings and sultans fight wars for power and possession; but creativity and talents enhance the art of living. The leaders of society draw their lessons from the past, keeping their sights on the future while moulding the present. Strifes and invasions, plunder and distrust, continued for almost two centuries. From the thirteenth century onwards, mutual acrimony between the rulers and the ruled, mellowed. The temperate climate of the country, prone to induce leisure, turned the once vigorous and sturdy warriors, to a life of ease and culture. Muslims from Turkey, Arabia, Persia and Afghanistan had made India their home. They shared a common lifestyle with those whom they ruled. The two religions slowly began the process of understanding each other. They were now enriching each other to evolve a common heritage. With communications between India and West-Asia thus established, trade and commerce, exchange of arts and literature became an intimate vehicle of regular contact.

This was a phase when the Arabs were leading the world in knowledge, closely interacting with the countries of the civilized world. They travelled from Varanasi to Baghdad in caravans for trade and commerce. This brought prosperity, understanding and exchange of knowledge. Medieval age was a period when men of valour governed; of action travelled and traded; and of imagination observed to create things of joy. The responsibility of this work fell on intellectuals, historians and sufi saints of the ruling community. Men like Al Beruni, Amir Khusrau and Al Gabr were to create a new force of unity for the forward movement of civilized life.

His early life

Amir Khusrau's parents had come to India from Turkey under the pressure of constant threat to peace by the Mongols. From his childhood, Khusrau was fond of everything he witnessed as a young boy. As he grew in age, his highly developed creativity, imagination and inventiveness began to be reflected in his career as a petty courtier. When these qualities blossomed, he rose to be an important functionary in the Sultan's court at Delhi. In this capacity he served successive sultans, watching their rise and fall for fifty years. His outstanding achievements however were in the field of literature, music, religion and producing a lively account of his times.

Contribution to literature

Khusrau in his recollections has described Indian climate, its flowers, birds and animals, its sciences and religious beliefs. On the fertility of Indian soil, he particularly writes:

> The soil of India is so fertile that it yields to little efforts, giving a wide variety of fruits, vegetables and grains. Peacock, is enchanting and a bird of paradise. To gladden hearts, there are flowers all the year round. In all other countries, flowers are for limited months. Indian flowers have a sweet smell, while in the flowers of cold countries, there is no smell.

He compares the philosophy of Greece in logic, astrology, physics, mathematics and astronomy with that of India. Besides Persian, Khusrau had also learnt Sanskrit. He was thus able to translate several Indian works to Persian. This enabled Indian thought to reach different countries while his writings became the wonder of the country. His works showcased India to the out side world and enabled others to continue their intellectual works to proceed further.

Besides:

1. Scholars from all parts of the world came to study in India.

2. The numerical system, specially the symbol zero, originated in India. The word 'Hindasa' in Arabic, is derived from 'Hind' (India) and 'Asa' a famous Indian mathematician.

3. The great book of wisdom *Kalila wa Dimna* was composed in India and acquired fame all over the world.

During Khusrau's period, Sanskrit had been replaced with Hindawi as the spoken language of the people around Delhi. Khusrau began to learn the language to be able to communicate with the common man. Soon he mastered the language and started writing poetry, often mixing it with Persian words. In one of his Persian poems "Nooh Sphir" (Nine Skies), he depicts life in India as he saw it in a new and novel country. Every thing Indian excited him with wonder and immense appreciation. In his writings, Khusrau charted the path for Urdu to develop with a combination of Persian, Arabic and Hindawi words:

> *Shabane higran daraz chun zulf o ruze waslat cho'umr kotah.* (Persian)
> *Sakhi piya ko jo main na dekhun to kaise katoon andheri ratian.* (Hindawi)

Amir Khusrau was a true representative of that age. Having learnt Hindi, he talked and wrote on different subjects in the local language. The popular songs in Hindi were understood by the village folks and soon became popular. Even after 800 years after they were written, these songs can be heard in north and central Indian villages. Besides, he was a master of riddles. These riddles still remain popular with children. At a time when language was vitally important for communication, Khusrau popularized the new language amongst the governing class. Later, during the Mughal period, this language would gradually develop into Urdu. Khusrau was proud of his Indian origin and his Hindi poetry. When asked why he wrote in Hindi when he was also a master of Persian, he would answer:

"I am an Indian Turk and can reply to you in Hindawi. I have no Egyptian sugar to talk of Arabic."

Such sentiments always helped in winning the hearts of both Hindus and Muslims.

Contribution to music

One of the Vedas, the *Sama Veda*, discusses the importance of music. From the beginning, it remained for centuries, an emotional expression of feelings. It needed to be organized to harmonious notes for reproduction. Khusrau provided the synthesis to Indian music that had been so far lacking. This also proved to be the most effective medium of cohesion between Hindus and Muslims. As new tunes began to be accepted by the masses, the rulers and the ruled began enjoying it. There would be regular musical sessions, when men, irrespective of religion or status, would demonstrate their talents, earning applause from the audience. Gradually, music became the strongest single factor of fusion. Even to this day we find Indian music to be the natural binding force between different communities of the country. Be it cinematography or organized programmers, the introduction brought all sections of society, to the same emotional wavelength.

Music, thereafter, became the common heritage of the whole subcontinent.

Music being the language of the soul, Khusrau integrated Indian music with Persian. This largely helped synthesis of cultures between the Hindus and the Muslims to evolve a culture common to both. In describing the beauties of the country, Khusrau has used particularly charming adjectives. Comparing women, with the flowers of India, he mentions of *bela, chameli, juhi, kevera, maulsari and karana*. These flowers are not only beautiful but possess a sweet and pleasant smell. In his times, women of Turkistan and Cathay were considered most renowned for their beauty. Khusrau, in his writings, compares them with the women of India. He admires their humility, submission, sweet and charming smile all delicately balanced to make them most attractive.

> The fair one sleeps on the bed with tresses scattered on the face.
>
> Oh Khusrau, come home now, for night has fallen all over.

Besides his keen intellect, he was blessed with spiritual strength to be able to perform great constructive deeds in his life time. One of his verses, both in original and its translation, are famous in India even to this day. They are sung in north Indian villages during the festival of spring:

> *Aaj Basant mana le Suhagan,*
> *Aaj Basant mana le.*
> *Anjan manjan kar piya mori,*
> *Lambe lahar lagae,*
> *Tu kiya soye neend ki maasi,*
> *So jage tere bhag, sohagan.*
> *Aaj Basant mana le...*
> *Oochi naar ke oonche chitvan.*
> *Aiso deo hai banai;*
> *Shaah-e-Amir tohe dekhan ko,*
> *Naino se Naina milaye, Suhagan.*
> *Aaj Basant Mana le.*

> Rejoice O bride, spring is here,
> Make up your face,
> Braid your hair.
> Do you sleep yet,
> Though your fate has woken?
> Proud beauty, it is spring, Rejoice!
> The king of king comes to see you.
> Meet his eyes.
> It is spring, O bride, Rejoice.

Sufi/Bhakti movements

During Khusrau's times, Sufi saints from the Islamic Empire, went to all corners of the world spreading the message of peace. This indeed was the need of the age. Being a rich and welcoming country a large number of Sufi saints came to India from various Islamic countries of the Middle East. One of the earliest to arrive was Kwaja Abdul Chisti. Initially preaching in Lahore, he came to Delhi and finally settled at Ajmer, then under the rule of Prithviraj Chauhan. Chisti believed in the spiritual value of music. He patronized proffessional singers, irrespecive of their religion. They soon began commanding deep respect from all communities. The message they delivered gradually caught the imagination of other religions. It spread amongst Hindus in the form of Bhakti. Mira Bai in Rajasthan and Chaitanya in Bengal were some of the most prominent devotees of the new cult. Having caught the imagination of the Hindus, it started the process of reformation. If Tulsi was inspired to write Ramayana as a text devoted to *bhakti* of Rama, the Bhakti movement of the thirteenth century was no less an inspiration. The closeness between the Sufi saints and the saints of Bhakti movement developed to such an extent that many Sufi saints had both Hindu and Muslim names like Pir Haji Mango and Lal Shah Qalandar. This helped bring the two warring communities closer.

Khusrau helped the movement by glorifying this phenomenon in literature and poetry. It helped build bridges between Hindus and Muslims. Ali Qalander's beautiful couplet was on the lips of most North Indians not long ago:

> *Sajan Sakare jainge aur nain marenge roe,*
> *Bidhna ause kijyo ke bhor kabhau na hoe.*

(My lover has to go early morning,
Lord do something, so there is no morning).

Process of sublimation

Intellectuals and men of knowledge in touch with progress in other parts of the world, and who possessed a wider view of changes in other countries, helped the crucial function of sublimation. They discovered the precious wealth in sciences and philosophy that lay buried in the Indian archives. Islamic scholars translated and transmitted this treasure for the larger good of humanity. We have read about men like Amir Khusrau who helped fusion of Indian and Persian cultures. The architectural skill of Turkey was employed to build Qutub Minar and other similar marvels in stone. Khusrau devised new musical instruments and improved the existing ones. *Khayals*, for the first time, were introduced in music with his deep knowledge of rhythms. One of the greatest contribution of this era was Sufism, the liberal face of Islam. In due course,

Sufism and Bhakti would combine to bring the two religions closer to each other. It would also provide a common platform to highlight love and compassion amongst communities. Countless *mazhars* and *darghas* all over India are a lasting tribute to such visionaries.

While artists, architects and intellectuals performed their constructive activities, kings and generals had fallen into venal and frivolous lives. Instead of providing good governance, they would rob the rich and extract the last drop of blood from the people. Such highhandedness in rule made the entire population of the country hostile towards them... even the warriors, who had enabled the sultans win the country, lost their earlier dynamism and fighting spirit.

The genius of Amir Khusrau lay in observation and imagination. He possessed a clear vision of the future. To that end, he worked ceaselessly, offering his strength and spirit. Never tired of glorifying all that was Indian, people occasionally inquired why he was so infatuated by the country of his adoption?

"Prophet Mohammed has advised that the love of one's country is a part of the Islamic faith," he would answer.

Amir Khusrau always offered the first flowers of spring (Basant) at Ajmer Sharif Dargah, the holiest Muslim shrine in South Asia.

The extraordinary work performed by men like Amir Khusrau can be seen in the synthesis and unity that binds the most complex diversities in the world. Amir Khusrau appeared in the country when the times desperately needed him. We will get to know about some such great men as we proceed. They struggled to reform Hindu religion in the light of challenging changes. We will follow the path that slowly led the two communities become the warp and woof of the Indian nation.

The 'unity in diversity', of which we are so proud today, is the work of such men. Khusrau was an outstanding representative of a new Hindu Muslim culture; his personality stands prominently unrivalled. He indeed was a true representative of the cultural life of mediveal India.

Ramanuja and Ramananda

Religion has always dominated the life of an Indian. In ancient times, Hinduism and Buddhism flourished. In mediveal India, with the arrival of Islam and introduction of new changes, reforms became imperative for harmony. The cultural weeds that had grown became so obvious that it required pruning. We read earlier how Acharya Shankara, with his forceful debating capacity, convinced the learned of the age to his way. During the Golden Era, Hinduism had remained subdued because of Buddhism's popularity. Arrival of Islam brought an immediate political and social change in society. Shankaracharya helped to revive the glory of Hinduism when political conditions did not need any radical change. He did not work for elimination of rituals and caste barriers; instead both were strengthened. Perhaps the system had dug deep into the Hindu psyche. But religions are also the outcome of the environment. When conditions change, as they are bound to, reforms become necessary for survival. The call of the time was not the revival of the past, but change and reforms. The governing religion of the period was Islam. It exposed utter redundancy of reviving the past. People could see, how every individual, following Islam, irrespective of his position was treated. Praying and eating together; there existed a permanent bond of love between the followers of the faith. There were no outcastes, based on professional heredity.

The deprived in society were impressed with the practice of this equality. They longed to enjoy a similar equality and social standing amongst their neighbours in the village. So long as there was no alternative, they remained wrapped in their misery. The new way they noticed in Islam, offered them a chance. They would not let this opportunity pass by. Such ideas must have sent shock waves amongst the priests as well as intellectuals. The time for serious introspection had arrived. The work done by Acharya Shankara had revived the vitality of the Hindu religion in which the caste system instead of being abolished was further strengthened. Circumstances had since dramatically changed. There was another religion, offering a different way of life. New forces were now required to meet this challenge.

The efforts of Ramanuja, Ramananda, Kabir and Guru Nanak were directed towards this goal.

Introduction of change

Shankaracharya, as a social expediency, had accepted the concept of worship of several gods. He had justified the arrangement with his extraordinary power of debate, keeping them all within the orbit of the Vedanta. But this was a rather loose arrangement. There were several questions, posed by the changed circumstances, for which there was no rational answer. Ramanuja set to reform the work of Shankaracharya, by emphasizing devotion to one God rather than rituals to several. Having observed Christianity in South India and Islam in the north, he saw the damaging effects of the caste system. Yet looking around and finding opposition to his ideas on caste, he discreetly left the subject alone. It was later more vigorously taken up by Ramananda and Guru Nanak. He, however, expressed his views in considerable details in his book *Sribhashya*. This was largely to effect the thinking of future spiritual leaders.

Ramananda thereafter took the task of linking the thoughts of Ramanuja expressed in his writings.

Ramananda (AD 1400-147)

Saint Ramananda lived during the age of the Tughlaqs. Islam was then gaining both in political and social strength. This was partly through migrations from Middle East countries, but mainly due to internal unrest in the Hindu religion. Ramananda picked up the social fabric from where it was left by the saint from the south. He must have observed the revolutionary changes amongst a particular section of castes; their attraction towards Islam. Being a saint living among the people of north India he could foresee the future. After all caste discrimination had been largely responsible for decay in society. On closer interaction with Islam, this fact became glaringly clear.

His revolt against caste system

Ramananda was the first Hindu saint of that period who preached dissolution of caste arrangement with total resoluteness. He would teach devotion to one God, without discrimination between different classes and castes. Like others before him, his philosophy was based on the Vedanta. The evil of the caste system was so deeply engrained that the issue became a controversy. It was so vehemently opposed that even his own followers started deserting him!

Varanasi has been the seat of Hindu orthodoxy since time immemorial. The Hindu priests denounced Ramananda in the strongest terms. The more he was denounced, the greater became his resolve to fight against evil. In spite of opposition from a particular class, the intellectuals always supported him. Ramananda was soon the most sought-after teacher of spiritual knowledge.

The detached (*Avadhuta*)

Ramananda founded a school to propagate and practice his philosophy. Calling it 'the detached', he would impart pure knowledge of the Vedanta, denouncing the superfluous rituals that had blurred knowledge during the course of time. After Shankaracharya, it was Ramananda who purged Hinduism of the 'mystical sensuality'.

Soon the school unleashed a wave of social change. Spiritual saints like Kabir and Nanak would sit by his side to seek his guidance. His personal influence was realized when Nanak founded the Sikh religion and Kabir became the greatest lyrical poet of medieval India. Both these masters often came to Ramananda. Kabir, later, became his disciple.

The change brought about by Ramananda in the environment taught devotion to one ideal. This was to generate a new awareness to devotion *(bhakti)*. In the next century, this change would result in the writing of the greatest devotional literary production, the Ramayana, by Tulsidas.

The phase of union

Sufism was another factor for change. It emphasized devotion to one God. So did spiritual leaders like Ramananda, Nanak and Kabir. It was indeed a period of change and adaptation in a new society that was emerging in the country. In the last few centuries, Islam and Hinduism had learnt much from each other. There were apparent differences in their conduct and rituals but their philosophy on morals and belief in one God was the same. The difference in conduct was because the two religions had developed in altogether different circumstances. Now, when such a difference did not exist, similarities like devotion to God, considering all human beings equal before Him, were facts that both religions preached.

Islam had brought with it definite and distinctive religious, social and cultural ideas. Many of its features differed from Hinduism. The two religions now had to co-exist. Ramananda would therefore emphasize the common features between the two cultures. He worked to accelerate this process of harmony.

The process of reforms in Hindu religion, initiated by Shankaracharya and continued by Ramanuja and Ramananda, gathered strength. It was now the turn of a poor orphan brought up by a Muslim weaver. He would seek Ramananda's blessings to take forward his work. With his blessings, Kabir influenced the masses and brought about a new awakening in Hindus and Muslims. His simple verses sent shivers down the spines of the pandits and maulvis of his time. He appealed straight to the hearts of the people. Born in a Hindu family and brought up by a Muslim, this simple saint of Varanasi was Kabir, the most revered and popular name in India after Gautama Buddha.

Chapter XXII
Founder of a Faith–Guru Nanak

Guru Nanak (AD 1469-1539) was born at a time when the Pathan-Lodhi rulers of India were sunk deep in sensuous luxuries, neglecting their primary function of maintaining law and order and defending the frontiers of the country. They, along with the Islamic priestly class, had degraded the rule. There was utter chaos. Nanak felt and understood the cause of misery within the Hindu society. Misunderstanding 'self' as selfishness, the community could not present a united front against oppression. Nanak, taking cue from Islam, realized this grave shortcoming. He introduced *sangat* (combined congregations) and *pangat* (eating together without regard to caste, creed or status of life). Nanak understood, how each time, the problem of disunity had been the cause of defeats and disasters. The change introduced by Guru Nanak, brought not only different castes of Hindus including the socially backward together, it also encouraged others to join the new faith.

Nanak homogenized the Hindu religion. Thus was he able to introduce reforms, desperately needed for peace and harmony in the society of those times.

As Babar's hordes fell on the helpless people of Punjab, they burnt, looted and killed without discriminating between Hindus and Muslims. Nanak describes the battle between Babar and Ibrahim Lodhi in his verses:

> Battle was joined between Mughals and Pathans,
> Freely were the swords plied in battle.
> Those led elephant charges,
> Swarms of females—Hindus and Muslims, Bhatias and Rajputs,
> Many were in tatters from head to foot;
> Many found abode in cremation ground.

It was unique, for an essentially spiritual person, to be so describing political degeneration. Until now, spiritual leaders had generally confined themselves to prayers and devotion. Nanak combined spiritual wisdom with a zest for social reforms. His heart felt the pain of others. Understanding its causes, he tried to remove them. A thousand years earlier, Prophet Mohammed had faced a similar situation in Arabia where cruelty and oppression dominated life. He had then raised his sword in defence of the innocent people. Now, his own followers were committing the same crimes against which Mohammed fought all his life! Every religion starts with the philosophy of love. It preaches everything that is conducive to bring varying factions together. Vested interests corrupt its true significance. Power seekers begin to use it for their personal gains. Instead of love, the core of religion is converted into hate.

Life and teachings of Nanak

Born near Lahore (Pakistan), Nanak from his childhood was of a contemplative nature. Rather than concentrating on professional attainment, he was ever eager to seek the company of saints and mystics. Yet, his family forced him to the service of the king. It was while serving as a keeper at Kapurthala that revelation dawned on the young Nanak. The first words that he uttered, were those that were uppermost in his mind:

"There is no Hindu and no Muslim."

Henceforth he would devote all his time and energy, preaching this truth. Unlike saints of his time, Nanak would not rest content merely preaching prayers and devotion. As a revolutionary, he worked for social upliftment which he thought was the real reason for people's misery. Nanak used religion to bring about a political revolution. He created a martial force to resist cruelty and injustice; to bring back the honour of a subjugated people oppressed by tyrants.

Nanak now became Guru Nanak. He preached devotion to one God. His main thrust for spiritual upliftment consisted in holy teachings, reflection and deep meditation. Service to fellowmen was an essential part of spiritual attainment. To those used to meditating in the Himalayas, he would ask them to come down to work amongst the masses. He refused to sit idle in slumbering meditation, while people groaned under the heels of the oppressors. He awakened them to a new consciousness saying:

"Kings are butchers; cruelty their knife, sense of duty (Dharma) has taken wings and vanished; only fools and idiots ruled without regard to the good of the people"

To be using such words against monarchy required extraordinary courage!

Division—the destiny of religions

Nanak noticed how Hindus and Muslims were divided into castes and sub-castes. Instead of serving humanity, each was serving his ego; proving his superiority over the other. After some years, he started composing 'Gurubani' and other sacred hymns. He denounced the emptiness of rituals, maintaining equal love towards all religions. Having witnessed caste discrimination amongst Hindus, he was particularly harsh on them for practising 'untouchability'.

Seen in retrospect, Guru Nanak gave India the elixir to survive the onslaughts that her people had brought on themselves. He created a new vision; gave new vigour to masses through his personal courage to oppose wrong. It helped to bind society together at a critical period. The spirit of self-sacrifice contributed to the world a faith embedded with the spirit of idealism, adventure and service. His verse amply sums up his mission:

> Degeneration occurred in this world,
> leading to the four caste divisions
> And enactment about four stages of life.
> The Sanyasis into ten,
> And the yogis into twelve sects were divided;
> Truth invisible was divided and sub-divided,
> Into numerous ugly shapes.

> Truly *Kalyuga* led men into mazes of illusion.
> Many were the streams that flowed,
> And so appeared Mohammed with his companions.
> His followers too were divided into seventy-two
> And spread strife in manifold ways;
> He made current the fast, Id and Namaz,
> And imposed a new ritual on the world.

> Amongst Muslims appeared various orders of religious teachers,
> Of various sects strife was wide spread amongst men,
> Who were filled with egoism, meanness and pride;
> Ganga and Banaras were sacred to Hindus,
> As was Mecca and Kaba to Mohammedans.
> Truth was cast aside and Brahmans and Mullahs
> Clashed each, with each, bitterly.

Considered as a lesson of the past, Guru Nanak provides a sober message when he declares:

"Religion is not meant to be a tool for strife!"

Principal compositions

Nanak expressed himself in various poetic compositions. They describe the path leading to human fulfillment. Morality is an integral part of all spiritual knowledge. Nanak explains his thoughts through similes for easier understanding of the common people. The most outstanding and principal composition of Nanak is *Japji* (the holy chant). Its regular recitation is believed to confer the boon of liberation to the seeker. Who are the ones who chant *Japji* everyday? Nanak gives himself the answer in the following couplet in *Japji*:

> Men of continence, charity, contentment,
> Indomitable heroes, all chant thy praises.
> Men of learning, mighty seers,
> All laud thee in holy text, age after age.

After *Japji*, is the *mul mantra*. The verses from this section are recited on all occasions for divine blessings. They are recited at the time of initiating persons into the Sikh faith.The other composition on morality in living, meant for early morning singing in large gatherings, is *Asi-di-vas*. It contains the message through similes for easier understanding:

> Avarice is the king; evil doing his minister;
> Falsehood his revenue collector.
> Lust is the counsellor, always consulted for advice,
> The subjects are purblind and thoughtless,
> Wretches who foolishly obey their evil rules.

Guru Granth Saheb

Guru Granth Saheb is the religious scripture of the Sikh religion. The Granth starts with *Ek Onkar* to explain the concept of God. It is a philosophy similar to what is contained in all great religions. This confirms the essential unity of all religions. On the relationship of the Creator and the Created, Nanak says;

> He is the sole Supreme Being; of eternal
> Manifestation, creator, reality, without fear
> Timeless Form; unincarnated; self existent;
> Realized by the grace of Holy Percept
>
> Why do you go to forests in search of God?
> He lives in all and is yet ever distinct;
> He abides with you too,
> As fragrance dwells in a flower
> So does God dwells in everything.
> Seek him, therefore, in your heart

On yoga, the Granth says :

> Yoga consists not in frequenting wild places,
> Tombs and cremation grounds,

> Nor does it go with wandering in the world,
> nor does ritual bathing help.

> To be able to live with impurities around,
> is indeed yoga in practice.

To the devotee, the scripture says:

> He who enjoys remembering Him
> All his fears and dreads are shed.
> He who enjoys remembering Him,
> He does not enjoy anything else.

Further, Nanak says in the Granth:

> Let Truth be your Namaz (Muslim Prayer)
> And faith be your Mussala (prayer mat)
> Kill desires that might be your support,
> Your body should be the mosque
> And your mind, the priest.

Crusade for reforms

Nanak considered social reforms an integral part of spiritual development. Welfare of the humble and the lowly was of concern to him. To the proud and the arrogant, his message was to dissolve their egos. A person of caste, harbouring within himself feelings of separateness and untouchability, were to his mind of foul thinking. He was a votary of a casteless society. It used to pain him to see the treatment meted out to untouchables of the period. He would say:

> Kshatriyas, Brahmins, Shudras and the Vaishya,
> all the four castes have a common gospel to unfold
> The devotee who remembers the name in *Kalyuga* is saved.
> Says Nanak that, God dwells in every soul.

Nanak was a born in an age when hate and violence flowed freely. Different faiths were virtually ever frowning at each other. The stronger looked forward to devouring the weak. But Nature sent Nanak as a messenger to restore the balance of civilized life at a critical juncture. He would not only transmit the message of good will, he would also himself work for it. Nanak transformed the prevailing environment through emphasizing compassion and oneness of all human beings. He sowed seeds for a sacrificing force of committed warriors, whose essential weapon was a sword.

The message of Guru Nanak revolutionized the minds of the masses. Having taught the way towards reconciliation and harmony, he also preached resistance to evil by force. After him, other Gurus, of whom Guru Gobind Singh was the last, took up the work in the same spirit of martyrdom.

Sikhism–truth against tyranny

After Prophet Mohammed, his successors, the Caliphs of Damascus and Bagdad had carved an Islamic empire with Babar conquering North India. After him the message of Guru Nanak was successively followed by: Guru Nanak Dev, Guru Angad, Guru Amar, Guru Arjun Mal, Guru Hargovind, Guru Har Rai, Guru Har Kisan, Guru Teg Bahadur, and Guru Gobind. Followers of Guru Nanak sacrificed their lives for the cause. Nanak and his ten successors, in a span of two hundred years, succeeded in ridding Punjab of Mughal rule. Not only this, when Timur, the plunderer from Afghanistan, was returning home with vast riches, he was relieved of a large part of the booty by the followers of Sikh religion. This wealth was distributed for service amongst poverty the stricken people of the Punjab.

Their sacrifices against cruelty created a tremendous martial force. Pledged to fight injustice and spread spiritual wisdom, the faith fought cruelty and malignancy of the rulers. One of the followers of Sikh faith, Raja Ranjit Singh, almost conquered the throne of Delhi. Sacrifices made by Sikhs, helped change the atmosphere of despondency. Instead, there prevailed a call for unity of the two communities. Even Aurengzeb's son, Dara Shikoh died a martyr; victim to the fanatical wrath of his father, who called himself a true follower of Islam. The book, *Majmua-ul-Bahrani* (The Mingling of Two Oceans), written by Dara, is a call for fusion of the Hindus and Muslims. Similarly, Aurangzeb's other son, also rebelled against the suicidal policies of his father.

As the call for sanity rose, religious fanatism of emperor Aurengzeb and disintegration of the Mughul Empire began!

Guru Nanak's successor, Guru Gobind Singh dared challenge the emperor thus:

"Smite not anyone mercilessly by sword, lest some one high may smite thee likewise! Even though thou art strong, oppress not the weak. Lay not the axe to thy kingdom."

Within a few years of such foreboding, the last of the Mughal emperor was lamenting his fate in a British prison in Rangoon. When religions becomes more concerned with power and politics, its inspirational energy is diverted towards conflicts. The natural tendency of tolerance taught by Guru Nanak, helped preserve truth by inspiring his followers to fight tyranny, first by reason and then by the sword. Followers of other religions of the country echoed the inspiration he provided. The multi-cultural and multi-religious ethos emphasized by Guru Nanak and the other Gurus helped send the right signals to the rulers. They realized that a country of such diversity could not be governed with narrow religiosity. Unlike the earlier sultans, the Mughals cared more for the rule of the law. This brought peace, stability and prosperity. India became one of the richest countries of the world. The stern and firm message that Guru Nanak gave to the Mughal rulers, through the action of his followers, was largely responsible for the transformation and consequent prosperity of the masses.

Chapter XXIII
Apostle of Truth–Kabir

Krishna came when the land of Bharata was in deep distress. Kabir too appeared in an age of grave religious confrontation when Indian society was divided in all types of unimaginable sections. Frustration and exploitation prevailed. Both Hindu and Muslim priests were ever engaged in manipulating their supremacy; *maulvis*, over the rulers; Hindu priests, over the ruled. This artificial division of society was not to the liking of nature. There appeared a pure hearted saint to replace suspicion and hatred with peace and harmony. He was like a bodiless spirit, indeed, descended from the realm of light to the earthly plane wearing a body. Kabir was presented as a gift by mother Ganga in response to the prayers of the masses. The child Kabir was found floating in river Ganga at Varanasi by a Muslim weaver. Born a Hindu and brought up by a Muslim, Kabir was a message to the people. With no formal knowledge of books or scriptures, Kabir sang his poetry from the heart. He called himself a child of Allah and Rama:

> I am a child of Rama and Allah,
> I accept all Gurus and Pirs.
> Call him Rama if you like,
> Call him Allah, one thing I know.
> Rama and Rahim are one,
> and so are Kashi and Kaba.

His early life

Kabir (AD 1398-1448) joined the family profession of weaving from his early childhood. He wove cloth during the day and sold it at the marketplace in the evening. He would charge the customer only that much as was necessary for his survival. This earned him the goodwill and love of all. Fond of singing from his childhood, whatever he sang was philosophy of the highest order but meant for understanding of the poorest. He would enjoy working on the loom of his foster-father, producing cloth to earn for the family.

After his marriage, Kabir brought his wife, Loi, to his old and dilapidated home. Seeing the condition of her new home, the young bride wept bitterly.

Kabir, finding his wife in grief, inquired the reason for her agony. After some persuasion, she confided. "There is a boy in our village. We were childhood friends, liking each other. Just when we were to be married my parents married, me to you."

Kabir laughed at her wailing description and said in his innocent, amiable tone. "Why did you not tell this to me earlier? I will take you to the village myself and get you married to the one you love. Now stop sobbing and get ready to leave." Next day both Loi and Kabir started on their journey. It was the rainy season. The rough and muddy village footpath made the going tough. After walking a few hours, the young bride was tired, unable to walk any more. Seeing her difficulty, Kabir asked her to sit on his shoulders. They had only gone some distance when Kabir again heard her sobs. "Now, what is it that you want me to do," he asked? Loi was pleading with him to return home to the dilapidated hut.

"Why do you now want to turn back?" Kabir asked.

"Where in the world will I find a husband like you?" she said.

His work begins

Kabir, during the early stage of his work, was deeply influenced by the saint Ramananda. He was anxious to seek his guidance. During this period, Narsi Mehta in Gujarat, Vidyapati in Bihar, and Guru Nanak and Kabir in North India, were preaching *bhakti* (devotion). Ramananda was teaching the Vedanta, leading to devotion. After some reluctance, he accepted Kabir as his disciple. Soon Kabir's popularity grew. Priests and mullahs were particularly offended at what he preached and said. Fearing that their business was endangered, they complained to the ruler of those days. They charged Kabir of inciting the simple people against them and disturbing peace.

Sikander Lodhi, who was then the king, asked for Kabir to be presented before him. The mullahs charged him for speaking like Mansoor, another Islamic reformer who lived during the reign of the Caliph of Baghdad. They charged that Kabir was pretending to be divine. They urged that he be put to death. The king, finding nothing of the sort to be true, was reluctant. Inwardly, he was impressed by the logic Kabir gave in his defence.

Fifteen hundred years ago, a similar complaint was presented to the then custodian of peace in Jerusalem. The Jewish priests had gone to the Roman Governor of Jerusalem, charging Jesus Christ for disturbing peace. Pilate, the governor, like Sikander Lodhi, examined the evidence but found nothing against the accused. Yet, to maintain peace, he took the easier route to maintain peace. He passed the death sentence on Christ. Perhaps the world had grown wiser when Sikander Lodhi, for exactly similar reason banished Kabir from the city of Varanasi. Thus, the singer of holy spirit; the man of peace; the teacher of brotherhood; the poet of life; the reconciler of Hindus and Muslims; the illuminated mystic, was punished by extradition. Henceforth, he was to roam around the country all his life with his *Ektara* (musical instrument like sitar) to enrich the people of the land.

It is a travesty of truth that in every age, liberals are usually indifferent to the wrongs. Under such conditions, the rulers tend to compromise and take the line of least resistance. From now on, Kabir would have no home, having to wander on the dusty roads of north India till his death in 1448, though many *Kabirpanthis* (followers of Kabir) say he lived till the age of 120 and died in 1518. The suffering he endured was to bestow the eternal truth not only to his generation, but also to the coming generations.

His words of truth

Kabir became an apostle of truth; the greatest medieval poet of India whose influence on the minds of men is unaltered even today. He had become a roving ambassador of truth, speaking truth in his poetry. Henceforth Kabir delivered his message of unity of all beings. His lyrics were compositions from daily life. People flanked to listen to his easy-to-understand verses. He was the first amongst saints to forcefully bring to the world the philosophies of the Quran and the Vedanta together:

> Some to Dwarka run; some to Kashi go;
> Some to Mathura travel far, forgetting that.
> The master and the Lord is in the heart within!

On self-realization and action

Kabir was a man of action. He made his living by weaving every day. His mysticism was not that of a quietist. He compared action to a flower and fruit from the flower as self-realization:

> Work is flower: realization is fruit.
> The flower blooms in beauty for the fruit,
> When fruit comes, the flower withers,
> Through work, we reach realization:
> And realisation is within!

To explain the same point, he says:

> The moon doth shines within my body;
> Alas! Mine eyes are blind and see not the light!
> Within me sound the drums of eternity—,

> The unstuck music of the spirit,
> Alas! Mine ears are deaf and cannot hear.!

On God and mind

People usually asked Kabir to define God. He explained to his audience that God is not known through intellect. His presence is not demonstrated by arguments. All pondering, polemics and debates on the subject are futile. He would laugh at the very question and reply:

> I laugh when I hear,
> that the fish in water is thirsty.

He would explain further :

> The deer carries the musk in his navel,
> But wanders for it, far in the forests!"
> So Rama abideth in the heart within,
> But the world beholds him not!
> You do not see what the real is within you,
> and wander from forest to forest, restlessly.

The way to God is from within the human body. The obstacles in the way have to be removed by mind and meditation:

> They are thieves who steal spiritual wealth,
> Through their mighty companion:
> Lust, Auger, Attachment, Greed, Avarice,
> Jealousy, Hate and most of all Ego.

Men, from time immemorial, have tried to tame their minds through austerities, penance, fasts, renunciation, self torture, self mortification, yoga and denial of food and comfort. Even seclusion in forest for long periods have not helped. He advises control of mind through understanding its origin and characteristics. Kabir starts quoting the learned that say 'mind is matter'. He says it is neither matter nor spirit; its origin is in the universal mind. When it enters the body, it turns into an individual mind, giving it a separate identity (ego).

Kabir advises that effort must be to bring it back to the universal mind. For this, the mind must be trained to go back to the 'unmind' or quietude stage of mind. Meditation helps one to reach that stage.

How does the 'universal mind' or 'cosmic mind', turn into an individual's mind?

Kabir answers this question saying, "the world and its objects present to the mind attractive material for desires and cravings. Again and again, therefore the mind comes back to the world of objects." Explaining the function of the mind, he says:

Mind was originally a means to function in the world. It was meant to associate and reciprocate with others; to know and experience the vicissitudes of physical surroundings taking place in the outside world. Instead, the universal mind, submitting to cravings and desires generated by the outer world, is made helpless before them; it keeps helplessly tossing around.

Three stages of life

Kabir divided life into three parts:

(a) The active life has to be a life of virtue and self control.

(b) The contemplative life must concern man to the love of God.

(c) The intuitive life is a blend of the active, and the contemplative. This brings silence and love, through which man learns the hidden secrets of heart.

The lyrics of Kabir reflect the state of society during his period. He suggests through his poems the right action that must be followed. Social evils are always a cause of tension in societies. During his days, intoxication was widely prevalent. Not only the rich, even the poor were its victims. Families were ruined by its ill effects. Kabir would awaken people with his message:

> In Kaliyuga, Kaal has sent,
> Tobacco, opium and wine
> As his agents to make man loose his head,
> Forget devotion, and stay in Kaal's confine.

Paying tribute to the value of good company, Kabir advocated this in verse, by comparing a person to a drop of dew. In the company of the good (plantain), the drop becomes a priceless jewel; in the company of evil (snake), it turns into poison.

> The drop of dew falls, on the root of a plantain,
> Into an oyster shell, on the mouth of a snake.
> All with different effects.

On human destiny

Kabir says that man is at the top of creation. He is a perfect combination of all the five elements that form the basis of life. Other creatures are not fully endowed. They are devoid of inner qualities of mind like discrimination, understanding and analysis. It is our attachment that pulls down the soul to the level of animals, he says:

> Kabir is standing in the marketplace,
> Inviting all seeking salvation.
> Let them be detached from worldly objects,
> Before they join my company.

For family men

To lead a happy life, Kabir advises following the middle path. He would suggest them:

> Those who followed the middle path, swim across.
> Those who go to one extreme, sink in the ocean of the world.
> O Kabir! Remain aloof from the two; Stick to the middle path...
> Things extremely hot and things extremely cold,
> Are both injurious, like fire.

For happiness in life, he had the simplest of formulae:

> Be just; and happiness is at your elbow.

Kabir remained continuously on the move, conveying his message with intensity; yet in direct and easy to understand verses. Tired and exhausted, he was advised to spend his last days in Varanasi. He refused, saying that "if sinners can reach heaven by just dying at Varansi, what is the difference between the sinner and the virtuous?"

After almost half a millennium of his death, men in villages and towns sing the songs of Kabir with devotion. Each morning, some wise old man can be heard reciting his verses in the company of his friends. Intellectual friends, emphasizing their point during conversation, always strengthen their wit with a suitable verse from Kabir. These convey the truth of existence and wisdom of daily living. Time seems to stop when we hear his songs being sung by a distant *fakir*. They appear as true today as when Kabir himself sang them on his *ektara*. Devoid of religious verbosity and ritualistic trapping, they serve as nectar to the ears. If Gautama Buddha was the greatest Indian to have influenced the minds of men all over the world; Kabir was the greatest Indian who will be quoted and sung by common men and women in villages and towns all over India. In his own words:

> His heart was like a large Banyan tree,
> On whose branches live innumerable singing birds.
> And they flew to the East and they flew to the West,
> Singing of the unstuck music of the depths.

Generations to come will admire the simplicity of his expression, benevolence of speech and boldness of his thoughts. Our prayers are:

Your songs, O master singer! Will live for ever,
In the sleepless memory of mankind.

The Magnificence of the Mughals

If there is a paradise
on earth,
it is here, it is here,
it is here!
(Inscription in Persian in the
Dewan-e-Khas in the fort of Delhi.)

Chapter XXIV
Foundation & Consolidation
of Mughal Empire

We may recollect how, during the fourth and fifth centuries BC, the world was enlightened by great thinkers and pathfinders. Socrates and Pythagoras in Greece; Confucious and Lao-Tse in China; Gautama Buddha and Kapila in India, laid the foundations of the modern civilization that spread to different corners of the world.

With establishment of the Mughal empire by Babar in 1483, a new era of cultural grandeur commenced in the country. During the earlier regime of Afghans and Turks, Indian spiritual life remained under pressure of religious discrimination. The Mughals brought with them the vigour and dynamism of a new culture. The Indian life had reached a stage of stagnancy and senility. It received nourishment from Persia and Arabia to recover. The Mughal Empire, in time, was destined to become one of the greatest and most prosperous empires in the world. India, that had hitherto appeared unchanging, started on the road to progress and prosperity. The ferocity faced during the rule of the Afghans, was replaced with a civilized and just rule.

Zahir-ud-din Babar (AD 1483-1530)

Babar, like the Macedonian Alexander, was a gifted ruler of outstanding ability. A lover of fine arts, intensely fond of nature, a keen observer of men and their psychology, he was equally gifted with an extraordinary physique and capacity for physical endurance. Free from religious bigotry, a poet of Persian language, lover of beauty, gardens and flowers, he longed for the 'lovely violets of Farghana', his home. His rule commenced the process of inter-mixing of Indian and Islamic cultures. This began a new synthesis in thoughts, language, economic activities and the way of life. Islamic and Hindu religions, so far in confrontation with each other, started to look at each other with friendly glances; a kind of new understanding began taking shape in the daily lives of the people.

Emergence and growth of a composite nation which had been lacking since the days of Samudragupta, had begun.

March of Mughals

Babar of Farghana had inherited a small state located at the tip of Afghanistan. Being small and lacking resources, it used to be under mortal fear of being usurped by neighbours. His father having died early, his mother, as his guide and protector, trained her son to be sturdy so that he could protect his father's estate. This training hardened the prince. It was however impossible to rule with empty coffers. He, therefore, began to use his skill and strength to extend his territory. This he did by gaining Kabul. Ambitious, skillful and innovative, he ruled in Kabul for more than a decade. Soon he would win India. With the blood of Chengiz Khan and Timur in him, his mother's training made young Babar particularly strong and tough. As he grew old, a burning flame to win new lands possessed him. His ambitious eyes found riches beyond the border. Failing in his earlier attempts, he was able to defeat Ibrahim Lodhi at Panipat in his fifth attempt. Babar had crossed the river Indus with a small but efficient army. He carried a 'secret weapon' of gunpowder with him. It would be used on the Indian soil for the first time. Ibrahim and Babar met in the fields of Panipat in 1483. On one side was a determined, well-trained warrior-general; on the other side a large assemblage of mercenary soldiers with no will to fight. Large elephants and cavalry commanded by an over-confident, over-indulgent, luxury-drenched Sultan, joined the battle. When Babar's guns oozed out fire, the scared animals ran amuck trampling their own soldiers in the chaos.

Babar was able to win the crown of India. Like his ancestor, Chengiz Khan who always surprised his enemies, Babar scared and spread terror amongst his enemy with gunpowder. Babar was one of those captivating and excellent warriors, who possessed the fortitude of the Turks, the grace of the Persians and the spiritual and moral discipline of Islam. A keen observer of men and environment, he was ever restless and active in mind and body. This was reflected in his decision to make Agra, instead of Delhi, his capital. During his short reign, he was always busy fighting the Rajputs who would not let him rest. A connoisseur of the finer things of life, his memoirs on India and his testament for his son, draw a graphic picture of those times. On the art of governance, they provide an insight to his imagination and vision.

Glimpses from his memoirs

For posterity, Babar was keen to preserve the history of his times in his memoirs. After attending the affairs of state, he would devote time to reading religious scriptures and write his memoirs. He showed an unusual sagacity by making Agra his capital, instead of Delhi. This was because of constant challenge from the princes of Rajasthan. In his memoirs, Babar made some interesting observations about India. He records that the country was indeed a rich country possessing immense gold and silver. Its soil yields bountiful crops with little effort. There are excellent artisans and craftsmen of various trades. The land is generally passed from father to son. He complains that the country has no fruits like those of Samarkand. He missed the grapes of Chaman, and watermelons of his native Farghana. Comparing the flora and fauna of the two countries, he found no gardens as beautiful as in his native land.

Babar appreciated Indian wildlife and forests. He writes longingly about the birds, frogs, lions and tigers with wonder. Yet, in the innermost corner of his heart, he longed to be in Kabul; around the snow-clad mountains and lush green valleys. No wonder he records how he missed cold drinking water in India. Immediately after settling down to rule, he invited architects from Istanbul for construction of the fort at Agra.

Testament for Humayun

His instructions to Humayun on how to rule, show his dexterity and future vision. They are proof of his deep understanding and perception of vision. These helped Humayun lay a strong foundation for the future of the Mughal empire:

1. "You should not allow religious prejudices to influence your mind, but administer impartial justice, having due regard for religious susceptibilities and religious customs of all sections of people."

2. "In particular, refrain from slaughter of cows, which will help you obtain a hold on the hearts of the people of India. Thus you shall bind the people of the land to yourself by ties of gratitude."

3. "You should never destroy places of worship of any community, but always be justice-loving so that relations between the king and his subjects remain cordial and thereby secure peace and contentment on land."

4. "The propagation of Islam would be better carried on with the sword of love and obligation than with the sword of oppression."

5. "Treat the different peculiarities of your subjects, as different seasons of the year, so that body politic may remain free from disease."

An incident in the fort at Agra reflects his sharp intellect and keen observation. One evening, while dining together with his commanders, Babar was struck by the action of a junior general. He noticed that the young general was not able to reach the food kept in the centre. The young man was thus unable to pick up his share of the delicious food. Exasperated with waiting, the young general jumped over the shoulders of those sitting in front. Picking up his choice with his dagger, he went back to his seat and nonchalantly resumed eating.

Babar, rather startled, discreetly inquired from his minister, "who is this young general?"

"Sher Khan," the minister replied.

"Be careful of him; he is too ambitious." Babar whispered to his minister.

After the death of Babar, a few years later, Sher Khan was to defeat Humayun and rule India for five years as Sher Shah Suri.

Personal traits of Babar

Babar was blessed with the virtues of a great prince and a good man. He was so jovial, frank and buoyant in spirit that no privation, distress, or misfortune ever disturbed the equanimity of his temper. Unlike the Turks and Afghans, Babar was a visionary, with a long family tradition to govern. He possessed a secular culture unlike those of earlier Islamic rulers. Other Mughal kings of the dynasty successively maintained this spirit. And when Aurangzeb abandoned it, the empire just vanished.

The episode about the illness of his son explains his character. When medical treatment failed to cure his son Humayun, he prayed for recovery of his son. Babar, in his prayers to God, offered his own life in exchange of the life of his son. Gradually, Humayun started to recover and Babar began to sink. When *hakeems* (doctors) tried to examine and prescribe Babar medicines, he contemptuously refused to be cured. He had made a promise to God to spare the life of his son in exchange to his own.

Babar would not betray an obligation or break a promise!

Humayun (AD 1508-1556)

Humayun inherited from his father, the taste and temperament of a noble man; love for literature and philosophy, comfort and luxury. Unlike Babar, he had no taste for wars. Generalship or swordmanship did not attract him as much as did books. Peace and tranquillity rather than the crown of India was what he loved more. After Sher Shah defeated him, instead of reorganizing his force, he was inclined to go and settle in Persia. Inspite of all odds, he could still regain the throne. Time, chance and destiny are often more powerful!

Humayun was generous to a fault. He pardoned the misdemeanour of his brothers and cousins even at the expense of losing his kingdom. Fond of learned company, he enjoyed discussions on sciences and philosophy. A cultured and kindly gentleman, Humayun was destined to face hardships for most of his life. Yet, more than his qualities as a soldier, he was a polite and charitable man. These qualities won him the friendship of the Persian king and the able generalship of Bairam Khan, which ultimately helped him regain the crown.

Going back to ancient times, we may recollect how Bindusar of the Mauryan dynasty was anxious to have a philosopher in his court. Though he could not get one as a gift from Syria; Nature blessed him with Ashoka his son. Similarly, the highly cultured, virtuous and charitable nature of Humayun, whose fondness for nobility and learning was no less, was blessed with a son, Akbar. Before we proceed, destiny had another great ruler to be introduced even though only for a short duration. This was the young, aggressive and uncouth but brave former general of Babar's army—Sher Khan.

Sher Khan becomes Sher Shah Suri

The Mughal empire had yet not been established firmly when Babar died. This placed a heavy burden on Humayun. Sher Khan, an Afghan, who was once in the service of his father, collected other Afghans who had not reconciled to the Mughal having won the Indian empire from them. They would persistently harass the young king. The trouble was further compounded by non-cooperation of his brothers. After some bitter fighting, Humayun was defeated and had to flee and take shelter in Persia.

Sher Khan became Sher Shah Suri, the king of Hindustan.

His rule was short but memorable. He was a visionary, who planned for the welfare of his people. Building better communications and creating an efficient mechanism of tax-collection are his legacies that continue even today; while Sher Shah ruled, Humayun lived the life of a fugitive. It was during this period of wanderings that Humayun's son, Jalal-ud-din, was born in the deserts of Rajasthan. Meanwhile, Sher Shah, as a worthy administrator, ruled with keenness to develop his empire. As a wise administrator, he soon established a powerful kingdom. A soldier of uncommon ability, he was extremely careful of being just and fair to his subjects. Yet, like most Afghan sultans before him, he too lacked the culture of Babar and Humayun. He realized the importance of communication to fecilitate a smooth transport system in a vast subcontinent. Sher Shah constructed links between several important states, joining strategic routes with Delhi and Agra. His entire personality comes out through his conviction. This he expresses in his own words:

"The cultivators are a source of prosperity. I have encouraged them and shall always watch over their condition that no man may oppress and injure them; for, if a ruler cannot protect the humble peasantry from the lawless, it is tyranny to extract revenue from them."

As the administration of Sher Shah grew stronger, Humayun did not want to come back to India. Destiny however was kind to India. While assaulting a fort in Bundelkhand, Sher Shah died due to a sudden explosion of gunpowder. His son tried to keep the administration running in the manner of his father. However, he lacked the talents to hold on to such a vast empire. The several chiefs in the kingdom fought each other to gain supremacy. Humayun saw his chance. With the help of the king of Persia, he entered India and regained the throne.

Return and exit of Humayun

Hardly had he been on the throne for one year that Humayun's life ended. Hurrying down from the library for his *namaz*, he fell down the stairs and died shortly. Akbar at this time was only two years of age. In his last moments, Humayun left his son to the care of his loyal and capable general, Bairam Khan. He taught the young lad, Jalal-ud-din Akbar, all the arts that a king needed to learn during those days. By the time Akbar was eighteen, he had grown into a passionate hunter of lions, the best horseman, the best swordsman and the greatest athlete in the empire.

Jalal-ud-din Akbar—the founder of a modern nation state

Akbar (AD 1542-1605) was an ideal combination of his ancestors. He was a rare gift who shaped India's destiny. If, during the same period, England was blessed with a great queen in Elizebeth I; France, with Henry IV; then the fate of India was altered by Akbar. He possessed the physique and energy of his grandfather Babar; love of knowledge and literature of his father Humayun and the ambitious vision of his great grandmother. Bestowed with a magnetic personality, athletic physique; being the best horseman and swordsman in the country; one of the great architects, he was like 'a sea in sunshine', when in a good mood. He could, when enraged, burst into anger, making others tremble with fear. Akbar was so fond of sports that he devised a ball with which he could play polo even at night. A strange glitter in his eyes bewitched all those who stood before him.

Yet, unlike other great warrior kings like Julius Caesar and Napoleon, he was never calculative. Given more to thought than action, he would melt with pity when royalty demanded resolve. Akbar achieved everything he set his mind on. Having conquered most parts of India, he was amongst the richest, strongest and the wisest emperor of the world. He belonged to the company of Cyrus of Persia, Julius Caesar of Rome and Ashoka of ancient India. He wanted to be more than just a great emperor; at heart a philosopher, he wished to be remembered as one. He says:

> I am the maker of so vast a kingdom. All appliances of government are in my hands; yet, since greatness consists in doing the will of God, my mind is not free in this diversity of sects and creeds (religions). Apart from outward pomp, with what satisfaction can I undertake to change the direction of my Empire!

His doubt takes a mystical turn, when he adds:

> I await the coming of a discreet man of principles, who will resolve the difficulties of my conscience. There was an Ashoka, who centuries earlier, after the Kalinga war felt a similar need for being not able to do enough. Such sacrificing nature and respect for life, is only possible on the soil and climate of this subcontinent!

Mode of governance

To consolidate the boundaries of his empire, young Akbar started his rule as a zealous warrior. He won almost every war he fought except the war with Mewar. When he had brought all of India under one umbrella, he turned to improving the administration. His principal advisors were a prime minister (*Vakil*), a finance minister (*Vazir*), a master of the court (*Bakshi*) and a *Sadr* who was head of the Mohammedan religion. Like Vikramaditya, Akbar surrounded himself with the best talents in different fields. They were all a collection of the keenest experts in their subjects that ever adorned the court of an emperor. Amongst the inner circle were Abul Fazal, Faizee and Birbal.

Aware that bias towards any religion in a land of multiple faiths could be an impediment to good governance, he conceived of a common faith. In a country long fed on religion, this was not acceptable even to his closest advisers. The concept proved a disaster. Not only his own co-religionists were up against him along with the clergy; followers of other religions were equally revolting. *Din-e-Ilahi* the new faith he had coined, died even before it was born. But his vision to see that Hindus, Muslims, Christians and all other faiths lived in peace with each other, never faltered. Akbar had realized that religious dogmas take time to get rooted in our minds. The changes he introduced were accepted more out of fear than conviction. When he departed, his vision of religion lay buried.

Faith permeates into the mind by slow reasoning.

To understand the religion of the country, he got the scriptures and epics like the Upanishads, Mahabharata and Ramayana translated from Sanskrit to Persian. At leisure, he would listen to them, participating in discussions of the learned. So fond was he of knowledge that he would invite Jains, Christians and Buddhists to speak of their teachings for the benefit of the learned.

Why was it that he placed so much emphasis on different religions?

The answer lies in his understanding that religion plays a crucial role in uniting or dividing the people of a country. As a passionate lover of his motherland, he sought to weld the Afghans, Turks, Mughals, Hindus and others into a common bond. This extract from a letter he wrote to the king of Persia reflect his sentiments:

> Various religious communities are divine treasures, entrusted to us by God. We must love them as such. It should be our firm faith that every religion is blessed by him and our earnest endeavour is to enjoy the bliss of the evergreen garden of universal toleration The Eternal King showers his blessings on all without distinction. Kings, who are shadows of God, should never give up this principle.

Development of Urdu

Earlier we read how Amir Khusrau, during the rule of the sultans, strived to produce a common language, spoken and understood by both the Hindus and Muslims. It was during Mughal rule that Urdu became the common language for literature and poetry, patronized equally by the intellectuals and the masses. Today, speakers on intellectual subjects, invariably quote a Sanskrit *shloka* from the scriptures; some others, similarly express themselves quoting an Urdu couplet for delight of their audience.

Urdu became popular only when it became useful to the common man. The camps of Mughal kings used to be a city on wheels. Spread in an area of 30 to 50 miles, it sustained a population of four to five lakhs. The people, comprising the royal troupe, were men drawn from all walks of life and from far and near. Without close and clear understanding, it was hard for them to perform their multifarious duties. Urdu, with a mixture of Hindi, Persian, Arabic and Sanskrit words, became the *lingua franca,* first of the royal camps and later of the people.

Urdu continues to flourish by bringing the emotional feelings of both communities to a common platform. Be it a song, a film, or an expression of culture in everyday life, Urdu helps join all parts of India with each other.

Respect for reason

Akbar's secular spirit yearned to see the diversity of different religions fusing into a single moral and spiritual code. He endeavoured to bring out the richness of morality, without the institution of religions. Being ahead of his times, he may not have succeeded in his rather grandiose plan of introducing a common religion for the entire humanity through *Din-e-Ilahi,* yet a firm foundation was laid for the future direction of India.

St. Francis Xavier, a Christian invitee of Akbar, records his observations thus:

> The King takes no stock in revelations and would accept nothing that would not
> justify itself with science and philosophy. It was not unusual for him to gather
> together friends and prelates of various sects together and discuss religion with
> them. When mullahs and Christian priests fought, Akbar would say that God
> should be worshipped through the intellect and not through blind adherence to
> supposed revelations. Each person, according to his condition, gives to his
> Supreme Being a name; but in reality to name the Unknowable is vain.

Akbar believed in reason rather than following traditions. The best way for
him to reach a decision was through discussions on diverse ideas. Akbar often
used to preside over such debates. This helped create an understanding between
groups thus furthering social cohesion. Maintaining the ancient practice, he
frequently invited scholars to review the Vedanta and Buddhism. Akbar
nourished the secular identity of India in which Hindus, Muslims, Christians,
Jews and Parsies were equal partners. He held that "pursuit of reason, rather
than reliance on traditions is the way to address difficult social problems." The
most effective manner to fight fundamentalist forces was to insist on reason.

It was only once in life that he did not obey commands of his mother. Angry
over an insult to the Quran in Ormus—a Christian country, she asked Akbar to
tie a Bible to the neck of a donkey and the animal be taken round the streets
of Agra.

Akbar told his mother, "What they did was abominable. To insult other religions
is to defile your own."

Religious zealots of the modern age in our country can learn a lesson in
religious tolerance!

Architect of the nation state

Lao-Tse, the ancient Chinese philosopher defines spirituality as 'non action'
which is really action in accordance to the laws of nature. Akbar's policies of
governance were guided by the Laws of Nature. This created wealth that
attracted European traders. The surplus so generated was used in construction
and other welfare activities. The judicious rule of Akbar brought such peace
and prosperity to India as was never seen for centuries. Art, literature and
trade reached a level of prosperity to make India the 'golden bird'. The rule
bound people of diverse races, religion and culture into a cohesive nation. The
wealth attracted the East India Company to send Sir Thomas Roe for
permission to do business in India. Before him, the Dutch and the Portuguese

were already engaged in trade and commerce. This induction would introduce vast and unforeseen changes.

Akbar used to plan splendid edifices and dressed the work of his mind and heart in the garment of stone and clay. He ruled from his capital at Agra. The grandeur of the city was the Red Fort with about one hundred buildings within it. In true devotion to Salim Chisti, a Sufi saint who had blessed him with a son, Akbar dedicated an entire city to his memory. At Fatehpur Sikri, near his grave, he built his own capital. The skill in the construction of Fatehpur Sikri demonstrates not only the architectural skill of the period, but also the application of Laws of Nature that govern scientific principles. The cooling system of the entire complex, with adequate provisions for comforts are marvels of their time. The *Buland Darwaza* built by Akbar to celeberate his victory in the south, is awe-inspiring. It is a sight to witness expert divers dive in to the pool below from a great height. At Sikandara, near Agra, even when alive, he had his own memorial built in a simple yet elegant style. For the welfare of his subjects and improvement of trade and commerce, he built rest houses. Akbar had a separate Public Works Department for construction of palaces, forts, tombs and mosques all over the country.

The three important constituents of civilization flourish only when there is peace and harmony in society. No amount of words of praise can match this fact. During Akbar's rule, some of the great poets and singers flourished under his patronage. Tulsi Das wrote *Ramcharita Manas;* Sur Das, was a poet of the royal court when he wrote *Sur Sagar* in praise of Lord Krishna. The wisdom studded poetry of Abdul Rahim Khan-e-Khana are even today present in the curriculum of young students. Mira Bai, the queen of Rajasthan, sang her devotional songs during Akbar's rule. Extensive work of translation from Sanskrit literature was reproduced in Arabic and Persian languages at his initiative. His mind always remained absorbed in devising means to cultivate greater understanding between religions and races to make India a haven of multi-cultural growth. Akbar possessed the insight to see beyond the superficial current in Indian life, an undercurrent of unity behind the outward diversity. This required a great visionary who was fortunately born on Indian soil when desperately needed. He had the large heartedness of a spiritualist who considered the entire world as one and the liberal nationalism of a great philosopher. He combined all the precious gifts of nature to unshackle India from her past prejudices and take her on the new path of greatness and glory.

Akbar had now ruled India for half a century, using his genius for the welfare of her people. The strength of great and outstanding rulers usually becomes the weakness of state. It is particularly so when heredity is the determining factor. The rule, during his tenure, entirely depended on his authority. This was destined to weaken with age. Akbar's quality of mind, would now also show signs of disintegration. True to understanding, at the time of his death he passed away in peace without benefit of prayers of any religion! Akbar had attempted to chalk out a great future for India. Alas, it was not to be. Mortals do not get enough time to complete their dreams. Succeeding generations need to be trained to ensure continuity. If the successor is not competent, (history considers Jahangir to be so), the effort is wasted. Instead of following the footsteps of his father, he is said to have unnaturally hastened his death! Akbar reigned when Elizabeth I ruled England. It was indeed an age of glory. Both rulers took their respective countries to great heights of achievement.

Period of spiritual refinement

In the West, growth of science coincided with refinement of spirituality in India. This awakening witnessed emergence of great saints, sages and sufis. They all preached devotion to one god. The process of synthesis started by them brought the new and the old cultures together. The messages of Guru Nanak and Kabir produced a climate of cooperation and goodwill. This reached a climax during the rule of Akbar. After several centuries, national unity of India was restored during the golden periods of Ashoka and Samudragupta. Indian genius, like that of Europe, had peace and harmony for creative activities to flourish. Significantly, science remained mostly ignored in India. Even during this period it did not get encouragement for growth. This was to become a severe cause of backwardness.

If the West could take pride in producing skills and knowledge in the material world, Indian genius excelled in spiritual growth. Since both are equally important for an integrated human growth, both remained incomplete without the other. This would emerge if science could achieve methods of controlling the ferocity of nature; if it could help us achieve a chosen end, it could not help us decide the end; it could not teach patience, sympathy, and a sense of human welfare. These emerge when the mind has been trained in spiritual wisdom.

Human life gets fulfilment when both science and spirituality are in a delicate balance. Nature keeps enforcing her immutable laws of creation and destruction. When the time is ripe, rulers and thinkers, saints and sufis, poets and architects appear on the world canvas. They perform their functions and then wither away. To meet the new challenges of time, India produced Ramanuja, Ramananda, Guru Nanak, Kabir, Abdul Rahim Khan-e-Khana, Tulsi Das, Sur Das, Salim Chishti, Chaitanya, Narsi Mehta, Chandidas, Tuka Ram. A galaxy of such persons hovered during the reign of Akbar.

Chapter XXV
Affluence and Decline of the Mughals

More than a century of efficient Mughul rule brought prosperity to the subcontinent. Law and order, agriculture, religious freedom, craftsmanship, trade both by land and sea; in many respects exceeded that of affluent countries of Europe. The courts of kings displayed such grandeur that their glitter dazzled European ambassadors and visitors. Peace and harmony in the land had created an atmosphere of affluence. The country was bursting with economic prosperity. Law and order permitted transport of gold and silver across hundred of miles, in full view of village folks, on elephants without any royal protection.

Jahangir–the merry monarch (AD 1569-1627)

Jahangir, born of a Hindu mother and Turkish father, possessed all the elements to rise to great heights of glory. Yet as an heir apparent, his indulgence in lechery and wine made Jahangir a degenerate. Punishing people with slow death was often his pastime. Drowned in wine, he had little care to govern. Extravagant, without any constructive approach either towards the throne or posterity, he would waste wealth. Fond of ostentation, he was keen only to keep the clergy in good humour. The liberal policy on religion, adopted by Akbar, began to go downhill unconsciously.

We often find great men who beget mediocre offsprings. Is it because the blood of their parents is absorbed and diluted in the immediate work at hand? Or is it because, getting no time from the exigencies of work, they have little time to discharge their filial obligations? Whatever be true it has been seen that the progeny of great men often do not get that stimulus which ambition usually provides to other youths.

Jahangir was an able administrator whose reign started in AD 1605. He had the capacity of appreciating the needs and circumstances of the age; he possessed the potential to understand the policies of his father and how to implement them. It was a lack of balance as an inherent instinct, which would not let him carry his ideas to their logical conclusion. Devoid of positive inspiration, he would always dither and revert to the safety of sensuous pleasures around him.

The climate of India had become conducive to a life of thought once again. Long ago Valmiki wrote the epic Ramayana and again Tulsi Das, in the Mughal period, produced a work based on the story of Rama from the Ramayana. He placed devotion of each relationship in the epic, as supreme. Being in the local dialect, it at once caught the imagination of the Hindu masses. When Tulsi Das sang the glory of Rama, Sur Das sang his poems in praise of Lord Krishna. Dara Shikoh, the eldest son of Shahjehan was to write *Majma-ul-Bharain*, a comparative study of both Hindu and Muslim philosophy.

Shahjahan–an architect of immortal love (AD 1628-1658)

Jahangir may have clandestinely hastened the death of his father; not so his son, Shahjahan. Instead, he had to liquidate his brothers to wear the crown. He inherited an empire, peaceful and well governed. There were distant territories, particularly in the south, which he was able to win because of his superior soldiering. The Mughal empire, during the reign of Shahjahan was not only the richest but the most powerful in the world. A kindly person by nature, he looked upon his subjects as his family. The empire was bursting with revenue. Afghans, Turks, Persians and Rajputs cooperated with the king in administering the far-flung territories.

As a young prince of 20 years, he was married to Mumtaz Mahal. Shahjehan got the crown after waiting for sixteen years. This must have produced in him intense desires to fulfil his natural instincts and spend on the luxuries of the court. Jewellery, pearls and diamonds were his ways to announce his majesty. His dual personality often makes future observers of his rule wonder. Perhaps he possessed some streaks of extravagance that forced him to impose the burden of extra taxation on his subjects!

Contribution to architecture

Shahjahan and Mumtaz Mahal lived together as king and queen only for three years. The agony of her death must have been too severe to bear. A later study of his character reveals a change in his attitude towards secularism. He started construction of the Taj Mahal immediately after Mumtaz's death. It took twenty-one years and 20,000 men, with the most renowned architects of the world, to complete the marvel. There was no dearth of money or material for its construction. The treasury was full with gold and the Maharaja of Jaipur was showing his friendship and munificence by providing the best marble available in the country.

The peacock throne, prepared at considerable cost, was the most valuable throne in the world. The envy of kings, studded with the famous Kohinoor, it was to invite ruin for the residents of Delhi. The famous Taj Mahal, the great Jama-Masjid, the Red Fort at Delhi with its white palace and its interior structure, *Dewan-i-Am* and *Dewan-i-Khas*, at Agra, were completed by Shahjahan in his lifetime. These marvels of human genius are a permanent reminder of India's affluence during the Mughal rule. They attract millions of tourists from all over the world every year

Besides the famous buildings, Mughals were meticulous in constructing their palaces with gardens, mosques and flower fountains. Their remnants silently narrate the history of their times. It is a wonder that such great works of art and architecture were conceived and completed in less than a human lifespan. Future generations remember the king who planned and financed these projects. They also remember the artisans who affectionately toiled to translate the dreams of their rulers into reality. The progeny of these artisans even today carry on their ancestral profession in the lanes and bylanes of Agra and Delhi. The craftsmanship in marble, the inlay work, and gold thread designing on silk, are some of the traditional handicrafts that still remind us of their ingenuity. Modern technology may have placed them temporarily on the sideline, but the immortality of their art will keep emerging and haunting technology itself.

Glamour follows greed

Shahjahan's acute fondness for glamour required more and more money. He therefore resolved to tax the population. He always esteemed valuable gifts from his nobles and subjects. Obsessed with power and glory, he changed the direction of policies laid down by Akbar and continued by his father. There was a decline in the quality of court management. Self-advancement of courtiers was weakening the administration. Bribery started from the top and filtered down below. Afghan, Persian and Turk governors of the kingdom started looking for opportunities to be independent. Religious priests, who had laid low since Akbar's rule, raised their heads to get back the powers they had enjoyed in the beginning The Mughal empire had reached its zenith. Greed for more money, hidden craving for independence by governors of distant territories announced that the decline had really started.

After the death of Mumtaz Mahal, a grief-stricken Shahjahan became incapable of managing the affairs of the court. He was being alienated from his people, who felt that the clergy was interfering in their religions freedom. Having seen better days during the rule of Akbar, they all the more felt this change. His wife no more by his side, he spent most of his time with wine. As old age weakened Shahjahan, his sons started to play the 'family sport'. Aurangzeb emerged the winner, killing his brothers. He put his father in the Red Fort as a prisoner. Shahjahan spent the rest of his life looking longingly at the Taj Mahal from his prison-cell. The only close companion to the broken man was his daughter, Jahan Ara. She would obediently look after her father for the rest of his miserable years, willingly choosing to lead the life of a prisoner.

Shahjahan's love for beauty

We learn history from the architecture and literature of the times. Personal likes and dislikes can influence written descriptions of events and their causes, the works left for future generations silently express the truth. The entire range of these works during the Mughal period illustrate the taste and calligraphy of the Mughal dynasty. The fortified palaces, designed for safety and elegant living, palaces of the nobles with imaginative arrangements for climatic changes, the large places for devotional assemblies, the expansive gardens throughout the country, remain a permanent tribute to their artistic culture, refinement of taste and immense love for the country.

We, in modern times, wonder how all these projects were conceived, planned and executed in a single generation! The zeal, energy and endeavour of not only the planners but also of the executors must have been enormous. The kings, nobles and above all, millions of men and women, contributed their labour and skills for creating a heritage which would last for generations. These works of architecture serve as monuments of their love and devotion for the country. They serve as reminders of how new cultures mingle with the established to produce a new, more robust culture than the earlier one. This is the secret of continuity in diversity; that is what makes an Indian feel proud of his/her heritage. It becomes the sacred duty for all who breathe her air, enjoy the romance of seasons, taste the vast variety of fruits and vegetables of her produce and enjoy freedom to follow any faith, not to squander but to preserve this precious heritage.

Shahjahan had set a bloody convention to reach the throne. He had physically removed his brothers. Now, when he himself was old, the same practice caught up with his sons, Aurangzeb, killed both his brothers to reach the peacock throne. One of them was Dara Shikoh, the favourite of Shahjahan, and also the most deserving and capable to be king of India.

The actions of elders leave a permanent impression on tender minds.

Aurangzeb—a victim of theocratic teaching (AD 1658-1707)

Young Aurangzeb began his education at the late age of 10 years. A mullah, well-versed in Quran, was given charge to teach and groom the young prince.

The mullah treated Aurangzeb like any other Muslim boy of his time. He made the prince cram the Quran sans understanding it. He gave lessons in Persian and Arabic grammar so as to be able to read and write. The teacher would lace his time with appropriate flattery; some abstract knowledge of geography and history. The sum and substance of his teachings was to put into the head of the prince that nothing exists beyond the great kingdom of his ancestors. He put into the head of his pupil that the knowledge he imparted was all there was to know in this world. Modern psychologists would not be surprised in the least, if such a boy when adult, would behave like an ordinary, narrow-minded, but aggressive adult!

Modern science considers that the nature and behaviour of man is moulded by his subconscious mind that he inherits and acquires during his childhood. A study of Aurangzeb's behaviour truly reflects this maxim. As a young student, he was totally possessed with what his mullah taught him. At one stage, he had even decided to relinquish the world to become a saint. As he grew in age, he realized the damage done to his personality by the kind of education, religious priests had given him. The 'education' imparted to him had made him a narrow-minded, religious bigot. As he grew, he would live in a make-belief world of religious rituals. So much so, that after he had fought his way to the throne, he considered stitching caps to make a 'living'.

Ambition without understanding

As Aurangzeb settled to govern, he started dreaming grand images of extending his territory with the strength of his army and religious faith. Without assessing the adminstrative condition of his empire, he aspired to reach Maharashtra and Rajasthan. He personally conducted several campaigns to bring Shivaji and other Jat chieftains under his dominion. Lacking perception, however, he did not understand the impossibility of governing them. In a country where distances were long and communications medieval, it was impossible to keep the line of supply protected. Besides, most of the chieftains had already accepted the suzerainty of the Mughal Empire. There was therefore no particular need to disturb this stability, more so when the loyalty of his governors was in doubt.

As for their passion for Islam, the Arabs, Turks, Afghans and later Mughal invaders came with similar slogans. With considerable intensity, zeal and even cruelty, they ruled India. Rulers had by now realized that a highly religion oriented people, following their own faiths, could not be made to change whatever be its tributes or tribulations. People of different religions, having long lived in India, had succeeded in developing a common language, culture, and a way of life in harmony with her environment. Yet, influenced by his earlier religious impregnation, he followed the dangerous path.

Ultimately, his wrong assessment of the political situation, religious fanaticism and a narrow outlook of the future, became the cause of the ruin of the Mughal empire.

A fatal fault

When the treasury desperately needed money, Aurangzeb introduced special taxes on other religious communities than his own. This did gladden the clergy but angered his subject. The work started by Akbar to assimilate different religions into nationhood, damaged by Jahangir and Shahjahan, was being eroded by Aurangzeb. Hindus, Sikhs and Christians considered the law 'repugnant to justice', as indeed it was. The policy may have succeeded in fetching some money and converting a few people to Islam, but it grievously destroyed the foundations of the Mughal empire. Aurangzeb remained blissfully unaware of dramatic changes in other parts of the world. These were to effect the empire soon enough. Living in a world of religious fantasies, stitching caps to 'make a living', he did not even had the foresight to inquire from the representatives of the East India Company, about the political situation in the West. His mind was engulfed in religious bigotry; more fit to be an insignificant teacher of some primary school, than to be the king of Hindustan; he neither possessed nor acquired the qualities that make rulers.

The Sikhs in the north had been facing prosecution for some time. Being a martial religion, it began gathering nationalist forces around the Jats from the mid-west. The Marathas from the south made governance difficult for Mughal chieftains. Soon pressure from north and south weakened the will of the army. Ranjit Singh and Shivaji challenged Mughal supremacy. Both carved out large territories for themselves. Aurangzeb's policy of delving in religion had become self-destructive. Having conquered a greater part of Punjab, Ranjit Singh even threatened Afghanistan. The famous Kohinoor was possessed during those days by the Amir of Afghanistan. The Amir, being much attached to the precious stone, always had it hidden in his turban. One of Ranjit Singh's spy passed on this secret to him. So, during the banquet given by the 'Lion of Punjab' to celebrate signing of a treaty between them, he insisted exchanging turbans with his honoured guest as a sign of friendship and thus got back the Kohinoor!

Wisdom in old age

In his old age, having grown wiser by experience, he regretted the past. Why was a teacher like Aristotle who taught Alexander, or a Chanakya who trained Chandragupta not available to him in his youth? He may have perhaps thought of Bairam Khan, who taught his great-grandfather Akbar the art of war and governance. The following lines reveal his regrets:

I know not, who I am, where shall I go, or what will happen to this sinner full of sins. God has been in my heart yet my eyes did not recognize light. There is no hope for me in future.

Ironically, his teacher having fallen on evil days, wrote his pupil a letter seeking favour for services rendered in the past. Aurangzeb's response to the plea, express the indignation and frustration of a failed emperor:

What is it you want for me? Do you dare desire me to make you a minister in my court? I will frankly tell: Had you taught me the manner a prince needs to be taught, I would have seen fairness in your request. I am convinced that if a boy is properly taught, he is eternally obliged to his teacher, as he is to his father. What, instead have you taught me? You taught me that their is a small island 'Frangistan' (England); that the greatest kings governed Portugal, Holland, France and Indonesia. You mentioned that they are petty kings compared to the kings of Hindustan. Now I know that this is fake history and false geography.

You ought to have taught me their strengths, weaknesses, customs, religions and their style of governance. You should have told me how they rose and fell. You did not even give me full details of my own grandfather and great-grandfather. How did they conquer, administer and rule such a vast empire for centuries?

Instead you taught me Arabic and Persian for ten years. Indeed I am obliged to you for wasting my time on learning a language that would make me a good scholar. The knowledge needed by a prince was not taught, but time was wasted on trifles.

You ought to know that childhood is the period to learn. This learning lasts for a long time. It keeps a mind active; it inspires to achieve great goals. To my father (Shahjehan) you told that you were teaching me philosophy. What you really taught were fanciful phrases of no use to society. Had you taught how to reason, had you given me the knowledge to raise oneself above prosperity or downfall; had you instilled in me thoughts that Aristotle taught Alexander, it would have been my duty to acknowledge them with reward.

So, go back to where you have come and don't let anyone know who you are.

Aurangzeb's rebuff is a grim reminder of the harm that misguided education inflicts on innocent minds. Fundamentalist education that does not teach love may succeed in exciting passions for hatred and violence. However, it leaves the student narrow-minded and deluded forever. The letter expresses Aurungzeb's urge for learning, when experience had enriched his wisdom. It reflects his sadness for not learning the history, the laws, the philosophy and political situation in other countries.

Rise of Marathas and Sikhs

The farmers beyond the Western Ghats have been traditionally peaceful. Rulers of Delhi occasionally required mercenaries to manage territories beyond Gujarat. Their local chiefs employed these farmers. In due course, they discovered in Marathas streaks of martial valour. Soon they were hired for more responsible functions in the south. With time, when they got aware of their own potential they thought; " When we are good at fighting, why not we be our own masters?" The feelings grew stronger as kings like Aurangzeb tempered their social and religious freedom. As the Mughal empire extended further south, greater grew their resolve. This went on until an intelligent strategist and a brave warrior with quick reflexes took over the command. Giving a taste of the enemy's own plans, he would tire out organized armies of Mughals in the hills and forts of his territory.

The might of this extraordinary general began to be felt throughout India. In the south even the Mughal officers felt terrified with the speed and surprise of Shivaji. Their concentration however remained more on gaining wealth than territories. The religious and patriotic feelings of people were thus aroused. After his death, others who followed, could only keep up the pressure. It was Bajirao, who after winning Gujarat and Malwa from the Mughals, reached the gates of Delhi. Just when the throne of Delhi was within their grasp, destiny disturbed their plans. Nadir Shah from Afghanistan descended on Delhi like a demon of death and destruction. He plundered and massacred the population; took the riches of kings, nobles and ordinary citizens to his home. It was Nadir Shah who looted the famous peacock throne and took it back with him to Persia where it remained in one piece.

Taking a cue from Nadir Shah, the glitter of gold, began attracting them as well. The farmers turned soldiers, began dissipating their energy in petty gains from areas still under their influence. They could however never make an impression of a joint force guided by a common purpose. Each looked to safeguard his interests; the gain of one was a loss to the other. Gaekwads, Holkars, Scindias, and other princes fell one by one. While one was fighting, his neighbour looked the other way. He would remain a mere spectator. We have noticed this tendency in the Indian psyche from the beginning. While reflecting on the events later, we may analyse how this poison of individuality unconsciously finds a corner in Indian minds?

The middle of the eighteenth century saw the Mughal Empire in tatters. Greedy eyes, from across the border were just waiting for such a situation. Taking advantage of the chaos, another Afghan, Ahmed Shah Abdali, came to loot and plunder. Here was the need of a leader who could assess comparative strength and plan for an effective resistance! This was not to be. From the earliest times, India's Achilles heel had been individuality and dissension amongst different sections at the time of crisis. The Marathas were no exception. Their forces fought Ahmed Shah on the fields of Panipat. Maratha chiefs, taking advantage of each other's weaknesses, could not unite to fight the common enemy. A crushing defeat and mass massacre amongst the Marathas cast a gloom in their camp.

After sometime, the tragedy was forgotten. The Marathas regrouped themselves. With a strong will power, they kept attacking Mughal forces wherever they found them weak. So doing, they reached even the southern banks of river Ganga in north India. Time and chance waits for none. The Marathas had lost their opportunity. They, out of sheer bravado, had attacked a robber and wasted their strength. Had they thought with unity of purpose, it should have occurred to the Marathas that Abdali was really helping them by weakening the Mughals. The Marathas were always in confrontation with three powerful enemies: the Nizam of Hyderabad, Haider Ali of Mysore and the English. The first two were won in wars; the English held others through diplomacy. The last Mughal emperor Bahadur Shah ruled only a few square miles of territory from inside the Red Fort.

The Delhi crown was to have been of Marathas, but for their individuality in action and concentration only on getting a share in the revenue (*chauth*).

Power equations were now rapidly changing. The British and the Sikhs in the north, were the rising stars. Both were struggling for ascendancy. One with better resources, diplomatic skill and superiority of arms and strategy, would ultimately be victorious. We have earlier read about the founder of the Sikh religion, Guru Nanak. An account of his followers will briefly provide an insight into their character.

Rise of Sikhs

The birth of the Mughal empire and the Sikh religion was almost in the same period. Like other saints of the fifteenth century, Guru Nanak preached brotherhood of Hindus and Muslims. His religious philosophy rested on oneness. This is what the Vedas and Upanishads, Jains and Buddhists had been advocating. With a philosophy of peace and brotherhood, there could hardly be any preparations or thoughts for struggle. For more than hundred years, Sikh religion kept expanding. Akbar, as a mark of respect for the religion, granted the Sikhs land for construction of the Golden Temple at Amritsar. Trouble started when Jahangir tortured to death the fifth Sikh guru Arjan Dev, charging him for militancy. This aroused the ire of the Sikhs. They launched a crusade against the death of their Guru. The sixth Guru Har Govind was imprisoned for ten years. From then on, the Mughals and Sikhs were on a warpath. This religious persecution intensified during the rein of Aurangzeb. The ninth Guru Teg Bahadur was asked to embrace Islam. His refusal to do so cost him his life. Therefore the tenth Guru Govind Singh made the Sikhs into a militant and powerful community. As they found their faith attacked, they resolved to destroy the Mughal Empire.

Decline of the Mughal empire

The political jigsaw that was India during this period had several players in the ring. Amongst the Europeans, there were the Portuguese, the French, the Dutch and the English. Within the empire, there were Mughal *satraps*, Maratha princes like Gaekward, and the rich merchants of Kolkata whose interests were being trampled. The Mughal king at Delhi was only a figurehead, confined to his own little world, writing good Urdu poetry which we listen to often even today. Amongst the religiously persecuted were the Rajputs, Jats, Marathas and Sikhs. These sons of the soil were carpenters, weavers, masons, tanners and sweepers. It was virtually a mini revolt against the empire, heralding the end of monarchy. Stray battles in different parts of India brought the Europeans powers to mediate between the two fighting factions. Like the story of a cunning monkey, they would take advantage from both the fighting factions— the disputants having to remain content with nothing.

Empires, in the past, have declined and fallen on losing their economic strength. Political events are not so much guided by moral forces as with economic reasons; if at all, they only serve as a cover. It is the rise or fall of economic activity that ultimately determines the curve of weakness and strength. 'Ideals' flaunted by the leader, are in reality a mere show; they only announce the material needs disguised as morals and faith. The Mughal empire suffered economic losses when the rulers started religious discrimination amidst their subjects. A large purse was spent to sustain wars in South India. This made the farmers flee from their lands. It made local governors bold enough to defy central authority. The soil turned barren and unproductive; the *satraps* did not let taxes reach the treasury. The fall of the empire became a natural consequence.

We have seen a similar thing happening three hundred years later with the British empire. Even after winning the war in 1945, the empire stood economically exhausted. It was wisdom's calling to make the liquidation of the empire in India an honourable affair.

To continue with our story, the sun of the British empire was on the rise. The next three hundred years were destined to transform Indian civilization as nothing had done in thousand years. Its progress in science and literature would take the world towards a global unity that the ancient Indian sages sang of in the Vedas. It would make different races, cultures and languages take a new direction. The universal play of 'unity in diversity' first discovered by Indian sages, would move towards realization of this truth. The West would bring material sciences to join hands with the spiritual philosophy of the East. Indian spiritual works would be translated from Sanskrit to European languages. India would commence her journey on the way to a synthesis of material and spiritual sciences.

Chapter XXVI
Contribution of Islamic Civilization

Banaa Banaa ke jo dunyia mitai jaati hai,
Zuroor koi kami hai jo pai jaati hai.
(There must be some shortcoming, for the
world to be destroyed and rebuilt again and again.)

—Jigar Muradabadi

Civilizations are like river water streams. Emerging from the high mountains, crisscrossing their way, they majestically flow and fertilize the plains. At the end of their journey, they become one with the ocean. This cycle starts again when the sun transforms waters of the ocean into clouds. The rains in the mountains keep perennially feeding the streams with freshness. Civilizations follow this eternal law of Nature. Each new civilization that is born helps fertilize life-giving elements. This enables a thousand flowers to bloom. Then, having served its purpose, the flowers that once bloomed, have to wither.

The Islamic civilization began from Syria. It reached the West as far as Spain and in the East it extended till Persia. The Syrians at that time adored Aristotle. The Arabs were thus able to acquire knowledge of philosophy from the Syrians. It was but natural that basic philosophical thinking in Islam is based on Aristotle's ideas. The Arabs had conquered a great part of the world in the name of religion. Initially ruthless, even cruel, in time they settled down as liberal rulers, keen to learn the higher cultures they had won. The seat of Islamic power was initially Damascus. It shifted later to Baghdad, on the main route of international commerce. Location of Baghdad encouraged trade and brought riches, prosperity and closer connection between people of the same faith. The Arabs translated the encyclopaedia on medicine and surgery compiled by Indian men of medicine, Sushruta and Charaka, in several languages. This enabled medical knowledge to reach different parts of the world.

Contribution to philosophy

During the ascendancy of Islam, the world's civilization was attended and cultivated through translations by people like Musa-ul-Qwarazini. He was an Arabic scholar who came to Varanasi and learned Sanskrit for the purpose.

He found in India that material in astronomy, mathematics and medicine, which was not to be found anywhere else. Simultaneously, Persian scholars studied the Greek civilization. They translated the wisdom and knowledge of Pythagoras, Socrates, Heraclitus, Hippocrates and several others. The civilization of Islam flourished when Christianity was passing through its 'Dark Age'. Knowledge of centuries, left by thinkers of Greece, Syria and India, was waiting to be co-ordinated in the service of humanity. Arab scholars took up the colossal and arduous task of its preservation and utilization through translations in different languages. To add to its knowledge, they translated ancient Sanskrit and Greek works into Arabic. Europe would later use it to enter the new era of science.

Two names dominate in philosophy: Ibn Sina of Bukhara (AD 930) taught philosophy and medicine. In his later years he thought like Aristotle and went to Europe to teach medicine. The other, Ibn Sina (AD 980-1037), essentially a man of medicine, was popular with the princes for his medical knowledge then taught by Ibn Rushid as a learned scholar of medicine, philosophy and mathematics. He worked at the court of Caliph Yakub. Ibn Rushid's successor was Al-Mansur. He was a liberal, reformist character who said, "God had decreed hellfire for those who thought that truth could be found by the unaided reason." Ibn Rushid, like the next generation of Islamic thinkers, did not encourage orthodox theology that considered all philosophy to be detrimental to religious orthodoxy. It was claimed that since necessary truth is in the scriptures, there was no need for independent speculation.

Being against orthodoxy, the Caliph had all his works destroyed.

Because of such restraints from the clergy and the caliph, inspiration for original thought could not flourish to its full potential. Another reason was the fast and action-oriented period in which Islam overwhelmed more mature societies in a short period. Original thought however takes its own time and leisure.

To poetry and literature

Poetry and literature, in Islamic society, has always been held high. Everyone has heard of the man, with a 'book of verse and cup of wine', enjoying the bounties of nature. The world knows him as Omar Khayyam (AD 1050), one of the greatest poets ever. The fact that he was also a mathematician and astronomer is however less known. As an astronomer in the royal court, he was engaged with several other scientists to reform the calendar. Their work helped adoption of a new Islamic era. As a writer on algebra, geometry and related subjects, Omar was the most noted mathematician of his time. The world however knows him for his *Rubaiyat*. Some of his popular couplets are:

It is dawn. A rise, o essence of delight.
Drink softly, playing the harp.
Leave those who are asleep. They will not find the truth.
Leave those who are gone. They will never return.
The world is now in its happy season
And every living heart wants to be out of town.
The blossoms shine like the light in Mose's hand
And the breeze revives like the breath of Jesus.

What I desire is a flask of ruby wine,
A book of poems, a half loaf of bread.
I and you alone in wilderness—
That is better than all the sultan's empire.

Before the lancer of death charges,
Ask for the scarlet wine.
You are not gold, You careless fool!
To be buried and dug up again.

Those flowers of human intellect
Ascending the heaven of thoughts.
Tried to discover the secret of the self;
But failing, because like the skies, errant, whirling and lost.

There was another great poet and philosopher–Khalil Gibran. Born in Syria, he settled in America in the beginning of the twentieth century. His proverbs, poetry and stories narrating moral lessons, contain a message for all. On knowledge, one of his poems says:

Knowledge is a light, enriching
The warmth of life, and all may
Partake who seek it out; but you
My countrymen seek out darkness
And flee the light, awaiting the
Coming of the water from the rock,
And your nation's misery is your
Crime...... I do not forgive you
Your sins, for you know what you
Are doing.

Humanity is a brilliant river
Singing its way and carrying with
It the mountains' secrets into
The heart of the sea; but you,
My countrymen are stagnant
Marshes infested with insects
And vipers.

Firdausi (AD 941) was both a poet and historian. At the initiative of Mohammed Ghazni, Firdausi is said to have written *Shahnama*– a description of war records between Alexander and Darius, the king of Persia, who was defeated in course of Alexander's march towards India. *Shahnama* also describes the achievements of Ghazni and several other kings.

Islam preserved the elements of civilization at a critical juncture when there was darkness all around. Through translations and mutual contact in different countries, Islamic writers translated international works of value. These helped the availability of collective wisdom without which progress is almost impossible. Before all these efforts could bear fruits, Mongolian hordes from North Asia came to destroy the edifice built with such hard labour, ruthlessly.

Urdu as a medium of communication in India developed during the Mughal rule. Several distinguished Urdu poets wrote verses which are still enjoyed by people of all communities in India. Mir Taqi Mir, Ghalib and Mohammed Iqbal and many others have made outstanding contribution to Urdu poetry. Their verses reveal both mystical and mundane ideas that dominated their times.

> When yesterday, by chance, I stepped on a skull
> Shattered it lay with a thousand knocks.
> "Walk warily, thou headless," thus spoke the skull,
> "I too, was someone's head, drunk deep with pride."
>
> —Mir Taqi Mir

> I now wish to live a lonesome place,
> With none to converse, none to communicate.
> I would build a house without a door or a wall,
> There shouldn't be a neighbour, there wouldn't be a watch
> If I fall sick, none should come to attend,
> And none to mourn, if I depart.
>
> —Mirza Ghalib

> "Do good and thou shall be blessed!"
> This is all a *darvesh* can say.
> Here I give my life for you,
> What else is prayer, I do not know.
>
> —Mirza Ghalib

Mohammed Iqbal was a great Urdu poet-philosopher of modern times. His life and work have been studied ahead. He lived in the times when British ruled India. Literature and poetry was again helping awaken a slumbering

Views of the palace of Delhi—the Red Fort.
The whole length of line from Shah Burj (Top) and a portion of
Dewan-i-Khas (Right)

The Koodseea Bagh or garden built by Koodseea Begum, the mother of Emperor Mahumud Shah

Artist's impressions of the impressive Qutub Minar in Delhi (Top and Below)

nation. We will come across Iqbal's poetry that shook the British Raj and infused such patriotism amongst Indians of his time!

To art and architecture

During the early momentum, Islam reached Cairo, Jerusalem, Istanbul, Baghdad and Delhi. After the quest for conquest subsided, the phase of refinement and culture commenced. Art and architecture being lasting creations, sultans and caliphs expressed themselves in bricks and mortar. With faith as their guide, they liked to transmit their feelings and emotions through construction of mosques. The great, spacious mosques in cities they conquered appeared to be ideal to follow in those tumultuous times. The are also a tribute to their intentions of ploughing back the wealth of the country for the good of local inhabitants.

In India, Qutub Minar is the first perfect work of architecture built by the Afghans. It signifies the maturity of construction and displays the glory of the rulers. The greatest contribution in architecture however was destined to be made by the Mughal rulers. Except for Babar and Humayum whose tenure was tumultuous and short, all others were devotees of the art of construction. With their love for grandeur, and a high sense of cultural refinement, they left behind monuments of marvel. Akbar was the first to build his father's tomb in Delhi and his own at Sikandra near Agra. True to his secular character, he built an entirely new city at Fatehpur Sikri near Agra. It is a perfect example of the vastness of space and thoroughness of planning. His vision of unity is visible in the designs that reflect an amalgam of Hindu and Islamic art. The marble tomb of Salim Chisti is a tribute of his sincerity towards a benefactor and friend. The significant factor of Islamic architecture is their use of flowers and geometrical designs for decoration to enhance the beauty of their works.

His son, Jehangir, true to his nature, confined his artistic expressions to making palaces of glass for himself.

Amongst Mughals, Shahjahan remains immortal. He planned the Jama Masjid and the Fort at Delhi. With their halls of public and private audience, they are amongst the best works. There is also the wonder of the world, one of the most perfect buildings on earth and the crowning glory of Islamic architecture–the Taj Mahal.

Reforms–the key

Mohammedan civilization, during its days of glory excelled in arts, poetry and technical innovations. We read how Al-Mansur, published and edited that "God has decreed hell for those who thought that truth can be found unaided by reason." The Caliph, out of fear of the orthodox, got all the books burnt. He deprived Al-Mansoor of his title and imprisoned him, accusing him of teaching ancient philosophy at the expense of faith.

Incidents like these, where reason is sacrificed, become a breeding ground of obscurantism and fantasia; fresh thought is stifled; faith, without new nourishment, is denied the warmth of enfolding and embracing other faiths. How often, such incidents in history suddenly reverse progress of societies? Repeatedly such a situation has occurred wherever reforms are resisted. Under the garb of scriptural authority, the priests in every religion tend to be greedy for power. They interpret every direction of the prophets to suit and serve themselves. Orthodoxy, under pretext of preservation of faith, does not accept change. This happened in the past; it is happening at present. Self-interest of the priestly class fights to dominate reason, sacrificing truth at the altar of faith! Thus do they deprive innocent followers of liberty. In the absence of impediments to think independently, adjustment in an ever changing world, becomes difficult for the common man and woman. In societies where education is still in its infancy, it falls on intellectuals and legislators to prescribe alternatives to check despotism. Past history is a witness that interpretation of religion by priests are governed by punishment and rewards of an invisible power. Under this garb does superstition flourish!

Environment, under which religions grow, keeps on changing. Every religion, after a period, requires reforms. Reforms are essentially introduction of compassion and homogeneity in human affairs. These become necessary to maintain a peaceful balance in societies. Reforms therefore are a continuing process. They are essential for optimum use of nature's resources. This requires application of new ideas that are ever growing, offering opportunities in education and better living conditions.

West Comes to East
(AD 1500-1947)

Oh, East is East and West is West.
And never the twain shall meet
Till Earth and sky stand presently
At God's great judgement seat!

—*Rudyard Kipling*

Chapter XXVII
Impact of European Renaissance

Nature and Nature's laws lay hid in night.
God said, 'Let Newton be', and all was light.

The campaigns of Alexander of Greece had helped spread knowledge from Greece to the countries in the East. It reached as far as the banks of river Indus enriching the Arabs on the way. After a period of darkness in Europe, it was the turn of the Arabs who introduced a great period of creative discoveries. Renaissance in the West began on the footprints of this knowledge with Roger Bacon (1294); it grew with the limitless Leonardo da Vinci, it reached fulfilment in the astronomy of Copernicus and Kepler. As knowledge grew, fear decreased. Men thought less of worshipping the unknown and more of overcoming it. There was confidence in the air.

Armed with the gift of reason and science, the new Intellectual class fought the orthodoxy of the priests. Powerful and adventure-loving nations were now daring to establish empires in different parts of the world. Men who took risk were ambitious, vigorous and inspired warriors, willing to create opportunities! The illusion of 'contemplative' life had, largely, ceased to impress the brave and intelligent in the West. The two pioneers who triggered the new era were Leonardo da Vinci and Galilei Galileo. When Galileo told the priests that the world was round, he was charged for inquisition because the scriptures said otherwise.

'But your Holiness, come with me to the seashore. I will show you that when a distant ship is approaching the coast, we first see the mast of the ship' so said Galileo to the Pope. He was however not prepared to listen to what was against the scriptures. Galileo had to face an inquisition. To save himself from ignominy, he reluctantly and under fear, apparently consented. However, truth goaded his conscience. He reverted to the truth. Galileo, for this effrontery had to suffer for the rest of his life. Galilio and Leonardo da Vinci were two extraordinarily talented and gifted men with sharp intellects. They applied their imagination to the arts and sciences of life. Leonardo da Vinci synthesized scientific investigations into artistic expressions. He conceived war machines, airplanes, submarines, parachutes and armoured cars, the kinds of machines in use today. He expressed his artistic emotions in immortal paintings like the *Mona Lisa* and the *Last Supper.*

Copernicus and Kepler, the two western astronomers, with their discovery, advanced astronomy. The indomitable human spirit accepted the challenge of untamed nature. The fearful roar of oceans that scared children by the seaside now became friendlier. The young lads longed to go sailing in distant lands. Adventurers, traders, merchants and even plunderers became more self-assured. Sailing the seas was no more a matter of chance. With the help of new scientific instruments, seamen knew their correct positions. Captains of ships, on dark, cloudy nights, faced the storms with confidence. The dread and uncertainties of the ocean no more deterred seamen from sailing on uncharted oceans. With bigger and better boats, men became bolder and more adventurous; economic activity received a big boost; sea routes to prized countries of wealth, were more easily accessible. Merchants were attracted to carry commodities by sea instead of land. In the excitement for adventure, not only new routes, but new continents were discovered. Columbus, a Spaniard, assigned by the king to find the sea route to India, landed up discovering America (1494). Vasco da Gama, a Portuguese, succeeded in reaching the West Coast of India (1498). Captain Cook, an Englishman, out on a mission to study planets, found the continent of Australia.

Growth of science—decline of religion

With science revealing the truth of nature, priests in the West started losing their high status. People were more prepared to accept what appealed to reason than what the priests asked them to believe. Truth had uncovered bigotry! The unholy bond between kings and priests loosened. Democracies began to emerge. In a few centuries, most of the kings would be gone. The authority of priests fell in direct proportion to awareness amongst the people. During the period of ignorance, priests had enjoyed absolute power, as in India. They quoted revelations and mystic tales from the scriptures to capture the minds of innocent people. The new class that now emerged used deductive reasoning in explaining natural phenomena. They studied the regular as well as periodical changes in nature, made observations, reasoned out conclusions and bravely contradicted the scriptures when they were against the truth. Rene Descartes of France was a pioneer in advocating the truth even while it contradicted faith. Descartes announced that "reason was an inborn light with us, and it is with this light that we must pursue discovery of truth."

Tools of progress now available soon altered the economic and political structure. So long as this knowledge was lacking, it was compulsive for people to seek consolation in faith and be humble before the 'representatives of gods'.

As scientific discoveries revealed nature and its secrets, there was greater confidence in human spirit. Rational explanations rather than blind faith would henceforth guide the material and spiritual life of the West. Science had made men look forward to the future with confidence.

The spirit of change

Great changes and movements in the world are generally due to economic reasons. A long period of peace in both the East and the West, improved the economy. This encouraged people towards creative activities. Men of genius, were encouraged to bring out their best in different fields of human endeavour. With development in sea-faring, geographical boundaries began to be threatened. Science was coming out with new knowledge. The new-found confidence made men achieve excellence in arts, architecture and philosophy. William Shakespeare excelled as a dramatist and playwright. His dramas reflected the struggle between the moral basis of truth and its conflicts. John Milton fought for freedom of the press through his poetry. Handel and Bach of Germany composed symphonies, in the later part of the seventeenth century, that elevated the soul. Amongst philosophers of the age, Francis Bacon of England became famous as a logician. Spinoza of Holland became famous for his *Ethics* and rules of logic. In architecture, Christopher Wren designed the St. Paul Cathedral in London. Isaac Newton from England harnessed astronomy in explaining the laws of motion and movements of planets. These helped the West to achieve supremacy on the seas. The light of rational inquiry, ignited by Descartes and Newton, now burnt brightly.

Following closely, were Harvey who discovered the science of blood circulation; Robert Boyle who is called the father of chemistry, established the laws of relationship between temperature and pressure; Napier became known for logarithms; co-ordinate geometry which was the result of the work of Rene Descartes; differential and integral calculus which emerged from the works of Newton and Leibniz; Torricelli who invented the barometer; and Guricka who made the first pump.

When men of science unravelled the truth, people ignored the belief that sun and planets were gods. As science started giving rational evidence of phenomena that had hitherto defied rational explanations, the hold of priests broke down. People would believe what they saw, rather than what the priests had been telling them. The curiosity that lay dormant, was awakened. The winds of change began to blow in all directions They began to have their effect all over the world. India would soon be influenced and have a taste of supremacy of science at the battle of Plassey. Geography cares but little for political frontiers. When an idea has matured, its vibrations are unstoppable. Suddenly, a fresh new wave began blowing all over the world. Authority of reason, instead of religion, had become supreme. Suddenly the aim of life was completely transformed. An ideal human being became the one whose aim was success in the world; not beyond it, as religion promised. This new image of a man ever-striving for success replaced the old religious view in which man's existence was conceived as a mere preparation for the promised life of luxury and happiness after death.

The gates of knowledge were now open. The new spirit of reflection and inquiry demolished old ideas and developed new ones. They were based not on heresy or mythology, but on sound observation and inference. The process let loose by science triggered a chain of development in generating wealth for a better life. By the end of the seventeenth century, science had completely displaced religion from its high pedestal. While minds of men in the sixteenth century remained old-fashioned, they turned progressive in the seventeenth century.

Thus science completely revolutionized man's place on earth. Most men of science were pious and well-meaning, but their works were not palatable to religious priests. As science triumphed, the sense of sin, inculcated by religion gave place to pride in achievement. This became the secret of success of Europeans in general and the Englishmen in particular. Thus inspired, they would go ahead to conquer the world. Knowledge that lay dormant due to control of education by men believing in superstition and persecution, had suddenly found freedom from the control of religion.

West comes to East

The Portuguese were, from the beginning, a sea-faring nation. Being first in finding the Indian sea-route, they started trading in Indian spices from the western coast. This business soon made the small country rich and prosperous. Watching Portugal prosper, their neighbours—France, Holland and England— also took the initiative to improve their ship-building industry. Like the Portugese, they developed their sea power for prosperity. Holland tried first to enter Indian markets. Greed for business soon triggered struggle between the two merchants. The Portuguese drove the Dutch out of India. Driven from India, they sought greener pastures in Indonesia. Entering that country as traders, the Dutch became her rulers.

France and Britain were, by now, ready with better and newer ships. Between the two, the French established their business at Pondicherry. Britain landed later at Goa, where the Portugese had their trading centre. Gradually the Portuguese proved weaker in comparison to the English. Even when the Portuguese tried, it became difficult to oust the English. In the battle at Surat Port, Portugal lost its possession. This left only France and Britain to compete with each other in India.

Indian internal situation

What was the internal situation in the country when the Europeans fought each other for trade in India?

Bound in blind belief, unable to enquire into the sequence of cause and effect, facing an uncertain future hostile to both reason and morality, men were led by priests rather than by their senses. Pursuing dead and fossilized traditions, irrational bigotry had choked the life stream of her people. The 'intellectuals' were busy inventing consolations for life after death. They were preaching better life in the next world by patiently bearing the present misfortunes. Anyone, who had some power, was prepared to fight, deceive, barter, negotiate and seek unscrupulous gains. The only law that governed was one of self interest at the expense of the weak. It was a game of survival at any cost.

Politically, the central authority of the Mughals lay in ruins due to persistent struggle with the Marathas, Rajputs and Jats in different parts of India. Struggle with the Marathas in south and central India, with the Sikhs in the north and the Jats, around Delhi, had strained the limited resources of Mughal armies. Their viceroys, finding central authority weakening, wanted to be masters of their territories themselves. They would lay claims to sovereignty on Imperial Provinces. Pretenders rose to challenge the usurpers; one who was strong in arms would win. In central India, Marathas saw and seized their chance. They would loot, raid and if possible rule. The country appeared heading towards anarchy.

In terms of defence, the greatest weakness of the Mughals was the neglect of sea power. Now, the Mughals were weak even on land. Such conditions of total turmoil must have been too tempting for plunderers across the border. If neglect of sea power invited unholy ambitions amongst western traders, its wealth invited looters and plunderers from across the border! Without much ado, Nadir Shah, the king of Persia, descended on the plains of Indus through the Khyber Pass. He had set his eyes on the fabulous wealth of the Mughals. Suddenly appearing in Delhi, during the summer of 1740, he ransacked that city, humiliated the emperor, slaughtered lakhs of her citizens and carried away loads of wealth including the famous peacock throne. The brutality he committed during his brief stay continued to send shivers of fear amongst the inhabitants of Delhi, where till not very long ago mothers would scare their children with the terror of Nadir Shah.

The raid, though short and swift, announced to the world that the once great Mughal empire was now permanently crippled. Whatever little dignity the king and the dynasty enjoyed, went away with the peacock throne.

Struggle between France and Britain

The plunder of Delhi by Nadir Shah changed the mood of both the British and the French. Meanwhile, another incident occurred that ignited the ambitions of both the trading nations. The Marathas from Pune, slaughtered the Nawab of Karnataka. The long coastline of Karnataka was punctuated with French and British business interests. Emboldened with their success, the Marathas even started threatening the business centres of the two western traders at Madras (now Chennai) and Bombay (now Mumbai). Under the circumstances, it was impossible for both trading companies to be passive onlookers and allow their business interests to suffer. The choice was either to quit the country or align with one of the fighting factions. Both chose not to quit. They realized that more than trade, there was fortune to gain in diplomacy and soldiery. The excellence of both in the affairs of warfare, found a profitable medium of expression. If England would support one faction, France would lend her martial skill to the opposite side. While both the fighting factions suffered, the 'two traders' had the best of the bargain. France and the English East India company now clearly perceived their opportunity. Who amongst the two would rule India in future? This would be decided between the two contenders on the battlefields of South India.

During the eighteenth century, European powers with their supremacy on the seas, were establishing their empires in different parts of the world. Anglo-French struggle for supremacy was not just confined to India. They were fighting each other in Europe, America and Africa; almost everywhere there was economic gains to achieve. In India, France had an able general and statesman in Dupleix. Besides strengthening business, he employed diplomacy and military tactics to secure territorial gains. He possessed a clear vision for the conquest of the country. In this respect, Dupleix was the first to have perceived the weak and chaotic conditions on the subcontinent.

In a decisive diplomatic stroke, Dupleix appealed to the Nawab of Karnataka to forbid hostilities within his business jurisdiction. This granted, the Nawab proceeded to attack Madras, where the English business interests were operating.

The English Governor sought similar neutrality as imposed at French business stations. Dupleix, along with his request, had however secretly followed it with a promise of military support to the Nawab if his request was accepted. He had also promised that after Madras, where the English were stationed, was conquered, it would be surrendered to the Nawab. Dupleix supported him with 230 French soldiers and 700 Indian mercenaries trained in the use of modern weapons.

Dupleix won this battle against an army of ten thousand opposing him and his ally.

The victory proved a morale booster for France. It further ignited the flame of greed to conquer the country, which, in any case, was waiting to be conquered. The British contingent, stationed at Chennai, had to seek refuge in the Fort. Amongst those hiding in the Fort, was a young clerk, Robert Clive. The result of this war on the policies of the trading companies was to be tremendous. Both the English and the French now inferred that Indian governance was impossible by any central Indian authority. From their experience of recruiting Indian mercenaries to fight their wars, they knew that patriotism in India was negotiable. Indians, they thought, could be hired and trained in the use of western weapons against their own compatriots.

After victory in Madras, contrary to his promise, Dupleix refused to surrender Madras to the Nawab. Clive was watching the entire struggle with awe and wonder. In the fight between two Indian pretenders, one was helped by France and the other by Britain. Mohammed Ali, supported by the British, was besieged in Trichinapoly. To relieve their ally, they proposed to come to his rescue at Trichinapoly. Clive suggested that instead of attacking the town, British forces attack Arcot, the capital of Karnataka. Clive argued that to save his capital, the Nawab would have to divert a large part of his force to Arcot. This policy worked according to plan. The potentate, dismayed by the fear of losing his capital, despatched a large part of his troops to Arcot. The struggle lasted for fifty-five days. One night Clive's forces attacked and routed their enemy.

With only two hundred British and six hundred Indians, Clive had not only won South India for his ally, but had laid the foundations of the British empire in India.

Dupleix now sought help from home. However, the French government was too engaged in internal unrest to listen to his request. Royalty that controlled the French company, was out of touch with realities. French vulnerability on the high seas was yet another fear. The British naval strength was a great deterrent. The French government refused to send any reinforcement. The collective will shown by London, was lacking in Paris. Instead of sending reinforcements, they ordered Dupleix to return home. The French fleet left South India in 1760. With it ended the French dream of conquering India!

The final stroke

The British conquest of India was stimulated by their rivalry with the French. The struggle between the two was then worldwide. It started with the Nawab of Murshidabad in Bengal ordering trading companies to pay the same taxes as their Indian counterparts. The French agreed but the British refused. The Nawab attacked Fort William forcing the British to retreat towards the sea, where they waited for reinforcement from South India. The reinforcement arrived soon. With them was Colonel. Clive. He, along with other British commanders, wove a complex web of intrigue, deceit and bargain with the Nawab's ministers and rich Indian merchants like Jagat Seth. They secretly engineered the ouster of the Nawab, promising them rewards for treachery. This was however only till the battle was won. They had secretly conspired to make Mir Jafar the Nawab. The battle of Plassey (1757) was an arranged affair in which economics played an important role. Mir Jafar commanded the major part of Nawab's army. This force did not take part in fighting at all. The Nawab was forced to flee and subsequently murdered. Thereafter started a chain of blackmail and extraction, of which there are few parallels.

Empires are seldom established by virtuous means; Satan governs the conduct of victors.

The battle of Plassey paved the road for British ascendancy in the whole of East India. The English now held all the strategic and fertile parts of the country. With the entire Gangetic valley under their control, the throne at Delhi was theirs for the asking. The riches of the fertile fields lay prostrate before the greed of the petty servants of the East India Company. Suspicion, in-fighting, opportunism, in fact every conceivable guile, recommended in Chanakya's *Arthashastra* and Machiavelli's *The Prince* were used on that day of 1757 at the small hemlet of Plassey. A small contingent of a few English and their trained Indian soldiers, with the help of deceit and treachery, opened the road to the crown of India.

Clive's triumph at Plassey created as many problems as it solved. The period that followed saw the throne of Bengal being auctioned to the highest bidder. The Company that had initially reached India for trading found its petty servants offered bribes and other attractions to the rich and wealthy of Calcutta. India would now pass through a dark and ugly period of ignominy, exploitation and shame.

Coming generations will realize how the conquest of India by Britain was stimulated by internecine quarrels within the country and trade rivalry between the British and the French. The government of England played little part. The british Empire in India emerged more under force of circumstances than by any wilful ambition.

Clive had now absolute authority over the fate of Bengal. With no laws but that of conscience, what happened was a logical conclusion of the ambitious, all-powerful 'brat', which Clive was from his early childhood. The East India Company having lost both its profits as well as its trading reputation was hurt.

The British Parliament tried him for corruption and fraud. His reply was remarkably sincere when he answered the charges. He said,

"Am I rather not deserving of praise for the moderation which marked my proceedings? Consider the situation which the victory at Plassey had placed me. Great princes were dependant on my pleasure; an opulent city lay at my mercy; its richest bankers bid against each other for my smiles."

After a long deliberation, British Parliament exonerated him. Perhaps the then members of Parliament were also shareholders of the East India Company. Yet his conscience kept troubling him. He ultimately committed suicide.

Time, chance and destiny brought centuries of knowledge in philosophy, sciences and arts that had by-passed India. As British administration consolidated, education brought her gifts. Indian intellectuals would grasp new opportunities to accelerate engines of growth.

Chapter XXVIII
Beginning of British Raj & Indian Renaissance

The responsibility of governing India
had been placed by the inscrutable
providence upon the shoulders
of the British race.

—Rudyard Kipling

British power was now reaching its zenith in maritime supremacy all over the world. Great naval and land battles were fought by British soldiers and seamen, who came from the school-playing fields of Eton, Rugby and Harrow. The youth who emerged as leaders from these institutions were men with the highest sense of discipline. The trial of Robert Clive by Parliament had shocked the conscience of the British people. The British Parliament realized that a company could not be allowed to rule the destiny of millions of inhabitants, just for making money and giving rich dividends to its shareholders. They were also ill prepared to take a direct responsibility for ruling a subcontinent from 3000 miles. As a compromise, they sent Warren Hastings, a capable administrator, to rule British territories as well as manage the trading affairs of the company.

> Ships, Ships, I will describe you,
> One goes abroad for merchandise and trading,
> Another stays to keep his country from invading,
> A third is coming home with rich and wealthy lading,
> Hello! my fancy, wither wilt thou go?

Warren Hastings

Warren Hastings came to India in 1772. He managed the Marathas, the Nizam, and Tipu Sultan in the south, with brilliant military tactics. The East India Company's administration was overhauled with better and devoted civil servants. This won him admiration of the company and his subordinates.

Modern India will consider the good that was done in that period of utter chaos. Imagine a condition where there was no authority to enforce law; no moral values to guide social interaction; and no promises to keep. It was a daunting task which only a disciplined and law-loving nation could have discharged. Some of the beneficial and far reaching changes in administration that have since blossomed, are a fitting epitaph for an otherwise kindly person:

1. Hastings was a connoisseur of literary works. As a lover of Indian literature and philosophy, he was the first to realize the spiritual value of Bhagwad Gita as a masterpiece of philosophy. To make it available to the world at large, he got it translated into English. This enabled the sacred book of the Hindus to be known all over the world. Therefore, the ancient philosophy of India, which may have otherwise remained buried, started gaining recognition. Thinkers in Europe, when they read the Gita, became aware of her rich ancient heritage for the first time. Hastings himself introduced the first translation thus:

   "The writings of the inhabitants of India will survive long after the British dominion in India shall have ceased to exist and the sources which it once yielded of wealth and power are lost to remembrance."

   Hastings had the understanding to recognize the wealth of thought in the Gita and the fallacy of power!

2. During those chaotic times, all sorts of conceivable evils had penetrated in to Hindu society. To provide a uniform law for all Hindus, Hastings directed codification of the Hindu laws. This would provide the foundation on which Raja Rammohun Roy of Bengal would later work to eradicate 'Suttee'.

3. Hastings formed the Asiatic Society of Bengal and helped in publication of the first English newspaper. This opened the world of thought and action to a country that had gone into a shell.

Hastings acted on the principle of understanding people through their language, literature, customs, poetry and mythology. As a leader with infinite responsibilities, he saw some subordinates of the company enriching themselves at the expense of the East India Company as well as the people. More than him, his men continued with the old traditions of bullying, grafting and creating division amongst princes as laid down by Clive. This policy helped the servants of the company acquire personal prosperity. Again, the wrath of the British people was aroused at the misdemeanour of Hastings. He was impeached by Burke, one of the finest orators of his period. The famous speech he delivered reflects the character and values held by the British race in the eighteenth century.

My lord, the business of this day is not the business of this man (Burke). It is not solely whether the prisoner (Hastings) at the bar be found innocent or guilty; but whether millions of mankind shall be made miserable or happy. We charge the offender with the offence that have roots in avarice, rapacity, pride, insolence, ferocity, treachery, cruelty, malignity of temper. In short, nothing that does not augur a total extinction of all moral principles, that does not manifest inveterate blackness of heart, dyed in grain with malice, vitiated, corrupted, gangrened to the very source. We have brought before you the chief of the tribe, the head of the whole body of eastern offenders; a captain general of inequality, under whom all the fraud, all the peculation, all the tyranny in India are embodied, disciplined, arrayed and paid. Warren Hastings has not left substance enough in India to rubric such another delinquent; it is with confidence that, ordered by the Commons, I impeach Warren Hastings Esquire of high crimes and misdemeanours. I impeach him in the name of Commons of Great Britain in Parliament assembled, whose national character he has dishonoured. I impeach him in the name of people of India whose laws, rights, and liberties, he has subverted, whose properties he has destroyed, whose country he has laid waste and desolate. I impeach him in the name and by virtue of those eternal laws of Justice, which he had violated. I impeach him in the name of human nature itself, which he has cruelly outraged, injured and oppressed in both sexes, in every age, rank, and condition of life.

The impeachment is part of history. It helps us understand the perishability of power and fallibility of contemporary assessment. It confirms that human nature is a combination of both good and bad. It is hard to determine when the angel in man may turn into a devil.

Members of Parliament, being also shareholders of the company, may have heard Burke with secret delight. There is no denying that Hastings and his men, in the early stage of British rule, did commit ignominious deeds usually warranted by circumstances and naivety. What however is important is the national spirit that recognized evil behind the action. It did not matter if it was committed against a foreign people.

Cornwallis

Cornwallis arrived in India in 1786. Devoted to improvement of the administration, he came to India when military situation around the country required an army man. He was a veteran of wars in America. Cornwallis drew a policy of non-intervention in the internal affairs of the country unless it effected the business interests of the company. One of his most beneficial acts was the system of revenue collection in Bengal. This helped the farmers and brought some prosperity to them after long deprivation. He worked to improve the administration and judicial system. He opened new departments of PWD and irrigation. He started the improvement of sea ports that, in due course, were to help sea trade. This enabled future governments to improve the infrastructure for modernization of India that had lagged behind for lack of appreciation of sea power.

Richard Wellesley

Wellesley came from one of the most distinguished families of England. Educated at Eton College, his other brother, the Duke of Wellington, was to defeat Napolean at Waterloo in 1825.

Wellesley's achievement lay in enlarging the control of the company through policy of subsidiary alliances. He subdued the Nizam of Hyderabad, King of Lucknow and the Maratha chiefs who were struggling to carve their own kingdoms. It may be fit to say that Welleseley turned a trading company into an imperial power during his stay in India (1798-1805). What Akbar did for the Mughal empire, Welleseley did for Britain. He had, with his far-sighted policies, ensured a united India for future. An imperialist by temperament, he possessed qualities of diplomacy, a clear vision, a soft but firm heart and sharp intellect. He encouraged Britishers to learn Indian languages and advance primary education.

Wellesley at that time acted in the British interest of creating an eastern empire. He however did good to India by consolidating different independent principalities into one cohesive state. Never before had the country been administratively united, not even during the reign of Ashoka or Akbar.

Advancement of science and knowledge

By the early decades of the nineteenth century, the political situation in India became increasingly clear. Induction of English language opened the gates for transmission of discoveries in science and thought. Men, instead of being absorbed in survival 'at any cost', looked for something higher and nobler. After a long interval, India had peace and some leisure. They could introspect into the causes that led to their degradation, suffering and misery. People now yearned to learn and value knowledge and reason that had helped Britain and Europe march towards a better life.

To introduce English education for study of science, technology and other subjects, in which the country had lagged behind, was a colossal work. Resources were insufficient to meet the demands of a wide and varied country. This motivated Christian missionaries to lend a helping hand. Men and women who volunteered their services to such schools were inspired with the noblest Christian sentiments. Their devotion to duty was exemplary. If a child was absent from the school without reason, they would not hesitate going to their homes to inquire from the parents, the cause of absence. Such gestures of consideration helped bridge the gulf between the Indians and Englishmen.

Advancement of science and new knowledge opened a new world with immense possibilities. On the material plane, it helped technology; on an intellectual plane, it gave rise to rationalism. All these inspired sensitive Indian intellectuals, besides acquiring a European texture. Dazzled by western civilization, this class tried to give Indian culture a new synthesis. This was confined to the few in the cities; village India remained completely aloof. Therefore, the new culture had no roots. The young would go for it with the zeal of youth. With age, as wisdom dawned, it was left behind as worn out clothes.

This legacy persists even today.

New knowledge and its fruits

As these institutions served the cause of education, hesitation of local inhabitants towards Europeans began to change into friendliness and regard. With growing demand, more missionaries were encouraged to open new schools at other centres. When the demand could not cope with the need, not only missionaries but businesspersons too responded to the requirements. Heads of schools, running such centres of education were called 'Fathers', 'Mothers' and 'Sisters'. This gesture made the rulers and the ruled closer to each other. Education and discipline was imparted on the pattern of schools in Europe. There was deep respect from children and the their guardians for school staff and management. On their part, these men and women of compassion, had left their hearths and homes, in a far away country only to serve the call of Jesus Christ. Such men and women bestowed abiding love towards their pupils. The guardians of Indian children, were overwhelmed with their courteous, sympathetic and devotional approach. The discipline and its enforcement over the children created a deep impression on all who noticed them work.

After receiving education from English schools and colleges, Indian youths, exposed to achievements in different arts and sciences, learnt new subjects of which they were so far ignorant. Gradually as the significance of learning was realized, knowledge began to be desired for its utility and value. History books made them aware of the struggle in Europe between Christian priesthood and the intellectuals of science and literature. They read how priests deliberately encouraged ignorance and poverty, ignoring logic and reason. The new generation read the romantic poetry of George Byron; the songs of nature and her beauty by William Wordsworth; the philosophy of John Milton's *Paradise Lost* and works of Shakespeare touching almost all aspects of history, romance, treachery, philosophy and diplomacy. They read with wonder the perfection and excellence of Leonardo da Vinci– how he combined physical experiments to mathematics and reason to become the first modern engineer. Then there was the seventeenth century theologian, Descartes, who drew distinction between reason and revelation, pointing out that at the core of all revelations, was the fundamental accord between revelation and the laws of nature. They learnt about the struggle of truth between the Papacy of Rome and the scientist Galileo; how he was made to suffer when he challenged the scriptures to maintain that the world was round and not flat. Also, what appealed to Indian youth was the patriotism and devotion of Mazinni and Garibaldi of Italy for the freedom of their country.

The regular flow of new books, journals, newspapers and other literature coming into the country, made intellectual India receive the impetus denied to her for centuries. Knowledge that was now freely available, enlightened intellect and inspired the hearts of the young. They wanted to do what others in progressive countries were doing or had done. Seventeenth century was a period of regeneration in Europe in which revival was triggered by forces of learning. In the nineteenth century, the young Indians were inspired to do what the youths of Europe had done in the seventeenth century. The instrument that helped the process was the learning and new knowledge fresh from Europe. England was at that time the most advanced country of the world. Indians were thus able to get the benefit of the best in every field. Whatever had been lost during her twilight period, was at her doorsteps. Thus started the Indian renaissance. As generally happens, it began first with creative destruction of the old system that was being followed for centuries. It was indeed a rebirth of new minds, initiated by thinkers trained in new ideas. This silent revolution in India coincided with the Industrial Revolution in England, the French Revolution of 1779 with its message of 'Liberty', 'Equality' and 'Fraternity' and the accounts of the American War of Independence.

Using machines for production of goods, India became both a market, as well as a springboard for future growth. The British traders took full advantage of this market to make England a rich country and centre of world trade. Indian entrepreneurs planned their commercial and industrial genius to fall in line with times. Introduction of new methods of production, the railways, post, telegraph, and other modern systems that were to follow were as much in their interest as was governing a vast subcontinent. Teachers, engineers, lawyers and civil servants, who came from Britain as professionals, were largely humane and gentle. They had come to India initially seeking jobs. Working for a while in the country, the environment of India would start effecting them just as it had done all others in the past. Gradually they started to love the country. Brought up under a disciplined lifestyle and Christian values of service, they always gave their best to the country they served.

Character and temperament largely effects the destiny of nations as it does of individuals. Englishmen in India set an example in times of crisis of inflatable cool. When all those around them were excited; they were always calm in panic situations. Allied to this was the sense of success. Englishmen of those times imbibed the natural arrogance of men 'born to rule'. Men who came in contact with them were mesmerized by the sheer absence of logic in behaviour of a handful, who refused to accept odds against them. Like Nelsons and Wellingtons, they were products of an age of chivalry and love for wealth and good living. Besides the qualities of character, possession of superior technology, and improved navigation, their nature and character became the source of British expansion in India. British navy ruled over the oceans. It could reach any part of the world unhindered, earlier than her competitors, with her sailors singing: 'Britannia rules the waves'.

William Bentinck

Bentinck (1828-1835) was the first Governor General of India. He was essentially a soldier who also turned out to be a political leader. He concluded the Yandabo Treaty of Burma in 1826 securing the eastern borders of India. His tenure as Governor General became memorable because of his farsighted vision. One of his prominent and famous advisors was Macaulay. Both together chalked out the grand policy of introducing the English language in India. Advancement of English had become an urgent necessity to govern such a vast country. It was getting harder to administer the country without involving Indians. This was not possible without their knowing English. Under the supervision of Macaulay, laws were framed to start English schools in large towns. Some other significant and beneficial works that Bentinck did, were:

1. Suppression of the most formidable murder association—the thugs operating in the country. This improved law and order providing security and peace to the people. They could now move about the country without fear.

2. The abominable custom of suttee under which the widow was compelled to immolate herself on the funeral pyre of her husband, was officially banned.

3. Introduction of English as the literary and official language of India in which Macaulay played a vital role. He induced the government to adopt English in schools. Macaulay and others in administration strongly felt that a vast subcontinent, to be unified, requires one common language. He records: "We must at present do our best to a class, who may be interpreters

between us and the millions we govern; a class Indian in blood and colour but English in taste, in opinions, in morals and in intellect. Whenever it comes, it would be the proudest day in English history."

The British officers of the Company encouraged Christian missionaries to take up education in a big way. They had realized that such a stupendous work could not be implemented by a few. Immersed in centuries of religious bigotry, they were initially suspicious of the new education. As the youth started getting advantage of jobs in government and access to vast knowledge in literature, poetry and sciences, their resolve to study in new schools increased. Bengal in this respect led the country. Raja Rammohan Roy, Ishwar Chandra Vidyasagar and other intellectuals, took up the leadership to educate the middle class. New knowledge from the history of the freedom struggles in America, Italy and France, helped awaken national sentiments amongst the Indians. It proved to be a catalyst for change.

Administrative and civic changes brought about by liberals like Bentinck and Rippon, induced a new vigour amongst the people. Fortunately the administration was headed by a person with a keen sense of administration. Lord Rippon deserves profound respect and sincere admiration for the manner of his administration. He brought such laws that were to help strengthen national unity and an urge for freedom. In this respect, Rippon is hailed as the man who introduced local self-government. With it, infant democracy was reborn on Indian soil.

As a friend of India, he first recognized that village India largely remained untouched with the blessings of education and science. Rippon worked to expand education, both amongst boys and girls. He ordered the first complete census of India when the population of united India was recorded to be 254 million; he also appointed an education commission that was to introduce mass education in the country.. Rippon considered education to be the chief harbinger of enlightenment. He worked to achieve this objective.

But Rippon was an exception. The rule in general at different levels of administration, remained impersonal, non-cultural and non-sovereign. This was hardly conducive to future political and cultural change. Yet, the rule did provide India the peace that allowed unhindered pursuit of knowledge.

More than anything, these steps gave India her taste of liberty, a step up the ladder. Let it be remembered that a composite nation, a heart aching for freedom, will remain the positive contribution of the Raj that enabled the country to rise on its feet again. It enabled India to gather the ingredients of modernization that it had lacked. The country could now distinctly see some light beyond the dark tunnel.

Urge for freedom

We have seen right from the dawn of Indian civilization, the Hindu penchant for academics and learning. When the flood gates of western education were opened, they were the first to adopt the new trends in education. Muslims had to await the arrival of Syed Ahmed Khan. He would inspire the community to benefit from English education. Soon the campaign to learn English and other sciences caught the imagination of the intellectual youth. Within a generation, English schools and language swept urban India, producing a class that would help the British govern the country by law. The intimate contact of Indians with the English at schools, offices, army, trade centres and industry, offered opportunities that would generate a longing for freedom.

The modern generation, without getting sentimental about 'ancient glory', may realize that English language helped bring people of India together when they were divided and disorganized! Growth of science and technology caused yet another revolution. This was in the field of industry. New machines and better methods of production transformed the economic and social laws of society. Mental attitudes towards creation of wealth changed. Negative factors of greed and unscrupulous methods of exploitation gradually surfaced. This disturbed the economic balance, draining the agricultural wealth of the country and damaged the traditional handicrafts followed by farmers as a subsidiary occupation. This brought acute distress amongst artisans. The intellectual class was deeply hurt by this neglect on the part of the rulers. Having learnt their lessons from western examples, they began finding ways to redress the wrong. British business had started from Bengal. Military success, administration and educational programs all had their roots in Bengal. A radical awareness arose amongst young Bengali intellectuals to mitigate the ills. One such young man was an Anglo-Indian, educated at Hindu College, Calcutta. He inspired the new generation with his patriotic poems:

> My country in the days of glory past
> A beauteous halo circled round thy brows.
> And worshipped as a deity thou wast,
> Where is that glory, where the reverence now?

There was another young man of intellect and extraordinary memory. He tirelessly studied the causes of India's degradation and poverty. Ram Mohan Roy was in the service of English rulers. After travelling extensively, he acquired first-hand knowledge of the country's condition. Thereafter, he left his job to become the first to fight social evils; first to create a parallel platform to the British rule and the first to awaken a slumbering nation.

Architect of modern India—Ram Mohan Roy

In the early nineteenth century, a thousand superstitions and beliefs swamped India. Priests of different religions had complete command on the minds of the masses. Education had reached only a very few people. Events in the country presented people as mere herds. Their worth was determined by the number of 'enemies' slaughtered rather than the nobility of adding to the capital of knowledge and prosperity. Impact of western culture provided a new awakening. Conquest by a distant race, with superiority in arms and political acumen, exposed the weaknesses of Indian society. Thoughtful Indians pondered over these defects and the means to remove them. Modern science and the doctrine of logic, reason and humanism impressed them. All sections, whether rich or poor, demanded change.

A new star on the Indian horizon lifted the fog of gloom. Born in a Brahmin family of Bengal in 1772, Ram Mohan inherited all the defects of religious conflicts. This helped him gain an early insight of the orthodox ideas. The stagnation and corruption of society dominated by caste and religion pained him. Hindus and Muslims, the two dominant religions, were full of superstition. The upper class was selfish, often working against its own larger interests. It would not hesitate to inflict mortal injury on the innocent masses for small gains.

Acquisition of knowledge

The educated young Bengali joined the East India Company as a tax collector. Ram Mohan was required to travel extensively, often in the interiors of Bengal. This offered a unique opportunity to study rural India and the extent of her deprivation. He witnessed how religious priests, using abominable rituals, were exploiting the ignorant masses. They would cover their criminal acts under the garb of the supernatural for which no rational explanation was required or given. Evil passions had made men incapable of seeing the truth; while false beliefs offered excuses for evil passions. The struggle between religion and reason that had pulled the West out of darkness, was absent in India.

Ram Mohan decided first to find the truth through enquiry instead of depending on past writings. He would henceforth accept only what would appeal to his reason. Debating with the learned, at famous seats of learning, in Varanasi, Mathura, and far away Lhasa (Tibet), he was convinced that reason alone was an instrument to understand the complexities of a changing world. From his study of western literature, he had arrived at the conclusion that struggle between religion and reason is vital. Ram Mohan decided to travel on the same route to eradicate social evils and religious pollution to bring modern education, and fight for liberty and self-respect. Ram Mohan would expose the tricks of crafty men, who attributed all misfortunes to the will of God. He would work to eradicate heinous crimes committed under the religious umbrella. Through his message, he would develop love instead of hatred and division between castes and communities.

As he immersed himself in the great task, he realized that remaining in his job, he would not be able to devote himself to his mission. Ram Mohan left his job with the East India Company and became a journalist.

Education through journalism

Ram Mohan now had a clear vision of the evils that ailed society. There were groups of people divided by languages and customs. To fight the evils and convey his message to the educated, he started journals in English, Hindi, Bangla and Persian. To impress unity in all religions, he was fond of quoting the famous Persian poem that said:

> Faqat Tafawat hai naam hi ka
> Dar asl.sab eka hi hai yaro!
> Jo-abe safi ki mauj mein hai,
> Usi ka jalwa habab mein hai.

(Only the names differ my friend; all are but the same. Both ocean and dew drop are but one living liquid frame.)

As a critic, he focussed on the deficiencies and drawbacks of the administration and the need to remove them. As a visionary, he had understood the importance of constructive agitation as well as education. Gradually, his writings began attracting the well-meaning people in India and abroad. Both Indians and Englishmen paid special attention to his views and looked seriously for finding ways to implement them. He had visualized that the future of India lay in modernizing education on English lines. He even advised the youth to learn English rather than Sanskrit at great personal risk from the conservative class. This was not possible unless more centres of western education were established. Ram Mohan took help from the government and businesspersons from Holland and England. He also sought assistance from charitable organizations in his mission to start scores of schools for imparting western education.

Fear-culture relationship

No society inspired by fear can further life. For the past several centuries, the rulers successfully employed the policy of fear in religion and governance. This had degraded life. Culture is a collective creation; a mould of collective consciousness of society that organizes life along certain common values. When culture becomes rigid, unable to change, it becomes a dead mass. Full of fear, without hope, beliefs amongst people become a delusion. Those who pretend to know more, exploit this in turn. Ram Mohan had understood that as a living organism, this cultural status-quo must change according to changing conditions. In his zeal for western education, he did not neglect India's ancient culture. Though committed to English education, he revived interest in the study of the *Vedanta* to balance the western assault on Indian heritage.

In 1828, Ram Mohan founded the Brahmo Samaj. He declared its purpose as, "a place of public meetings of all sorts and descriptions of people without distinction for worship and adoration of the Eternal and Immutable." Brahmo Samaj was based on reason, knowledge and human dignity. Instead of fear, it encouraged knowledge with hope. One of the great evils of his time was the practice of burning widows. The custodians of Hindu religion would burn the woman on the same funeral pyre as her dead husband. Ram Mohan built up public opinion against this practice. The english administrators fully concurred and supported him against this barbaric practice. In due course, the practice of 'Suttee' was banned by law. His forceful advocacy had emboldened the government to act decisively against the shameful practice.

Brahmos were also against the caste-system and child-marriage prevalent amongst the Hindus. Ram Mohan took up the cause and worked to bring laws for a change. He went to England to plead with the British Parliament. So deeply were these evils engraved in the Hindu psyche, that none dared to enforce the change even by law. The crusader Ram Mohan Roy was however determined to move mountains. Gradually with his persistent efforts, evils, at one time accepted as natural, began to be doubted. He was bold enough to chart out the future path of modern India at a time when fear held back the high and the mighty.

Reason and Faith

Faith and reason have been eternally at war with each other. No saint has ever accepted the knowledge obtained from senses or by reason. Yet, darkness follows faith. When reason dominates, there is enlightenment. Ram Mohan studied from European history, how with the advent of reason and science, a new era of renaissance dawned in Europe. He learnt Sanskrit to read Vedas; Pali to study Buddhism; Persian and Arabic to understand Islam and Koran; Hebrew to master Christianity and Greek to study the Old and New Testaments. If it was Rene Descartes of France who, in the seventeenth century, challenged and doubted Christian scriptures; in the nineteenth century India, it was Ram Mohan Roy who condemned the blind beliefs of his time.

Both triggered renaissance with the help of knowledge in their respective time. Europe, during the nineteenth century, was exploding with new ideas. In India, the minds of men, regularly fed through books and journals that reached her shores, advanced learning and knowledge. Literary works of Charles Dickens and Leo Tolstoy, gave a vivid description of conditions of deprivation in their countries. They described interesting but direct measures to fight them. French philosophers like Rousseau and Voltaire wrote about both the good and evil in society. They gave convincing reasons of solutions without mystical delusion. The spirit of science that brought steam engine, electricity and other tools to human service, all helped Ram Mohan convince people in favour of reason. Ram Mohan would impress that if a child speaks something reasonable, accept it; but even if Brahma says something which does not appeal, reject it. He defined reason as the "knowledge of truth that is conducive to our well being". He would argue that blind belief does not inspire enquiry. This in turn allows domination of superstition and belief in the supernatural. So far, priests were preaching that all calamities, be they man-made or natural, were punishments for our sins. Ram Mohan pleaded that to shape our spiritual and cultural life, we needed to revert to our heritage. But for the reconstruction of political and economic life, we must not hesitate to apply western knowledge. He even said that:

"Creator has no power to do impossible things". He would even challenge the idea that "God's will is made known through prophets."

After a long time, leadership of ideas began to shift from the bigots to rationalists. Amongst the deaf and dumb self-seekers, there was at last some one to speak the truth. It did not matter if others, depressed, dejected and fearful, sought solace in ignorance. With perseverance and courage, Ram Mohan helped focus the attention of people on the evils in society. He was thus able to build the broad bridge of confidence between the East and West. The coming generations could now use this passage to go forward.

Revival

The new generation gradually began ridiculing the priests, doubting existence of either heaven or hell. Reincarnation, which helped reduce fear of death, was questioned. The entire edifice, on which religious beliefs rested, started shaking. They dared challenge even some of the Upanishads as 'metaphysical illusions' Such revolutionary thoughts gave birth to fresh vigour. Others, appreciating the change, looked forward to pursue not only western education but also reform the age old customs and rituals that had ruined the spirit of India.

A century had now rolled by since the East India Company started to commercialize warfare as a source of profit. Destiny had brought western civilization to India in order to awaken the masses from deep slumber. The enlightened intellectuals of both the East and West helped create awareness and understanding. They started to review the ancient traditions in the light of new thoughts learnt from English books. Ram Mohan Roy was the first to apply to the Indian milieu the basic social and political ideas of Liberty, Fraternity and Equality from the American and French revolutions. Ram Mohan represented the first glimmer of the rising national consciousness. A grand vision of resurgent India always guided his thoughts and actions. Tagore said of him:

"Ram Mohan Roy was the only person of his time, in the whole world of men, to realize completely the significance of the modern age."

The spirit of a silent revolution ushered by Ram Mohan Roy became the beginning to break the feudal structure of the period. True to the land of Buddha, he had initiated a peaceful but effective method for change. The candle lighted by him was carried forward by others of the coming generations. Resurgence of India that he visualized continued to gather momentum and fulfilment. Ram Mohan Roy had lighted the lamp; others would now carry it forward to its destination.

There was however some more time before those 'others' would appear on the Indian scene to carry the torch forward. So, in the meantime let us follow the developments in the political arena.

Dalhousie

If Bentinck and Macualay, knowingly or unknowingly, prepared the foundations for a modern India, Dalhousie was responsible for creating its political boundaries. He expanded the territory of British India, defining its boundaries that stayed until the partition in 1947. Educated at Oxford University, it was during his governance (1845-1856) that railways and telegraph lines were laid, helping communication in a vast subcontinent. It improved administration, and travel at a time when such facilities of science were confined only to Europe.

Dalhousie enforced his 'Doctrine of Lapse', on Indian rulers. According to it, if a ruler had no direct heirs to the throne, his territory was to be merged with British India. This proved to be a major cause of the Mutiny of 1857. The revolt of the Rani of Jhansi was entirely for this highhandedness. Besides railways, posts and telegraphs, Dalhousie constructed a network of roads and canals. These developments helped irrigation and communication in remote villages.

The sea ports of Bombay and Calcutta were improved, making flow of goods at the ports easy. What benefitted rulers, in the end, were to help the people of India even more.

The British effort had been to strengthen their rule and increase trade so that surplus generated by industrialization brought riches home. It provided India blessings of western technology, a system of canals for irrigation and better roads for communication. More than these appurtenances of civilization, it fired the imagination of youth with the spirit of freedom. Awakening brought by interaction of the cultures and exchange of knowledge between the East and the West inspired intellectuals with a will that would be free to draw her own destiny. Urban India got involved in industry and business. New machines and tools attracted Indians to start new industries in jute, cotton and engineering. As infrastructure for ports and communication increased, new ancillaries began to be established.

While urban India started receiving commercial benefits of western contact, rural India remained utterly neglected and depraved. This was to cause occasional famine and shortage of food even in towns. Rural India lived in neglect until schemes for irrigation and road building were implemented.

Social and religious reforms

The impact of western education and ideas affected the religious sensibilities of both Hinds and Muslims. The old fossilized order that had rested on religious morality, instead of the law of the land, was no longer able to face intellectual scrutiny. Intellectual India would henceforth clamour to abolish such tyrannical practices. They would discreetly propagate cleaning of religion from bigotry, superstition and obscurantism. The young intellectuals were realizing that traditional customs and irrational beliefs were choking the life stream of society. Having noticed Englishmen working in India at close quarters, they started holding progressive views. Mutual co-operation that had been woefully missing returned in an endeavour to do well for the country. This helped development of regional togetherness, placing emphasis on united efforts.

The resurgence of India had commenced.

Chapter XXIX
Trials and Triumphs
in a 'Strange' Land

If you can keep your head when all about you
Are losing theirs, and blaming it on you,
If you can trust yourself when all men doubt you,
But make allowance for their doubting too;
If you can wait and not be tired of waiting,
Or being lied about, don't deal in lies,
Or being hated don't give way to hating,
And yet don't look too good; nor talk too wise:

If you can talk with crowds and keep your virtue,
Or walk with kings—nor loose the common touch,
If neither foes nor loving friends can hurt you,
If all men count with you, but none too much;
If you can fill the unforgiving minds,
With sixty seconds worth of distance run,
Yours is the Earth, and everything that's in it,
And which is more—you'll be a Man my son!

—Rudyard Kipling

Most English officers and men, serving in India, followed the ideals laid down by the poet Kipling in his poem above. Having overcome initial inertia, they settled in their respective duties according to their education and training. Power and authority now rested in the Governor General of East India Company. For the common person there was gradual easing of suspicion; violence, banditry and thuggery. Power and profits of the Company grew rapidly. Practice of 'suttee' was abolished, but only legally. Bands of murderers known as 'Thugs' who preyed upon travellers, had been hunted down. 'John Company' employed Indians of every caste and religion to collect taxes and do other clerical duties. Indians, with visions of the future, understood which way the wind was blowing. It was wisdom to understand and learn the techniques that had made Britain master of the subcontinent.

Who were these 'supermen', from a small island, three thousand miles away? What was so outstanding in them that they were able to control millions of people with a force of a few thousand? If science and technology was responsible, why not make the new generation learn about the new gods that bestow such enormous power? Why not practice their morals and manners; their aspirations and adventures; their discipline, forbearance and steadfastness?

Questions of this nature amongst the intellectual youth triggered the Indian Renaissance. Within a few decades, India had partially caught up with the lost centuries. Henceforth they would keenly observe working of these people as a model for themselves and their children. Action followed thought. In a short time, the average Indians had adjusted their new pattern of lives. It must be to the credit of Indian genius in adaptation and assimilation that during a short period they were able to pick up the language and a quest for science and knowledge. They had also learnt to imitate the English gentlemen in dress and style. The more affluent would send their young men for studies in Britain. The foundations of modern India were laid during that otherwise bleak age of shame and ignominy.

Builders of the Empire

Britons who came to serve East India Company were professional youths who looked forward to the adventure of the East. They usually received training at the Institute of the Company at Addiscombe, England. The young recruits got exhaustive training as soldiers, administrators and business managers. Their seniors, having earned laurels on land and sea, were models for the new entrants. After serving India, they usually looked forward to spend their retirement at 'home'. Sitting by the fireside in their old age, they would narrate unbelievable tales of lion, elephant and tiger hunting to their grandchildren. Following their footsteps, their children came to the 'land of snake charmers'.

Amongst hundreds of such English youths, who arrived in India every year, there was a typical young lad of 18 years. At home, he was never interested in studies. He would often organize adolescent ruffians, to extort money or local produce, like apples, from traders of the town. In return, the gang would promise not to break their glass windows. Soon, fed up of the 'business', he managed a petty job with the East India Company. This was destined to make him famous as Lord Clive, the architect of the British Empire in India.

We have earlier read how he won crucial battles with his daring and strategy against tremendous odds. The victories he gained in South India against the French and at Plassey against the Nawab of Bengal, were decisive. His political assessment, in a complex environment, was always accurate. Clive would understand, analyse, and act in a manner as to leave no choice to his enemies. At one time, the King of Delhi invited him to take over the entire North India for revenue collection. Knowing his limitation, Clive refused. He waited for the fruit to ripen and fall by its own weight.

Later, when he was charged in the British Parliament for bribery and corruption, he contemptuously remarked:

"By my assertions, the company has acquired an empire more extensive than any kingdom in Europe." Poet Kipling was not far from the truth when he wrote that the "British Empire of India was an inscrutable design of destiny."

The slow boat to China

Jet travellers of modern age may find it difficult to comprehend the ordeals and uncertainties of sea travel before introduction of steam engines. During those early days of British domination of India, sails and masts moved ships. The Suez Canal was still a distant dream. To cover 5000 miles used to be punctuated with months of adventure and uncertainties. Ports in Europe had 'Weeping Halls'. Relatives and friends, who came to bid goodbye, were never sure if they would ever meet each other again. The ladies, after bidding good bye to their loved ones, went into these halls and wept in seclusion. Departure scenes at the ports were always painful. A chill passed through people when the 'Big Bell' announced departure of the ship. Mothers and wives, bidding goodbyes, these days, are seen to be wishing with flowers and cheers. The modern certainties of travel have changed the entire outlook. During those days, such partings shook the near and dear ones to the bones.

Has not easy travel facilities and satellite communication deprived people of such rare moments of refined emotions?

As ships sailed from the British docks and the coastline of England receded around the Isle of Wright, the last post of the British Isles, faded into oblivion. Many a heart in the boat would sink, wondering if ever such a sight would be seen again. Travelling by land, one has the continuity of persons and incidences. Sea voyage and now air travel, on the contrary, at once severes relationship. It makes one conscious of being cast loose from the secure anchorage of a settled life, sent adrift upon a doubtful world.

Sailing the rough sea of the Bay of Biscay in the Atlantic ocean, with the creaking of masts, the straining and groaning of the bulk heads, the boat would labour in the weltering sea to reach Gibraltar. The next stoppage of the boat would be Malta where the sea breeze helps wild growth of foliage and fruits. From Malta to Alexandria, the distance on the map appears short. In those days it took three days to reach the beautiful port built by Alexander. Here, the boat had to be abandoned. Journey would then be resumed on a barge that sailed on the Mohammedi Canal to reach Cairo (Suez Canal was opened in 1869). Cairo then was a great cosmopolitan centre where the East met the West. There was a regular flow of new arrivals and departures. From Cairo, passengers were required to take horse-driven carriages to reach the port on the Red Sea. Here, the Peninsular and Oriental lines waited to take passengers to India and China. The journey on the dusty roads of Cairo, with indifferent local drivers, was perhaps the toughest test of physical endurance.

After nearly seven days of ordeal in Egypt, the comfort of berths on the "P and O" ships was a welcome change. A fine day, a tranquil sea, and a favouring breeze gladdened the hearts. With the ship decked out in all her canvas, every sail swelled, carrying the ship gaily on the curving waves. The pleasant journey got a break when scant greenery announced the approach of the Arabian Desert. At the port of Aden, the ship anchored for passengers to have another bout of bargaining with clever Arab merchants.

Next, commenced another long and often rough journey towards the destination. The breeze in the Arabian Sea would begin to blow violently. There would be the same creaking of the masts as in the Bay of Biscay, the same straining and groaning of the bulk heads as the ship laboured in the weltering sea. Passengers, particularly ladies, usually went into a frightful state. When the passengers reached Indian ports after nearly two to three months, scenes of anguish, similar to those witnessed at the port of embarkation, were repeated at Calcutta. Separated families, joining after years; anxious parents seeking news of their children at home; first timers to the East struck with wonder; newspapers bringing news of happenings at home, everything made the docks a centre of deepest emotions and excitement.

Rudyard Kipling, the English poet and writer, born and brought up in India during the same period has described sea travel by Englishmen during that period by Peninsular and Oriental Lines, in his poem the "Exile Line":

> Exile Line, brings out of exile and ships them home,
> When their work is done....
> "For all the soul of our sad East is there,
> Beneath the house flag of P and O.

For thousands of Englishmen, who travelled to the East each year, P and O stood for adventure, romance and the magic spell of the East. To those returning home, it meant release from 'exile' after hard work, hard fighting, in a strange land where they were temporarily in exile!

P and O boats plied for some years after Indian independence. Those amongst us, who may have travelled in their ships, may have fond recollections of a three-week trip. Science and Suez Canal has made a tremendous change. Speed and sound of modern times had not yet confined life to excitement alone. Boarding the boat from Gateway of India at Bombay, stuffed with plenty of provisions, there was the same Victorian elegance right from the captain to the crews. The fragrance of that era still lingered. Breakfast, lunches and dinners, served with personal attention to individual tastes, became lasting memories. The pantry remained open day and night for self-help; all kinds of eatables, tea and coffee, could be picked up from the pantry at any time of the day or night.

There was leisure and recreation; deck tennis, swimming pool, and indoor games never permitted a dull moment. Two hundred and five hundred passengers, depending upon the capacity of the boat, made friends to their tastes; the library satisfied travellers' fondness for reading. When the sea was calm around the Mediterranean, sitting on the top deck, watching the moon brought recollections of the rich history of Greece and Rome. What labour must have gone in the construction of such massive works as the Pyramids? How Moses led Jews to the promised land of Sinai across the Red Sea? How Alexander and Julius Caesar, loved and fought in the region? The whole history of the land passed through the corridors of memory.

The Jet Age has robbed some such sublime moments!

Reaching destination from Calcutta

For European passengers going on duties to various stations in north India, Calcutta was the main port for transit to the destination. Railroads had not yet arrived. The long journey, often deep into north India, was by barges on the river Ganga. During those days, the river Ganga was navigable up to Allahabad. There was the choice of travelling either on the roads, drawn by horses with frequent stoppages or by barges on the river. Road travel being more economical, was preferred by the young single officers and men. River travel was expensive but more comfortable, particularly for families. The journey by barges offered opportunity to see nature at comparative leisure. Passengers could watch life on the riverside, with children swimming and playing and elders bathing and praying. Excitement of the journey increased when suddenly from the river appeared a crocodile in search of food. The stories of a land where wild animals roamed freely and snake charmers displayed their expertise to children, came to the minds of new comers. Some of the crocodiles and turtles were so huge that even Indian operators were scared of frontal attacks. Talking about crocodiles, the boatmen narrated both true and fictional stories. They would start that "how once during summers, a hungry crocodile dared to come out of deep waters of the river to catch an innocent human prey from the banks of the river and how the child was just swallowed!" Once on friendly terms with the passengers, they freely narrated tales of terror in forests of the countryside.

When the barge reached the ancient city of Varanasi, the rising sun sprinkled its golden rays over the placid water of the river. With the barge moving slowly, the metalled domes of temples and mosques sparkled in the bright sun making the entire riverbed shine like a golden sheet. Excited passengers went down the ghats to see the old and lovely jumble of palaces, temples and mosques. Unlike all ancient cities, one has not been able to dig out the beginning of the city. Time appears to stop at this holy place of the Hindus. Nearly a thousand years ago, Shankaracharya from Kerala, came here to discuss Vedanta with the *Acharyas* of Varanasi; Tulsi Das five hundred years later wrote *Ram Charitra Manas* on the banks of the Ganga. Kabir sang here the essence of all religions in his verses.

The next stoppage for the barge was at Allahabad, the largest centre of pilgrimage for the Hindus. Here, Hindus have been trekking for thousands of years on Kumbh, held every twelve years. This grand congregation has remained the largest assembly of human beings in the world. Here the river Jamuna becomes one with the Ganga. Legend says that those and only those who can truly claim to be sinless can see a line of ripples that marks the place where an unseen river Saraswati becomes one with Ganga. Those who bathe at the 'Sangam' are said to acquire great merit. At the time of Kumbh, all kinds of followers of Hindu faith assemble here to display their talents. Allahabad being the end of the river travel, the journey to respective destinations is continued on the Grand Trunk Road.

Rest houses, bungalows and barracks

The East India Company, to facilitate travel in the large subcontinent, established rest houses. For military and civil officers and men it constructed bungalows and barracks at strategic centres. One such station was Kanpur in UP. Under the Faizabad treaty between the English East India Company and the Nawab of Oudh in 1775, a brigade was hired for defence of Lucknow, its capital. This became necessary because of persistent onslaughts on the Nawab by the Marathas and tribals from central India. The then King of Oudh, unable to pay the hire charges, the revenue accuring from the districts, was legally assigned to the East India Company. Governor General Wellesely, who loved to deal with matters with an imperial air, closed the mortgage when the amount remained unpaid for several years.

The pledged territory of Kanpur thus lapsed to the company. The town, along with its adjoining territory, was the first in UP to legally belong to the British Company. Thus started the first, establishment of the army and its barracks in the Cantonment. British businessmen and their massive bungalows by the side of the river, followed. As industrial development created markets in India, farsighted Englishmen set up new factories, with European technology.

Responsibilities of adminstration and business multiplied and with it an organized plan for construction of essential services was implemented. At Kanpur, the English brigade, stationed in the cantonment constructed barracks and bungalows. The model of cantonments with their barracks and bungalows was identical all over the country. Their construction and furnishings announced that the occupants were merely sojourners, likely to move at short notice. The furniture usually consisted of a large rickety table strewn with empty soda-water bottles, brandy, a corkscrew and few glasses. There were playing cards, chess, a vernacular-English dictionary, inkstand, a revolver, boxes of cigars, newspaper supplements from England and a few books obtained from the regimental library. The officers were provided with a reference book containing symptoms and cure for Indian tropical diseases. Married officers lived more comfortably. The lady of the house, if she was not away 'home,' would adorn it with a feminine touch of perfume, curtains and a battery of domestic servants. Behind it all lay the same style of a sojourner, announcing the temporary attitude towards his stay in the country. When not engaged in work, they enjoyed themselves remembering their home.

> This is my own my native land!
> Whose heart hath ne'er within him burn'd
> As home his footsteps he hath turn'd
> From wandering on a foreign strand?

> —Sir Walter Scott

The gathering storm

Amongst 'the jolly old fellows' who enjoyed risks and life in a strange land, there were also sensitive and wise administrators. They always had hands on the pulse of the people. Lord Canning, who came as Governor General in 1855, was one of them. In the light of events that were to overwhelm British rulers, they were prophetic words indeed! At a dinner hosted by East India Company, he said:

"We must not forget that in the sky of India, serene as it is, a small cloud may arise at first no bigger than a man's hand, but which growing bigger and bigger may at last threaten us with ruin."

This was to become true immediately after his departure from India.

Lord Rippon was made the Governor General of India in 1856. He was the first to introduce steps towards self-government. As father of local self-government in India, he enforced laws for elections to civic bodies. Like his predecessors, he had studied the intellectual capacity of resurgent India. His contribution in modernizing and introducing new techniques remains memorable for their sincerity and purpose. Another pioneer achievement of his administration was the prompt introduction of railways in India. Railway network had started in the country of its origin only a few years ago. Rippon began work on the layout of railway lines in India. One of the earliest beneficiaries of rail communications was Kanpur and Bombay. Establishment of post and telegraph services and opening of nearly a thousand post offices all over the country laid the foundations of a strong and unitary government for later years. The vast length and breadth of the country was connected. Quicker movement throughout India became gradually possible.

We saw how leaders of the renaissance like Rammohun Roy, Ishwar Chandra Vidyasagar and Debendra Nath Tagore encouraged female education. Rippon, by making laws, facilitated their efforts. To help farmers, who often suffered from drought due to the uncertain monsoons, Rippon started construction of more canals and roads. There was no distinction on account of race, colour, language, culture or religion in providing the benefits of science and technology.

Undercurrent of dissatisfaction

Life in India has always centred around debating at leisure. This does develop sensibility of perception; it however also destroys the ability for action. Following its tendency, it turns inward, where the self dominates. This kills the spirit of common interest; the determination to create a commonwealth fades; there are no citizens now; there are only individuals. Repeatedly, instead of facing danger together, each one tries settling issues individually.

Gradually, life of rulers and the ruled appeared to fall into a routine. One became used to power; the other to morbidity, expecting the ruler to do everything for him. It appeared that this arrangement suited the nature of both and would therefore go on and on. History, on the contrary, informs that periods of peace generally loosen the sinews of control. Those in high places, out of touch with feelings and opinions of people, are oblivious of the signs and mutterings on the ground level. These mutterings brewed dissatisfaction that soon exploded. For mischief makers, use of religion has always been a handy tool to exploit. In illiterate societies, it is indeed a potent and effective instrument of self-aggrandizement. When power seekers are not able to reach their goal through the right road, they take the short cut of inciting simple people with religious delusions. The unfair usurpation of Oudh, the grievances of the Marathas in the west and the Nawabs in the east, were all waiting for a religious spark to ignite the gunpowder. This appeared soon enough in the form of new Enfield cartridges from Britain.

What happened thereafter has been termed as the First War of Independence by those whose rights had been forfeited; historians call it a mutiny.

Chapter XXX
Indian Freedom Struggle–The Mutiny
(AD 1857)

In this our age of infamy, men's choice is but to be
a tyrant, a traitor, prisoner. No other choice has he.

—Pushkin

When novel situations and events do not readily lend themselves to natural explanations, ordinary minds ascribe them to supernatural causes and thus feel satisfied and rested. The ancient Roman Empire, the Abbasid Caliphate, the Ottoman and Mughal empires at their zenith, considered themselves invincible. Hundred years after the battle of Plassey, the British Empire appeared to be in the same mood. Any Englishman, in any part of the world, thought that the glory of the Empire would continue for a thousand years. They ruled the seven seas, won wars in almost all parts of the earth; were generating wealth from machines invented after the Industrial Revolution. British people thought they were born to rule.

Post-Plassey, the East India Company, with their red coat soldiers, had beaten the Marathas, won over Punjab and threatened the rich plains of Ganga. Governor General Wellesley had annexed Oudh in 1856 and cancelled the treaty signed between the company and the Nawab of Oudh. After the Nawab was sent to exile, his wife, Hazrat Mahal, a courageous woman, collected people, both Hindus and Muslims, to revolt. Kanpur, was placed strategically on the road to Lucknow, the largest contingent of British force in northern India, was stationed there. The Mughals had grown so weak that Nana Saheb, who was in possession of Bithoor in the province, considered only this English force to be in his way to reach Delhi to capture the Mughal throne. Similarly, there was Rani of Jhansi and several other small Rajas and nawabs who were victims of the British policies by which their principalities were annexed. They had been nursing their grudges for long and were waiting for an opportune time to strike.

There was yet another factor. A keen guardian, Governor General Canning, could perceive an undercurrent of dissatisfaction amongst the sepoys caused by inadequate compensation. They had incessantly fought with English soldiers in Afganistan and Burma to protect business interests of the East India Company. The insolence and greed of the soldiers, their impatience, and their lust for money and power, were effective causes for the break out of the mutiny. For long had the East India Company and its administrators taken the loyalty of the people for granted. A streak of complacency had crept in the administrators after a long stay. Perhaps the tropical heat of India was playing its part. The company administrators, in the last few years had framed laws of collecting revenue that was harming the interests of princes and other petty Rajas, nawabs and *jagirdars*. Usurpation of territories on grounds of heredity, deteriorating economic plight, increasing awareness amongst the middle class as a result of western education, these factors combined to cause dissatisfaction amongst the princes and the Indian servants of the company.

They all waited for an excitable cause to strike. For both Hindus and Muslims, what could be more inspiring than a religious cause? This appeared in the form of introduction of new Enfield rifles and their cartridges. Immediately the Indian rumour market linked the change to religious sentiments. Rumours were circulated that Britain wished both Hindus and Muslims to be converted into Christianity by despoiling their religions. The new cartridges needed to be bitten open with the teeth. The rumour mill circulated that the cartridges were smeared with cow and hog fat.

This was enough to incite religious sentiments of both the Hindus and Muslims.

The deluge starts

"To Delhi!, To Delhi!" suddenly cried Indian soldiers led by Mangal Pandey of Meerut cantonment in U.P and some others in Barrakpur cantonment on a hot summer day in 4 May 1857. The month was wisely chosen as during this period heat in North India is at its most unbearable intensity. By the end of the month, entire northern India was in ferment. Small government stations, with a handful of British officials, looked in vain for support from outside. They were ill prepared for the catastrophe. No support was forthcoming; no British troops came to fill the vacuum. To the wonderstruck British administrators, the European and their families, it was a surprise.

Revolts are however never an accident of the present. Their cause is hidden in the past. A wind blows and nobody knows where it came from. Now, after more than a century, if we analyse and review the events, it would be remarkably significant that religious feelings in India were always easily aroused amongst the illiterate masses by clever men seeking power. It is perhaps the easiest emotion to take people up the garden path. Religion is the art of intoxicating people with enthusiasm so that they are unable to see events with logic and reasoning. Instead of morality, masses are fed miraculous fables that are hostile to reason. Instead of listening to reason, they are taught to rely on the wisdom of others. In a perpetually evolving world, this is a highly risky business. The moral code may change in time, but religion would not let it alter.

We will see how during the mutiny, religious sentiments were woven in fantasy! How vested interests exploited religious sensibilities with lies and half-truths!

The company, after winning at Plassey had, by force or sef-interest, brought the Holkars, Gaekwads, Scindias, Nizam of Hyderabad and Tippu Sultan to become their collaborators. The soldiers, seeking higher wages, found a convenient cause to revolt. An opportunity suddenly appeared in which the disgruntled elements could seek personal gains.

Shock and determination

Englishmen in India, were initially shocked with such an outburst of hatred and cruelty. For a long time, British army and civil servants had been enjoying a life of oriental luxury never seen in the West. Mutual confidence amongst the governors and the governed, made living carefree. This allowed complacency and over confidence in their temperament. More than anything, intoxicated with successes all over the world, they felt the fatal aura of self- belief. Where lay the spark? What was really the cause that ignited the dry chaff? Questions were debated amongst themselves at different levels without a conclusion. As we proceed towards the various acts perpetrated and methods adopted during the high tide of the mutiny, we find economic self-interest of the few was at the back of it all. The big fish exploited religious sentiments of Indian sepoys by offering them rewards for revolt. The few weeks that the mutiny lasted saw some of the most inhuman, barbarous and shameful acts. In the end, the mutiny expressed man's capacity for debasement on both sides. It showed that if a people can rise to the height of sublimation, they could also sink to the lowest level of degradation.

Oudh and Kanpur—the epicentres

The King of Oudh, Wajid Ali was a weak and old man. His wife Hazrat Mahal was dynamic, young and prepared to take full opportunity of the situation. She appealed to both Hindus and Muslims of Lucknow to drive out the English. She succeeded in her resolve. English headquarters at the Residency was invaded and won. The remnants of British forces had to retire to Alambagh awaiting reinforcements. Hazrat Mahal herself, riding on an elephant, commanded the force. Meanwhile the English received the awaited reinforcements from Calcutta. This time, the reinforcements of guns and artillery proved too much for a disorganized, uncoordinated and ill-equipped assemblage.

London Times of England had deputed an Irishman, Russell, to cover the mutiny. He apprised himself of the annexation of Oudh and the circumstances leading to the exile of ex-king Wajid Ali. In his despatch to the paper he wrote:

> The menagarie of the king of Oudh, as much as his private property, his watch and his turban, were sold under discreditable circumstances. The king's jewels were seized and impounded, although we had no more claim on them than on the crown diamonds of Russia. Do the English care for these things? Do they know them? The hundred million people of Hindustan know them well, and care about them too!

Kanpur in UP, before the mutiny, had a sizeable European population in North India, trading or soldiering for quite some time. The Maratha chief of Bithoor, Nana Saheb was in command on this side of river Ganga. He was fighting out a legal battle for territory with his relatives and was not unfriendly to the English. The sepoy mutiny however suddenly offered him an opportunity. He planned to take his army to Delhi and gain independent control. So far, he had to depend on British support. Others in his command advised that he should rather first settle with the English at Kanpur, gain greater strength and then move on to Delhi. Thus persuaded, a conspiracy was hatched to bring Indian sepoys to join his force. A *firman* that makes interesting reading reveals conditions existing in the world only two centuries ago. The message read:

> A traveller just arrived in Cawnpore from Allahabad states that before cartridges were distributed a council was held for the purpose of taking away the religion and rites of the people of Hindustan. The members of council arrived to the conclusion that, as the matter was one affecting religion, seven or eight thousand Europeans would be required and it would cost the lives of fifty thousand Hindus and Muslims. At this price, the natives of Hindustan would become Christians. The matter was therefore, represented in a dispatch to Queen Victoria, who gave her consent. A second council was then held at which the English merchants were present. It was then resolved to ask for assistance of a body of European troops equal in number to the native army, so as to ensure success when the excitement should be at the highest.

> When the despatch containing this application was received in England, thirty five thousand Europeans, were rapidly embarked on ships and started for Hindustan, and the intelligence of their despatches reached Calcutta. Then the English in Calcutta issued the order for the distribution of the cartridges.

The object was to make Hindustan Christian; as it was thought that the people would come over with the army. The cartridges were smeared with hog and cow's fat. One man who let out this secret was hung and one imprisoned.

Lord of Egypt assembled his army in the city of Alexandria which is on the road to India, before the Europeans arrived. As soon as the troops arrived, Egyptian troops began to fire into them with guns on all sides, and sank all their ships, so that not even a single European escaped. The English in Calcutta, after issuing orders, were looking for assistance of the army from London. But the Almighty, by the exercise of His powers made an end of them all at the very outset. When intelligence of the destruction of the army from London arrived, the Governor General was much grieved and distressed and beat his head. At even tide he intended murder and plunder, neither had his body a head, nor his head a cover.

In one revolution of the blue heavens, neither Nadir remained nor a follower of Nadir.

(Issued by order of his Grace the Peshwa 1273 of the Hegira).

Post-mutiny scenario

In the early stages of the mutiny, the English garrisons, with their wives and children, faced the fury of the mutineers with characteristic calm the British people display in danger. Contrary to the *firman* from Peshwa, reinforcements passed through Alexandria without hindrance, reaching Calcutta in time. As these contingents began reinforcing the trapped English forces in different cities, the face of the revolt started changing. Being sporadic, unplanned and uncoordinated, it soon lost momentum. Besides, equipped with superior weaponry, and strong feelings of anger and rage for brutal killings of women and children, the British soon regained the initiative. Incidence like the massacre of more than 200 British wives and children by deceit at the Massacre ghat of Kanpur and death by suffocation at Calcutta, sent the British soldiers to a frenzy. These and several other incidents generated feelings of revenge. An average Englishman in India had earlier thought Indians to be gentle. Now what mattered was revenge and teaching a lesson.

On the other hand, the Indian initiative, lacking leadership, fighting with crude, often outdated weapons, disorganized with divergent interests and a general indifference of people, soon dissolved the revolt. The suffering to the European community during the conflict left an indelible mark on Englishmen and women. It revealed how rumours and rancour; fraud and fear; cowardice and cool self-interest; greed and guile could drive men to perpetuate such inhuman and unpardonable crimes as were committed during the mutiny.

After the storm had blown over, an era of punishment, revenge, and rehabilitation of the administration commenced. British civil servants, who showed signs of panic during the crisis, were punished; but this was confined to North India. U.P. and Bihar were the main centres of the mutiny; Kanpur was at the core, where the cruellest deeds were committed on both sides. Little respect was given to the British tradition of justice. The flimsiest evidence was sufficient for a conviction as a mutineer. With revenge on their minds, the British listened to arguments of defence with a prejudiced mind. It is painful to recall how the events generated a wave of hatred, fear and revenge. An illusion was however destroyed in both the Indian and the English mind. The degree of trust amongst the two races, developed earlier, was destroyed. Trade, conquest and administration had brought the two widely divergent races, together. In the honeymoon period that followed the Maratha and Pindari wars, 'freebooters paradise' was substituted for English rule of law. The common man felt more at ease with his life and property. All this stood shattered now.

How did the two races react to the mutiny?

The British had no choice; they were Victorian Englishmen and women. For them, cowardice from childhood was taught to be dishonourable. They had to fight or die. The Indians, who allied with them had a choice. They had no more love for Britain than for others. Pressed by economic needs, they had joined the armed forces of John Company as its servants, they had sworn loyalty to it. They merely wanted to be true to their oath.

Who were the others?

They were feudal chiefs, whose territories was annexed by force of arms. Without a plan of action, they reacted to a situation that was not of their making.

Calm was restored on the subcontinent within a year of the uprising. Business as usual started again. Yet, attitudes of the two races changed dramatically. An undercurrent of dissatisfaction amongst the people and an air of superiority and arrogance in the other became too obvious to be borne by a shaken people. Used to hardships of reprisals, those inflicted by the rulers were too much to bear. Much could be said of the heinous crimes committed against English women and children; so were the punishments equally barbaric. The earlier congeniality, therefore, was now absent. A new relationship of suspicion and arrogance replaced the friendlier, even compassionate attitude. British Parliament realized that a commercial company, seeking profits, could not be allowed to govern a subcontinent. The imperial ambitions of the new Victorian age demanded change. Henceforth the British government would be directly responsible in governing Hindustan.

Chapter XXXI
Imperial Arrogance–Winds of Change

Men like power so long as they believe
in their own competence to handle
the business in question;
But when they know their incompetence,
they prefer to follow.

—Bertrand Russell

With annexation of India into the British Empire, a new relationship was now established. The Britons, at this stage excelled in every field of human endeavour. Their power on land and sea helped the empire to extend her wings in all parts of the globe. Science had long placed religion at the back burner. The spirit of self-discipline found nourishment in pursuit of truth. Determination, courage and resolution produced such strength in pursuit of set goals that people called them possessing the tenacity of 'bull dogs'. British people proudly proclaimed that 'the sun never sets in their Empire.' Their navy ruled the oceans of the world and defended her coastline. Her poet Alfred Tennyson, was singing the deeds of discipline and valour in the 'Charge of the Light Brigade.'

The destiny of India was tied to such a tough, tenacious and law-abiding nation!

After the mutiny, the British Parliament took over governance of India from the East India Company. A secretary of state, answerable to Parliament, henceforth was to direct the affairs of administration from London. Britain, in her characteristic style, went in to generate and earn wealth. Simultaneously it introduced instruments of modern civilization of which India had remained deprived so far . India was waking up to resume her onward journey again. Nature, with the new arrangement, was only fulfilling the immutable laws of growth and decay; glory and disgrace. Lord Lawrence, the Governor General, after the mutiny, started the process of reconciliation and a fresh adminstrative and military build up. The impact of the mutiny was Queen Victoria's proclamation for the Indian people. This said, "We declare to be our royal will and pleasure, that none is in any way favoured, nor molested or discriminated by reason of their faith or observance, but that all shall alike enjoy the equal and impartial protection of the law. In their (Indian people's) prosperity will be our strength, in their contentment our security, and in their gratitude, our best rewards."

Governance of Empire

From the dawn of history, Indians had been witness to their growth into a Hindu religious state; thereafter, for several centuries, it was the Buddhist moral state; then there was the rule of the Afghans and the Mughals for nearly eight hundred years. In all the periods, races that came to conquer settled here in due course. They made the country their home and their kings ruled the country. It was for the first time in history that a Queen, bound by a democratic parliament, was ruling a subcontinent from across the seven seas. The British government, with the active help of her chosen civil servants governed the country. Theirs was an impersonal, non-cultural and non-sovereign rule that made no direct contribution to the welfare of the people. It helped inflate the importance of the civil servants to maintain law and order so that wealth produced was without any hindrance. The consequences of the rule that followed were therefore both direct and indirect. Whenever an opportunity appeared, in either cultural, moral or infrastructure improvement, its positive impact reached the people. Having passed through depravity and neglect, Indian society was now in a position to reassess and plan her own future. The British administrators, engineers, judges and businessmen, who now arrived in India, were trained for public places from their boyhood. Most went to schools at Eton, Rugby and Harrow. Completing college education at Oxford and Cambridge, they would start their career with apprenticeship to govern India. These young men were pioneers of the modern age in their specific fields. Sailing to a distant land, they were dedicated to perform their duty, forgetting trade and finance. They were destined to illuminate other minds while ruling millions of voiceless Indians. Brimming with self-confidence and pride, they possessed a genuine spirit to bring blessings of science and technology to the country they had come. The *Times* correspondent in India during this period wrote to his paper in London:

> There is no bond of union between two races (Europeans and Indians) in language or faith or nationality. The West rules, collects taxes, gives balls (Western dance), drives in carriages, attends horse races, goes to Church, improves its roads, builds theatres, forms Masonic lodges, holds kutchehrees (court) and drinks pale ale (beer), The East pays taxes in the shape of what it eats, grown on taxed land, grumbles, propagates, squabbles, sits in its decaying temples, haunts its rotting shrines, washes in its failing tanks, and drinks its semi-putrid water.

The sketch of rural India, drawn by him, a hundred and fifty years ago, has improved but little since then!

Years of regeneration

Taking to English education and eradication of social evils initiated by the leaders of the renaissance was accepted with enthusiasm by the urban middle class; rural India however was to await this transformation until independence. They were now ready for the next step in which science and technological education would dominate. As new academic institutions were started, Indians began attending them in larger numbers. Young men who came out of these institutions successfully fulfilled their responsibilities. Management and construction of roads, maintenance and planning for new canals, forests and irrigation, laying down of railways tracks, establishment of post and telegraph network under guidance of experienced English engineers and administrators, brought a resurgence in the entire country. There was a certain urgency amongst the young men on their jobs to catch up with the lost time. There was demand for more post offices, extenuation of telegraphy and railways, more roads and canals and other new facilities of life. Fruits of the new age, delayed for over a century, were now reaching the interiors. Indians, in ever increasing numbers, sought European centres of learning for higher education. They surprised their university professors with their mental qualities. A deluge in development of education soon helped India join the mainstream of the world of knowledge. Confined to a section of the middle class, modest in the beginning, they gradually started challenging the mightiest and the highest of their subjects.

India was able to receive in abundant measure the gifts of science, technology and new thoughts. In the last twentyfive years after the mutiny, it was understood that Britain had conquered India for her economic interests, subordinating India's interests to British gains. This realization was further strengthened when they allowed British-made surplus goods, to be freely imported into the country, ruining the Indian cottage and rural industries. There was in this a hidden benefit. It indirectly started the process of industrialization in India when textile machines began to be imported from Oldham in England, to establish new manufacturing units.

Influence of western culture

Culture is a collective creation, a mould of collective consciousness of a people that organizes life along values evolved in time. As a living organism it changes according to changing conditions. When a culture becomes rigid, unable to change, it becomes a dead mass. Cultures, to be able to interact amongst themselves freely, require meeting as equals. Western culture met Indian culture, as rulers and subjects. Indians looked upon the English race to be of a superior class with a higher culture. There were some who considered themselves of a superior culture. Living a shelled and stagnant life, with little contact, they shunned everything that was new. As subjects of a powerful culture, they were required to go along appreciating it. Indians, who met Englishmen, did so for either business or administration. In both, the rulers were in a position to give. Culture is however not a commercial commodity; it is nourished when people are inspired by hope, tolerance, and the realization that strife is foolish. Observing interaction of the two cultures in this light we find that the association with the English was a superficial relationship. Being not from the heart, it always remained imitative and mindless.

The new culture therefore could not absorb the good of either. Confined to wearing English dresses, eating western food with knives and forks, possessing imported furniture, decorations and speaking in English was all they could do in acceptance. It was deprived of the vitalizing food of the intellect and scholarship and developed an uncongenial, social inequality. It developed in the atmosphere a lack of free exchange of ideas. An essential ingredient for evolution of synthesis in cultures was missing. As a result, the English character, expressed in self-respect, self-control, and strength of will combined with adaptability, moral courage, the 'sportsman and gentleman' spirit, was not fully exposed to learning. Instead, the upper and middle class Indians adopted what they had seen or understood in appearance. It brought some uniformity but failed to influence in essence. It was a half-baked culture that neglected the real and adopted the visible.

Even after more than half a century of independence this struggle continues. New techniques keep opening new systems. On the upper crust of observation, the present day youths derive some delight. As soon as the effervescence of age subsides, the call of experience and wisdom draws them back to their cherished values and habits.

In this respect, the Islamic culture, represented by Afghans and Mughal kings, fulfilled the parameters mentioned above. Both cultures lived sharing each others' joys and sorrows, celebrating festivals, speaking the same language, enjoying similar music and eating the same quality of food. Their social and cultural attitudes, with passage of time, virtually became indistinguishable. It therefore became permanently absorbed in the body and soul of India.

Although politically, Britain had established her supremacy in India, people at large took them as one of the many usurpers who come to plunder, collect their wealth and depart. What however did impress them and invited their admiration were the technological gifts that made life easy. Social life therefore went on merrily in the same way as before the mutiny except for some big cities like Calcutta and Madras. While science and her gifts that enlightened the mind was accepted, there was no particular effort to imbibe western culture.

Educated Indians are today more in tune with western culture. The part of culture connected with technique, is readily accepted. When it comes to the social and spiritual, they find fulfillment only in their heritage.

Transformation after the mutiny

The relationship between Britain and India can be divided into two phases. The first was over; in the second, confidence of the common man, after the mutiny, was shattered. They now began looking towards the British as a race armed with supernatural powers. The English educated class began to imitate what apparently met their eyes. The boyhood training had however not equipped them to intelligent imitation based on correct understanding. As such, they could only form a superficial view of English character. They saw that Englishmen attached more importance to material values, while at their home they had learnt just the opposite. They also mistook the healthy individualism of Englishmen as egoism. Therefore, the middle class Indians could merely touch the outer surface of English character and thought, without understanding the basic strength that had made them world leaders. There were some amongst intellectuals of keener observation. Inspired by acquired arts, sciences and technologies of the West, they started analysing and understanding their past mistakes in the right perspective. Having realized their faults, they would work to improve their conditions. The new environment would produce leaders in political, social and religious field. A new class of 'gentlemen leaders,' learned and well versed in their respective professions, would take up new challenges.

Dignity or arrogance!

Meanwhile, the Britons in India went about their business with an acquired arrogance and racial superiority that comes from a sense of power. In the evenings, they would assemble in the clubs, exclusively established for their pleasure. With cigars pressed to their lips, they discussed the business of the day with friends and colleagues. The younger and more energetic amongst them, would take to the wooden dancing floor of the great halls within army premises. They danced and made merry with their wives and women friends in India. The remnants of these clubs, their culture and plaques still hangs in district clubs. Who were these new high-brow, tight-lipped supermen? They were the members of Indian Civil Service (ICS) who governed India under the new law of the Queen. These brilliant young men were the cream of English intelligentsia. Selected after stringent tests of scholarship and sports, they were imparted with vigorous training. The youth possessed a strong will, unimpeachable integrity and devotion to duty. Working with total commitment, in a short period, they established a reputation amongst the village folks of their power to govern. Amongst them were other Englishmen, mostly bachelors, whom call of duty had brought to India. Mothers in England would send their daughters to find suitable matches. These new 'arrivals', nicknamed by their male counterparts, as the 'fishing fleet' joined parties organized by the mature army and civil officers. The lucky ones got married in the cantonment churches. They would settle and gradually get used to the slow pace of life in Indian summers. The couple usually enjoyed their memorable stay in India. They would fondly describe the country in letters during their stay thus:

> ... The chance to wake up early at dawn and see from our window, the long line of Himalyas spanning the horizon, and to watch the peaks catch fire, one after another, as the sun comes up. To see the enormous stretch of the plains at evenings, where the smoke from the cooking fires draws out like long blue veils and cattle come straggling back from the grazing grounds, and every canebrake is full of fireflies. To watch the enormous Indian moon lift slowly up through the dusty green twilight to glimmer on marble domes and minarets and carved temples that were old when Queen Elizabeth was young! To stroll through the clamor and the colour of bazzars, listen to sitars and tom-toms, and to smell the scent of Jassmine and sprinkled water on hot, dry grounds.

Some amongst the intellectual civil servants, showing interest in India's past, acquired more knowledge about her rich heritage. They admired, translated and compared literary works of Indian writers with similar works of their country. New scientific instruments enabled these devoted 'archeologists' to dig out the past that lay buried in ruins of time and neglect. It was amongst such daring and devoted men who, with the help of professionals, discovered the ancient civilization of India, before Aryan immigration. Such men uncovered dunes of time from Mohen-jo-daro and Harrappa the remnants of ancient Indian civilization, appreciated the invaluable paintings in the caves of Ajanta and Ellora; the majesty and beauty of the Taj Mahal that lay neglected so far was revealed to posterity. Such diverse and multi-coloured panoramas sparked awe and wonder in every European heart.

The educated class that came to serve in India brought literature and poetry that flourished in England. Indian writers and admirers came to know about books on different subjects almost at the same time they appeared in the West. The ignited Indian minds started to project local problems in their own works of fiction and poetry; they would combine the new with the old oriental tradition. Enrichment of literary activities was given a big boost. These novels and dramas, vividly describe the life and time of that period; it triggered in the new generation of Indians, a resolve to regain lost self-confidence.

Almost twenty years after the mutiny, Queen Victoria was crowned as Empress of India at the Darbar held at Delhi in 1877. Lord Canning, who was then the Viceroy, read out her message:

There is one thing above all which the British Empire means. That all her subjects shall live in peace with each other; that all of them shall be free to grow rich in their own way provided their way is not the criminal one; that every one will be free to hold and follow his own religious beliefs without assailing the beliefs of other people and live unmolested by his neighbours.

Winds of change

Events are the results not only of preceding conditions, but also of conditions around them in other fields. Change of governance from the East India Company to British Parliament, hardly made much difference in the fundamental British policy. The natural conflict that arose out of trading interests of Britain and India, continued to be invariably decided in favour of the rulers. British economist, and author of *'Wealth of Nations'* Adam Smith, refers this position in the following terms:

> The Government of an exclusive company of merchants, is perhaps the worst of Governments for any country. It is the interest of East India Company that European goods should be sold in Indian dominion as cheaply as possible; and that the Indian goods brought from there should be sold as dear as possible. As sovereigns, their interest is exactly the same as the country they govern; as merchants, their interest is directly opposite to that interest. Britain's primary interest in India was initially trade. Her domination was more from a sense of destiny than design.

Economic scenario

At this period of history, new inventions in science were laying foundations of technological triumphs. Machines were beginning to liberate man from manual labour and toil. Railroads and steamboats were cutting short distances. Nations and cultures were getting uniting. Exchange of ideas and trading were getting more frequent, developing as a result, a closer relationship between man and man. Mechanization in England was producing goods far in excess of her needs. India as a British dominion, having a large market, was ideally suited for trading this surplus. British economic interest therefore induced authorities to permit import of such goods indiscriminately. Devoid of scientific skill, Indian artisans produced goods for local consumption, earning their livelihood through handicrafts. The sudden change in methods of produce signalled their ruin. The looms that engaged the entire family, became suddenly silent. Textiles from Manchester created an economic chaos amongst the poor weavers of India. Trade in iron and steel items were no different.

Not content with textiles, the greedy eyes of the profiteers fell on agriculture. In indigo plantation, the traders found a gold mine of wealth. Farmers, who earlier cultivated grains were forced to plant indigo. The grain that fed them and their cattle was soon converted into an industrial raw material that denied them an adequate survival wage. Having destroyed the old and established economic system, in the name of progress, they reduced India into a half-starving, famine-ridden country, with complete disaster. Soon every section of Indian society started understanding that their interests were not safe. British rule was becoming a cause of economic backwardness and ultimate ruin. Rational, democratic and national political outlook acquired by the new generation began to feel the humiliation of slavery of rulers who were bent on profits at all costs.

There is some wise counsel on economic exploitation, from an ancient sage of China, that goes as follows:

> Menicus, a wise sage of ancient China, was asked by his king, what advice he could give the king to profit his kingdom? Menicus replied, why must your Majesty use the word profit? I only possess benevolence and righteousness; for if your majesty says, what is to be done to profit my kingdom; ministers will ask, what is to be done to profit our families; common people will say, what is to be done to profit our person; superiors and inferiors will try to take profit from one another, and the state will be endangered."

Is the ancient message also applicable to modern times? Reviewing the present state of governance in many countries, do we find corruption a way of life. The root of evil lies in the impersonal rule of civil servants. Since the 'king' seeks profits, his civil servants serve themselves and their families with 'profits'. The British policy of economic neglect of the Indian people invited resistance from intellectuals who understood economics. They realized the damage British policy was doing to the country.

Sparks of awakening

Amongst the first to take up the cause was Dadabhoy Naoroji. He invited the first ever assembly in London in 1866 to influence British public opinion against economic exploitation. It was a brave step. He was the first Indian to raise the banner against exploitation. To gather public opinion, he talked to like-minded Indians that the economic ruin, if unchecked, would bring disaster to the country and her people. During speeches, Dadabhoy would ridicule the benefits of law and order for security claimed by the rulers. He said:

> There is security of life and property, but for England's own grasp; for others, there is no security. Britain is perfectly secure in taking nearly 30/40 million Pounds Sterling a year from India. To Indians, life is simply half feeding or starvation, or famine or disease.

Between Menicus of China and Adam Smith of England, there is a gap of two millenium. Yet, the economic truth does not seem to have altered in two thousand years! Because of a selfish economic policy, people's welfare remained subordinated. Earning wealth and making profits was the primary concern. First the East India company, as a trading organization, and later the Government of Britain, were single minded in its pursuit. What the Chinese sage feared, was happening. One governor general after another was charged with corruption. The bureaucracy had become the 'impersonal rulers'. They were to leave this legacy for the future. After more than fifty years of independence, we find in civil services that the best have slowly gravitated to the bottom, the worst of them have floated on to the top and the criminals are being replaced by greater criminals. Brilliant Indian youths gave their first preference in joining the Indian Civil Service. In this service, they learnt the art of governance. Watching their seniors, they picked up snobbishness, and a sense of arrogance. Neglecting the good of the people, members of the service often acted more in Imperial interests than that of their own people. It was through them that a handful of British officers ruled India.

Amongst the first few Indians who entered the ICS was a brilliant youth from Bengal. Surendra Nath Banerji joined the service with high ideals but soon realized that he was merely serving the cause of Imperialism. When a choice appeared, he preferred to be loyal to his country rather than the interest of its rulers. This did not go well with the rulers; he was dismissed from the service with dishonour. Thus dishonored, he took to a teaching job so that he could join the increasing number of active nationalists to agitate against the government polices that were harmful to national interests. Journalism, even in those days, was an effective instrument to propagate ideas and influence public opinion.

The 'bad ruler' was Lord Lytton , the then viceroy. He had, during his tenure, exhibited racial arrogance, not felt before by educated Indians. First, he had reduced the maximum age limit for the ICS to put Indians at a disadvantage. Secondly, a badge of inferiority was placed on Indians with the law that even though they may be members of ICS, they could not try a European in their courts. The worst discrimination was that Indians were not to travel in the compartment occupied by a European. Bad, as the laws were, they came as the ruler's reaction to the growing nationalism. In a short period of two decades, India—docile and stagnant—began to vibrate with dynamism. Such expressions of nationalism began to appear through newspapers in English and other regional languages. Government policies, adversely affecting the common man, were now openly criticized. Great novelists and poets wrote soul stirring works to arouse national consciousness. Bankim Chandra Chatterji wrote in Bangla, Subramanya Bharati in Tamil, Vishnu Shastri in Marathi and

Altaf Hussain Hali in Urdu. Their creations stirred the nation. There were
patriotic songs on the lips of the youths of the new generation.

Birth of a new India

While introducing English in Indian schools, Macualay planned to produce
office assistants. This would, he thought, help Britain govern India better and
longer. He forgot that knowledge is that light which permanently swallows
darkness. English language helped bring what Indian youths desperately needed.
The new knowledge exposed the generation to developments in different
fields. They learnt how, through organized struggles, nations around the world
had lifted themselves. They saw British engineers, professors, doctors, lawyers
and civil servants meticulously performing their duties. Having lived through
the worst economic exploitation, Indian enterpenuership received stimulus.
For fifty years until the middle of the nineteenth century, Indian society was
literally stagnant. With introduction of English, Indians learnt both the theory
and practice employed in the material world. Facing new realities they established
the first textile mill at Bombay in 1850 and a jute mill at Calcutta in 1854. This
was followed by several core industries like cement, sugar, paper, leather, wool,
and rice and flour mills.

As demand and competition increased, British entrepreneurs started production
in India. Calcutta, Kanpur, and Bombay became premier cities where
Englishmen established textile, jute and other engineering factories. Towns with
traditional cottage and village industries provided men and raw materials for
mechanized production. Within a few years, a decent network of core industries
was producing goods for mass consumption. Fast changes in the political and
technological fields broke through the status quo. With increased awareness,
cottage and village industries introduced new methods of production. New
tools improved the skills of artisans. Industrial revolution that started in England
and other European countries did not finally fail to benefit India.
Industrialization, besides economic change, influenced the traditional social
base of society. Men of different casts and religions worked side by side in
textile factories. Besides economic prosperity, it was bringing the inevitable
social kinship and new fertilization and pollination of ideas.

The silent revolution brought by illumination of minds, intellect and wisdom,
was generating tremendous other forces. The period saw the birth of great
political and social reformers. As in the past, with it also appeared protagonists
of dogmas and obscurantism. Several centuries ago, in similar circumstances,
they had succeeded in fuelling the logic and reason of Gautama. They had
then fought and neutralized his plea to reform the Hindu religion. But this

could happen because science had not revolutionized communication and thinking. Now when interaction between mystic beliefs and truth was easy to ascertain, people were not prepared to accept myths of unreason any more. India extricated herself from centuries of isolation and ignorance.

We now arrive to the period that determined the destiny of the country for centuries. The national movement had come of age. It had ignited a new zeal amongst the Indians. This period will go down in modern history as one in which centuries of backwardness was fought. Not confined to only the political field, literature, poetry, art, industry, agriculture all the ingredients that accelerate civilization started finding fulfilment.

Rise of Nationalism, Thought and Literature

Superior leaders are like catalysts;
though things would not get done as well
if they were not there;
when they succeed, they take no credit:
credit never leaves them.

Lao Tse

Chapter XXXII
Rise of Nationalism

Bulwark of liberty is in love of liberty
which God has planted in us.
Our defense is in the spirit
which prizes liberty as the heritage of all men,
in all lands, everywhere. Destroy this seed and
you have planted the seeds of despotism at your own doors.

—Abraham Lincoln

In the seventeenth century, people were talking of salvation and divinity. With advent of science, reason dominated thinking; by the nineteenth century, economics had taken the centre stage. In the twentieth century, men and women were more concerned with security. At the start of the twenty-first century, is not mortal fear dominating minds all over the world?.

The Indian subcontinent, during the seventeenth and the first half of the eighteenth century, wasted her energy in in-fighting. In the second half of the eighteenth and first half of the nineteenth century, part of urban India was engaged in seeking knowledge of western literature, science, philosophy and western culture. This acquisition of knowledge brought the realization of loss of liberty. As rulers imposed greater restrictions, the loss turned into a passion. Sensitive intellectuals responded with an adverse reaction. This was a period when British race was at the pinnacle of their glory. Contact with Britain, even as her dominion, was taking the country towards modern thinking. This appeared in steamboats, railways and other facilities that were uniting people speaking different languages and separate cultures.

The change brought by imported technology and its services was dramatic. A wave of change was sweeping the lives and minds of people. It provided an inspiration to catch up with the lost opportunities. For the next few decades, a divided country, low in spirits, bound in mental blocks, woke up from its long slumber by new forces released by science and technology. Aligned and bound with the mightiest empire on earth, the country began vibrating with hope. With the teaching of Buddha's compassion; the fighting spirit against injustice taught by the sermons of Guru Nanak and the wisdom of Kabir, India produced some of her greatest sons and daughters. Not since the Golden Age were such men born. They would change a bewildered, heterogeneous, and self-centred people, into a vibrant nation. Suddenly the people were prepared to face the toughest challenges and sufferings for the sake of liberty.

Repression of rulers

We noticed earlier how economic self-interest always guided British policy of governance. With mechanization helping mass production of goods, they sought markets all around the world. In the field of textiles, India, with a vast population, offered a good market. As rulers, Britain had full access to it. Lord Lytton, the viceroy, allowed free import of textiles from Lancashire in England. Indian textiles, famous throughout the world for their quality and craftsmanship, were unable to stand against machine-made, mass produced goods. Instead of protecting goods made in India, the import policy of foreign goods, ruined the entire economy. Indian families, dependent on handlooms, were devastated. The once famous artisans faced starvation. Those who had made India famous for its fine muslin and silk, all over the world, were on the road seeking subsistence. Cities like Murshidabad, Varanasi, and Surat, once flourishing towns, were deserted. The weavers were looking for jobs anywhere to keep the home fires burning.

Soon after, there was another cause to arouse indignation. There appeared an ordinance for possession of arms for personal safety. The Arms Act of 1878 prohibited Indians to keep arms. The act indirectly required them to depend only on government for their personal protection. In an age when security from robbers and thieves required utmost vigilance, this was an indirect attack on individual self respect of people of status.

As education in India spread, intelligent Indians aspired to get into the ICS. This alarmed the powers in London, the centre for examinations. To make entrance for local English boys easy, the age limit for ICS examination was reduced. Therefore, Indian youths found it difficult to go to England and compete in examinations. This only allowed them to find lower positions which were extremely difficult. Yet another humiliating law prohibited Indian members of the ICS try European offenders in their courts. This was racial arrogance at its worst. It was another way of the rulers to impose humiliation on the ruled. The sensitive Indian mind was inwardly revolting at such insults.

Such incidences, in quick succession, led Indian leaders to consider them as challenges that required to be met resolutely. The prophetic comments of Surendra Nath Bannerji came to their mind. The repressive laws of Lytton annoyed Indian leadership. They recollected the mistakes of 1857 and analysed their weaknesses.

The burning question was how to fight the injustice of a mighty empire?

Birth of Indian National Congress

Leaders deliberating the problem, realized that it was impossible to fight injustice of a strong and powerful Empire through violence. The British race, during their rule, had shown deep respect for constitutional and reasonable means. They loved democracy. Why not use the same qualities as weapons of war? As an enlightened race, trade and greed had temporarily blinded their discretion and wisdom. Laws of good governance, for which the Britons were once famous, were forgotten at the altar of wealth. Leaders decided to use petitions, discussions and agitation. This would enable them to mobilize public opinion as well as send the right message to the government.

It had its effect. The die-hard Lytton was replaced with Rippon, who had earlier earned the reputation as a liberal Governor General. The agitator's morale was boosted. It encouraged Indian leaders take up fresh causes that were harmful to Indian interests. More and more petitions started flowing to the viceroy. Some of them had identical grievances. Leaders thought that representation on a collective basis would perhaps be more rewarding. The need for a common platform on an all-India basis, was considered imperative for more effective results.

A retired English ICS officer, having completed his service innings, was enjoying a peaceful life playing golf in the foothills of Simla. He thought it in the interest of both India and Britain, that differences between the two may be resolved through peaceful discussions. The issue was informally taken up with other Indian friends. All well meaning and senior people liked the idea. It was decided to form an organization that could cover the entire country. This they thought would help both rulers and subjects, evolve mutually acceptable solutions, making governance smooth. AO Hume, a retired ICS officer, laid the foundation of Indian National Congress in 1885 to provide a link between Britain and India. For the next, more than fifty years, the Indian National Congress would relentlessly pursue the interests of Indian freedom. The spirit of cordiality that existed during the days of its formation, continued till the last day of freedom.

The first session of the Indian National Congress, formed with efforts of enlightened intellectuals and an English civil servant, was held at Mumbai on 28 December 1885 with WC Banerji as its first president. It was the first gathering comprising of a rising middle class devoted to peaceful political reforms. The delegates to the Congress comprised of lawyers, journalists, businessmen, landowners and other professionals. Mostly products of universities of Bombay, Calcutta and Madras, they had been exposed to ideas in social sciences of eminent scholars of England like Jeremy Bentham, John Stuart Mill and Thomas Macaulay. These young men aimed to improve the political and social conditions of Indian society on the pattern of knowledge acquired from British social and political thinkers of that period.

The Indian National Congress defined its objectives as follows:

1. The first priority was given to promotion of friendly relations between nationalists of different provinces of the country. Before any meaningful programme could be followed, unity of people speaking different languages, following separate social customs, had to be brought on one platform.

2. The next important factor emphasized by leaders of the first session, was to strengthen national unity amongst different communities living in the country.

3. It decided to consolidate grievances of people on an all India basis. These were to be represented by the Congress to the government for remedial measures.

4. To strengthen the organization and expand its base further, it decided to organize public opinion to lend strength and force to their appeals.

Working with these objectives, Congress, in a few years, grew into a strong political force. That it brought diverse elements from all over the country, into one homogeneous body was itself a great achievement during those difficult days of considerable chaos!

Besides economic issues, one of the early issues taken up by the Congress, was representation of elected members in the council that framed laws of governance. In 1892, it succeeded in persuading the viceroy to allow some members of the council to be elected by the people. This provided an effective platform where public grievances could be placed and frankly debated. For those days, it was a revolutionary change brought by love of liberty in the British race and Indian devotion to peaceful means.

Dominance of economic issues

Dadabhoy Naoroji had been a pioneer in raising economic issues before the rulers. Gopal Krishna Gokhale, a mild and articulate teacher of Poona, now joined him. They would examine pubic spending more critically. Finding public funds recklessly spent, leaders criticized the government for its policies detrimental to Indian interests. They squarely blamed the government for the poverty of people being directly connected to the waste of public money. "No taxation without representation" the slogan of the American War of Independence, became a common cry of Congress leaders in and outside the council chambers. They were now able to blame the government for the annihilation of cottage and village industries. Dadabhoy could only plead in 1881 that "everlasting, everyday increasing, foreign economic invasion was utterly destroying the country". Now he could more forcefully place the point in the council by threatening agitation.

Congress leaders now started advocating use of 'Swadeshi'(country made) goods, especially textiles, in preference to imported material. This had its reaction amongst the youth. The students held the first positive demonstration of its kind in Poona in 1896, where imported goods, for the first time were burnt in public. Later, for leaders it was to become a magic weapon to follow.

So far the government had been quite liberal in allowing free speech. When they found their own economic interests threatened, they decided to act. Bal Gangadhar Tilak had lately been advocating militancy in his journal. He was too vociferous for toleration by the government. Tilak was arrested. Contrary to expectations of government, Tilak at once became a national hero. Instead of creating fear in Indian minds, the challenge was courageously accepted. The influence and stature of Tilak, and with him of the Congress, jumped overnight. Tilak's influence, which was until now confined to upper middle-class intellectuals, reached the people. Surendra Nath Banerji, in one of his prophetic writings had ridiculed the Raj with a philosophy that proved to be true:

"In the evolution of political progress, bad rulers are often a blessing in disguise. They help to stir a community into life, a result that years of agitation would perhaps have failed to achieve." The popularity Tilak's arrest fetched the Congress, could have taken decades in the normal course!

Fateful decade—seeds of division

Britain, to justify her autocratic rule, was propagating a new theory. She advertised that Indians were a divided people, who fought with each other. Being incapable to rule themselves, the English were obliging Indians by providing some elements of civilized life. There was some ground for them to say so. In Congress, there were three prominent leaders at that time. There was the eloquent Surendra Nath Banerji; the mild and constitutional teacher, Gopal Krishna Gokhale; and the fiery, extremist journalist, Gangadhar Tilak. Education and learning was playing its role amongst all sections. The social inequalities that lay buried were now emerging. Leaders of different groups were bringing out their grievances; some of them no doubt genuine.

The rise in national consciousness had created a class of fundamentalists amongst both Hindus and Muslims. They aroused communal consciousness within the illiterate Indian population. The leaders of backward Hindu community took this opportunity to dig out the long history of their exploitation. This turmoil in society brought out centuries of suppressed feelings. Each section, to gain sympathy of a particular class, exaggerated their grievances to form a solid block of its support.

Hindu fundamentalists started the cry of 'Back to the Vedas'. Each community was tempted to take up a new road to nationalism. A new definition, a new angle of citizenship was being evolved without taking any notice of changes that had occurred. It was like denial of history of last several centuries during which tremendous changes in governance and culture had occurred. It was like an ostrich digging his neck in the sand and crying that he saw nothing. This cry was a denial of reality. Fundamentalists behaved like old cynics, who refused to accept change. For such men, time had stopped. For them the age of Buddha, Nanak, Kabir, Shiekh Farid, Rahim who of the ancient and medieval era, were mere ripples, were insignificant before their own faith.

The communal division amongst people of the country did not miss the keen observation of foreign rulers. As the national movement picked up speed, the government used the fractured polity to its advantage. As we proceed, this would keep repeatedly appearing in one form or the other. Instead of joining hands to give an effective answer, rulers used religion to stifle and choke the national movement.

If 'Swaraj' (liberty) was the slogan of the nationalists, the British *mantra* was Divide and Rule.

Partition of Bengal

Bengal, from the beginning had been leading in all social and political battles. Rulers considered the state a menace. As an efficient surgeon, to safeguard the interest of the crown, the Viceroy Lord Curzon, partitioned Bengal. He envisaged that such an act would create a wedge between the two major religious communities. West Bengal comprised of a Hindu majority; East Bengal had mostly Muslims.

With the partition of Bengal, the foundation of the Partition of India in 1947 was laid almost fifty years earlier.

The partition of Bengal, implemented in 1905, offered an ideal platform for Congress and Muslim League to expand their constituency. When Congress started an agitation for re-unification of Bengal, it had the support of all communities, including a section of intellectual Muslims. The League countered the agitation with appeal to Muslim religious sentiments. Having governed the country for several centuries, they referred to martial superiority of their community. The fundamentalists, in this manner, sought to revive the old glory of Islam when Turks and Arabs had conquered a great part of the world. A delegation of Muslim leaders, led by Aga Khan met the Viceroy Lord Minto. They demanded separate safeguards for the Muslim community.

Religion had given Britain the chance to play the politics of divide and rule. Since it played such a pivotal role, it would be interesting to know the how and why of religion and knowledge, particularly scientific knowledge, which had been crossing swords with each other.

Chapter XXXIII
Glimpes of The Past

Trust no future however pleasant!
Let the dead past bury its dead!
Act, act in the living present!
Heart within, and God overhead.

—HW Longfellow

New religions and their characteristic civilizations in history have taken birth and flourished together. When their vigour is exhausted, they have decayed side by side. We may well regard this process of decay and growth, as cause and effect. What is regarded as the birth of a new religion, is really only a reaffirmation and revivification by the extraordinary personality of the 'reproclaimer'. The new religions were only necessitated by changed circumstance when earlier values got wrapped with non-essentials and harmful formalism. Not able to meet new challenges, religions and civilizations start decaying. Since all religions are the same essentialy, an atmosphere of peace and happiness is created when men highlight similarities instead of differences.

Is it a coincidence that all great religions were born in Asia? Is it again chance that most great religions were either born or flowed and flourished in the country? We are aware that some came to escape torture at place of their birth; others arrived with a missionary spirit and some others for wealth and fame. Once in India, whatever their initial design, they made the country their home. In course of time, they were absorbed lending diversity and strength to their ideas. This has helped fertilize and enrich Indian culture, lending the country, the beauty of diversity of colours like in a rainbow. Together they all help nourish this multifarious nation and so sustain her ancient civilization!

What is unique in India that makes different religions adopt this commonality?

The middle path

Let us get some clue from an Arab traveller! Musa-ul-Qwarazini had come to India, several centuries earlier, looking for an answer to the same question. The traveller was anxious to meet some saint who might be able to impart knowledge of Indian metaphysics. Varanasi was then the centre of Vedanta knowledge. At Varanasi, he was guided to a learned scholar on the subject, who had been preaching religious philosophy and giving discourses for the last forty years.

The traveller extensively discussed the subject; both the learned men had a hearty discussion. The Arab was satisfied and happy. Before his departure, the traveller inquired:

> "I am satisfied with the talks we had. Are you too satisfied with your knowledge on the subject as I am of yours?"

> The scholar replied, "I have been studying and teaching scriptures for the last forty years. After all these years, I realize that I know little about them. Placed between two extremes of ignorance and knowledge, I have not been able to comprehend time, space or eternity. I try to find out what is it that produces thought? I do not know why I exist? My disciples often ask questions on these subject. I answer them. They apparently feel satisfied, but I, in my own self, remain confounded and in doubt."

> "Can I meet some one who is satisfied in himself" the traveller asked.

> The scholar advised him to go and meet an old woman living nearby.

> The traveller reached her house and found the woman happily singing devotional song before her god. He asked her, "What is it that makes you so utterly happy?"

> She answered, " I remain extremely busy serving my Lord Shiva. In the morning, I go every day to take bath in the holy river and bring Ganges-water. Cleaning the floor, I give a bath to my Lord God; decorate the seat with flowers and sit chanting His name. This gives me great satisfaction. I feel myself to be the happiest woman on earth."

> The traveller went back and narrated the whole story.

> "You are right," the scholar admitted. "I have always said I would be happy if I was ignorant; yet it is not the kind of happiness that I would ever cherish."

The happiness of the woman was derived from a faith that is an inheritance from knowledge of the past. Looking from a wider perspective, both were deriving happiness and peace from the same source. The old woman drew it from faith, the scholar from study. Religion is a ceaseless pursuit that elevates the spirit for a purpose. While the learned and the ignorant are its extreme, the wise in every age, have pleaded for a middle path, a golden mean. India has followed the middle path that helps her people to be at peace in times of distress. It has provided the country a resilience to meet challenges of adversity with indifference. The dos and don'ts of religion are like centripetal and centrifugal forces to maintain a balance in the physical world. The law, by which nature operates in the world, is also the same.

Zarathushtra, the Parsi god says about the two principles of light and darkness, good and ill, that seem apart from one another, yet are bound inseparably together, each to each.

> O Mighty Lord of wisdom, Mazada!
> Supreme, Infinite, Universal mind
> This "lower mind" of mind, this egoism,
> And put an end to all duality.
> Ahura! Thou that giveth life to all,
> Grant me the power to control the mind.

Buddha and Mahavira advise the following non-extremism in their scriptures:

> Even as the dairy-maid, pulling and slacking,
> The two ends of the churning-string by turns,
> Churns out the golden butter from the milk,
> E'en as the sage working alternately,
> At both the two inevitable sides
> Of every question, finds the perfect truth.

The Mahabharata, in Shantiparva, emphasizing the same point advises:

> Be religious, not bigoted; vitreous, not self righteous;
> gather wealth, not cruelty; enjoy without elation;
> be generous, not wasteful;
> give, not indiscriminately;
> serve your interest, without hurting others;
> be angry, not without a strong cause;
> be gentle, not to the mischievous;
> worship Deity, without display.

The Sufi saints of Islam define the middle path thus:

"Oceans of sweet and bitter serge abreast,
Between them rests the razor-line of Rest,
The essence of Godhead rests amidst the pairs,
 Maintaining even justice for all.

All religions therefore endeavour to be in harmony with the envoirnment in which they are born. They are a guide to furnish us with the daily duties. But gradually, the custodians of religions begin to do the 'ordering', become over conservative, rigid, narrow, domineering, greedy, immoral, despotic, loose their elastic touch with changing times, forget the essentials, insisting over much on non-essentials and thus corrupt the religion by their own excesses. Then 'politics' and 'science' begin to do the ordering and go even to the worst extremes.

Role of orthodoxy in religion

Religion in India, has been a source of both her strength and weakness. Geographical location and physical features blessed the country to be host to all great religions of the world. In a country of such diversity, glorifying any particular religion is possible only at the risk of her fundamental unity. Even when Vedanta, as the earliest philosophy, prevailed in the country, there were tribes following different gods and performing varying rituals. It preached oneness amongst all human beings. With passage of time, new thoughts produced new religions. It is in the nature of men that they corner privileges when in power. After they are gone, their descendents try to retain them. Under the circumstances, sticking to the past becomes most convenient. However, no society has ever rested on its laurels. They keep being moulded with changing nature and needs. The change being not in personal interests of fundamentalists, they try to negate reforms as anti-religious. To prove their point they do not hesitate to present twisted interpretations of scriptures before their constituency. New mythologies and new 'facts' are cleverly fabricated to prove what would ensure the old mood of blind devotion and dedication.

In ancient Hindu India, kings ruled their territories along with religious priests. This bestowed on priests the power to interpret scriptures suiting royal interest. The kings and priests were thus made dependent on each other. Again, during Islamic rule, in the medieval period, kings followed the same arrangement. They also sought guidance and interpretation of scriptures from the Islamic priests. The king-priest duo was sharing power. Since it suited both, the arrangement continued. Like kings, the priests followed the same tradition of bestowing their charge to their progeny. They argued that if, after the king was dead, his kingdom could be passed on to the next generation, why the same principle could not be applied to the priests? To maintain their hegemony, they could always produce new methods, fabricate new tales, to entice people. New stories were spun to keep the faithful enchanted! This glorification served another useful purpose. In periods of humiliation and distress, glorification of the past became the balm for the sufferings of the present.

Then, arrived science in the West. The collective knowledge of all countries was put to the service of man. The unexplainable causes that gave birth to fear and produced religion, began to be explained with logic and reason. Countries blessed with the new knowledge unfettered themselves from beliefs fabricated in earlier ages. Englishmen of logical and scientific temparament arrived in India. This helped evoke nationalism amongst western-educated Indians. Besides political, religious and social reformers were equally inspired to work against the evils that grew with the shackles of ignorance. Another class, silently suffering for ages, clamoured for justice. The 'backwards', for centuries, were leading a miserable life. Inspired by winds of change, their leaders took up their cause. Jotirao Phule in Maharashtra, Chatrapati Sahu Maharaj in north India and Ramaswami Naicker in south India, endeavoured to redress injustice and improve the lot of their community. Jotirao Phule even sent a petition to Queen Victoria, the Empress of India, writing:

"You have set a wonderful lesson to the whole world by banning slavery in the (British) empire. It will be a blot on your fair reputation if you don't free these unfortunate brethren of mine".

His plea for reservation in government services had to wait until the independence of the country. One of the early actions taken after independence, was to bring the backward classes of societies to the mainstream of Hindu society.

Divisive tendencies: erosion of nationalism

Religious divisiveness succeeded in creating a wedge between the two communities. If Hindus sought their identity in the Vedic age, the other inhabitants of India could not be blamed for finding their identity and support in Buddha who was the first to have condemned the caste system. Muslims, having been masters of a great part of the world during the medieval period, looked for their inspiration from Arabia, and other West Asian countries. The religious tug of war, so started, damaged the rhythm of the national movement. Hindu religious fundamentalists came out eulogizing the heroism of Maharana Pratap and Shivaji fighting 'foreigners'. Hot-headed fundamentalists amongst Hindus, Muslims and Sikhs, gradually began suspecting each other's intentions. There was a sudden growth of fundamentalist organizations to threaten the national fabric. In due course, such a twisted version of religion, was only to create uneasiness amongst religious minorities. Again, when India was on its way to move forward, religious fundamentalism stifled progress. Somehow, the past has always obsessed Indian thinking at different stages of history.

Scrapping a thousand years' history was ignoring the contribution of kings like Akbar; religious saints like Salim Chisti, Farid, Kabir, Guru Nanak; cultural reformers like Amir Khusrau who helped develop a common culture, music and arts; of musicians like Tansen who made Indian music what it is today; Ghalib the immortal poet whose *ghazals* enchant Indians of every age. There were many great Muslims of the era who held a prominent place in the history of the nation. How could anyone forget them? It was like denying the existence of Qutub Minar, the Red Forts at Agra and Delhi and Taj Mahal, not acknowledging a part of Indian heritage.

To ignore changes in religion, culture and language introduced in medieval India was a denial of history. It was a false glorification, confined to only one community. The backlash of such a policy would be felt when Hindu and Muslim religious nationalism would start spreading their tentacles to damage the national movement. It would be felt at the final phase of negotiations for independence when the third party would use one against the other.

Finding response to ideas that were meant to arouse divisive religious feelings, several other fundamentalist organizations spoke of Maharana Pratap and Shivaji, as their ideal for fighting 'foreigners'. Who were these 'foreigners?' This was a mischievous version, of a purely territorial struggle of Hindu leaders fighting Muslim kings of their time. It would be false to equate it with freedom from English rule. Such an approach, would be a denial of cultural changes of centuries. History informs that religions and their characteristic civilizations have grown and decayed together. We may well regard the two as side effects. What is regarded as a birth of a new religion is really a re-proclamation when the earlier one gets wrapped up with non-essentials and harmful formalism. As religions, at their roots, are the same, men only need to be friendly, highlighting similarities instead of differences. This can be easily done with love as the guiding force:

> Sole remedy of all life's ills and sadness.
> Prime antidote of pride and perjury,
> Art, Sciences, Scriptures, art thou to me.
> Vedas, Avesta, Bible, Al Quran,
> Temples, Pagodas, Churches and Ka'aba stone.
> All these are near my heart doth close embrace,
> Since my religion now is Love alone.

Religious orthodoxy invariably seeks stick to the past. In a world subject to change, this is an utterly impractical approach. The past is to be remembered for drawing lessons from old mistakes. The present has to be based on changes brought by time. Instead of presenting a united identity, that the national movement required at this critical juncture, different forms of religion began surfacing. National consciousness instead of moving towards its goal, got diverted towards communal consciousness. Vivekanada repeatedly condemned this conservative approach. He called even "to forget religion for some time". His was the voice of sanity. We will know more about him in the next chapter.

Tearing down barriers

Religion and science with varying degrees influence civilizations. Both together involve moral values, create institutions, and discipline in thinking and believing.

Each civilization starts with vigour. When it has reached the peak of fulfilment, it starts claiming to be the best that could happen. It begins to consider itself invincible. So thought the ancient Indians about the Vedantic age; the Greeks of the age of Pericles, the Romans of the rule of Julius Ceasar, and the Mohammedans of the days of Caliphate. The onward march of civilization is like a man trying to climb a greasy pole. So long as his effort to climb continues, it continues to go up with a slow or fast momentum. As soon as he stops, the fall downward, starts. Once down, he is required to start all over again. The past he had created, never returns. A new foundation for a fresh structure has to be built again; but hoping to bring it back with the same vigour and velocity, has never been possible. Striving for return of the past glory only remains an obsession, a myth of self-satisfaction; a cause of conflict and indeed a mirage.

Indian civilization decayed after the fall of Harsha Vardhana. Soon after it was influenced by Islam. The Mohammedens had come with their own culture and religion. The Indian spiritual climate of multiplicity, the vastness of the subcontinent and above all its emphasis on peace and non-violence, saved the continuity of her civilization even when its culture and language underwent a change. Language, morals and manners, music, and art all changed, but the change remained within the wider parameters of her core culture. By denying this cosmopolitanism, we shall unwittingly destroy the very foundations of our strength. Civilization is not something material in nature. It is the outcome of complex combination of cultural creations. If the ground at some other place is conducive and receptive, the ingredients move on to their new place of habitation. The Greek civilization in which Homer sang his songs and Pericles encouraged thoughts, died; Indian civilization did not die because of her inbuilt capacity of accommodation and absorption; instead of resisting change, it accepted this change.

During the brief domination of India by Britain, there was again an invasion on her modified culture. This time, it was not an exchange like what occurred when Islam had arrived in the country; it was unidirectional. Western culture dominated the minds, particularly of the intellectual class. In spite of change in language and culture, India has been able to maintain her continuity. She has been able to accommodate Christianity as it did Islam, a thousand years earlier.

However, the star of India was now ascending. Against all hurdles and complexities, India would continue her march. To inspire the nation, nature gifted the country with three great revolutionaries: one, that roared like a lion on religion. The other two announced India's awakening of India through poetry. They sang the songs of their social and emotional life, of patriotism and the infirmities of religion, responsible for her political and economic stagnancy. They, in their speeches and writings, changed the complexion of the game of life. There was the passionate Urdu poet and philosopher, Mohammed Iqbal, who would not be afraid to question the religious bigotry of the high and mighty. He inspired his compatriots with poetry and condemned religious priests for leading people astray. In a short spell of time, three great intellectual leaders sent a thrill amongst the people of India. Vivekananda strived to reform religion and improve the quality of life. Tagore and Mohammed Iqbal were true representatives of their time when the entire country was afire with patriotism. These extraordinary men helped awaken the spirit of India with their inspiring thoughts, speeches, writings and action.

Chapter XXXIV
Reformers and Philosophers
The New Era

If one religion was allowed, the Government
and people would become arbitrary.
If there were two,
people will cut each other's throat.
But if there were a multitude,
they all live happily and in peace.

—Swami Vivekananda

English language and Christianity, during the last few decades of the Renaissance, profoundly influenced the youth, particularly in urban India. The early impression made on young minds in missionary schools and the fascinating figure of Christ had deep impressions on them. The tree of knowledge now started bearing fruits. The new wave helped produce such men of genius, not witnessed for centuries. Within decades, new stars appeared on the Indian sky. Enriched with creative ideas, they produced a symphony between the metaphysics of Vedanta, Islam and Christianity and the material world of science. A new bond of collective unity and wellbeing, established amongst people following different faiths, was now clearly visible. We will have the opportunity to get glimpses of these men whose wisdom gave the country a new line of thought and action. Inspired with a common base of togetherness, these men and women of the new generation, would help bring a unique revolution, the world had not seen before.

One of them was the simple saint of Dakhshineshwar. Sri Ramkrishna of Bengal was an ordinary priest in the temple of Mother Kali. Not involved much in intellectual pursuits, he was happy serving her in the temple. He would silently serve the Divine Mother, caring little for religious scriptures. His heart was ever flowing with tenderness and affection towards all who visited the temple. If some visitor would ask him to say something for guidance, he would repeat, "that all religions are good; each leading to God, or a stage on way to the essence of his faith. All rivers overflow to the ocean. Flow and let others flow too."

Amongst the many who accepted Sri Ramkrishna as his guru was Narendra Nath Dutta, an idealist and a seeker of the Truth with an intensely analytical mind. In his first meeting with Sri Ramkrishna, Narendra sang some devotional songs. Thereafter, during fierce discussions on religion, he spoke from his heart. He always subordinated his imagination to the demands of reason. Although overwhelming inner experiences marked his visits to Sri Ramkrishna, his great respect for material western sciences, made him want to test each. He would accept only those that stood the test. In a short time, Sri Ram Krishna and Narendra Nath had mentally merged with each other.

When Sri Ramkrishna died, Narendra was 23 years of age. He had promised the Guru to continue with his resolve and serve humankind. Becoming Swami Vivekananda, after the death of Sri Ramkrishna, for the next ten years, this restless monk roaring like a lion, created a new India. Henceforth, every action of this monk would be dedicated to the service of the poor.

An ideal spiritualist–Swami Vivekananda (1863-1902)

If man is guided by the spirit of the sub-conscious mind, national behaviour follows this collective spirit of her people. Thousand of years of culture and civilization has moulded Indian character to be individualistic, intuitive, non-violent and generally content, debating subjects they like. The tropical climate has influenced them to be contemplative. They care more for spiritual life than the mundane and the material. This may have been India's weakness in violent actions; it has perpetually provided inner nourishment to the soul. Indian mind, from ancient times, has focussed on the metaphysical phenomenon of nature. When science began dominating religion in the West, its effects reached the entire world. Indians, with their ancient heritage, sought a vision wider than the material; they looked for something more balanced; something between both science and spirituality. Men of intellect strove to fuse this knowledge of science and spirit.

Who were the extraordinary geniuses whose wisdom helped to give the country a chain of leaders in a short period? Why, at their call, people left their high profile professions for a cause that appeared so distant? What was the magic that turned them into great leaders of Indian history?

Indian environment

Indian Renaissance, triggered by Rammohun Roy, had awakened a slumbering nation. She now awaited men of vision to give a suitable expression. Nature produced such men when the time was right. These extraordinary men, developed a symphony between the outer world, enriched by western science and the message of Vedanta, Islam and Christ. Armed with similar thought, Vivekanada infused daring, courage and vigour to act. The leaders succeeded in developing a silent revolution in the mind of men. They so charged the atmosphere that people followed the path they trod. Vivekananda introduced true spirituality in his mission. He used his sharp intellect with such discretion that it changed the direction of formal religious practices. He had synthesized his intellect with the inner enlightenment of Sri Ramkrishna, when he said, "For next fifty years…let all other vain gods disappear from our minds…The first of all worships, is the worship of those around us…".

There would be many more like him whose words of wisdom unfettered the chained minds of a depressed people.

Early life

Narendra Nath Dutta, from an early age, was blessed with a sharp intellect, keen concentration, self-confidence and inexhaustible resourcefulness. While at college, he was deeply influenced by the use of logic and reasoning to arrive at conclusions. New discoveries in science were encouraging a scientific temper. Young Narendra was not prepared to accept beliefs, whose only claim was that they were contained in scriptures. He would not accept anything that could not stand the test of reason. Existence of God had remained a favourite subject on which the priests had always had their say. Narendra caught exactly this point to challenge the priests. Being an idealist, he sought truth that could meet analytical reasoning for acceptance. "Have you seen God?" was his favourite query to them. They all fumbled, giving vague answers that did not satisfy his intellect. Ramkrishna, the simple saint of Dakshineshwar could only guide him. When he asked his usual question, Ramkrishna answered, "Yes. I have seen God; I see Him as I see you here, only much more clearly!"

Ramkrishna, an enlightened saint; Narendra, an idealist-intellectual, became master and disciple. Narendra knew that without intellectual questioning and inner struggle, no one can arrive at illumination. In Narendra, he found the energy, the will and the inner instruments for such questioning. Ramkrishna yearned to test his experience through the dynamic intellect of Narendra. As a youth, Narendra was possessed with a mental dilemma. He had learnt that science gave power to conquer the world. Scriptures, on the other hand, advised renouncing everything to reach God. Narendra placed his conflict before the master. Ramkrishna, having seen and experienced both the inner and outer world, added a third dimension. This was, "direct contact with human misery." What had driven Gautama Buddha to solve this enigma, several thousand

years ago, was the search for the cause for human misery. Ramkrishna advised
his pupil to find an answer to this question in the misery of the Indians. He at
once accepted the formula that "the way to reach God was to help remove
human misery." Henceforth he devoted himself to eradicate misery amongst
his people.

Having so inspired Narendra, Ramkrishna felt relieved. He thought that he
had achieved the mission of his life. Now it was for Narendra to carry it
forward. This Narendra did. Ramkrishna passed away soon after; Narendra
was now Swami Vivekananda.

Swami Vivekanada starts his mission

Vivekanada had noticed how religion had corrupted society. To cleanse it from
bigotry became his mission. He dreamt of a religion that would "develop
confidence and awareness, self respect, power to feed and educate the poor,
and relieve the miseries around me." He began propagating the mantra of
his master:

If you want to find God, serve man.

For the first two years, he went round the country to assess and strengthen the
several spiritual centres that existed. Thereafter, he travelled to western countries
to develop rapport with the people following other religions. On his return,
he tested his experiences in the crucible of human misery. Flinging away all his
earlier conflicts, he set out to implement the *mantra* of his master.

His religion–universal religion

All religions preach tolerance, mutual respect, and control of sensuous pleasure,
a code for peace and progress, pursuit of knowledge with wisdom, control
of anger, and non-violence. Indian philosophy has termed them as 'dharma'.
These qualities, contain the essence of factors that promote human progress.
Vivekananda believed that religion formed the centre, the keynote of the entire
music of Indian national life. It was natural for him to apply the Vedantic
philosophy of inter-dependence. In practice, he found that this valuable principle
was merely repeated only in words and glorified in debates. In action, it was
not implemented. The great Indian king Akbar, a few centuries ago, had
conceived a similar idea in *Din–i-Ilahi*, the religion of humanity. Vivekananda
also thought of a universal religion. Finding wide variety existing in different
societies, he concluded that unless the human race was enlightened enough, a
universal religion was an impossibility.

How was it possible to bring enlightenment? This was the question facing the
young Swami.

Vivkenanda explained that, "a common sense approach, guided by logic and reason, without caring for forms, ceremonies, or rituals, alone satisfies and enlightens man. Commonality of interests, which is the essence of all religions, has continued to be ignored as impractical." He considered this "understanding to be essential for the existence of the human race; it was true enlightenment." In a letter to his Muslim friend, Vivekananda wrote:

> Whether we call it Vedantism or any ism, the truth is that Advaitism (Oneness) is the last word of religion and thought. It is the only position from which one can look upon all religions and sects as one and the same. I believe it is the religion of future enlightened humanity. The Hindus may get the credit of arriving at it earlier than other races, they being an old race than either Hebrews or Arabs. Practical Advaitism that looks upon and behaves with all humankind as one's own soul was developed amongst the Hindus. On the other hand, my experience is that if ever any religion approached to equality in an appreciable manner, it is Islam and Islam alone.
>
> Therefore, I am firmly persuaded that without the help of particle Islam, theories of Vedantism, however fine and wonderful they may be, are valueless for the entire mass of mankind.

We notice how the modern world is realigning its joints. Development in science is making the world go global. Vivekananda addressed the Parliament of Religions, on 11 September 1893. His ideas transformed the beliefs of the millennia. Man, to be able to achieve this objective has still to cover a long journey on the road to enlightenment. Vivekananda had the vision to speak of this journey in his address, thus:

> …I am proud to belong to a religion which had taught the world, both tolerance and universal acceptance, which has sheltered and is still fostering the remnants of the grand Zoroastrian nations. I will quote to you, brethren, a few lines from a hymn which I remember to have repeated from my earliest boyhood, which is everyday repeated by millions of human beings,
>
> "As the streams have their source in different places, all mingle their water in the sea, so O Lord, the different paths which men take through different tendencies, various though they appear, crooked or straight, all lead to thee."

Vivekananda further said:

> I accept all religions that were in the past and worship them all. I worship God with every one of them, in whatever form they worship him. I shall go to the mosque of the Mohammedan, I shall enter the Buddhist temple, where I shall take refuge in Buddha, and his laws. I shall go to the forest, and sit down in meditation with the Hindu, who is trying to see light, which enlightens the heart of everyone. The Bible, the Vedas, the Koran and all other sacred books are but so many pages, while an infinite number of pages remain to be unfolded.

We stand in the present, but open ourselves to the infinite future. Salutations
to all the prophets of the past, to all the great ones of the present, and to all
that are to come in the future!

Fusion of matter and spirit

With the introduction of science, knowledge of the outer world gained
momentum. India's aim had been not to acquire but to release, to enlarge his
consciousness by growing with and growing into their surroundings. It was
felt that truth is all comprehensive, that there is no isolation in existence. It was
realizing this harmony between man's spirit with the spirit of the world. The
more we learnt about the outer world, the more enigmatic it appeared.
Mysteries of the universe were far beyond comprehension; they remain today;
they will continue to be so. Qualities like patience, sympathy, sense of human
destiny, essential for a harmonious human relationship, are thus born.

Vivekanada explained the limitation of science: "Man instead of materializing
spirit into matter, must spiritualize the matter". Since our present lives are
based on the opposite principle; it is causing disharmony in conduct of men,
women and nations. "The gift of science to life needs to be measured on the
scales of human happiness. The material life can only be made full of purity
and peace, when it is spiritualized."

Vivekananda explains spiritualism saying, "No man, no nation can hate others
without degenerating itself. India's downfall was sealed the very day, they used
the word 'malechha' (untouchable) and stopped communion with others."
Vivekananda never tired of blaming priests for distorting religion and the
philosophy of Vedanta.

Nationalism and internationalism

Vivekananda appeared on the Indian scene when the realities of existence
were goading the country for action. She was realizing how excessive thought,
not backed by action, had been the cause of her misfortune. Vivekananda
toured the country relentlessly proclaiming, "Be moral. Be brave; brave unto
desperation. Do not bother your head with religious theories. Only cowards
sin. Try to love everybody." Induction of science in the last few centuries had
increased the common man's love for materialism. He warned intellectuals to
learn only what was good in science–

> No religion is against acceptance of fresh ideas or things good for the country.
> The test, whether they are so, is to put them in the crucible of morality. If they
> create greed, hatred, jealousy and suspicion, they at once turn against harmonious

human relationship. This life is short. The vanities of world are transient.
They alone live, who live for others; the rest are more dead than alive.

Vivekananda's patriotism was not just love for the country, it was service to the poor of the world:

Leave to the next life the reading of Vedanta and the practice of meditation.
Let the body which is here be put to the service of others...The first of all worships is the worship of those around us. They are all our god... man and animals; and the first gods we have to worship are our own countrymen. Truth is my god; Universe my country,

Vivekananda considered excessive respect for past, self-destructive. He was highly impressed by the American struggle for independence. In appreciation, he even wrote a poem that embodies his internationalism:

To the fourth of July,
Move on, Oh Lord, in thy restless path,
Till thy high noon overspreads the world,
Till every land reflects thy light,
Till men and women with uplifted heads,
Behold their shackles, broken and know,
In springing joy, their life renowned!

March towards the universal

A century of scientific and technological development has helped globalization, and convergence of interests. It is gradually helping strengthen bonds between different races and cultures. Human rights, not national rights, are acquiring a higher position in the world community. Travelling on this route, humanity will reach enlightenment. All great thinkers and religious reformers, from time to time, have impressed the same to universalize religion. New technologies, in the field of information and communications, have for the first time in human history, opened geographical frontiers. The path of enlightenment, which they preached, but could not practice, can now be followed without hindrance.

Beginning of the twentieth century was springtime for mother India. Beautiful flowers bloomed in her garden. A generation of political leaders appeared on the Indian scene one after another. The nation that is advanced economically also holds political leadership. Vivekanada's dream will become a reality when world leadership is guided by a combination of political, economic and spiritual elements.

Chapter XXXV
A Lover of Life—Rabindranath Tagore

Deliverance for me is not in renunciation
I feel the embrace of freedom in a thousand bonds of delight.
No, I will never shut the doors of my senses,
The delight of sight and hearing will beautify delight.

—Rabindranth Tagore

Rabindranath (1861-1941) was born in challenging times. Absence of knowledge that had created a state of stagnation for centuries was no longer existent. The doors of knowledge now opened to those who sought it. India, having assimilated several cultural invasions, was now face to face with western culture. The magnificent East-West encounter of the eighteenth and nineteenth century had given birth to a new dynamism that had long lived buried in ignorance. It was now being received with fresh strength. Men of learning were catching up in art and literature, science and technology. There was another class of political leaders, who were prepared to sacrifice everything to be in the forefront of freedom struggle. J.C. Bose received renown in discoveries of electricity, C.V. Raman received the Nobel Prize in Physics, and Chandrashekhar got outstanding fame in astro-physics. Vivekananda was an ideal spiritualist who was also a great religious parliamentarian. Tilak, Gokhale and Lajpat Rai were loved for their fearlessness. There were also shining examples like Sri Aurobindo, Dayananda, Annie Besant, Badruddin Tyabji and many more. All these men and women were fruits of the Indian Renaissance and were doing India proud in their specific spheres. The new age was bringing change; gradually obliterating the weaknesses of the past.

The Tagores, for two generations, were a renowned family of India. Bengal had been the home of art, music, drama and culture. Rabindranath's grandfather had taken over the Presidentship of the Brahmo Samaj. Most members of the family had achieved fame in art, paintings or music. Rabindranath excelled in philosophical poetry. Through it, he expressed the romanticism of nature, blending the East and the West. He would write lyrics and literature, providing wings for the imagination to admire the beauty and tenderness of nature in all its manifestations. When Tagore was sailing for the third time to England, a co-passenger on the ship inquired: "What was so great that takes you undertake the voyage again?"

Tagore answered, "To rediscover a country, that produced leaders like the captain of the luxury liner, Titanic."(This ship had sunk in the Arctic Ocean after hitting an iceberg. The captain, with traditional British courage and discipline, organized rescue operations to save as many lives as possible. Finally, closing himself in his cabin, he went down to the bottom of the ocean with the ship.) The bravery, the courage and tradition that governed such actions of a foreign race were the source of inspiration for his love for the country. This would, time and again be expressed in poetry for the world to wonder.

Face to face with new culture

Only a few years ago, no one could dare criticize ancient Hindu scriptures. Tagore took the initiative and wrote "the ancient civilization of India, had its own ideals of perfection. Its aim was not attaining power as it generally neglected to organize men for defensive and offensive purposes, for co-operation in the acquisition of wealth and for military and political ascendancy." The ideal that India tried to release her best men to the isolation of a contemplative life was not to his liking. He complains, "In this lies the secret of India's misfortune as well as her glory. Just as people learn from past mistakes, civilizations also do so to meet growing challenges!"

While Tagore admired the West for her scientific achievements, he was averse to their propensity for its use in exploitation. He considered greed and lust for political power, self-destructive. Tagore emphasized that India is the epitome of the historical concept of unity in diversity. Indian civilization has relentlessly dreamt of oneness in the world. It never built boundaries of segregation to keep foreigners and their ideas from entering the country; she has on the other hand, welcomed them. Tagore expresses these sentiments in his famous poem:

> Where the mind is without fear,
> And the head held high;
> Where the world has not been broken up
> Into fragments by narrow domestic walls.
> In that heaven of freedom, my father,
> Let my country awake!

Political condition in his period

There was considerable turbulence when Curzon, the Viceroy of India, announced partition of Bengal, in 1905. This was under the British policy of 'divide and rule'. The works of Tagore however found an affectionate response amongst both Hindus and Muslims. He wrote stirring patriotic songs against the artificial division of Bengal, done with the sole motive to create a wedge between the Hindus and Muslims. Although the partition had to be eventually annulled under persistent agitation, Curzon had sown the seed of dividing the subcontinent. In 1971, after the formation of Bangladesh, one of his patriotic songs, namely '*amar sonar Bangla…*' was adopted as her national anthem.

Tagore enthusiastically supported the agitation launched by the Congress, both for Swedeshi and against partition of Bengal. He wrote patriotic songs in favour of non-cooperation, Hindu-Muslim unity, untouchability and rural education. His heart always turned to the voiceless Indian, living in remote villages, with no one to pay attention to his plight.

> To the dumb, languishing and the stupefied,
> Must we give voice;
> These hearts, wilted, withered and broken
> Must be galvanized with New Hope;
> Beckoning them, we must exhort.
>
> Lift up your heads this very instant
> And stand united,
> They before whom you quake in fear, quake more
> Than you in their guilt.
> They will take to their heels the moment
> You are aroused ….

Immediately after World War I, in 1919, the tragedy of Jallianwala Bagh occurred at Amritsar. Hundreds of innocent people, with no chance to escape, were gunned down, deliberately. Tagore was deeply hurt by the tragedy. As a protest, he surrendered his knighthood.

His imaginative philosophy

Tagore, from his childhood, was brought up in refinement and comfort in a place where music and poetry held all the expressions of life. Gentle in spirit, so affectionate was his nature that birds perched on his hands for food. Observant, and receptive to mystic sensitivity, some of his works take long flights of imagination:

> Tell me if this be true, my love, tell me if this be true,
> When these eyes flash their lightening, the dark clouds in
> your breast
> Make stormy answer.

Is it true that my lips are sweet like the opening bud of the
first conscious love?
Do the memories of vanished months of May linger in my
limbs?
Does the Earth, like a harp, shiver into songs with the
touch of my feet?
Is it true that the dewdrops from the eyes of night when I
am seen,
In addition, the morning light is glad when it wraps my
body round?
Is it true, is it true, that your love travelled alone through
ages and worlds in search of one?
That when you found me at last, your age long desire, found
utter peace.
In my gentle face and my eyes and lips and flowing hair?
Is it then true, that the mystery of Infinite on this little
forehead of mine,
Tell me, my love, if all this is true?

The poem delicately brings out the feminine understanding of love between man and woman; nature and man. It gives an insight into the philosophical thoughts of India, wherein each woman is endowed with beauty; each man infatuated by woman, death and God.

Indians have accepted different moods of nature with awe and respect in a compromising spirit!

Political statesmanship

In the first gush of freedom struggle, there were streaks of militancy. Tagore was, at heart, an internationalist. He denounced aggressive nationalism and would condemn narrow nationalism thus: "The cult of nationalism is professionalism of leaders. This cult is becoming a greater danger because it is bringing them enormous success. Ideals and morals find no place in their scheme. Man becomes the greatest menace to man. Therefore, the continuous presence of panic goads that very nationalism into an ever increasing menace." In his condemnation lay the missing element of spirituality for internationalism. Modern political attitudes confirm this philosophy of Tagore. In modern times, the menace of militancy has engulfed almost the entire world. The present political scenario has proved Tagore's worst fears true. He had warned in his observations that 'crowd psychology is a blind force and that rulers of men exploit it to their purpose.'

The phenomenon is now practiced worldwide. Nations taking pride in their morals and values, are its victims. Analysing the anatomy of nationalism, Tagore says, "with unchecked growth of nationalism, the moral foundation of man's civilization is unconsciously undergoing change." Narrow notions of patriotism and nationalism are producing fanatics in the coming generation. Growth of terrorist activities, all over the world, is an example of misguided nationalism with religious faiths abetting it. They are consequently damaging the forward march towards internationalism. The values that built modern civilization are in danger of destruction. Misplaced nationalism, devoid of proper perception of truth, is inviting clashes between societies with increasing frequency. Tagore was one of the earliest philosophers to point out the negativity of patriotism, and instead, encouraged cultivating internationalism.

Tagore considered the shift towards material success in commerce, deplorable. He never favoured material progress at the expense of social values. Sceptical about organized institutions, he put little faith in them. He placed greater faith in individual effort. Do we not see that values are valued more by individuals and exploited by organizations? What Tagore said was to abjure violence, restrain greed, and respect the supremacy of moral values.

Philosopher-thinker

Tagore's writings sought inspiration from the Upanishads. His thought covered the whole gamut of nature in his songs. Like Vivekananda, impact of western education merged his intellect with the spirit. He explains, "Material as material is savage; they are solitary; they are ready to hurt each other; they are like our individual impulses, seeing the unlimited freedom of willfulness. Left to themselves, they are destructive."

Tagore's message is simple and straight. He learned from the Upanishads to 'enjoy without greed.' His life was simple and clean, at times bordering on the austere. He knew that Hindu spiritual tradition had overstated the case for self-denial and had made life seen as a bleak desert. He wanted to correct this balance and teach his people the art of enjoying life without vulgarizing it. It conveys that pushing materialism does not lead to creation; it defies the natural law of evolution. It indeed leads backwards; towards barbarism, not civility. When a close relationship between spirit and intellect is stuck, there emerge the most pleasant and harmonious notes of life.

> Alas my cheerless country,
> Donning the worn-out garment of decrepitude,
> Loaded with the burden of wisdom,
> You imagine you have seen the fraud of creation."

Tagore, in thoughts, words and deeds, was tenderness personified. Whether it was poetry, literature, music, art, or education, sophistication dominated his works. In 1913 he was awarded the Nobel prize for literature. Asked to define the role and extent of poetry, he said, "To detach individual idea from its confinement of everyday facts and to give it soaring wings–the freedom of the universal."

Shahjehan built the wonder of the world, Taj Mahal, to immortalize his love for his queen. Tagore provides soaring wings to his imagination in poetry thus:

> You allowed your kingly power to vanish,
> Shahjehan, but your wish was to make imperishable a
> teardrop of love.
> Time has no pity for the human heart,
> He laughs at its sad struggle to remember.
> You allured him with beauty, made him captive, and
> crowned the form
> Formless death with fadeless form.
> The secret whispered in the hush of night to the ear of
> your love is
> Wrought in the perpetual silence of stone
> Though empires crumble to dust, and centuries are lost in
> shadows,
> The marble still sighs to the stars, 'I remember'.
> 'I remember,' But life forgets, for she has her call to the
> endless;
> And she goes on her voyage unburdened,
> Leaving her memories to the forlorn form of beauty.

Tagore truly represented the *rishis* of ancient India in modern times. He was essentially a teacher who radiated knowledge through his songs. Rabindranath established Shantiniketan as an ideal institution for the youth. The great educational and cultural centre, established in natural surroundings, educated youths who took pride in placing their services for the country. Throughout the national movement, Shantiniketan served as a lighthouse to leaders of the movement. The great centre of education was to produce some of the finest brains of the world. They not only helped the national movement but proved their brilliance in the arts and sciences.

Then at 80, old of age, his wife having departed from him early in life, the delicate heart of the poet was broken. The colour of his poetry turned melancholy. He would sit under the banyan tree and sing his lyrics to the chirruping birds in the soft moist breeze of Bengal. In love with nature, he lived with nature but thought globally.

> "Ah, poet, the evening draws near; your hair is turning grey,
> Do you in your lonely musing hear the message of the hereafter?"

The poet gives his reply to the question:

> "It is trifle that my hair is turning grey.
> I am ever as young or as old as the youngest and the oldest of this village.
>
> They all have need for me,
> And I have no time to brood over the after-life
> I am of an age with each; what matters if my hair turns grey?"

Rabindranath Tagore had expressed that his last parting words be:

> What I have seen is unsurpassable.

Chapter XXXVI
The Philosopher-Poet: Mohammed Iqbal

Life is preserved by purpose
Because of the goal, its caravan bells tinkle
Life is latent in seeking,
Its origin is hidden in desire
Keep desire alive in the heart
Lest thy little dust becomes a tomb.

—Mohammed Iqbal.

Mohammed Iqbal was born in 1875. Indians, in this period, were indifferent to the British administration. With each day, the latter's grip on the country was getting tighter, the economy was geared to consume mass produced goods produced in English factories. Village India was indifferent to what went on in the cities. Iqbal watched the decay of the Indian spirit and his voice against it was raised through poetry. An ardent fighter of obscurantism in religion, Iqbal advocated in his works, a life of action. Quiet contemplation and resignation, was not acceptable in an age when the country was in chains. He advocated young men to go for western education. Iqbal, lived during the age of Tagore and Vivekananda, who were similarly emphasizing the virtue of action. He said that through constant endeavour, following the laws of nature, man should mould nature. Passive acceptance of situations to him was a sign of weakness; asceticism and rituals were merely an escape from the realities of the world.

Iqbal (1875-1938), wanted people to achieve happiness in the living world, rather then idly exist in an imaginary world created by the priests.

Early life

Iqbal started his educational career with philosophy as his subject. Blessed with a brilliant mind, he studied philosophy from an English teacher at the Lahore College. Appreciating Iqbal's extraordinary qualities of mind, his teacher advised him to proceed abroad for higher learning. After obtaining his degree from Lahore, Iqbal sailed to Germany. The University of Berlin, during those days, was one of the great seats of learning in Europe. Seekers of knowledge used to come from all parts of the world. During his stay in Europe, he worked on his subject in Paris and London. After completing his studies, Iqbal returned to India. His stay abroad, broadened his vision and he returned home pulsating with new ideas and convictions. The knowledge within, now sought release in action. He decided to start teaching at Lahore University. After some time, the daily routine of teaching did not satisfy him. India, during this period, was slowly awakening to the spirit of freedom. Iqbal however felt the incompetence of a people who were still bound by old religious traditions. Disturbed by the prevailing religious attitude, he decided to plunge into action. The grave humiliation of foreign rule had always agitated his mind.

Iqbal decided to forget his profession of philosophy and act. He would go around the country with his message to reform religion and inspire people to work for freedom from foreign rule. Poetry would henceforth be his instruments of inspiration. Mirza Ghalib and the last Mughal king, Bahadur Shah Zafar, were the earlier two great Urdu poets of the old generation. Iqbal joined the new generation of poets in which Tagore was the brightest star. While Iqbal expressed himself in Urdu, Tagore wrote in Bangla and English. Both the poets of the new age wrote some immortal patriotic poetry that are still sung in India. A public function, a social gathering or a school prayer, is always studded with some of their works. They continue to provide moral courage and inspiration, touching the hearts of both the singers and listeners.

Iqbal's patriotism

One of the most enchanting and inspiring poem, "Tarana-e-Hind" will ever remain his most renowned poem that once dominated hearts of the entire country. Before partition of India, the poem was the morning prayer of most schools in northern India. During the national movement, the song was the beginning of all-public meetings and assemblies. Even today, a national programme remains incomplete without it:

> *Sare jahan se achha Hindostan hamara,*
> *Hum Bulbulen hain uske, who Gulsitan hamara.*
> *Furqat mein hon agar hum rehta hai dil watan mein,*
> *Samjho vahein hame bhi, dil ho jahan hamara.*
>
> *Parbat who sabse uncha, hamsaya asman ka,*
> *Who santari hamara, who pasbaan hamara.*
> *Godi mein khelti hain jiski hazaron nadian,*
> *Gulshan hai jinke dam se rashk-e-jahan hamara.*

Aai abrode ganga, who din hai yaad tujhko,
Utra tere kinare jab karavan hamara.
Mazhab nahin sikhata apasme bair rakhna,
Hindi hain, humwatan hain, Hindostan hamara.

Unan-o-Misr, Roma, sub mit gai jahan se,
Abtak magar hai baaqi namo nishan hamara.
Kuch baat hai ki hasti mit ti nahein jehan se,
Sadyon raha hai dushman dourey zaman hamara.

'Iqbal' koi mehrum apna nahein jahan mein,
Maloom kya kisi ko darde nehain hamara.

Fight against religious fundamentalism

Iqbal considered that in a changing world, reforms in religion were necessary. He was of the view that spiritual bankruptcy started in religion when a fundamental stability is imparted to it. In one of his dramatic poems, Iqbal imagines himself to be in the presence of God in heaven. A priest from earth is brought before God, to be rewarded with heaven, for services rendered to his community on earth. In all humility, Iqbal pleads to God, saying:

Being present when Lord granted Mullah heaven.
Unable to control, respectfully submitted I,

"Pardon my Lord, Heaven's beauty and wine shall suit him not,
In heaven, no discussions, no debates or mutual quarrels are,
Causing communities to quarrel, his job is.
While no Mandir, Masjid or church there exists."

Such bold ideas were penned even when utterances of this nature could invite immense unpopularity.

Expressing the fallacy of rituals, in another verse, he says:

Oh! Priests, may I respectfully speak the truth,
That idols of your worship are mere fossils.
Discontent, I heed no sermons and fables,
And I have left Mandir and Masjid.
You believe that God dwells in stones,
He sparkles in tiny dust of my country.

Love for humanism

Like the "Tarana-e-Hind", the following prayer has been popular from the beginning amongst young children. It reflects Iqbal's concern for human values that he wished children to acquire from their childhood.

How I wish my life to be,
A lamp that would illuminate the world.
May my life be like that of a moth,
To love learning as a moth loves lamp.

May my efforts help remove ignorance,
While my presence radiate knowledge.
Ever I may feel sympathy with poor and infirm,
Always loving care, for the old and needy

My Lord! I pray thee to keep me away from evil,
So I may tread the noble and kindly way.

His love for environment

Nature and its preservation has been a concern of all worthy men. Iqbal, in his vision for the future, sounded a note of warning to the coming generation against indiscriminate industrialization. In his poem, he makes God directly chastise man for wanton destruction of his great gift. He says:

I scriptured a world with earth.
You changed it into Turkey, Iran and Tartar,
I bestowed iron in earth,
You made arrows, daggers and swords.

With the carcass of fallen green trees,
You made cages for the singing birds.

Iqbal had sounded the warning bells long before the West even realized the importance of man's interdependence with nature.

The philosopher

The education that Iqbal received in India and Europe made him appreciate scientific achievements. Like his contemporary, Tagore, he acknowledged the need for science as far as it served human beings. His sharp intellect however cautioned against its indiscriminate and unbridled use. As a visionary, he feared that its misuse might drag humanity towards self-destruction. He expressed this fear in his verses:

Oh the West, God's earth is not just a shop,
What you consider right will soon show its colours.
One day, you will destroy your own civilization
What you build on a weak base, is all fragile.

Are we not face to face with the fearful reality that Iqbal had warned against, a century ago?

The Atomic theory, discovered by the great scientist Albert Einstien was expressed by Iqbal in his verse below:

Hakikat Ek Hai har shai ke, Khaki ho ke noori ho,
Lahu Khursheed ka tapke, agar zarrey ka dil chirain.

(Truth is the same, be it dull or shining,
Splitting an atom, produces the light of sun.)

Describing the relative importance of feelings over intelligence, Iqbal says that intelligence must be used to control emotions, but occasionally, it is well worth to let emotions reign supreme.

Achha hai Dil ke pass rahey pasbane akl,
Laykin kabhi kabhi ise tanhan bhi chor de.

(It is good for intellect to guide the heart;
but occasionally, let the heart do what it craves.)

Iqbal was fond of describing his philosophy through imaginary dialogues. One such work is a long poem "Shikwa" (Grievance). In this poem, a faithful devotee places his grievances before God. In reply, God explains the cause of man's sufferance and Iqbal, through poetry conveys the high philosophy:

Oh God! This from humble faithful devotees,
Listen to their little grievance.

The poem then describes how man has always remained His ardent and faithful devotee. Even when he has been faithfully obeying his commands, why is it that he is always miserable. Thereafter he lists the grievances with which man is suffering on earth. The 'grievances' are a long list of common problems, man has to normally face during his life. This stretches into several pages. Complaints to God are made in the manner of a child who places his grievances before his parents.

God, in turn, replies in the verses. He accepts that prayers, if offered with deep devotion, are accepted. But prayers alone would not help, God says, but honest efforts must also follow them. Impressing the importance of effort, God asks man to perform, rather than consider that his job is finished after praying!

The entire dialogue between Man and God impresses the significance and value of 'Self effort' (karma).

Whatever comes out from the heart, yields power,
Yet, it does not contain the power of action
Division amongst sects; elsewhere, in castes,
Do these qualities, in time, prosperity bring?

God, in his answer to the prayer, informs that praying does have an effect, but only when they are followed by right action. Man, divided in sects and castes, can hardly be prosperous and happy.

Iqbal, in his poetical style, conveyed desperately needed practical philosophy for man. Instead of entering into metaphysical jargons, Iqbal explains life in a pragmatic language, understandable to common intelligence. In the verse below, he refuses to be guided by those who call themselves wise. He would rather depend on his work for a better ending:

> Why should I ask the wise, whence have I come,
> I am troubled by the thought, 'what would be my end?'
> Raise your selfhood so high, that'fore allotting fate,
> God Himself asks man, 'Tell me what you will'.

Here again is his philosophy of action that destroys or builds man. Iqbal exhorted people to work in the present. Past is remembered by those who have no present. He wanted the new generation to learn from the discoveries of English botanist Charles Darwin and German philosopher Immanuel Kant. This alone would make their future bright. To bring change in society, he used the word 'Inqilab' (Revolution) for the first time in his poetry. As people began understanding its significance, it became the most popular slogan of the freedom movement.

Lest we forget

Iqbal was not only a poet but a great revolutionary of ideas in his times. He helped mould the spirit of the national movement. Equipped with wide knowledge, blessed with a strong memory, he never needed notes while reciting his poems in poetic assemblies *(mushairas)*. Even while appearing to be critical of religion, he was not against religion but only against its distortion.

Mohommed Iqbal was a fearless man. In one of his verses, he says:

> Oh my countrymen, wake up from slumber,
> If not, from existence you will go.

A study of the life and works of Iqbal reveal that his earlier feelings of nationalism got diverted to the interest of his community. The political climate of the country was charged with upheavals. Instincts of survival occupied most minds. This changed earlier comprehension.

Why was it so? What were the ground realities of that period to bring such a drastic change?

The early decades of the twentieth century saw nationalism gathering considerable momentum. The light of freedom began to appear at the end of the tunnel. An important pre-requisite of a diverse society like India is:

Majority rules; but the rights of minorities are preserved!

This golden rule was not to the liking of religious bigots. Finding the going good, the government was very willing to look the other way. The zealous fundamentalist elements, started distorting history. They tried to bring back the same old reactionary attitudes of 'ancient glory', ignoring realities of a thousand years of change. Eagerness for new knowledge, emphasized by all progressive leaders of the period, was condemned as a sin of foolish pride. They introduced the dead vision of the past, revived again.

This developed deadly distrust between the two major communities of the country. Consequently, even western educated Muslims like Syed Ahmed Khan and Mohammed Iqbal, finding ground realities different, changed. This gives an important lesson for the future. "Let us, in the twentieth century, not repeat the same old mistakes. Let us strengthen the bonds of trust between all communities. Let us not express them in mere words. They are required to be followed in our daily action and speech." Iqbal said so in half-zest: Giving lectures is rather easy, let our actions show our intentions!

> *Iqbal bara updeshak hai, mun batoan me moh leta hai,*
> *Guftar ko yeh Gazi to bana, Kirdar ka Gazi bun na saka.*

(Iqbal is good at lectures, wins hearts only by talking,

In conversation, he is an expert; but could not be great in action.)

Readers, of the work of these three notable and worthy men would have an insight of the country's mood in that crucial era. A refreshed feeling had fired the imagination of her intelligence. Areas like religion, in which the brave feared to tread, were condemned. Logic and reason, taboo to religion and politics, were asked by these men to be tested before acceptance. A revolutionary spirit, not of the violent kind, possessed her leading men. Writers, in their literature and poetry, sought freedom of thought and action. They brought out the true essence of India's spiritual heritage. The fanatical and fundamentalist approach was condemned in no uncertain terms. Their writings helped awaken the middle class of India to their responsibilities. The philosophies of Vivekananda, the idealist, Tagore's love of mankind and Iqbal's revolutionary spirit, expressed in their works, opened new vistas for the country's emancipation.

Science—its application for human welfare

Science, in the present times, has brought the world closer to each other. Its knowledge has placed economics in a dominating position. Every individual and nation is engaged in the race. It is no doubt true that knowledge is power. But we would find in our daily lives that it is as much a power for good as for evil. If used with wisdom, it brings happiness. It is equally true that it brings misery, if used wrongly. In the present world scenario, leadership in economics also gives strength for leadership in politics. World leadership presently guides opinion within nations. Yet the force that leads to action is missing. Leading

Indians emphasized forming of opinions conducive to the growth of entire mankind; it was not just one's own country that matter to them. Brought up in a spiritual atmosphere, they followed rules of nature observed in daily living. Whatever contradicted, even if of short-term benefit, was rejected. They understood that science and technology could only answer 'what is'; it cannot advise 'what should be'. World civilization, to move happily forward, has to await the one who could give an answer to 'what should be'. Poet Iqbal, who lived in those times, in one of his verses, provides the answer. In a rare moment of imagination, he finds God in distress at the plight of the poor and the miserable. God exhorts his Angel to go down to earth and redress the condition of the downtrodden:

> Resurrect the poverty-stricken lot of the world,
> Demolish the palaces of the rich and mighty.
> So set heart of slaves on fire that success assured,
> The 'little bird' may bravely fight the Eagle mighty.
> Break free from the prison of the past,
> Democracy is the order of the day.

The message of the three great poets and spiritualists of the era are similar. It is fusion of religion, economics and science with spirituality and use of human intelligence with discretion for the welfare of mankind.

The Spirit of India— Mahatma Gandhi

A leader of his people,
unsupported by any outside authority;
a politician whose success rests not on craft,
nor mastery of technical devices, but simply on the
convincing power of his personality;
a victorious fighter who has always scorned the use of force;
a man of wisdom and humility.
Armed with resolve and inflexible consistency,
who has devoted all his strength
to uplifting of his people and the betterment of their lot;
a man who has confronted the brutality of Europe with
the dignity of the simple human being,
and thus at all times risen superior.
Generations to come, it may be, will scarce believe that
such a one as this ever in flesh and blood
walked upon this earth.

—Albert Einstien

Chapter XXXVII
Experiments with Truth

That man is true
who taketh to his bosom the afflicted.
In such a man
Dwelleth augustly present.
God himself.

—Tukaram

Power is control over others to achieve an end. Be they individuals, social groups or nations, all seek power. When the British Empire reached its zenith, Indian nationalism, inspired by her leaders, was fighting for self-rule. Officers and men, who governed her vast empire, served with the feeling of a nation born to rule. Britain, with her strong sea power and spirit of adventure, had conquered the dwindling might of the Mughals. A sea-faring nation, with the spirit of adventure and ambition to get rich, had succeeded in colonizing the most fertile land in the five continents. While ruling subjugated countries and inducting their language and culture, they used trade to get rich. Britain governed India, following Akbar's policy of non-interference in religion. She, after a long time, succeeded in unifying the subcontinent, establishing law and order amongst people of several faiths, speaking many languages and following different customs. It was an extraordinary achievement to unite the India of Akbar and Ashoka.

Conditions in South Africa

Besides India, South Africa was another country conquered by the Europeans. Asian immigrants from poorer countries of Asia, came to South Africa in search of work and for business. Amongst those who came, most were Indians and Chinese. They were largely doing manual work, serving as 'coolies'. The better-off Indians were in business. Indians, who came to South Africa comprised of Hindus, Muslims, Christians and Parsis. The treatment meted out to Indians and other similar immigrants was generally inhuman. Therefore, the Indian businessmen hesitated to even call themselves Indians. Instead, the

Muslim merchants in South Africa called themselves Arabs; the Parsi clerks called themselves Persians while Indian labourers, speaking Tamil and Telegu, were addressed as 'coolies'.

Both India and South Africa, were undergoing similar political and economic conditions in many respects. It was a perfect reproduction of Indian conditions; a conglomerate of people seeking survival, a mighty Christian colonizer having conquered the country, expanding its trade, culture and religion. As in India, so in South Africa, the black African race patiently bore the humiliations and injuries. South Africa, as a carbon copy of India, served as a perfect laboratory where experiments on Indian nationalism could be ideally conducted. The imperial rule was going on merrily. Everyone thought the rule would continue forever and ever.

Then, suddenly, the immutable laws of nature intervened.

Experiments with truth begin

It so happened that a Muslim merchant needed a lawyer to argue a business case in South Africa. Incidentally, he belonged to Porbandar in Gujarat. By time and chance, a young barrister from Porbandar happened to have just arrived from England, looking for an opening in the profession. As a barrister, being competent to practice in the British Commonwealth, the Muslim merchant hired and arranged his departure to South Africa. Mohan Das Karam Chand Gandhi, the young barrister, sailed to South Africa to plead the merchant's case. The young barrister, dressed in a frock coat and turban, duly appeared before the European magistrate on the due date. Noticing his strange head wear, the judge ordered the barrister to remove his turban before pleading the case.

Gandhi, the young barrister, was taken aback. He refused to obey the insulting command. The presiding judge asked Gandhi to leave the court. Gandhi had his first brush with the arrogance of power! The humiliation struck a sensitive chord within him. Gandhi would henceforth use the South African laboratory for his 'experiments with truth'. Gandhi's armoury of struggle would evolve and be refined in South Africa. For the next fifteen years, Gandhi the social scientist, would practise and refine his simple and truthful means. The fight would continue until he had ensured dignity of existence for his people.

Shortly after the incidence, in another case of the merchant, the 'coolie barrister' as Gandhi was nicknamed by Europeans, was required to reach Pretoria from Durban. A first class ticket was booked for his journey. When the train reached

Maritzburg at night, a white man, who did not like a brown man sitting by his side, asked the railway official to get Gandhi out from the compartment. As in the court, so in the railway compartment, Gandhi refused to move out. The indignant official called the police constable. He pulled Gandhi out of the compartment and threw him on the platform.

Gandhi sat shivering and wondering again at the arrogance of power!

The humiliation of that night stirred his sensitivities. A storm arose in him to fight the indignities arising from the arrogance of power. Conditions in South Africa had ignited a resolve within him to fight this ignominy. Pursuing his profession suddenly did not matter to him any more. From now on, his consciousness would have only one objective:

To fight insolence of injustice and power!

This predetermination remained his companion throughout his life. The future of struggle in India had started taking shape! Collecting his thoughts, Gandhi took another train to reach Charlestown. Here he hired a horse driven carriage. Sitting by the side of the coachman, he was instead, asked to sit by his feet. Gandhi politely refused. The refusal annoyed the coachman. He boxed Gandhi to dare disobey. Reaching Johannesburg somehow, Gandhi went to a hotel for accommodation. Here too, he met with the same arrogance. Gandhi was refused accommodation in the hotel.

The young barrister from Temple Inn, in a brief stay, had to swallow successive humiliations! He thought how men, living in such conditions, loose their self-confidence? He decided to stay in the country and learn. He would study conditions and causes prevailing in South Africa that had so brutalized the people! The experiments in the laboratory had ensued with full vigour.

Gandhi started with inviting Indians in Natal to speak out their grievances. During his brief stay in South Africa, he noticed how Indians were living an individualistic life without any regard to cleanliness. They were generally living an isolated life, in unclean surroundings, and disunited amongst themselves. Gandhi, in his meetings, stressed the need for truthfulness in business, cleanliness in living and unity among themselves. Within one year of his stay in South Africa, Gandhi had contacted Indians of all classes. His advice led Indians to improve their relationship with each other. Making cleanliness a habit, they started living a healthier life, pleasing the local population. Gandhi followed his routine of spending the day in professional work. This offered him opportunity to discuss with the Indians, their problems. During his leisure, Gandhi studied books on religion, philosophy and economics. The study and the ground realities, he faced during his stay, were to influence his future life.

The man of India's destiny was gradually crystallizing his future working philosophy in self-chastisement and truth. Gandhi, during this period, developed the ancient Indian philosophy of truth and non-violence, as weapons to fight wrongs.

Making of the Mahatma

Gandhi's popularity was now established in the Indian community of South Africa. Other Asiatic people, who like Indians, lived to earn their livelihood, watched with admiration the 'strange' pursuits of the young barrister. The class that usually exploited labourers from abroad mostly consisted of Europeans owning large farms and factories. They were used to humiliating and treating the Asians as worse than animals. In Gandhi, they saw someone who dared to challenge their system. The Europeans, as a superior race, considered exploiting others, their natural right. In Gandhi and his activities, they saw seeds of discontent. They felt that if this tendency was left unchecked, it would damage their interests permanently. Consequently, to meet the challenge, they organized themselves and called a meeting to draw the future line of action. They approached the government to make laws to restrict and regulate immigration of Asiatic nationals. To strengthen their resolution, they held a public demonstration for imposing restrictions on migrating Asians.

Europeans, whose interests were at stake, attended the meeting. Gandhi was one of those who also came. As soon as the crowd saw him, they yelled, "We must get him. We must get him." Some amongst the demonstrators started lynching him. Finding the situation getting out of control, the police threw a ring around him. They asked Gandhi to move out for safety. He refused to take any help from the police. As the situation worsened, some amongst the Indians, took him to safety. Here the police asked Gandhi to lodge a report so that the identified culprits could be brought before the law.

Gandhi, to the utter surprise of the police, refused even to lodge any complaint against the culprits. The incidence of lynching and Gandhi's subsequent refusal to lodge any complaint against the culprits had an effect on the demonstrators. They were touched by his noble gesture. In not seeking revenge for the wrong done to him, Gandhi immortalized truth and non-violence. The culprits realized their fault; they felt ashamed for what they did. The prestige of the entire Indian community was at once elevated all over.

During all this period, Gandhi was in regular touch with leaders of the Indian National Congress. He attended its meeting at Calcutta in 1901 for the first time. He also registered himself as a volunteer. Working as an ordinary clerk in Congress, he trained others in personally performing duties of sweeping and scavenging. Gokhale helped him to move resolutions on situations in South

Africa to attract the attention of the Indians. On advice from Gokhale, Gandhi undertook an all India tour to apprise him with the political and economic conditions prevailing in the country. Gandhi's selfless service was regularly in news. This had made many Indian leaders, his admirers. During his tours of different provinces in India, the leaders he met formed an image of Gandhi as a kindly and patriotic Indian.

Reaction of the government

The South African government was now getting apprehensive of Gandhi's taking up 'uncomfortable' issues. As a measure to protect the interests of the Europeans, the government planned new obstacles for Asians entering South Africa. They brought an act, requiring all immigrants to first get themselves registered. Gandhi at once opposed the act calling it a 'Black Act'. He mobilized the Indian community to oppose the act vigorously. For this act of disobedience, Gandhi was tried and imprisoned to serve his first term in jail. This infuriated the entire Indian community. They collectively and resolutely started defying the act. Having undergone imprisonment once, its fear did not haunt them any more. They would rather defy and go to jails, than get themselves registered under the act! Negotiations between the government and the movement leaders did not help. The Act was finally enforced.

The Indian community, under the leadership of Gandhi, decided to start 'passive resistance' against the Act. Now, besides Indians, some Chinese migrants joined the Satyagraha. The Satyagrahis would picket at District Permit Offices. Gandhi, along with hundreds of his followers, was tried in courts. Instead of pleading in defence, he asked for the heaviest penalty. The judge duly announced this. Gandhi, along with some others, got imprisoned again.

Congress leaders in India were closely following the events in South Africa. They decided to send Gokhale to help the movement and negotiate a settlement. Meanwhile Gandhi was arrested for the third time. Next day, the marchers were carried in three long trains to Natal to be imprisoned. The result of this action was that nearly twenty thousand workers in Natal struck work leading to repression and bloodshed. The agitation had turned into a mass movement.

The Congress session, held at Karachi, voted its admiration for the 'heroic endeavour of Gandhi and his followers'. The Governor General of South Africa General Smuts, considered it wiser to release Gandhi and his followers. Thus ended Gandhi's first great Satyagraha. He evolved and then practised the principles of non-cooperation, non-violence and collective discipline in South Africa. Gandhi had perfected his tools of struggle for the Indian freedom. Readers will see how Gandhi never deviated from his principles.

The agony and ecstasy

During his experiments with truth, Gandhi suffered deep agony. This was to transform his entire being. Despite endless humiliations, he stayed bearing the agony and sufferance inflicted by an arrogant and powerful race. With the help of the common people, he fought the might of the British Empire. His non-violent and passive resistance, won the hearts of not only the sufferers but also of those who made them suffer. Gen. Smuts, the Governor General, listened to him with due regard. Leo Tolstoy, the Russian philosopher-poet, considered Gandhi's work in South Africa, as the "most important of all the works now being done in the world". Gandhi, deliberately selected non-cooperation and non-violence for his struggle as weapons. He had realized that for people to be fighting unarmed, their action might at any time, take the form of unorganized violence, provoking the government to unleash their organized strength. He had studied the biographies of many great men. They entered men's minds only to destroy human fellowship and goodwill. Gandhi, working in South Africa, promoted only love in the hearts of both his followers and adversaries. This was to become his policy in all the future struggles. In modern India, we often find instances when a peaceful protest suddenly erupts into violence giving the government an excuse to release organized force! Gandhi had understood that the Indian characteristic from ancient times has been to love peace and shun violence.

Meanwhile, the Indian national movement was grievously hurt at a time when it was faced with historical challenges. The partition of Bengal had introduced communal antagonism amongst Hindus and Muslims. Congress leaders, used to making petitions and agitation, found themselves incapable of challenging the government. With all their earnestness, the movement lacked mass support. They needed someone to create a miracle. How could a weak, disunited and confidence lacking nation, face the might of a great empire? In Gandhi, the true spirit of India appeared on the Indian scene. Lord Krishna in Gita says the he appears in person when dharma is endangered. True to the promise Gandhi appeared on the Indian scene as an 'Angel' sent by God! Besides leading the struggle for independence, Gandhi maintained the continuity of the Indian heritage in the glory of truth and non-violence.

Chapter XXXVIII
Communalism for Power

Hindus, if they want unity amongst different races
must have the courage to trust minorities.
Adjustment is only possible
when the more powerful take the initiative
without waiting for response from the weaker.

—M.K. Gandhi

As in the life of individuals, so in nations, certain events determine their destiny for ages. What happened between 1905-1915, was to mould the Indian political scenario for centuries. The congress leadership, during the last two decades, was able to alter the Indian temper from pessimism and indifference to determination and self-confidence. The new spirit, brought vibrancy and a will for action. It introduced a new strength and encouragement to the national movement. This awareness, besides outlining the positive element of nationalism, also allowed a look into its negative aspects. Men, to gain power for their group, looked upon the leaders to help them get it. The leaders, taking advantage of this human weakness, instead of going for the more arduous task of strengthening nationalism, were tempted to take the easier road for power through communalism and factionalism.

Politics of communalism

Indian heritage has always been admirable for its capacity to absorb differences in religion and races. For a long period, Hindus, Muslims, Christians, Sikhs, Buddhists, Parsis, almost all religions of the world, were co-existing in the country. Suddenly, the short-sighted leaders, to grind their political axes, brought religion in the struggle for freedom. They dug out the past, exaggerating and distorting what suited their interests. Attainment of power for themselves and their group was now their only objective. To garner support of their co-religionists, they twisted the past and did not hesitate to incite hatred amongst different communities. Pursuing their objective, if the Hindu Mahasabha looked exclusively towards Hindus, the Muslims turned to the Muslim League. Earlier, the Congress movement against partition of Bengal, boycott of foreign goods, clamour for unification of two Bengals, had added to its popularity.

But, when the Muslim League, with the new bait, started drawing rich property owners and Nawabs, the Congress base in the Muslim community weakened. The emotional approach to politics, introduced by communal forces, ran exactly opposite to the Congress policies. If the Congress agitated for revoking partition of Bengal and exhorting the nation to boycott foreign goods, the Muslim League demanded partition and condemned boycott of foreign goods.

The ploy worked. There was shift of the Muslim community towards the League. The intellectual and professional Muslims, who understood the difference between communalism and nationalism, continued to support the Congress. Prominent men like Hakim Ajmal Khan, Hasan Imam and Maulana Zafar were moved by the ideals of self-government. There was another great Muslim, Maulana Abul Kalam Azad, from Al Azhar University in Cairo, who propagated nationalist ideas through his newspaper *Al Hilal*. With separatist and loyalist tendencies growing amongst a section of Muslim landlords and Nawabs, a superhuman effort was needed to harmonise varying interests. For the Imperial power, differences between the League and Congress was a bonanza, that could now be used to keep the Congress under control. From now on, their policy remained centred on playing one against the other.

There were other moderates in the community who understood the policies of an alien government. They considered that social upliftment of the community should remain in the mainstream. This was prone to exploitation, manifesting itself in communal self-interest. Amongst Muslims, Syed Ahmed Khan took the initiative for betterment of the Muslim community. More than religious reforms, he considered education important for welfare of the community. He at once plunged into creating an atmosphere of education amongst Muslims. With this view, he started schools and colleges in different cities and worked to establish a great centre of learning in U.P. This materialized in the shape of the Aligarh Muslim University. Besides education, he advised Muslims to work together for the independence of the country. To imbibe the spirit of nationalism, he exhorted:

> Both of us (Hindus and Muslims) live on the air of India, drink the holy water of Ganges and Jamuna. We both feed on the products of Indian soil. We are together in life and death. Mussalmans have adopted several Hindu customs, the Hindus have accepted many Muslim traits of conduct, and we both belong to the same country. We are one nation. Progress and welfare of our country depends on our unity, mutual sympathy and love, while our mutual disagreements, obstinacy, and opposition is sure to destroy us.

Divide and rule

Bengal, during this period, was the cradle of Indian nationalism. It was in full tide of a literary, social and political renaissance. Imperial rulers were convinced that a united Bengal could create grave problems to their rule. On the other hand, Bengal divided and pulled in different directions, could neutralize this power. Any measure, that would divide the Bengali-speaking population, would encourage independent centres of activity. This would dethrone Calcutta from its place as the centre of successful intrigue. Thus the viceroy assessed the political situation of his period. Since East Bengal had Muslim majority, the League favoured partition. The rulers now found a force to be used to their advantage. Henceforth, they would support demands of the Muslim League. The national movement now lacked support of the East Bengal Muslims. With some brutal actions by the East Bengal government, the Congress movement petered. Encouraged by the developments, the viceroy declared that "partition was final as it would invest Mohammedans with unity which they have not enjoyed since the days of old Mussalman Viceroys and Kings". Such a dream of past glory, of returning back to the Muslim community, was too much to be resisted by Muslim masses.

Both the Hindus and Muslims became victims to the lure of the past: one wanted 'Back to Vedas'; the other, 'return of rule of Muslim viceroys and kings'. Such a gullible wish would not enter the minds of men for the first or last time. It would keep raising its ugly head, impairing national identity for the sake of power. Finding its divide and rule policy succeeding, the government was further encouraged to introduce separate electorates for Hindus and Muslims. This strengthened the view that economic and political interests of the two communities were different. In growth of communalism, introduction of separate electorates was to provide nourishment to the seeds of partition of India.

Ascendancy of religious nationalism

Lords and Knights of Parliament in London, getting regular information and advice from their officers, were carefully monitoring the political struggle in India. Bengal led the Indian Renaissance with Rammohun Roy. Thereafter she produced such patriotic visionaries as Surendra Nath Banerji, Bipin Chandra Pal, Ishwar Chandra Vidyasagar, Rabindranath Tagore and Vivekananda. United Bengal appeared to them as a power; but 'a divided Bengal would pull in different directions', so they thought in England. Incidentally, Muslims largely populated the eastern part of Bengal; the Hindu majority inhabited the western part. Lord Curzon, the Viceroy, divided the province. So doing, he fertilized the seed of division.

The Indian National Congress started to vehemently oppose partition. On the other hand, All India Muslim League, formed 'to protect and advance the rights of Mussalmans of India' favoured it. Amongst the resolutions passed by the League, one was to support partition of Bengal; the other was to condemn the 'boycott movement'. In other words its policy was now only to oppose the Congress. This was to continue until the final partition of the country. Rulers, in their own self-interest, consciously encouraged separatist tendencies. Imperial 'reforms' in future would reflect this tendency. The policy had hit at the root of Indian nationalism. Henceforth, instead of concentrating on economic and political freedom, national energy got diverted to religious and communal issues.

Present and future political leaders may draw some lessons from such a suicidal policy for short term gains. What Imperialism gained, lasted only for another few decades; but the damage done to the country was incalculable. Present day politicians, with their narrow-minded politics, may achieve some short-term gains; but they are purely temporary.

The air of liberty

The spirit of patriotism, sacrifice and fearlessness was now blowing over the five continents. There were revolutionary movements in Ireland, Russia, Egypt, Turkey and China. It was only a matter of time before the hurricane would strike India! Bengal and Maharashtra were particularly nourishing revolutionary and democratic sentiments. They needed a cause to light the spark. Failure of liberal nationalism and growth of petty communalism was not to the liking of the young generation. They longed to look ahead. Liberal nationalism had also reached a dead end. The youth, particularly of Maharashtra and Bengal, were no more satisfied by petitions, agitation and slogan shouting. They, particularly the young, wanted action.

The youth of Bengal and Maharashtra, would use force. They would take to militancy!

Growth of militancy

The national movement had so far centred on opposition to the partition of Bengal, boycott of foreign goods and self-rule. This however could not pick up the requisite momentum. Governments of East and West Bengal, used their respective strength to alienate the two communities as completely as possible. Anger against partition of Bengal resulted in youths of Bengal taking to militancy. Soon it spread all over the country. Aurobindo Ghosh, Bipin Chandra Pal, Tilak and Lajpat Rai gave a call 'to make administration in the present conditions impossible'. They called for an organized refusal to do anything which would help either British commerce or the British official machinery. The movement, started by leaders, however remained confined to cities. Strong government repression and lack of mass support, weakened the movement. The youth, though aroused for action, yet did not exactly know how to harness this new energy. Breaking the law here and there, using weapons in isolated quarrels with the law, was all they did. Forerunners, who led the militancy, were soon arrested. The dumb and inert Indian masses hardly knew how to respond. With their leaders in jail, the government was able to subdue the movement without much difficulty.

Politics of religion

Britain was now convinced of the usefulness of religious politics for retaining her hold on the Indian Empire.. Her core policy, around which government actions would henceforth revolve, lay in manipulating support of one community at the expense of the other. This was done by bringing laws in the shape of 'reforms'. Division of Bengal and introduction of separate electorates was followed by subtle interpretation of ancient and medieval history of the country on religious lines. Works of historians was employed to popularize them. A well-tried approach was used to hoodwink the innocent and illiterate masses. The new interpretations of history made the Hindus glorify their ancient past with a cry of: 'Back to the Vedas'. The ideological support to Hinduism was the route to revive religious nationalism. This route, attractive to innocent masses, would continue to be taken by seekers of political power without caring for the damage it would do to the complex fabric of national unity! Political leaders, who until the other day were exhibiting nationalist feelings, identified themselves with the Muslim League. Even though some intellectual Muslims remained with the Congress, landlords and their followers, strengthened the League. The two communities, at the same time, got busy organizing their separate religion-oriented leagues, sanghs and mahasabhas.

The English were watching this division with morbid pleasure. They saw in this tendency, their weapon to fight the national movement. For quite some time, they had been groping in the dark for instruments to handle the growing Congress strength. In the divisive approach of the two communities, they found what they were looking for.

For the common person, 'the Back to Vedas' slogan was translated by references to mythologies and scriptures out of context. On the contrary, for harmonious relationship between man and environment, and man and man, it is reasonable analysis alone that nourishes the mind to evolve solutions. Similarly, dealing with human relationship in a pluralistic society, almost all scriptures advise this approach. If understood with relation to period and place of their origin, they convey an identical message. The difference is only in period and constitution. As times and values changed; new knowledge and ideas keep changing; sometimes for the good, at other times for evil.

In response to Hindu glorification of ancient India, Muslim leadership responded by taking pride in the history of medieval India. They referred to the rule of the Turks, Afghans and Mughals kings in the country. How India was enriched in art, architecture, music and poetry by their arrival. They would glorify the West Asian history of Islam when the great Mohammedan civilization contributed to the growth of science, and culture of medieval western civilization. With both communities epitomizing their own religions, claiming to be superior to the other, it was natural for communal feelings to take hold of the minds of masses. Gandhi would however continue to advise, saying, "Islam was not intolerant in its brilliant days. It commanded admiration of the world. Let Hindus study it reverentially and they would love it even as I do."

The fact that the ancient and medieval policy of Indian kings was generally based on economic and political considerations was deliberately ignored. Instead, the atrocities of invasions, the wars with Maharana Pratap Singh and Shivaji, which were essentially political struggles for territories, were emphasized (this is being quoted even today). The soldiers fighting these wars on either side comprised members of both communities. The merchants of hate would cleverly refrain from mentioning these facts. Instead, they emphasized areas of differences and distorted joint patriotic feelings. Such negative propagation produced religious 'reformers' amongst Hindus and Muslims. They would operate within their own narrow mental spheres. The rulers overtly gave encouragement to one against the other. Therefore, the common heritage of centuries became suspect. This weakened the capacity to fight the common enemy and allowed safe sailing for the British Raj.

Nature has its own method of correcting wrongs. Forces were at work in Europe that would weaken Imperial powers. European countries were pioneers in controlling the seas. Amongst the large countries, Europe, Britain, France, Russia, Italy and Spain had their empires in different parts of the world. Germany was the only powerful nation without any territory to govern abroad. It therefore always nursed a deep grievance. The First World War in 1914 lasted for four years. During this period, it exhausted not only Germany, but also both Britain and France. This was to have an impact on the colonies of Imperial powers all over the world. The urge for freedom picked up momentum.

Arrival of Gandhi

It was during the war years that Gandhi returned to India from South Africa. After a brief study of the political climate in the country, he said:

> My Hindu instincts tell me that all religions are more or less true. All proceed from the same God, but all are imperfect because they have come down to us from imperfect human instrumentality. The real reform movement should consist in each one trying to arrive at perfection in his or her own faith. In such a plan, character could be the only test. What is the use of crossing from one compartment into another, if it does not mean a moral rise? What is the meaning of my trying to convert to the service of God, when those who are within my fold are everyday denying God by their action?

He had understood that religious antagonism was at the root of India's present misfortune. His effort would be to blend politics with religions, so that different religions of the country may appear complimentary to each other.

State and religion

The politics of states and religion are wedded to citizen's welfare. Religion functions through faith and spiritual force; reason governs politics. Primary function of a state is to attend to physical welfare of the citizen. Religion helps strengthen morals and virtue for harmonious relationship. Politics and religion are two diametrically opposite ends. Politics, employing reason, works for the welfare of her citizens; religion, by developing faith, helps bring peace of mind. When state politics and religion interact between themselves, they merely help dissipation of energy at the cost of human welfare. When reason, the driving force of the state, weakens, it tends to 'borrow' faith from the religion, not for citizen's welfare, but for its own aggrandizement.

Buddha, Socrates, Confucious and Gandhi preached and practised reason. They were able to contribute most for human welfare in the history of mankind.

Ascendancy of religious nationalism

Man is the work of Nature; he exists in Nature; he is bound to her laws. He cannot remove himself from them. Nature has an in-built arrangement to harmonize man-made contradictions.

Just when religious nationalism amongst Hindus and Muslims was at its height, war broke out between Turkey and the Italian Empire in 1911. It appeared to be Nature's way to respond to the Imperial exploitation. It so happened that most of the Muslim religious centres were located within the Turkish Empire. A wave of sympathy therefore swept for Turkey in the Muslim world. The Muslims, who were so far supporting the British power, suddenly found themselves on the wrong side of the popular opinion. Pro-Turkish and pro-Caliph or Khalifat sentiments made the Muslim community rise against British Imperialism. The Muslim League, so far thriving on opposing Indian nationalism, suddenly found itself abandoned by her own constituents. The conflict brought the forces of nationalism and religious nationalism, face to face. Indian national movement under Congress at once espoused the cause of Islam. The Muslim League concentrated on protecting holy places and the status quo in Turkey. The Congress opposed the far more deep malady of economic and political consequences of imperialism. The habit of looking at political questions with a religious angle however started fanning communal feelings all over the country. Hindus and Muslims, instead of developing a secular approach started giving a religious twist, adversely affecting the national movement.

In future, this approach would continue to damage Indian unity. Actors will change; but purpose will remain the same.

> Alike for those who for today prepare,
> And those that after some Tomorrow stare,
> A Muezzin the from Tower of darkness tries
> Fools! your reward is neither Here nor There.

—Omar Khayam

Beginning of the end

Amongst the countries of Europe, Britain, France, Italy and Spain, had taken an early lead in developing sea power. With growth of industries, foreign markets became a necessity. Germany, having no imperial territory but equally industrialized, was anxious to sell its surplus production. War appeared the only alternative for getting markets. Germany decided in 1914 to go to war with the leading European powers—Britain, France and Italy. The cause lay in not sharing economic exploitation of Asian and African countries. In India, although nationalism had come of age, it still lacked unity and vision of future. Rural India was still indifferent to the political and communal activities of National Congress and the Muslim League. They adopted a pro-British attitude in the fond hope that India's loyalty at a critical juncture would earn them the gratitude of Britain. They did not realize that the war the imperialists were fighting was not for democracy, as they claimed, but precisely to protect their empires.

With India still caught up in communal infighting, she awaited arrival of the man of her destiny from South Africa. Gandhi arrived on a clear January day in 1915 at Appollo Bundar, Mumbai. He would apply the conclusions derived at the 'South African laboratory' without being influenced by the temptation of power.

Chapter XXXIX
The Spirit of India–Gandhi

Show us not the aim without the way,
for ends and means on earth are entangled
That changing one, you change the other too,
Each different path, brings other ends in view.

–Ferdinand Lasselle

Time, chance and destiny often play a decisive role in the making of man and nations. Gandhi had gone to South Africa at the call of his profession. Once there, circumstances took such a turn that he cast his lot with his fellow citizens suffering injustice in a foreign land. He fought their battles, developed instruments of struggle, putting his entire being in the cause. By so doing, Gandhi compressed in a few decades the collective consciousness and the spirit of Indian civilization of three millenium. The teachings of Mahavira, Buddha and Kabir became the weapons of his struggle. The collective consciousness of Ashoka, Vikramaditya and Akbar, operated through one person—Mohan Das Karam Chand Gandhi.

It all started with Natal in South Africa. On an October day of 1913, a vast crowd of Indian miners collected to protest against the imposition of a tax on them by the Imperial government. They had their wives and children with them, evicted from the houses they lived. They came to Gandhi, expecting him to lead their struggle against the government. He took up the challenge; converted the unruly mob into disciplined soldiers to be able to offer collective resistance to defy the law. Marching day and night without material resource, three thousand men and women, travelled to the forbidden district of Transval. There, Gandhi, with several other men, was arrested. The crowd exhibited complete discipline, self-suffering and non-violence. The unruly crowd that had come to him only the other day, under his leadership, was suddenly converted into a patient and disciplined force. Such an exhibition from the crowd, melted the heart of the oppressors.

The government yielded; it withdrew the tax imposed. The trial conducted by Gandhi having succeeded in South Africa, would soon be put to awaken the entire subcontinent with a similar march from Ahemedabad to Dandi on the western coast of Gujarat.

Programmes and policy

Gandhi had returned to India with the realization that imperialism had to be fought in India. To non-violence in South Africa, Gandhi added direct action. So doing, he compromised caution with dynamism. This became the middle way for toil and trouble. Such human approach blunted the aggressive intentions of the oppressor, making him more humane. During the first year of arrival in Mumbai, Gandhi travelled extensively all over the country. At Calcutta, he would condemn assassinations and militancy at a time when secret societies and terrorism were popular with the youth of Bengal. At Madras, he proposed a toast to the British Empire and defined the 'right to rebel', as a right of all British citizens. In other cities and towns, he talked of non-violence, untouchability, swadeshi and the right to rebel. This enabled him to meet both the common men and local leaders. It gave him an opportunity to assess the impact of his approach on the masses. His work in South Africa had given him an insight into the minds of British imperialists and his own instruments of struggle. He was now well aware of available 'resources'. Within a decade, Gandhi would convert them into an inspired and disciplined force that could challenge the might of a great empire.

In the planning of his programs, Gandhi counted no cost; did not hesitate to sacrifice in order to uphold truth; always remaining wedded to non-violence. In this manner, through setting personal examples, he elevated the weak to be resolute; the unruly mobs into a disciplined force; the self-centred, to give and suffer for others.

What was the force that worked behind the idea?

In Gandhi's words,

> Satyagraha and its off shoots, non-violence and civil disobedience are nothing but the new names for the law of suffering. The thinkers of India, who discovered this law of non-violence, were men of greater genius than Newton; they were greater warriors than Wellington. Having themselves known the use of arms, they had realized their uselessness and taught a weary world that its salvation lay not in violence but through non-violence.

The lesson he preached almost a hundred years ago, now appears relevant in the present context of highly destructive weapons.

Gandhi considered truth and non-violence, the basic principles of organized life for civilization itself. All through his life, he used the two with unfailing conduct in all his dealings. As a man of action, Gandhi did not merely depend on conversion of hearts or the good will of the opponents. His endeavour always remained to organize and strengthen those suffering from injustice and inequality, shedding all division and fear as well as petty self interest. To instill courage and self-confidence, through truth and non-violence, was the objective behind all his movements. Once his followers were possessed with indomitable courage, opponents were bound to change.

Reforming a new revolution

Gandhi was not only a great political leader but also a great thinker who gave mankind a new message of hope and rational living. The revolutionary significance of Gandhi lies in his attempt to release the contained energies in endurance of suffering of the people. This ancient gift was adversely affected due to a divided consciousness amongst the masses. Certain others, who had received western education, were also responsible for this division amongst the people. Gandhi had studied this serious flaw that he thought would eventually retard the progress of the impending movement He looked for a link that would join the opposing forces to the national mainstream.

Advancement of science and technology had opened a new world with immense possibilities. Indian intellectuals were completely overawed by its magnificence. Earlier leaders were themselves mostly the product of western education. Their sense of superiority would not let them join the common cause with the masses; it prevented them from identifying themselves with them. Political activities, in the past therefore had remained centred around the middle and upper classes. The inert and inactive, who formed the masses of India, hardly understood them to be able to respond.

Gandhi transformed this inaction and inertia into a source of energy and strength. He had found a function for them in the political life of the country. This was to be one of his greatest achievements. Instead of an aggressive and militant struggle, Gandhi built a movement on nonviolence and passive endurance of the people.

Gandhi, from his study of industrialization in the West, had understood, how political liberty conceals economic slavery, bringing unbearable hardships to labour and their families. His introduction of the spinning wheel, Khadi and village industries were part of a programme of self-interdependence. This integrated approach to the national movement was to demolish barriers that hindered social interaction between the masses and intellectuals. The history of earlier revolutions had taught him how, after the initial success of revolutions, they are often faced with counter-revolutions, changing both its contents and character.

In revolutionary fights, actual struggle is of as much importance as a period when there is a pause. At such times, to keep national spirits active, Gandhi introduced constructive work. The spinning wheel, Khadi weaving, village industries and national education programmes, Harijan welfare and eradication of untouchability were programmes that not only provided immediate economic self-sufficiency to the economically deprived, but also helped social interdependence. These programmes kept the spirit of Satyagraha attuned to the goal of freedom.

The struggle that started with philosophy of truth and non-violence was in complete harmony with the nature of Indian masses. It brought an immediate response. Amongst the inhabitants of a dependent country, a new life was thus infused. Removal of hatred of all kinds and fostering interdependence amongst different social groups, was to be at the root of activities started by Gandhi. The emergence of a single individual, as an epitome of desire of an entire people, signifies that people were as much responsible in making Gandhi what he was, even as he moulded the masses. From the silent language of millions of people all over India, at that moment in history, Gandhi read and understood what they wanted.

Thus was he able to infuse a new life and spirit amongst the people!

The Plunge—marches and campaigns

The first call for action came from a remote town in North India in 1917. The rulers had promulgated a law that the farmers of Champaran must cultivate three-twentieth of their land holdings with indigo—an industrial raw material required by the textile industry in Lancashire. Not content with this, the government levied a tax that was beyond the capacity of farmers to pay. They had been agitating for its removal, but the government would pay no attention. Gandhi went to investigate the grievances and to find out the truth.

The District Magistrate of Champaran did not like this interference. He served Gandhi with a notice to quit the town. Gandhi refused saying, "My desire purely and singly is in general search for knowledge." This argument was not accepted by the authorities. Gandhi was tried in the court. Meanwhile, thousands of farmers, hearing about the visit of a stranger for their cause, collected in the court. The law could award no punishment, as Gandhi had infringed none. The developments upset the Commissioner. Gandhi was allowed to conduct the inquiry. This offered him the opportunity to travel to the interiors of the district. There he met tenants, planters and other officials. The Congress organization, not known in the area till then, became popular and associated with public good. The Lt. Governor even invited Gandhi for discussions.

After his talks, he appointed a committee, with Gandhi as its member. This committee submitted its report. The inquiry report found the grievances of the farmers to be genuine. The government accepted the report. Satyagraha had recorded its first success, gaining both prestige and popularity.

Indian Immigration Act 1917

Indian labour, during those days, used to be sent to work in sugar plantations of the British colonies in different parts of the world. The labourers mostly belonged to South India, Bihar and east UP. Besides being low paid, the social cost of having to neglect their families was incalculable. It was a torture for families and children to be separated for long periods. The Indian National Congress decided to take up the issue with the government. It gave a notice that if indentured labour was not stopped, they would picket the ships carrying them to different countries. This was a period when the World War was at a high pitch. The viceroy, realizing the delicacy of war, was not prepared to take any risk of agitation. He invited Gandhi for talks; indentured labour was abolished.

Gandhi, as a statesman was supple of mind, visionary in concept and bold in execution.

Satyagraha against humiliation

The British government was now feeling the heat of an awakened India. This was noticeable in the complexities of different kinds of causes taken up by the Congress. There was terrorism and militancy in some parts and peaceful demonstrations in others. The speeches and writings of leaders were gradually taking the element of fear out of ordinary citizens. Fear, the unseen demon, was gradually losing its sheen. Going to jails was no more the terror it used to be earlier.

The first phase of a peaceful revolution, to remove fear of authority, had succeeded.

The government, watching the situation, introduced the Rowlatt Act in 1919. The act deprived citizens of their civic right in trial for sedition. National Congress, represented by Gandhi, reacted to the derogatory act. One day, Gandhi while talking to Rajagopalachari, said, "The idea came to me last night in a dream that we should call upon the country to observe a general Hartal." This was Gandhi's way to start momentous programmes. The call for 'Hartal' (strike) was to be the first all-India campaign to be led by Gandhi for a cause that affected the entire country. He called upon people to fast, pray, close business establishments and hold protest meetings. The day, 6 April, was fixed as the day when both Hindus and Muslims participated in the Hartal. Muslim friends invited Gandhi and Sarojini Naidu to deliver speeches in mosques. The level of unity between the two communities was once again revived by a common cause. The Hartal invited the wrath of the government. There was police firing at Lahore and Amritsar and skirmishes with the people in streets.

Fearing serious trouble ahead, police arrested Gandhi. This incited the mob to violence, followed by acts of sabotage like removing rails from tracks. The government imposed the Martial Law. Gandhi declared a penitential fast for three days by his followers. He advised those who had committed violence, to confess their guilt. To the world outside this may have looked the rarest of acts; in India, it was promptly implemented. Gandhi himself took the lead by confessing that his launching the kind of a movement at this stage was a 'Himalayan Blunder', a miscalculation. Realizing that civil disobedience required greater training, he raised a corp of satyagrahi volunteers to teach the significance of satyagraha. While Gandhi worked in Mumbai, the government was active in suppressing the movement in the Punjab. Police arrested the leaders of satyagraha. This act annoyed the people. Their reaction to the arrests caused the death of five Englishmen. The government was in a frenzy. They waited for an opportunity to teach the people a lesson. The massacre of Jalianwala Bagh was indeed a consequence of the killings of Englishmen.

Jalianwala Bagh, Amritsar 1919

Man is the product of various experiences and circumstances. The genius amongst them only adds the last step to work done before. Gandhi, by doing so, infuriated the government to commit blunders. These mistakes by mature rulers would not have otherwise happened, which thus started a chain of reactions. The western rulers took Gandhi's appeal for confession as a sign of weakness. It decided to react boldly to regain the lost prestige by regenerating fear.

It was Vaisakhi day on 13 April 1919. A protest meeting was held in Jalianwala Bagh. The night before, General Dyer had forbidden holding public meetings; but none had heard of the order. The General came with his armed troops and ordered his men to open fire on defenseless, unarmed people. This lasted for ten minutes in which more than 400 innocent people died and several thousands were injured. Thereafter followed a reign of terror in which civic amenities like water and electricity were denied. The degrading 'crawling order' was enforced on suspects. They handcuffed one Hindu and another Muslim, together. Students in colleges were flogged for joining the meeting. To the Hindus and Muslims, who were presenting a united front, such acts were not to their liking. Having got rid of the fear complex, they were growing conscious of their self respect.

A dark and abominable deed would now blow a storm of uncontrollable fury. The news of the incident at Jalianwala Bagh stirred the conscience of India. They could now see the ugliness and façade of western civilization. Greater and vastly different challenges waited next year. Circumstances would develop that would bring the varying factions and communities nearer on one platform. The caravan of Indian freedom had reached its first stage. There would now be an interval to rest and regroup. The superiority of race, because of technological and scientific progress, had initially dazzled intellectuals of India. Now, its barbarity stood exposed against a revolution born from the ancient Indian philosophy and culture. It brought the relationship between the rulers and the ruled to a point of no return. The thought once fondly entertained, to make a part of India their home, on the South African pattern, died with the tragedy of Jalianwala Bagh.

Gandhi put to practice the ancient Indian philosophy to practical use after its successful experimentation in South Africa. Village, as well as urban India, responded to what they understood and believed in. We come across even today, the 'Dharnas', 'Hartals', 'Fasting', and 'Yatras'. Different people for different reasons today undertake similar satyagrahas. In concept, they are the same as what Gandhi practised during the freedom struggle. People then understood his silent language; now, when leaders make similar demonstrations, they appear as mere rituals for spectators. The spirit is missing.

Chapter XL
Philosophy of Action in Non-action

The phenomenal awakening of masses
during the last twenty-five years has been
entirely due to purity of our means.

—M.K. Gandhi

If economic imbalance is a cause of wars, it is also a force that inspires and nourishes nationalism. More often it becomes nature's way to rejuvenate its laws. The Industrial Revolution in Britain helped establish industries in India. During the first World War of 1914–18, these industries had a good time supplying war material to allied armies, offering job opportunities to Indians. Soon after the war, when demand dried up, people were jobless once again. To look after their interest, only a government of the people could bring counter measures; a foreign government would engage herself once again in her old game. During the four years of fighting in Europe, India helped war effort by providing both men and material. So long as the war lasted, Britain was never tired of claiming that it was being fought to save the world for democracy. Once victory was achieved, people realized that war was fought, not for its liquidation, but for its preservation, even expansion. This became clear, when after the defeat of Turkey, the largest Islamic empire, was divided and a part of it was occupied by foreigners. The Sultan, who then ruled Turkey, was also the Caliph of Islamic religion. Besides, most Muslim holy places fell in the territory, now under foreign rule.

The Indian masses had only recently borne the brutality of Jalianwala Bagh. Its wounds were still fresh. With the new hurt inflicted on the Muslim community, the entire country was again agitated. Khilafat movement started to give vent to their feelings. Gandhi, who took the initiative, understood the mind and mood of the Muslim community. He channelled their pent-up feelings and energies into a collective nationalist movement involving the whole country. This identification of Indian nationalism with the Khilafat movement at once brought a unity between the two communities, not seen for a long time. Gandhi, a veteran of the non-cooperation movement, promptly started the movement. Hindus and Muslims alike whole-heartedly supported it.

Non-Cooperation/Khilafat movement

The Gandhian philosophy of *ahimsa* in action was derived from the ancient theory of Karma. Suddenly, a new wind of patriotism began blowing all over the country. A spirit of unity, when the entire nation had one objective, rarely seen, was visible in every heart. Events and circumstances had aroused the entire people. Gandhi, after making common cause with the Khilafat movement, expressed himself saying that "Non-Cooperation is the only remedy with us. It becomes a duty when cooperation means degradation or humiliation or injury to ones cherished religious sentiments."

Ever since Congress was established, its leaders functioned within the constitutional limits. Leaders like Firozshah Mehta, S N Banerji, Madan Mohan Malaviya and Bal Gangadhar Tilak had opposed the government within the framework of the law.

Non-cooperation meant going a step beyond. The new approach was to be a non-violent agitation against injustice that would touch the conscience of the oppressor. It was Satyagraha, the force of the spirit, that Gandhi used as a weapon to pierce the conscience of the wrong doer. The movement represented the deep anguish felt by the people against the rulers. In Gandhi's new approach, masses fathomed fulfilment of their sacred longing. It started with a letter to the Viceroy that said, "I have advised my Muslim friends to withdraw support from your Excellency's government and advised Hindus to join them." He thereafter announced that the movement would commence with fasting and prayers. The Congress, representing nationalist forces and the Khilafat organizations were now at Gandhi's full command. He had carefully drawn the strategy to fight physical power with non-violence and political manoeuvres with sincerity of action. As a leader, his success rested on his convincing power. People considered him a man of wisdom and humility, armed with resolve and inflexible consistency. Now that Gandhi was the sole leader, the Ali brothers, Maulana Muhammad Ali and Maulana Shaukat Ali, who were leading the Khilafat movement, worked closely with him. To mobilize the masses, Gandhi and the Ali brothers, went on all India tours together. They spoke identical language of defiance against the government assuring people that the British did not really want to do justice. It was therefore their bounden duty to bring down the empire.

Such an open challenge for struggle had never been delivered by anyone in the empire ever before! It was a direct call for revolution, but of a different kind. As the non-cooperation intensified, differences in approach began to appear. There were some Congress leaders who believed in other methods. They did not agree with Gandhi's non-cooperation. Those advocating violent methods, considered militancy; some others, intellectually inclined, favoured the earlier method of constitutional agitation. Bipin Chandra Pal, Annie Besant and Mohammed Ali Jinnah, were amongst those who left the Congress over choosing an aggressive approach of non-cooperation. It was strange politics that at the time when Gandhi took up Khilafat—an Islamic cause, Jinnah, who was to be so vehement for Pakistan, was not in its favour!

The call for non-cooperation had thousands of students from schools and colleges joining road demonstrations, during which, they burnt foreign goods. Police, in turn, used force and firing against agitators, who burnt foreign goods and shouted slogans. With the burst of a new spirit of patriotism, everyone found pride in disobeying the law; every participant had his heart and soul in the movement. Such moments are rare in the history of nations when every individual becomes a part of the whole.

Magic of the man

The tour that Gandhi undertook with the Ali brothers was instrumental in creating a new awaking in the masses. Such enthusiasm had not been witnessed before. Gandhi travelled from Aligarh to Dibrugarh in Assam and to Tinnavelly, in south India. He would travel from village to village, from town to town, speaking at road crossings and town halls, temples and mosques. Gandhi would meet priests and Imams; write letters in trains; sleep on bare platforms amongst motley crowd and cross rivers in dilapidated boats to reach inaccessible places. He would deliver his message of non-cooperation in every field. With his soft and simple words, Gandhi would make his listeners delirious with enthusiasm; that would make them obey his commands.

On these tours, every local problem that adversely affected the people interested him. If it was the grazing tax in Andhra, he would take up the issue with local authorities; in Malabar he would try to understand the 'Mohab' trouble. He would study why the Tamils, who were such good workers in South Africa, was slow in taking to Khadi here? In the tour, Gandhi saw misery and the poverty of Indians in all its manifestation. He noticed the stark poverty that did not allow men and women to cover themselves. This touched his very being. He contemplated on the wonder that made masses accept such a state of existence with comparative contentment! In one such soul searching moment of excruciating self inquisition, Gandhi decided to discard his formal dress. He decided that from now on, like millions and millions of Indian men and women, he too would wear just a loin cloth around him.

For his compatriots, the English educated barrister was now Mahatma Gandhi; the imperialists would call him a 'half-naked fakir'.

During one of his tours in a Bihar village, his party was stranded due to the rain. An old woman seeking out Gandhi said, "Sir, I am a 104-year-old woman and my sight is dim. I have visited several holy places. In my own house, I have dedicated temples. Just as we had Ram and Krishna as Avatars (incarnations), so has Mahatma Gandhi appeared as an Avatar. I believe that unless I have seen him, death will not appear."

The Mahatma, with his vision of the future India, had succeeded in stirring the soul of India. By his simple, easy to understand methods that were in tune with the psyche of the people, he ignited within them the flame of patriotism. His simple and sincere words were always followed by action. Everything he said or did, touched their hearts. The entire country was delirious; it was drowned in a rare mood of self surrender that comes with absolute faith once in a thousand years. People would wait from dusk to dawn for him to arrive. At night, they brought torches just to have his *darshan* (physical presence) in its light.

"The trials"– Chauri Chaura episode

Gandhi's call for non-cooperation was in full swing in 1921-22. His declaration was that it was contrary to national dignity and interest of any Indian to engage or remain in service of the government in any capacity. Such words, during his extensive tours in last two years, his personal contact with people, the mild yet firm speeches, had electrified the masses in the farthest corners of India. They had started courting arrests, and resigning from official positions. Over 50,000 men and women were in different jails for defiance of the law.

As a part of the non-cooperation movement in east UP, a group of two thousand farmers had taken out a procession, shouting slogans against the government. Suddenly the police started firing on demonstrators. The cruelty displayed by the police, infuriated the demonstrators, who in a fit of rage, burnt the entire police station along with some officers and men in it.

Gandhi received the news of the tragedy with deep sorrow. He was pained at the loss of lives in a non-violent movement. To atone for the violence he called off the movement and undertook a fast for five days. To the leaders of the Congress, years of hard work and suffering appeared lost. The government saw in this retracing of steps, Gandhi's weakness and their triumph. They arrested Gandhi and put him on trial. When presented before the judge, he took complete responsibility for whatever had happened and said, "I will still do the same thing…the only course open to you Mr. Judge is either to resign or inflict on me the severest penalty."

Gandhi got six years of imprisonment.

Khalifat movement–analysis with 'reason'.

The Khilafat movement received a shock when suddenly the Sultan of Turkey fled to Malta. Kamal Pasha, a great revolutionary and a religious reformer, forced the Sultan to leave Turkey. Wars in many ways are nature's way to impose her laws. The cascading effect of the First World War was not only the Russian revolution, it was followed with reformation of religion in Turkey, then centre of the Islamic world. Suddenly both the non-cooperation and Khilafat movements petered out. It had however succeeded in energizing spirits of the nation generated during the movement. The awareness for freedom, built with patience and courage, made people conscious of their power to change. The tremendous energy released by the new spirit of patriotism having thus been fractured, would seek outlet in other areas. Communal strifes appeared to be the best method to express themselves. Reactionary elements, amongst both Hindus and Muslims, were looking for such a situation. Patriotic enthusiasm that had united both communities to work for a cause, was drowned in communal clashes. Men of wisdom thought, why religion from time to time, overwhelms and possesses the mind of a people who took pride in heterogeneity and openness?

So the frustrated spirits of the people found fulfilment in communal strifes. This suddenly engulfed the country, making Gandhi a sad man. The Muslim League and Hindu Mahasabha, born during the war years of 1914-18, again became active. The growing feelings of a common nationhood, were again dimmed. Those who encouraged this tendency were the very same who were never tired of glorifying the past. They kept supporting their thinking amongst illiterate masses with supernatural myths, as historical happenings. Gandhi tried to intervene and retrieve the situation. He undertook a fast of twenty-one days at Maulana Mohammed Ali's house against the inhumanities committed during the communal rioting. The feelings at that time ran so high that his efforts failed. Gandhi reluctantly, but temporarily, disassociated himself from political work. Instead, he got busy with constructive work. This included spinning Khadi, village industries, Harijan welfare, and removal of 'untouchability'. His mind was however busy planning the next move. He only marked time, waiting for an opportunity when the people would be ready for action.

In an age when knowledge rules, reason holds the key to chronic problems. We are aware how religions are strengthened by faith. The myths, created by the priests, hold a grip over the minds. It begins to believe abstract notions that are contrary to reason. At a time when science had not been able to discover the causes, reason was helpless before faith. As knowledge unfolds different phenomenon, faith replaces reason. We reiterate its commitment only when it stands the test of reason. India's divergent customs, with people holding numerous beliefs, demands a sharpness of mind to reiterate the tradition of great Indian kings, confronted with a similar situation.

Gautama Buddha, during his life and his disciples after his death, preached reasoning as means to social harmony. Buddhist councils used to be regularly held after his death in different parts of the country including Kashmir. After Gautama, Ashoka, in ancient India, was guided by a similar practice. He would encourage debates and meetings, keeping himself interested in all religious activities, participating equally in all of them. In medieval India, Akbar was careful to treat all religious communities in his kingdom with equal regard. He would invite their learned to hold debates, with himself presiding over them. He would always apply reason instead of believing in tradition to solve difficult problems posed by religious priests. In present times, there is a revolution in communication technology. Truth is easily ascertainable; when exposed amongst opposing elements, with initial reticence, it is accepted. The old practice of debates and dialogues, will continue to be needed to strengthen reason. These are questions answered by the wise of every age in different ways. Without going too far back in the past, modern civilization considers that religion is not just a matter of faith. It includes culture, habits, beliefs and prejudices prevalent in society. Gandhi practised this philosophy and followed it throughout his life. Others, in the name of religion, only consider it a matter of faith alone. Gandhi had a knack of mixing religion and politics. It is true that religion and politics, to serve society, are best kept separate. For this to succeed, education, that enables the use of logic and reason, is an essential pre-condition. Intentions and purpose are important to decide its worth. Gandhi, at that point of history when illiteracy widely prevailed, mixed politics with religion, to unite the two major communities of India for the freedom struggle. Perhaps it was the only alternative.

The opportunity appeared in a letter from the viceroy that informed about the visit of Simon Commission. The forces unleashed during non-cooperation movement were only temporarily lying low. The fire within just needed another spark to ignite. Gandhi drew a new blueprint for the movement. Its philosophy lay in breaking the law without breaking heads, as had happened at Jalianwala Bagh and Chauri Chaura. He would himself take command of breaking the law with his trained lieutenants from the Sabarmati Ashram, seeking only moral, support from the people.

In the history of revolutions, the Dandi march goes down as a tale of right against wrong, a struggle between the spirit of the oppressed with the arrogance of the oppressor. The importance at once grows when an assessment is made of the results achieved without using violence. It infused a kind of zealous courage amongst the people of the country with a firm curiosity for liberty. A silent revolution spiritually united both rural and urban India. If asked to name the most crucial and historic incidence in the struggle for Indian independence, it would be Gandhi's Dandi march!

The mid-night arrests—an artist's (V. Masoji) impression. Masoji accompanied Gandhiji on Dandi march.

All India Congress Committee Session on August 8, 1942—drawn by Babu Herur.

Chapter XLI
The Silent Revolution
Dandi March

Generations to come, it may be,
Will scarce believe
That such a one as this
Ever in flesh and blood
Walked upon this earth.

—Albert Einstein
(on the death of Gandhi)

Gandhi had gradually created the grounds to usher in change. By far, he had succeeded in rousing the masses against injustice. They had been bearing this humiliation for centuries. Educated people were tired of talking from different platforms, seeking redress to their annoyance and discontent. Exasperated, they wanted a command for action. Gandhi could read this from the restlessness on their faces. Finding the conditions conducive, he immediately started dropping ominous hints of an impending struggle. He said, "A man who is made for freedom has got to take tremendous risks and stake everything." The air of dissatisfaction that was prevailing in the country, only needed action.

Preparations for the march

We noticed earlier how international circumstances necessitated slowing down of the non-cooperation movement. The first requirement had therefore to be to rejuvenate it. Feeling the economic pulse in favour of the poor, Gandhi had been for quite some time demanding withdrawl of the tax on salt. Gandhi now sent an eleven point ultimatum to the Viceroy saying, "if you cannot see your way to deal with these evils and my letter makes no appeal to your heart, on the 11th day of this month, I shall proceed with such co-workers of the Ashram as I can take, to disregard the provisions of the Salt Laws."

The Viceroy's reply was cold and curt. That was signal enough for action. Gandhi decided that he, along with a few of his followers from the Ashram, would march a distance of 200 miles in Gujarat. Reaching the small town of Dandi by the side of the sea at Dandi, they would defy the law by making salt themselves.

Gandhi selected seventy-nine of his co-workers from the Ashram in the age group of 16–61. They included Khadi students, graduates of Gujarat Vidyapeeth, untouchable weavers, a former postal worker from Burma, a dairy expert, a dyeing teacher, an editor, and a Sanskrit scholar in charge of the Ashram tannery. Being entirely a male dominated team, women of the Ashram clamoured to join in the march. Gandhi, in his characteristic humour told the women inmates that, "I must be considerate to the opponent. If we put women in the front, the Government may hesitate to inflict on us the penalty that they might otherwise inflict. A delicate sense of chivalry is what decides me against including women in the first batch."

The Dandi march

The twentieth century saw two historic marches that changed the history of their countries. Both were led by great revolutionaries of the age, but their methods differed. The Long march led by Mao Joe Tung of China in 1934 along with his Red Army, was a guerilla war wherein force was used against the enemies of revolution. The Dandi march led by Gandhi in 1930 was a non-violent and disciplined struggle in self surrender. The objective of both was to force change in their respective countries. One was a conventional revolution, witnessed in the world from time to time; this was imaginative, original and first in the field of revolutionary movements.

On 11 March 1930, Gandhi gave his parting message before leaving the banks of Sabarmati. He said, "Our case is strong; our means the purest and God is with us. There is no defeat for satyagrahis, until they give up the truth themselves. I pray for the success of the battle which begins tomorrow." Gandhi gave instructions that in case he was arrested, Abbas Tyabji would lead the march; if he was also arrested, then Sarojini Naidu would lead.

What was the difference between the two marches? The Long march excelled in inflicting suffering on the enemy; the Dandi march was prepared for self-suffering for the cause that was, for them, right.

The seventy-nine followers in the march left for their fateful journey on 12 March. On the entire route, there was delirious excitement amongst the villagers. Roads through which the party was to pass, were swept by village folks and water sprinkled for the dust to settle. It was like celebrating a festival. People waited for arrival of the party patiently with reverence. Homes on the wayside were decorated with flags, prepared from green mango leaves. Just as a bride's father waits to welcome the bridegroom's marriage party villagers waited for Gandhi walking his way, staff in hand, clear eyed, firm in steps and determination in his entire being.

Travelling twelve to fifteen miles a day, the party would camp in the night under mango groves near villages, cooking their own provisions. Equipped entirely with their own camping kits, they erected their own huts with palm and date leaves. As the party proceeded towards their destination, the message of non-cooperation and civil disobedience spread through the whole country. In the camp, volunteers talked to people on social evils and their eradication. In the evenings, volunteers and the villagers assembled for prayers. There, the list of satyagrahis, arrested by the police during the day was read out in the dim lantern light. With each preceding day, the enthusiasm of the crowd on the wayside villages and towns, kept swelling until it developed into a hurricane.

The two hundred mile march, from north to south of Gujarat ended on 5 April. Next day Gandhi took his volunteers to the sea. The party, led by Gandhi, broke the salt law by picking up salt on the seashore. There was no police, no resentment from authorities and no blood letting. Yet, the effect proved to be a silent revolution. Its psychological effects were to change the destiny of the subcontinent. The non-violent and peaceful breaking of the law sent the entire country into patriotic ecstasy. Each day, Gandhi visited surrounding villages and gave the message and meaning of civil disobedience. He brought home to the people that the 1920 call for non-cooperation was just a preparation; the 1930 movement had to be final.

While peace prevailed around Gandhi, the entire country was suddenly excited with enthusiasm. The government had not expected such a sudden uprising amongst them. It now woke up to meet the growing challenge with all its might. In Peshawar, the military opened fire causing many deaths. There was firing in Karachi, Patna, Madras and several other places. Gandhi continued with his aggressive defiance the of law. He had prepared a note for the viceroy. Before its delivery, he was arrested while fast asleep in the camp on his way back. (see illustration)

Next day, India woke up to the news of his arrest. The country reacted sharply to it and people all over the country came out on the streets shouting slogans against the government. Nearly 50,000 workers of the textile industry immediately went on strike. The railways later joined it. Government servants and other honorary government appointees resigned from their jobs. Outside the country, American clergymen urged the British Prime Minister "to come to terms and save a catastrophe for mankind".

The entire country demonstrated a patriotic spirit never experienced before. They were all ready to follow Gandhi. People were all in a mood to stand every trial at the call of Gandhi. Each morning men and women went around their villages, towns and cities singing patriotic songs in different regional languages. As a young boy, I vividly remember the sense of excitement, honour and pride to be a part of such 'Prabhat Pheris' (morning rounds). The parents would encourage their children to join the small group. They expected no reward and their names never appeared anywhere. There was only one objective with which the towns and cities were tied together. There was an invisible bond of affection between all. A tricolour flag in hand, singing a song popular during those days, we took round of sections of the town, delivering Gandhi's message of ending British rule.

Avatar Mahatma Gandhi hain,
Bharat Ka Bhaar Utarun ko.
Shri Rama ke saath mein Laxman thay,
Shri Krishna ke saath mein Baladao.
Shri Ram ne mara Ravan ko,
Shri Krishna ne mara tha Kansa.
Ab Gandhi parghat bhaey jag mein,
Is Government ke maran ko.

(Gandhi an incarnation is,
To unburden Bharata's load of misery.
If Laxman accompanied Rama,.
Baladao with Krishna was,
With Gandhi, Nehru is,
For ending this ruthless rule.)

The rebel and prophet

The silent revolution started by Gandhi with his Dandi march and the discipline exhibited by his followers at once generated a spontaneous spirit amongst the people. It gave a new hope and self respect to a battered and oppressed nation. Having practised his weapons of non-violence in South Africa, he found them to be most suitable in the Indian environment. In this respect, Gandhi became the greatest political leader of the age. He understood the minds and moods of his people as none before him had done. As a practical man of wisdom, he exemplified the principles of Christianity that formed the basis of western civilization. In the choice of his weapon, he selected non-violence, the spirit of ancient India. Gandhi did not quarrel with the facts. Instead, he used them for his purpose. The usual revolutionary practice of employing militancy and violence, he realized, was not conducive to the nature and temper of India. India, from the ancient past, has been always averse to violence. Consistent with the nature of the people, Gandhi developed the principle of non-cooperation. Simultaneously, it touched the Christian chord of the rulers.

Modern culture came into shape during the twentieth century after three bloody revolutions. The first was the Russian revolution of 1917 led by Lenin; the other was the Chinese revolution in 1934 commanded by Mao Joe Tung. They were based on the political philosophy of Marx and Angles. Both were bloody changes that caused misery to millions, destroying their cultures and dramatically changing their lives. The third revolution, brought about by Gandhi in 1930 was unique from the other two. It brought on centre-stage, a projection of Indian culture in truth and non-violence against the democratic traditions of justice and fair play of rulers. In the past, Indian traditions and thinking had never extolled the ways of war. Its culture considered that a hero was one who renounced the good things of life rather than a victorious king who had killed countless sons of the soil to achieve success.

Mission achieved

Within two decades, Gandhi had achieved his mission. He had brought awareness to a crestfallen nation. He had brought them at the gates of liberty. From now on it was only a matter of time when freedom bells would ring announcing independence. The thirty-five million Indians could see the golden rays of the rising sun of independence. For the next couple of years there would be missions arriving from England to discuss modalities of self-government. There would be conferences, debates, dialogues, constitutional changes, and delegation of power to Indians. This would go on until the commencement of the Second World War in 1939 when Britain herself got busy with its own survival.

We may recollect how, ever since the Renaissance, Indian intellectuals and political leaders had been trying to inspire the rural masses. Thus far, they could only succeed in bringing to their fold the urban educated. Gandhi, during his travels had seen the indifference of village India. So far, masses living in villages remained largely, unaware. Gandhi, after the Dandi march, succeeded in bringing a silent revolution. Unlike the other two revolutions that changed the culture of their respective countries, Gandhi succeeded in achieving the objective without disturbing the civilizational continuity of India.

The Congress session in 1934 indirectly confirmed that his job was now over. This was proved when Gandhi introduced an amendment to a resolution that for his "experiment of non-violence in thought, words and deed, I need complete detachment and absolute freedom of action". Instead, the amendment was modified. Instead of truth and non-violence, the committee amended it with 'peaceful and legitimate'. This was a simple test of Congress sincerity towards the principles so dear to him. Gandhi's amendment was surprisingly not accepted by the Congress Committee. Non-acceptance was the acid test in which the Congress perhaps failed him. Gandhi resigned from the Congress. Henceforth, he would only be their advisor. Gandhi, after the Dandi march, had fulfilled the mission destiny had allotted. He awakened the Indian masses from centuries of despondent slumber, infusing a new zeal for action; boldness to face violence and a confidence that freedom was in sight. He broke the myth of invincibility of British imperialism. The next ten years followed with bitter communal clashes that could make even savages grin at their moderation. Once successful in exciting the masses, the leaders themselves were unable to control the gene they had released. The contradiction of the past, Gandhi was trying to bring together, lay in pieces. Merchants of hate, operating on both sides, had led people on to the garden path.

Chapter XLII
Beginning of The End

We must know that war is common to
all and strife is justice; and all things come
in to being and pass away through strife.

—Heraclitus

During the early period of the sixteenth century, European nations established their empires all around the world. Knowledge of science and spirit of adventure, had enabled Britain, France, Holland and several other countries, conquer distant lands. They freely exploited the natural resources of their colonies to get rich. Germany was one large European nation that continued creating wealth through self-effort. Soon, pursuit of science and agriculture helped the fatherland to produce more than it could consume. She also needed a market not only to sell her surplus, but also to import raw materials. So had started the World War (1914-18). Germany was defeated in the war by the collective strength of UK, supported by resources from the colonies and the USA.

A nation, developed in almost all branches of human endeavour, could not digest this defeat. Within a short period, she regained her strength as a leading European nation in arts, sciences and philosophy. Students from all over the world now came to German universities, in the same way as, nowadays, they go to the United States. Nature produced Adolf Hitler to impose her immutable laws. Hitler harnessed the unquenchable thirst of Prussian warriors from the province of Germany to challenge Imperial nations again. On 1 September 1939, the Second World War started.

This would ultimately hasten the destruction of the evil of Imperialism.

An English poet WH Auden has described how Nature sends evil, to destroy evil—In his poem, "1st September":

Find what occurred at* Linz,

What huge imago made.

A psychopathic god;

The public and I know.

What all school children learn,
Those to whom evil is done
Do evil in return
But who can live for long

In an euphoric dream;
Out of the mirror they stare
Imperialism's face,
And the International wrong.

(*A port on river Danube in Austria where Hitler was born.)

High road to freedom

The Dandi march succeeded in awakening a silent, non-violent revolution in the masses. It was now not confined to the educated middle class. The Gandhian light had illumined Indian hearts in the remotest corner of the country. Everyone was inspired with the spirit of patriotism; they longed, now, to suffer for the cause. The whole world wondered how a frail little man, could convert Indian inertia and inaction into a source of strength and energy? What was so revolutionary in preparing a pinch of salt by the seaside with a batch of a few disciplined volunteers that fired the imagination of a subcontinent?

The answer lay in his complete understanding of Indian masses, their culture, their religious understanding, indeed their core characteristics. Gandhi totally identified himself with them. Having spent a good part of his early years in South Africa, studying ancient Indian and western literature, he applied their ideals and methods to harness the suppressed energies that lay dormant within the people. Gandhi, through his personal examples, aroused their moral sense of self-suffering giving it the name of 'Satyagraha'. Gandhi did not quarrel with facts, but used them for his purpose. Instead of an aggressive and militant struggle, he built a movement of non-cooperation based on the passivity and endurance of the people. In the last twenty years of his public life, amongst Indians from different states, he had analysed their potential as well as weakness. The novel method of Satyagraha fitted the culture and temperament of the people.

The awakening and elevation of spirit, brought reminiscences of the Golden Age. As if by magic, the atmosphere of the country was completely transformed. A spirit of sacrifice possessed each individual. Hatred amongst each other was replaced with love; fear was replaced with fearlessness; and killing with dying. To a people, long oppressed, there at last arose hope. It was like a bewildered traveller, who, struggling on the long, serpentine and high road, finds himself at the top of hill. Suddenly, he clearly sees his destination, down in the valley!

Non-violence in a violent world

Before Gandhi experimented with his new technique of non-violence, the world knew only one kind of revolution. It was to kill or be killed. Gandhi's revolution was about elevation of the spirit in man. Gautama Buddha and Jesus Christ used this science. Gandhi followed their example. He cared for the sufferer as much as for the one inflicting suffering. Throughout the non-cooperation movement, he always preached love for the people of Britain. It took the country six to seven years, punctuated by communal rioting to develop non-violence. The role of civil disobedience in Gandhi's armoury was a well thought out plan. After breaking the civil laws, Gandhi would offer himself to be punished and sent to jail. This strategy, in due course, removed the fear and stigma of jail. It broke the first link in the chain that had restricted 'political advancement' amongst the urban middle class.

The five years that followed the Dandi march were decisive. The entire country was delirious for participation; everyone, irrespective of the community he belonged, humbly sought participation. The farmers in the countryside burnt their crops to come to the adjoining towns to join the struggle. Men and women would come out shouting slogans against the government, voluntarily facing police lathis and bullets. The movement of non-cooperation and boycott of foreign goods was revived with renewed vigour. The rich would refuse paying taxes and the poor farmers, their land revenue. Women, bringing the state revenue down, picketed liquor shops. As agitation reached a climax, the Gorkha military refused to open fire on the unarmed satyagrahis. They would rather face court martial than fire on their own people. The British, Indian ICS bureaucrats, and their subordinate officers were socially boycotted.

The 'silent revolution' lasted for a brief period. It compelled the government to start the process of negotiations. From now on, freedom remained only a matter of time.

The changing scene

The world political scenario was undergoing a rapid change. It was overwhelmingly turning towards aggression and war. Hitler in Germany, Mussolini in Italy, and Japan in the East, were unleashing aggression in their regions of influence. In India, the new generation leaders like CR Das, Subhas Chandra Bose, and Jawaharlal Nehru were influencing Congress decisions. Gandhi's weapon of non-violence, to some, appeared too weak to be successful in a world where power of the gun ruled. Within fifteen years, Gandhi had brought a nation of 350 millions at the gates of freedom against the most powerful country of the world. He had performed the duty destiny had allotted him. It was time for others to take charge. An ancient philosopher, Empedocles, two thousand years ago had said:

"The change in this world are not governed by any purpose, but only by chance and necessity. There is a cycle when the elements have been thoroughly mixed by Love, strife gradually sorts them out. Again: when strife has separated them out; Love generally unites them."

Prelude to Independence

India was now impatient. The situation in the world was quickly changing. Imperialism was not tolerable to Indians. There was now a transformation in the British policy. It was a twilight period between slavery and freedom. After negotiation with Indian leaders, Britain came out with the Government of India Act, 1935. It was a step forward towards self-government. The Act, along with the communal award, provided for elections to Provincial Legislatures in British India, leaving princely states to govern themselves.

The first elections were held in 1936. There were in all 1585 seats based on separate electorates. There were 402 seats reserved for the Muslim community. Congress fought 1161 and won 716 seat in five states; Muslim League won 109 seats. The states of UP, MP, Bihar, Orrisa and Tamil Nadu gave a clear majority to the Congress. Sindh and Bengal had a coalition and Punjab a Unionist government. In North-West Frontier Province, a Muslim majority state, it was a Congress government. India was one nation during the first assembly elections with two major communities sharing power, until fault lines that developed during the functioning of legislatures, broke the hearts of togetherness. Britain, playing politics during this crucial phase, cared only for her narrow self-interest. By the time she realized that she was playing with fire, it was too late. The die was cast.

In the working of provincial assemblies, particularly in states where coalitions were formed, there was intense bargaining to share power. Double talk, bargaining on numerical strength, broken promises and distrust, broadened differences. In retrospect, this period may be termed as the one when the feeling of partition developed into a passion. So far it used to be casually discussed. From now on, it was used as an instrument to generate fear amongst the minorities. To strengthen their position, leaders of minorities themselves generated this fear. It is noteworthy that all Muslim majority states, now a part of Pakistan, did not initially favour the Muslim League and therefore, partition. It was the fear-complex amongst Hindu majority provinces that Muslim League won overwhelmingly. Posterity, for partition, will blame leadership of the period for their inability to rise above their petty, castes and egoistic nature. Leaders would neither listen to what Gandhi advised or what sociology taught. First, let us see what Gandhi said:

"Hindus, if they want unity amongst different races, must have the courage to trust minorities. Adjustment is only possible when the more powerful takes the initiative without waiting for a response from the weaker."

Social science advises that "in a democracy, majority rules but the rights of minorities are preserved."

Results of the elections in 1936, proved to be so. Muslim majority provinces being secure in majority, did not care for partition. The Muslim minority provinces however dreaded, being overwhelmed by the majority, and voted for partition. The fault lay with the manner of functioning of the state legislatures after 1936 elections when the two basic principles were ignored.

Glimpses of democracy

Kings have from ancient times, governed Indian people. Britishers were witness to the pomp and show of the Mughals. They copied them and lived in the same style when posted East. This example made the seat of power, a hallowed centre of authority, that generated fear in the common person. With the entry of the elected representatives of people in legislatures, the standard of glory at once fell down. The urban and rural population that had voted came to see their representatives for removal of their grievances. Often some of them came to see their representatives seated in the hallowed chambers, debating schemes for their welfare. The British and Indian bureaucrats, who had so far enjoyed unlimited powers and authority over their destiny, were now looking towards the Khadi-clad, Gandhi cap-wearing, rustic members of the assemblies for instructions. No more were visitors to the secretariat scared of the scarlet uniform-wearing attendants of the sahebs. Instead of the bureaucrats directing the affairs of state, it was now the familiar faces of Gandhi and Fez cap wearing legislators in the assemblies of the country.

The English and Indian secretaries of departments in the secretariats awaited with some anxiety the result of implementation of the new arrangement. Occupying stately rooms, with a hierarchy of subordinates in attendance, they would still enjoy their imported cigars. There was a distinct air of anxiety and despondency in their conduct. Earlier, relaxing and smoking their imported cigars, they placidly used to smoke out small rings in the air; now, the smoke was just exhaled in the thin air. There was a definite streak of concern for the future. In contrast, members of legislative assemblies brought their '*hookahs*'(Indian contraption for smoking tobacco) to smoke in the new surroundings Easier access to the seat of power made the common man shed the fear-complex. It was this fear that had enabled a few thousand Englishmen govern a subcontinent.

The few fateful years, legislatures in different provinces of British India functioned, exposing the inner contradictions of the complex Indian society. The cooperation and emotional coordination between the people and their leaders was no more to be observed in their working. Instead, there appeared an air of suspicion in which interests of the community rather than of the country, came first. As one looked more minutely, elected leaders showed interest in caste and family. It was while running provincial governments in different provinces that the Muslim League found itself weak in bargaining a share in the power. Gandhi was always in favour of granting unqualified trust. His advice was respected, slilently appeared to have been agreed, but never wholeheartedly followed.

The bitterness over power sharing, generated during this period, was to change the destiny of the country. As time began unfolding itself, communal harmony that Gandhi had so assiduously built, began to crumble. He expected Congress to "represent even those who are hostile to it and those who will even crush it if they can. Not until we make good this claim will we be in a position to displace the British Government and function as an independent nation."

This truth is as applicable today, as it was then.

Gandhi, during the later stage of freedom struggle, was increasingly finding himself isolated. By 1938, this fact became apparent during the Congress presidential election. There were two candidates for presidency of the Congress party: Subhash Chandra Bose and Pattabhi Sitaramiah. Gandhi preferred Sitaramiah. He said so in so many words that "the defeat of Sitaramiah would be his defeat". Against clear indications of his will, Subhas Chandra Bose won. It was a symbol of the new mood. It reminds of the lines of Alexander Pope, when he says:

> All nature is but art, unknown to thee,
> And chance, direction, which thou can't see,
> All discord, harmony, not understood;
> All partial evil, universal good;
> And spite of pride, in erring response spite,
> One truth is clear, whatever is, is right.

Yet another remark from Gandhi, giving reference to the wise C Rajagopalachari, shows the pain within when he said, "Independence they (The English) cannot withhold unless Government in its wisdom is as much blurred as Rajaji (Rajagopalachari) claims mine is."

While Gandhi's non-violent policies was getting a cold reception, a storm was gathering in Europe. This would soon engulf the entire world into war.

Germany had not forgotten its humiliation of 1918. It had missed the rush of the eighteenth century to establish colonies in different parts of the world. Now it was a leading industrial nation, desperately requiring '*libensraum* (living space).' Adolf Hitler represented Germany's accumulated anger. The war was nature's way to bring change. Although, Imperial powers represented by UK and France were victorious, they had all grown weak. Post-war, it was impossible to control the awakening within different countries of the empire. The sun of democracy was rising; that of imperialism was setting. In the background of war, was laid the political chessboard. The urge for self-government had started with the formation of the Indian National Congress more than sixty years ago. The Muslim League was another player that was gaining strength into a third force. Each player now awaited the other to make the move.

The political chess-board

The Viceroy made the first move. As soon as war started, Linlithgow, unilaterally pledged India's total support for war. The Congress reacted to the announcement with a call to various provincial legislatures, where it was in power, to resign. This was an indication of the pending confrontation between the two. The country was being geared for a non-violent, non-cooperation movement in the midst of war. Even while Gandhi was pledged to non-violence; the younger generation of Congressmen were not so deeply committed to the creed. There was violence not only abroad but even in the Indian environment. The younger generation was not committed to any ideology but freedom of India from the British rule. This had become clear after the election of Subhash Chandra Bose, a young and dynamic leader, as the President of the Congress. Besides, veteran Congress representatives from south India did not agree with the policy of withdrawal from legislatures in an emergency. They rightly guessed, that if the Congress surrendered power, the other contending force, like the Muslim League, would fill the vacuum created by them.

The Muslim League, not yet possessing sufficient strength as reflected by the elections of 1936, had found an emotional issue to attract the Muslim community. The League declared the Congress announcement to boycott provincial legislators as a Thanksgiving Day. This sent a message to the rulers that the League was with them in their hour of need. It simultaneously considered the time ripe to lay their claim. In its 1940 annual meeting, the League passed a resolution demanding creation of Pakistan. This was to be carved out of all Muslim majority provinces of the country.

Theology, practised as religion is both food for the soul and an art of intoxicating men to make people commit abominable acts their priests/leaders desire. In India, particularly, it is a very powerful weapon. The announcement made by the League touched Muslims sentiments. Surprisingly, while none of the Muslim majority provinces showed any keen interest in the call for Pakistan, it found overwhelming support in the provinces where the Muslims were in a minority.

What was the reason for such an anomaly?

Social scientists are of the view that man, after his need for food, seeks security. Wherever Muslims were in a majority, they did not care for secuirity. It was in the provinces where they were in a minority that the Muslim League's call received the greatest support. Security for the minorities in a society brings tranquillity in relationship. A civilized society cannot stay peaceful if her minorities exist in fear. India suffered in the past; her growth, time and again, was hampered when the wielders or seekers of power, directly or through jugglery of words, disturbed social harmony!

Individual satyagraha

Gandhi, in order to keep alive the spirit of struggle, decided on individual satyagraha. Vinoba Bhave was honoured to be the first. He possessed Gandhi's characteristics. Vinoba started with anti-war speeches, explaining virtues of non-violence to the rural audience. Bhave was soon arrested under the Defense of India Rules. Thereafter, other Congressmen including Maulana Azad, the Congress President, followed. Gandhi now sensed that a grim struggle lay ahead when younger blood would be required to lead the nation. He announced Jawahar Lal Nehru to be his successor.

Thereafter, Gandhi was respected, formally consulted, but hardly understood, and much less followed.

War comes to East

While the war continued with renewed intensity, it soon involved almost the entire world. Germany attacked Russia in June 1941. Japan attacked the US Fleet at Pearl Harbour in Philippines on 7 December 1941. In a swift swipe of a few months, Japan over ran Philippines, Indo-China, Indonesia, Malaya and Burma. The colonies of Britain, France and Holland in the Far East, collapsed before the might of the Japanese. She now stood at the gates of India, threatening the jewel of the British Crown. In a matter of months, Japan had liquidated the empires of powerful western countries. This would trigger the liquidation of the remnants of imperialism.

Britain now desperately needed people's cooperation to resist Japanese from over running east India. Subhash Chandra Bose, was in Japan training the Indian National Army to cooperate with the Japanese for its attack on India. To keep the political situation in the country within control, the British government announced sending a delegation for negotiations with the Indian leaders. The Muslim League had all along been covertly helping the British war effort, giving full cooperation to the government. Its representation in the fighting forces had already exceeded their numerical strength. The Muslim League was therefore quite content playing the waiting game. It deliberately allowed Congress to do the agitating and face consequences involving sacrifice, suffering and antipathy of the rulers. Such a myopic view, of non-participation in the struggle for freedom, grievously harmed the interests of those, whom the League claimed to represent. Even after independence of India and formation of Pakistan, there remained a political vacuum in the mental consciousness of the region. The people, powered by a common culture, living for centuries together, sharing each others happiness and sorrows, could not be isolated from the mainstream of the subcontinent. Non-participation in the freedom struggle may have pleased the British civil servants in India. It struck at the root of a common national purpose. Repeated emphasis on difference in objective gave an erroneous impression. While the Congress was non-violently fighting in the streets of India for independence, the League, guided by design, was opposed to it. This was to create different perceptions about independence and its meaning of freedom! This also became apparent in British and Pakistani civil servants' apathy in Pakistan during the transfer of population.

Nature, after independence, rewarded the two countries with different results. After creation of Pakistan, it was frequently saddled with army dictatorship; violence and further division. India took the road of building her economy, healthcare and education and eradicating her centuries old social aberrations. She had learnt the lesson of living in diverse circumstances peacefully, concentrating on empowerment of the neglected in society. The process may be slow, but it goes on in the right direction. The two roads perused by their leaders, is clearly visible in the comparative progress made by India and Pakistan after more than fifty years of independence.

Cripps' Mission

During the war, as a British colony, India was expected to play a significant role. With Indian textile, leather and jute industries being of world standards, the allied armies depended on her for supplies. So to bring the agitating Indian leaders on the negotiating table, the government in Britain sent a mission under Sir Stafford Cripps, a man of cold logic. He arrived in India on a pleasant

March 1942 day. The proposals he brought from London, were drawn under leadership of Clement Attlee, the socialist leader of the opposition. They broadly provided for establishment of a loose federation of states. There was to be a Constituent Assembly for framing a constitution for the country. It mentioned that "British Policy in India was the earliest possible realization of self-government." It made clear that during the period of war, defence of India would be entirely in the hands of the British government.

Maulana Azad, who led the Congress delegation to discuss with the British mission, at the initial stages of discussions, caused some misunderstanding in the method of functioning of a future National Government. Azad announced that Cripps had proposed a National Government that would function as a Cabinet. Cripps backed out from it. Negotiations ended in failure with Gandhi calling the proposals, 'a post-dated cheque'. Cripps' effort ended in failure.

There was one political leader of vision and foresight from south India, C. Rajagopalachari, who as a member of the Congress working committee, and until recently the Chief Minister of Madras State, proposed acceptance of Cripps' proposals. He brought two resolutions passed by the Congress legislatures of Madras State. One asked a responsible government to start functioning in the state again (this was because, under directive from the Congress working committee, all Congress MLAs had resigned). The other was acceptance of Pakistan as the basis of settlement between Congress and the Muslim League. CWC rejected both the proposals. Rajagopalachari resigned from the Congress Working Committee after his proposal was turned down.

Destiny plays its role in several ways. With hindsight, it is possible that acceptance of the proposals at that time, would have brought out the impossibilities of partition. It would have given time for the colossal change that was to follow. Moreover, the change would have proceeded in as natural a manner as possible. Congress representatives in the south, were able to assess the political condition of the country better than those of north India.

Rajagopalachari was able to distinctly read the writings of destiny much before rest of the Indian leaders.

Cripps' Mission was the first serious encounter between the British and Indian leaders towards transfer of power. It found the hearts and minds of the negotiators full of suspicion towards each other's intentions. Britain had made it clear that until, at least the end of war, she was not prepared to loosen her control. She created differences between the League and the Congress whenever the situation demanded. Congress was suspicious because of its experience after the 1919 War, when earlier promises had remained unfulfilled.

Quit India movement

During the negotiations, the parties concerned discussed each others' position on independence. The Muslim League felt that the best policy for them would be to wait and watch. The League planned to work out how the provisions offered in Cripps' proposals for a loose 'Federation of Provinces' could be utilized to press for its goal; it had reasons to smile when Cripps backed out of a 'National Government' at the centre. It now became imperative for the Congress to continue with its struggle for independence. The war situation offered an opportunity to exert pressure on Britain. Congressmen considered the time ripe for the final blow to Imperialism. While Gandhi was calling his countrymen to mobilize for a movement to end Imperialism, far away in Britain, their Prime Minister, Winston Churchill, was calling his nation to gird themselves and protect Imperialism. He was asking the nation to:

> Come then, let us to the task, to the battle, to the toil-each to our part, each
> to our station. Fill the armies, rule the air, pour out the ammunitions, strangle
> the U-boats, sweep the mines, plough the land, build the ships, guard the
> streets, scour the wounded, uplift the downcast and honour the brave. Let us
> go forward together in all parts of the Empire, in all parts of the island. There
> is not a week, not a day, not an hour to loose.

"Let us therefore so brace ourselves to our duties, and so bear ourselves that, if the British Empire lasts for a thousand years, men will say, 'This was their finest hour.'

The All India Congress Committee passed a resolve on 8 August 1942, asking Britain to quit India. Next day, Gandhi was due to go and meet the Viceroy and challenge him with the resolution. The British governor-general, during those crucial and perilous days, was following Churchill's policy. Before the provincial Congress committees could be informed and opinion mobilized, the British Government in a midnight sweep, arrested Gandhi, the members of the Congress Working Committee, and prominent Congressmen under Defense of India rules. The press was restricted from publishing any news of Congress activities or any of their instructions. It became clear from the intentions of the government that it meant to keep full control and deal with an iron hand with anything that hampered the war effort.

9 August 1942

On the morning of 9 August, leaders being in jails, youths from schools and colleges all over India came out on the streets. In the absence of any guidance, they stoned and damaged telegraph, telephone and electricity poles. Anything that represented authority became their target. British soldiers patrolled the streets to display their strength. The first few days of the movement were a sporadic expression of enthusiasm, anticipation and anger. There was no planning or objective in the demonstrations. Since the leading city Congress leaders were under arrest, there was a vacuum in leadership. Besides, the Muslim League having other ideas, it refrained from the movement. In the absence of any programme and devoid of guidance, but full of patriotic spirit, the youth did what they thought Gandhi would have liked them to do.

Their's was a spontaneous upsurge; like a volcano ejecting lava on eruption. Demonstrations, slogan shouting, and clashes with the police and military were a manifestation of the anger at the arrest of their national heroes. To them, Gandhi's practice of non-violence meant damaging government property and hindering normal life. This appeared the only way to release their suppressed emotions.

The government on its part was equally determined to crush opposition in any form. Police would resort to lathi charge, firing and other tough measures. Within a month of such disturbances, the situation cooled down. There were individual acts of heroism on both sides. In one instance, in which the writer was involved as a student in Kanpur, a large batch of students marched towards the area inhabited by English managers of textile mills. Without any former plans, each one began to attack government property. Suddenly, trucks loaded with British army men passed the crowd. They had their rifles aimed at the students. Scared, the boys melted away only to reassemble after the truck had passed. The soldiers knew how not to provoke leaderless youths!

Meanwhile, other patriots worked out plans to continue the movement with better organization and planning. Jayprakash Narayan, a young socialist, showed the way. He went underground and started guerrilla campaigns. Senior students from various colleges and universities took part in these activities engaging the entire Government machinery. The police and army would open fire on the demonstrators; it would search for underground 'saboteurs', arrest and punish them. The secret service would keep a constant vigil on the youth. In the absence of Congress leadership, the mob usually turned violent, receiving bullets from the police and the army in return.

At a time when the Japanese were knocking on the eastern gates of India, maintenance of law and order was both a compulsion and responsibility of the government. The freedom movement was brought under control with a heavy hand. This had become an urgent necessity for the government to be able to continue war production in civil and military establishments. Their highest priority was to keep allied armed forces in different places of war, adequately provided with food and clothing.

World history shows that political divisions are a result of ambitious leaders, seeking personal revenge of some kind or the other. The quest for glory by great warrior kings and generals has led in the past to great human tragedies. With prominent congressional representatives in jails, the Muslim League, found itself master of the situation. Thus far, they were merely playing their waiting game. Continuing with their policy of cooperation with government, the League, to catch the imagination of the Muslim masses in North India, intensified its demand for Pakistan. This was necessary to broaden their base amongst the Muslim community. Now, when Congress leaders were in jails, it was easy to accomplish the task. The campaign of hate thus started, which disturbed the social fabric of the nation. Soon others found the policy paying rich dividends. It also weakened the Congress movement. During street demonstrations, the slogan-shouting groups of both sides would often clash with each other making the rulers laugh at the situation.

The divide and rule policy was making maintenance of law and order easy for the British. It was however creating a far more dangerous demon of communal rioting. The divide so created, led to repeated communal tensions. The League leadership's introduction of religion in politics, especially during the period between 1942–44, saw its popularity graph rapidly rising. The divisive course taken up by the League got them gains, but with it grew a distorted desire for liberty amongst their followers. The goal of two political parties was entirely at variance; one cared for all; the other, for religious autocracy. The atmosphere created by the League infected other communities. Hindu organizations saw their opportunity to broaden their base. Instead of pursuing the goal for freedom, each one was engaged in serving their petty projects. The Quit India movement was a constitutional, non-violent, struggle. The cause required a display of unity amongst all people of the country. Instead, there was not only total disunity, but an organized campaign of suspicion, artificially generated by the government. The seeds of hate sown would be ready to yield their ugly fruits in due course. One of the greatest human tragedies would befall the entire subcontinent.

Glimpses of war years

In the subcontinent, during the years of war, even when political reactions were often disturbing, civil and military establishments worked twenty-four hours a day, seven days a week. What was the secret of such an enthusiastic response from the people to cooperate in the war effort? Inspite of an undercurrent of anger against the government, why were people generally devotedly working on their duties?

India is a land of contrasts where contentment in everyday life dominates the senses. Her people believe in diversity and hence freedom to pursue any path. To be content with little is in her people's very nature. This has been the secret of happiness of her people. An average Indian, during the years of war, considered Britain to be fighting a war for her existence. She could not do anything more than to concentrate on its successful conclusion. Besides, it provided them work and wages. Economics moves man more. Co-operation coupled with agitation; the message that India could no more be kept in bondage reached powers that be. Those engaged in moulding the emerging new world from the ashes of the old, knew their time was up.

So near, yet so far

Gandhi, after his arrest, was kept in the Agha Khan palace at Pune for more than two years. During this period, the Muslim League was passively silent. Its policy was to let the Congress do the fighting for them. Indirectly, it meant earning the good will of the rulers. Gandhi, in order to give the League a more positive role, felt it was time to get in touch with Jinnah, the all powerful League leader. He sent a letter to the Viceroy for transmission to Jinnah. The Viceroy, instead of sending the letter to him, released it to the press. That is not so important, as Jinnah's comments after the release of the letter to the press. It speak volumes of the cold calculations that guided him to express such feelings.

Jinnah's press note said, "The letter of Mr. Gandhi can only be construed as a move on his part to embroil the Muslims to come into clash with the British Government solely for purpose of his release."

What will history make of such an insinuation? Was it revenge for a personal humiliation suffered decades ago in 1920 when Jinnah was a Congressman, who considered the Congress party 'a party of gentlemen'? Was it his personal distaste of Nehru, with whom he would not even share a seat in the interim government? Or does the answer lie in an interwiew he gave to a foreign correspondant after the establishment of Pakistan?

The correspondant wanted to know which other leaders of the Muslim League helped him in the establishment of Pakistan? His answer was a cryptic two-worded phrase: "I and my stenographer!"

Lao-Tse, the ancient Chinese philosopher said long ago:

"Man's heart may be forced down or stirred up. In each case, the issue is fatal. By gentleness, the hardest heart may be softened. But try to cut it and polish it, it will glow like fire or freeze like ice."

By 1944, the end of war was clearly in sight. Germany in Europe and Japan in the East, were in retreat. While the war curtains were drawn in May 1945 in Europe, Japanese surrendered when the USA used the atomic bomb a few months later. War had exhausted both the victorious as well as the defeated nations. Gandhi declared that "end of war would make for liberation of all exploited nations of the world." Immediately after the war, general elections were held in Great Britain. To the surprise of the Conservatives led by Winston Churchill, a socialist Government, under Clement Attlee came into power. The new government had earlier pledged to grant self-government to India. They began the process to implement their promise.

Events of history, it may be noticed, have been given greater space in these chapters than the subject deserves. To understand an age or a nation, we must understand its history. This therefore, requires close familiarity with the events and the characters influencing them. This would help in deeper understanding of the nature and culture of the Indian people.

The beginning of parleys

Wavell, the then Viceroy and a soldier of outstanding ability began dialogues with Indian leaders. Initial discussions showed each party holding on to its old prejudices. As a straightforward planner and executor of strategies, Wavell chalked out how power could be transferred without resorting to partition. It was unfortunate that during 1945-46, when the destiny of the country was being decided, there prevailed an atmosphere of suspicion, revenge, personality clashes and trickiness. In spite of marathon consultations, at one point or the other, leaders would find a reason to break off. India never appeared so divided as when the Viceroy wanted to surrender his authority! This was perhaps the darkest period when a honest soldier, with sincere intentions, was considered a villain.

The government in London announced elections to the central and provincial legislatures to enable them to assess afresh the respective strength of the Congress and the Muslim League. The elections kept politicians busy with explaining to the people what was going to be good for them.

The result of the elections in 1946 was to prove to be the year of destiny for India. The fate of the subcontinent was decided by events that occurred during this momentous year.

Chapter XLIII
End of an Empire

The United States of America established her influence as a super power to end World War II, using the atomic bomb. This incident conveyed the fallibility of human existence. Great Britain used the charm and will-for-achievement of Admiral Mountbatten to liquidate its empire in India. Both, not only brought misery to millions, the impact they have had on humanity at large, have been colossal. Transfer of power, like the early end of war, had one thing in common. The wise of both countries did not care for its impact on the future of humanity—narrow patriotism that could not foresee beyond the moment. When truth looks like untruth and vice versa, the rulers are apt to be confused. To know the true course to be followed in matters of far reaching significance, use of logic and intelligence for the right course of action does not suffice. In spiritual terms, it is determined by results. The result, whether it is true or untrue, is determined by its universal beneficence, the greater good of humanity. Even if it is true in the immediate present but is not in the interest of humanity, it is untrue.

Empires die when exhausted. Empires of Ashoka and Chandragupta II in ancient India, the Sultanate and the Mughal Empires in medieval times and the British Empire in 1947 ended when their course was exhausted.

Wisdom and expediency

Men of wisdom and experience wanted transfer of power from Britain to India to be a gradual affair that would provide time for adjustments. The plan of Britain, the advice of more mature minds, and reaction of elder statesmen in India and Great Britain, was in favour of a phased programme to usher in the complex change. This, they thought, would enable people of the subcontinent to settle down. Confronted with people in a hurry, like an efficient Admiral, Mountbatten charmed his 'enemies', giving them no time to 'regroup their forces'. Ordered to complete an assignment, he did so with speed and alertness in line with his naval training.

The citizens of Britain, through ballot, showed this maturity by practical example. Immediately after the war, Attlee became the Prime Minister defeating

Winston Churchill, who had led them to victory. Committed to Indian independence, Atlee immediately set the ball rolling. The first step in this direction was to ascertain the will of people of India. Ever since the introduction of elections, Hindus and Muslims were separately exercising their franchise. When the first election was held in 1936, the Muslim League had gained phenomenon popularity amongst Muslims. The results of the 1946 elections confirmed identical results. For the Central Legislature, the League won all the reserved seats; Congress getting all but five of the unreserved seats. In provincial elections, held on a wider franchise, the League gained 439 of the 494 seats reserved for Muslims; Congress sweeping the rest. The Congress, in 1946, could form governments in eight provinces; the League, only in Sindh and Bengal.

Post-elections, a grim struggle followed between the Congress and the Muslim League. This was on expected lines. The Muslim League had promised Pakistan to their constituency; the Congress had fought for a united India. The farsighted realism of Congressmen like Rajagopalachari had advised in 1942 that "if Muslims want Pakistan, let them have it". Maulana Azad was proposing that partition, may only follow when trial of a united India is unsuccessful. Gandhi's pledge for a united India was undisturbed. The new Governor General, Lord Wavell, a straightforward soldier, was given the assignment to satisfy both political parties holding diametrically opposite mandates. The initial dialogues held with leaders of different political parties confirmed that an unbridgeable gap existed between the two major contenders. After a few rounds of parleys, it became obvious that the problem was too complicated to be solved by the Governor General alone.

His Majesty's Government in London also realized this position. The government therefore decided to send a high powered Cabinet Mission to examine the complexities and seek a solution acceptable to both so that power could be transferred to Indian leaders at the earliest.

The Cabinet Mission

The Cabinet Mission arrived in India and listened to the different opinions. Maulana Abul Kalam Azad, a learned Muslim scholar, was the President of the Indian National Congress. He circulated a statement prepared by him on the subject. The document reflects the deep study of a scholar and a sagacious political leader. Impressed by the plan, the Cabinet Mission considered the proposals. After detailed considerations, they found it to be closest to the demands of the two political parties:

> I have considered from every point of view, the scheme of Pakistan as
> formulated by Muslim League. As an Indian I have examined its implication

for India as a whole. As a Muslim, I have examined its likely effect upon the future of Muslims in India. Considering the scheme in all its aspect, I have come to the conclusion that it is harmful to India as a whole and Muslims in particular. It is a confession that Indian Muslims cannot hold their own in India and would be content to withdraw to a corner specially reserved for them...To me it seems a sign of cowardice to give up what is my patrimony and content myself with a mere fragment of it. I am one of those who consider the present chapter of communal bitterness and differences as a transient phase in Indian life. I firmly hold that they will disappear when India assumes the responsibility of her own destiny....

Differences will no doubt persist, but they will be economic, not communal. Opposition amongst political parties will continue, but they will be based not on religion but on economic and political issues, Class and not community will be the basis of future alignments and policies will be shaped accordingly...I would say that in any case the nine crore Muslims (total Indian population was 35 crores) constitute a factor which no body can ignore, and whatever the circumstances, they are strong enough to safeguard their destiny.

The Cabinet Mission plan offered to Indian leaders the fundamentals envisaged in Azad's statement. They offered a united India, where Defence, Foreign Affairs and Communications would be under the central Government. The country was to be divided into three groups. The first group would comprise Hindu majority provinces, the second would contain Punjab, Sindh and NWFP and British Baluchistan, where the Muslims were in majority. The third group was to consist of Assam and Bengal where Muslims were in a thin majority. Thus, the Muslim majority would control all the provinces they were in a majority.

The great blackmail

Political leaders of different parties considered the Cabinet Plan in considerable detail. After long discussions and clarifications, the Congress and Muslim League both gave their consent. Gandhi, although not officially involved, gave his indirect consent. Everyone was happy that partition had been avoided.

When everything appeared to be moving in a positive direction, the subtle hand of destiny appeared in all its ugliness. The Congress, after completion of Maulana's term, was to elect a new president. Maulana Azad proposed Jawaharlal Nehru's name to replace him. This was duly accepted and Nehru elected as the new President of Congress. Nehru was now face to face with Jinnah. After formally assuming Presidentship, while briefing the press, Nehru said in answer to a question that "Congress was completely unfettered by the agreement and was free to meet all situations." This in other words meant repudiation of the agreement made in the Cabinet Mission plan already announced by Maulana Azad and informally agreed by concerned parties.

Such a statement, particularly in the year 1946, when only suspicion, egoism, and arrogance governed the minds of Indian political leaders, wrecked everything built so assiduously. Indeed, negative tendencies had taken a strong hold on the minds of leaders that year in which all qualities of leadership were left asunder.

Was it because their physical bodies were getting old and their minds, foggy? Was it because they were all too anxious to enjoy the fruits of their life long labour? Or was it the way all things end? It reminds us of the lines of the poet, TS Eliot:

> We are the hollow men
> We are the stuffed men
> Leaning together
> Headpiece filled with straw. Alas!...
> This is the way the world ends
> Not with a bang but with a whimper.

It had the unintended but disastrous effect on the negotiations. Jinnah promptly called a meeting of the Muslim League and declared that his earlier consent to the proposals stoond withdrawn. Stung by the rebuff, Muslim League declared 16 August as a Direct Action Day. The states in India under the control of The Muslim League were Bengal and Sindh. Hasan Surhawardy governed Bengal, a man used to strong arm tactics and supported by the hooligans of Howrah. Sindh, in the west, had a strong governor who issued strict instructions against any violence. Surhawardy, the chief minister, had prepared the grounds to make the day a turning point of history. He was possessed with a madness like Shakespeare's King Lear:

> I will do such things
> What they are, I know not,
> But they shall be
> The terror of the Earth.

Jinnah had assessed the situation to perfection. He and Surhawardy had anticipated what 16 August had in store for Calcutta on that day. Both were now determined that the violence would ultimately bring the reality of Pakistan before both the Congress and the British government. All along, during the last five-six years, Jinnah had been candid about Pakistan. Yet, none of the Congress leaders could reconcile to the idea or produce convincing alternatives as beautifully as Maulana Azad had done before the Cabinet Mission.

It needed the mayhem of 16 August to wake up the leaders to reality!

The day that was to be a Protest Day against British policy turned into terror and communal carnage. The message it conveyed reached the people it was intended for. From now on, Wavell feared that a civil war, in the near future, could be a reality. The English ICS officers, having realized that their days were numbered, wanted to leave the country at the earliest. The tired leaders understood that a compromise with the League was impossible. If Indian Renaissance had started from Bengal more than a century ago, the stage for partition was ironically set by the Calcutta carnage!

It is an inherent gift in the nature of the Indian people that they tend to forget the miserable quite soon. The 16 August mayhem lasted for three-four days. Even during the worst phase, while the killings went on, men and women of both communities saved the victims from the mad fury. Meanwhile the communal frenzy spread to other parts of Bengal. While leaders were busy tackling the political puzzle, there was one man whose heart bled for what was happening. Like a one-man fire fighting squad, he went where he was needed to provide the healing touch. "Lead kindly light amongst the encircling gloom" was the only message he delivered. With his saintly wisdom and fearlessness, he brought peace and amity wherever he reached. What army battalions could not do in Punjab and Bengal at their worst, Gandhi did all by himself. No one leader had either the patience or the foresight to awaken the true characteristics of kindness and contentment of the Indian people.

Gandhi understood India as no one had!

Abdication of reason and trust

The closing months of the year saw Wavell desperately seeking contending the parties to reach a common ground to start the process of transferring power. However, both the Congress and the Muslim League were so full of venom that alternatives put up with best intentions before them were considered vile, with a hidden meaning in them. Mistrust had overpowered the leaders. They were a tired lot, most of them had at the back of their minds, personal insults inflicted on each other during their long political careers.

How could Jinnah forget the insult in the Congress meeting of 1920 when he was a Congressman? He had just stood to speak that 'illiterate masses were to have no place in Congress' when instead of being listened, he was hooted down. Again, there were old accounts to be settled between Nehru and Jinnah. How could Nehru forget that Jinnah had described him "an arrogant Brahmin, who covers his Hindu trickiness with a veneer of western education?"

So, Jinnah did not trust Nehru; Gandhi and Nehru found Wavell a person 'ignorant of law'; Wavell did not get full support of the British Prime Minister so that squabbling and litigious arguments between Indian leaders could be stopped. The top leadership of the country were obsessed with their prejudices towards each other. During that fateful year, everyone seemed to have forgotten everything of value–wisdom and welfare of the millions who would suffer as a consequence of their shortsightedness in the fateful year of 1946.

After the failure of the Cabinet Mission Plan, the British Prime Minister lost confidence in his Viceroy, Wavell. A Sandhurst-educated Field Marshal, he was no match for the legal wiles of squabbling politicians. As an honest soldier, he was genuinely concerned with the unity and integrity of India. Wavell felt that the Cabinet Mission plan was an ideal solution for the complex problem. Yet, the Congress and the Muslim League, in sheer egoism, unceremoniously dumped it. This decision was to cause suffering to millions. In the coming days, panic, fright and phobia reigned over the minds of the otherwise wise and patriotic leaders.

An Admiral replaces the Field Marshal

The end of war had thrown successful seamen and soldiers out of job. The prime minister was looking around for a suitable viceroy to handle the Indian Independence. Attlee, the Prime Minister, had noticed the speed, determination and charm of Admiral Mountbatten. During the arduous campaigns in South-East Asia, he had succeeded in overcoming odds during crucial battles. He had successfully commanded millions of soldiers and seamen during his campaigns. He delivered what he was ordered to achieve. Besides, he was a cousin of the king. Who could be more qualified to liquidate the king's sovereignty than his own cousin?

The first reaction of the Admiral, who loved sea life, was one of reluctance. Then he thought, "instead of directly rejecting the offer, let me consult the king". He went to King George V and confided in him, "They want me to go to India as a viceroy to liquidate the Empire. Would it not be improper for a member of the Royal family to be so doing; besides, imagine the loss of prestige if I failed."

The king calmly answered with another question!

"How much will it enhance the Royal prestige, if you succeed?"

Viscount and Visountess Mountbatten reached India on 22 March 1947, accepting the great challenge that was to alter the fate of the subcontinent for a few centuries. Before he left, learning from the experience of his predecessor, he had extracted sufficient powers to take on the spot decisions. This was to prove disastrous to the cause. It never allowed time for mature wisdom to consider all the aspects. Besides, he had obtained a firm date for the transfer of power. What Wavell had been repeatedly seeking from the Prime Minster, Mountbatten had in his baggage.

Getting to business

The Viceroy's House, with official and personal staff, employed a staff of nearly 25,000. Out of these, nearly 4000 were directly attached to the household. The first thing Lady Mountbatten did was to dismantle the regal structure. This immediately gave a signal that the Mountbattens had come to end the old Imperial glory. It was a positive sign for the Indian leaders and the people. In less than a week, Mountbatten had streamlined the entire viceregal establishment. He was now ready for the great 'Battle of Wits' with the Indian leaders.

During the five months that he took in formalizing the transfer of power, he used his charismatic personality to hypnotize almost all political leaders. Like a magician, he would use seduction, dissembling, angling, shuffling, and leg-pulling; in fact every trick a magician uses to achieve his objective.

Mountbatten had, within a week, sent invitations to Gandhi, Jinnah, Nehru and other Congress leaders for talks to get a first-hand knowledge of the men and issues he was required to tackle. Military training had taught him to study and understand the men he would be required to deal with. In the first round therefore he concentrated on studying the men who mattered. It was only after this that he worked on the problem, dispassionately and objectively, disentangling one knot after another. In the subsequent round, he was to draw a plan of action with focus on the goal. Once the plan was tested and found to meet the aspirations of divergent views, the final phase would be to forcefully implement it.

The very first meeting of Mountbatten with Gandhi was remarkable in its brevity. Mountbatten casually inquired from Gandhi an alternative to Jinnah's demand for Pakistan. Gandhi, with graceful simplicity, replied, "Invite Jinnah to form the Government, leaving him to decide whether it should be all Muslim or contain both Hindus and Muslims." This very vital remark disentangled the first knot. He was to use this suggestion whenever he was discussing delicate issues with Congress leaders.

"Bapu conceding to give all powers to Jinnah; leaving the vast majority powerless!" The Congress leaders were all 'practical men' who had toiled a lifetime to reach this stage. It was something they could never fathom.

The other two Congress leaders he needed to win over were Jawaharlal Nehru and Sardar Vallabhai Patel. He always found himself at ease talking to Nehru;

with Patel, he was at times tough. In Nehru, he found an openness and could talk frankly, a typically Indian trait where one finds the other side is appreciative of the person. Mountbatten used it at crucial stages when both of them would discuss the problem with frankness. The knowledge so gained allowed him to know more about Indian leaders, their weaknesses and strength. This considerably helped him in his task. Mountbatten always admired the flexibility of Nehru and even confided in him that, "I want you to regard me not as a last viceroy of India, but the first to lead the way to the new India." Mountbatten considered Jinnah cold as ice, but honest in his pursuit of the objective.

Both Wavell and Mountbatten came as viceroys with the brief from the Prime Minister that transfer of power was to be accomplished for a unitary India. Thereafter the Constituent Assembly was to work out its own constitution. In this respect, both of them never wavered. Mountbatten kept pressing the objective. One day, during a discussion in Montbatten's study, Jinnah said with his characteristic clarity and conviction:

"There is only one solution to the Indian impasse: a 'surgical operation'; otherwise India will perish."

Mountbatten, like Wavell and governors of different states, even when convinced of the disastrous consequences of division, decided to go ahead with partition. Once the goal was determined, he pursued it with thoroughness and devotion. After all, he had a deadline to meet. Mountbatten's first loyalty was to his king and the country that had sent him to achieve an objective. As the Admiral of the British Fleet, he would accomplish the assigned task, whatever be the consequences. If history gives us ways of looking at things; ways with no finality, The Bhagwad Gita, for such decisions says:

"Action undertaken from delusion, without regard to capacity and to consequences—loss and injury to others—this is declared to be dark."

Mountbatten had dexterously handled leaders of both the Congress and the Muslim League, who could not fathom the repercussions of their agreement and the impending tragedy. If there was anyone who had an inkling of the deluge that was to follow, they were the English governors of North Indian Provinces and English ICS civil servants of the crown. From time to time, some amongst the well meaning had been conveying to the Governor General at Delhi, how the temperature of communal passion was rising, particularly in Punjab and Bengal. The Viceroy, during his parleys with Indian leaders, would obliquely mention the fact appraising them of these fears. However, events that year were moving faster then the minds of political leaders. Everyone involved had personal targets. The government in Britain had a date to get out of the 'mess'; Mountbatten had his date to join the navy; and political leaders of all hues, had by now, hurt egos. They would refuse to think beyond 15 August 1947.

So be it! Mountbatten had arrived at the conclusion that a division of India was inevitable.

Often the greatest men of history, deliberately acquiesce against their conscience! This was so with the Admiral. Having once decided, he initiated the exercise of partition with full vigour. As a friend of India, he redeemed himself during the crucial negotiations for integration of the Indian princely states. Some of the larger states had been dreaming of an independent existence after 15 August 1947. The Viceroy, with his personality and position, gave the message that the days of princedom were over. This helped Patel and Menon get 'all the apples in the Indian basket'. There was another grave situation where Mountbatten's qualities of leadership saved India from disaster. This was when the Indian administration, under pressure of mass transfer of population, faced a near collapse. During those days of crisis, he employed all his charm, personal charisma and authority to ensure that India came out safe and sound.

The princely games

There are instances, when a deserving player of history, does not find a legitimate place in it. Worldly success seldom comes to such men, but they inspire love and admiration of those with whom they work. Amongst such men was a member of the viceregal staff. This man of wisdom was VP Menon, the Reforms Commissioner. Working for nearly two decades, without being a member of the ICS or any other important central service, Menon with his extraordinary qualities of future vision, advised everyone concerned what was best in the interest of India. Preferring to stay away from the limelight, he had the knack of producing the right solution to intricate problems. He had complete understanding of the complexities of Indian politics. A true son of his country, he admired Patel and often confided in him what lay hidden in the minds of the rulers.

Vallabhai Patel, like Nehru, was close to Gandhi. He looked after the organizational and financial matters of Congress. Menon and Patel often exchanged notes on the future of India. Now that the transfer of power was going to be a reality, it was necessary to be politically alert. The proposed state of Pakistan was to have the two most prosperous and fertile provinces of India—Punjab and Bengal. Menon had a hunch that if, like the division of the country, partitioning of Bengal and Punjab was demanded, Jinnah might be inclined to agree. He floated this information into the ears of both Patel and the Viceroy.

Patel had been in search of an issue to confront Jinnah with his own aberration. Patel and members of the Congress Working Committee felt that once Jinnah was confronted with the division of the two provinces, a large part of the fertile lands would be denied to the proposed state. After all east Punjab and west Bengal had the majority of Hindus. If therefore religion was to be a basis for division of the country, why not the adjoining provinces? Patel moved a resolution in the Congress Working Committee demanding partition of the two provinces. The resolution was adopted. It was significant that Gandhi was not consulted; Maulana Azad, incidentally also happened to be ill on that day. Congressmen fondly hoped that the resolution would deter Jinnah from pressing for Pakistan.

The Congress resolution was taken over by Mountbatten. He confronted Jinnah with his own logic on partition. Thus cornered, he had no alternative but to yield. Now it was the turn of Patel and the Congress Working Committee to be surprised with the new solution. Mountbatten, working on the hunch of his Reforms Commissioner, had brought both the Congress and Muslim League, to agree to transfer of power. It was now time to act quick and fast. Mountbatten was now devoid of any doubt; he was full of confidence. Everything was going his way. Gandhi and Azad, the two exponents of united India were virtually isolated. Patel and Nehru had a feeling of 'good riddance' Jinnah was happy to get more than what he ever dreamt.

Drafting plan for transfer of power

After obtaining broad sanction from Indian leaders, it was necessary that the operation was completed at the earliest. It was now common knowledge that Britain was shortly leaving India. Her authority therefore gradually started declining; the long campaign of hatred had raised the communal temperature. Lawless elements were getting fearless. Even the Viceroy's interim council, comprising of four Muslim and nine Hindu members, only met to disagree on almost everything.

The draft plan was prepared. This was to be sent to London for approval. Menon insisted on a last minute provision. It was to propose that the two dominions would be new members of the British Commonwealth. Working informally behind the curtain, he had earlier obtained the consent of Patel. Jinnah had always been in favour of remaining in the Commonwealth. As for the other two important members of the Congress party, Nehru and Patel, Mountbatten brought them around; explaining its long term benefits. One stroke of genius from Menon had ensured safe passage for the bill in the British Parliament. It would not only get the sanction of the labour party, but also of the Conservative members headed by Winston Churchill.

The clause that the two dominions would remain members of the British Commonwealth of nations was an emotional chord that had its effect. In a record period, the bill was cleared by the British Parliament. Conservative party members had been showing their reluctance in favour of an early transfer of power. The law passed by Parliament fixed the dates of 14 August for Pakistan and the midnight of 14/15 August, 1947 for India. The first Governor General of Pakistan was to be Jinnah; Admiral Mountbatten was to be the Governor General of India.

Miracle of princely states

According to the Act of Parliament, nearly six hundred small and big princely states of united India were to accede to either India or Pakistan. Except for three or four small states that fell within Pakistan, the rest was located in and around India except Kashmir which had borders with both India as well as Pakistan.

To begin the process of integration, Mountbatten, as Viceroy and the King's representative, invited all the princes, formally conveying them to join either of the two dominions. He warned that "if they failed, they would be outside the British Commonwealth and therefore ineligible for future decorations by the King." During informal conversation with the princes, he advised them to willingly accede to India before popular opinion in their states turned unfavourable. This had a positive effect. Most of the smaller states signed the instrument of accession to India.

Menon and Patel were now working in close cooperation to bring together the larger states. Instead of taking up minor issues, they sought accession to India for Defence, External Affairs and Communications. Menon suggested to Patel that Mountbatten may ask the princes to accede to India only on these three subjects. On 25 July, 1947 another meeting of princes was called by the Viceroy. He displaying all his charm, power, influence, diplomatic skill and logical persuasion. Mountbatten advised them that to accede to India was in their interest. He made it clear that on these three subjects they were, in any case, never independent of British India. He made it clear that the offer being made now would not be repeated after 15 August, when he would cease to mediate on their behalf.

The administrative dexterity displayed by Menon; the political wisdom and iron will of Patel, and clear vision of Mountbatten at a critical period of history ensured absorption of all princely states by 15 August. There remained only Hyderabad and Kashmir, whose rulers were still dreaming the golden dream of independence.

With the completion of the stupendous task of integrating the states, India was made into a strong, united and independent country. The disintegration caused by separation was in this manner considerably offset by nearly half of Punjab and Bengal coming to the union of India. The problem of Hyderabad got solved when the over ambitious Nizam and his advisers instigated an internal uprising by the Razakars. To maintain law and order, the Government of India sent the army. In a few days, Hyderabad became a part of greater Andhra Pradesh.

The Kashmir story

Jinnah was confident that Kashmir would eventually accede to Pakistan. He was patiently waiting for this to happen. His prime minister was however anxious to show some genius of his own. The Maharaja of Kashmir, like the Nizam of Hyderabad, dreamt of an independent state. For the plan to succeed, Pakistan, clandestinely, organized Pathan tribesmen from the border of North West Frontier Province and Afghanistan, who suddenly raided Murshidabad in large numbers, ransacked the town and proceeded towards the capital Srinagar. The private army of the Maharaja, on whom he depended for defence of the state, was nowhere to be seen. They had all ran away into the hills to save themselves. The Maharaja, in desperation, sought Mountbatten's help. Only a few weeks back, he had refused even to discuss the issue with him while playing golf. As a constitutional head, Mountbatten advised the Maharaja to sign the instrument of accession to enable India to send her army and meet the challenge. This, the Maharaja did.

The Indian army flew to Srinagar just in time to save the capital from the raiders. They drove off the tribals. Pakistan's political gamble just missed the mark. What followed, still continues to establish Jinnah's theory that Hindus and Muslims are not two communities, but two nations. Kashmir, with an overwhelmingly Muslim population, joined the Indian Union. This was thoroughly unpalatable and against the very basis of establishment of Pakistan. It defied the very basis of Pakistan.

15 August 1947

People of India are remarkably spiritual in accepting both joys and sorrows with equal magnanimity. Because of this attitude in life, they are able to accept change with equal indifference. This is one of the secrets of the continuity of her civilization. On the living surface, they are of the world; within, they remain attached to the spirit. Whether it is their religious philosophy or climate of the country, this duality was evident during Independence Day celebrations. Millions, with broken hearts, were trekking hundreds of miles, leaving behind their homes where they and their ancestors had lived. On the way, seeking safety in the 'otherland', they were confronted with barbaric atrocities that would bring shame to the medieval tribes of Attila and Chengis Khan. Against such a background of misery and terror, people in several cites in India and Pakistan were dancing with joy!

People in cities and Congressmen in Delhi got the first thrill of power. The Father of the Nation, Mahatma Gandhi was lamenting the fate of the Hindus in an insignificant village of East Bengal. Gandhi's non-violent satyagraha could bend the will of the most powerful Empire, but could not influence his own people. Emotional India has faced this enigma in every age. Britain governed India for two centuries. Her governors and ICS officers, in their dispatches, were indicating the bitterness that had grown during the last few years. Besides politicians, there were millions of innocent and voiceless people. They and their leaders, did not fathom what was in store for them. Perhaps exhaustion had overtaken the rulers of a declining empire! In spite of these indications, Mountbatten's casual remark on bloodshed during Partition days, reflects that everyone amongst the decision makers, were in a desperate hurry. To a question before leaving India, he said:

"What did really matter to Indians except independence?"

It is true that she has indeed lived through such massacres before and yet remained unscathed. The dawn of freedom ushered in a new era in which events provided new dimensions and new opportunities. Nature has blessed her people with sufficient tolerance, contentment and capacity for assimilation. This is what her poets sing in their songs:

> On the shores of Bharat,
> Where men of all races have come together,
> Awake, O my mind!
> Standing here with outstretched arms,
> I send my salutations for the God of humanity.
> And in solemn chant sing His praise.
>
> At whose call no one knows,
> Come floating streams of men,
> And merge into the sea of Bharat.
>
> The Aryans, the Non Aryans, the Dravidians,
> The Huns, the Pathans and the Mughals,
> They have all merged here into one body.
> Today the West has opened its doors,
> And from thence come gifts,
> Giving and Taking.

> (Tagore—Translation: A Bose)

Chapter XLIV
A Vision of The Future

> Knowledge is power, but it is power for evil
> as much as for good: It follows that unless
> man increases in wisdom as much as in
> knowledge; increase of knowledge will be
> increase of sorrow.

—Bertrand Russell

When a clerk of the British Parliament said, 'Indian Independence Bill', the Crown clerk replied, 'Le Roi le Veult'.

In four French words, it was all over. The British Imperial power voluntarily abdicated their rule in India on 15 August 1947. The Mughal Empire had died of its own self-inflicted wounds; the British Empire did not fade away like so many others in history. Britain handed over to her successors, two modern functioning and vibrant countries, whose foundations were laid in decency, respect for law and acknowledgement of the universal values of civilization.

Ecstasy and agony

To celebrate the Indian Independence, Jawaharlal Nehru ceremonially released pigeons into the sky. But the Partition split the heart of India into two. The two newly created states suffered one of the greatest migrations of population recorded in world history. During this period of ecstasy, a kind of bewitchment had overtaken people of both the new born states. The two-nation theory, relentlessly followed, succeeded in igniting flames of hatred. It did not just create political division, it vertically split the heart of the nation. A people, living together for centuries in a compact geographical region, speaking similar language, holding identical moral values and a common culture, were suddenly declared to be two separate nations.

Yet, it was no separation but a result of the relentless pursuit of power on the part of the leaders. If religion alone was to be its cause, more than half a century later, there are more Muslims living in India than in either Pakistan or

Bangladesh. Pakistan, with mass migration of Hindus, is bereft of pluralism and secularism that had been the spiritual bond binding the different communities. India, not having shut her doors on its past, enjoys this continuity in political, social and economic advancement. The seed of hatred sown as means to achieve the goal did not end after the establishment of Pakistan. Even when the immediate purpose of hatred was served, bitterness continues the cause of in which lies the means adopted to reach the end.

Means and ends

India and Pakistan have a common civilization. One political party employed religion to serve its political interest. What is simply an ethical framework for conduct of daily life, was used to manipulate public opinion. During the struggle for freedom, the two mainstream political parties, the Muslim League and the Indian National Congress, followed different means to achieve their ends. Instead of participating in the struggle for freedom, the League preferred to let the party led by Mahatma Gandhi, struggle and face suffering. During the freedom struggle, the sly politicians focussed on seeking power, preferred to cooperate and earn the goodwill of the rulers. The large masses, led by Gandhi, laid emphasis on the means. The crafty politicians cunningly left the work of suffering to those who cared for the means. They waited to strike, bidding their time. Therefore, when nationalists were courting imprisonment, suffering humiliations and death, others were earning patronage of the rulers. Nature has not remained indifferent to the practice. Both countries would reap fruits of two diverse policies. India and Pakistan had started their journey at the same time. Within half a century, there is a perceptible difference in their national balance sheet. What is that changed? Why is it that society across the border is not able to come out of feudalism? Why does she still await the birth of democracy and reforms?

The answer to such questions lies in the expediency of politics over principles of morality; it lies in not using the right means to achieve the noble end!

Present scenario

India, with all her complex problems, is engaged in tackling the impediments on the road to progress. Centuries of social and caste differences are dissolving in the race for new knowledge for human welfare. Education at all levels has ushered a silent social and economic revolution. Grave social problems inherited from past centuries are being resolved in a democratic and free environment. To a casual observer, twenty-first century India may give the impression of chaos, even violence. It must however not be overlooked that fighting poverty, eradicating caste discrimination and dominance of feudalism, have long remained neglected. The secular constitution of the country is a source of strength for pluralism and secularism. Old fogeys of the hate brigade do occasionally keep raising their heads only to feel ashamed within themselves later. Their capacity to bluff the innocent masses is gradually fading.

Religion, which politicians used as a department of politics, is being understood in its true perspective. Rather than be a tool to exploit sentiments, it is being understood and regarded as a matter of personal faith!

Science for human happiness

Science has been and continues to be the greatest cause of change. It is enabling us to know the means to any chosen end. Yet, it is helpless to decide the end. It does not possess within it, the capacity to teach us the emotions of sympathy or kindness that nourish human relationship. In a way, science has snatched from us the base of our morality. We see in our daily lives how every one around seems engaged in thoughtless individuality. The more we learn, the less we know. Every new discovery reveals new mysteries and new uncertainties, throwing new challenges. Consequently, the knowledge we derive from science is getting dangerous; it has triggered economic growth, but with it, has also brought economic ills. When ordinary men and women seek redress to these ills, economists suggest still more economic growth as a cure.

In the modern world, men of knowledge are enriching us with new ideas for a better world. The clever and the naive are in power. Men of knowledge have become like the Djinn in the Arabian Nights and are using the ingenuity of such Djinns to strengthen their own position instead of using it for good of the masses. World over, such leaders appear incapable of realizing that they are leading their flock towards disaster.

How then can science be employed in creative pursuits? The answer lies in application of intellectual wisdom, as a guide to action.

Use of intelligence with discretion

Spiritualism is to use intelligence with discretion.

There are signs that western civilization is getting tired of its own achievements. In spite of far reaching developments in the material world, the average man and woman, inexorably yearns for strength of spirit. Science and technology has reduced the youth to prepare for an animal life, caring merely for self-preservation and self-advancement at all costs. The young after a short period of consuming the variegated luxuries of life are confronted with weariness, fatigue, suffering and tedium. As they grow in age, a feeling that all is vanity overtakes them. Science may have thus enormously increased external changes, it has not yet discovered the power of hastening psychological change that develops power of discretion with intelligence. This, in a true sense, is spirituality. To the Indian people, this is a gift of nature.

All men and women, besides material goods, need more outlets for creativity, wider opportunities for joy in living and greater cooperation with his fellow men. More than anything, they need some end outside the life of physical existence. From the dawn of civilization, India has always been devoted to metaphysics. An average Indian understands that personal separateness is an illusion. From childhood he learns from his elders that what exists is a vast evolving and dissolving process that goes on endlessly. Such a philosophy at once takes the mind outside life where suffering and happiness merge. The ancient practice of yoga, meditation and contemplation, are powerful teachers to this end. Even today, these qualities remain a common feature of the Indian way of life.

Interdependence–the key

Philosophers and religious preachers, from time immemorial, have advised that life on planet earth is interdependent. In every age, the message remained in the domain of metaphysical imagination. It was a pious subject of sermons for churches, temples and mosques. In the twenty-first century, all boundaries, natural and human, are being dismantled under force of science. Man is beginning to understand that there are both positive and negative forces acting simultaneously. Virtue exists with evil; love with hate and kindness with cruelty. Such is the fate of humankind. To make human existence less conflicting, a conscious feeling of interdependence at once dilutes the diverging tendencies. Knowledge grows. Man begins to realize its sanctity. Pride in success and achievement is diminished. As the ego in him dissolves, he begins to feel like all others. Then the entire universe starts being a picture of unity.

India, from the ancient past, has been giving the message of 'One World', delivering the mystic consciousness of the Infinite. To explain the phenomenon, poet Tagore says:

"Truth has its nest as well as its sky. The nest is definite in structure; accurate in law of construction.... For some centuries the East has neglected the nest-building of Truth... Trying to cross the trackless infinite; the East has relied solely upon her wings. She has spurned the earth till buffeted by storms, her wings are hurt and she is tired, solely needing help...."

To enable science contribute towards constructive and creative functions, India's spiritual attitude towards life, needs fusion with science. A common man in

India possesses a liberal attitude. He not only tolerates what he likes, but has the capacity to accept what he does not like. A light of this wisdom and knowledge from the East awaits to guide material knowledge towards the call of the spirit!.

Shadows of future

Religious rituals are gradually diminishing as knowledge and science grow and globalization brings different cultures nearer. Closer interaction amongst societies are making political boundaries irrelevant. In due course, this would help strengthen a commonality in various cultures. So far, individuals formed societies; in future, societies will influence the individual. Different societies will cooperate more and more with each other. Present times place considerable emphasis on economic prosperity. This has instilled an unduly large emphasis on producers of wealth and holders of political power, who covertly help them in their socially destructive hypes. Economic progress, to be of service, has to depend more on collective cooperation instead of individual or corporate gains. In future, the creators and possessors of wealth will only get what they help the masses to get. The needs of the latter shall have to be addressed first if they desire their own to be satisfied.

In the new age of knowledge, the principles that governed the Industrial age will have to be forgotten. We now need a philosophy of peace as a normal condition of living in the present as applied to the home, the nation and the world. At present, either economics or political science governs the western social thought. The techniques of peaceful domestic living, for example, have hardly developed. This becomes a major factor of tension.

As societies reach the pinnacle of their glory, they generally begin to suffer from petrification. An arrogance ensuing in a feeling of invincibility and immortality sets in them. This deadens creativity. So went down the Roman Empire, the Caliphate of Baghdad, the Mughals of Delhi and later the great British Empire. In each case, having nourished other forces, they themselves perished.

Buddha in ancient times, Kabir in medieval India, Vivekananda, Tagore and Gandhi in modern India, all emphasized the search for God, Truth and Beauty (*Satyam, Shivam, Sundaram.*). They all preached and practiced an instinctive union with the mainstream of life that guides material life. India is now entering an exciting passage of history. She is making all efforts to possess the experience of modern 'nest-building.' Arts and sciences are being fast developed in the hands of the new generation. A vibrant politics and good governance are on the national agenda. India, with the help of new knowledge will be able to reconstruct her 'nest', walking on the high road of intellectual advancement along with economic progress. This is what the poet 'Tagore' hints at in the example of the bird and her nest. While it is the natural tendency of a bird to fly over the vast sky on her wings, rebuilding the nest for rest after the flight is equally necessary. Having had enough of flying in the sky, India is presently engaged in reconstruction of her nest. She may often appear slow, but like a lumbering elephant, she shall get along majestically. She has one unique advantage. Her spiritual power, gained during flights in the sky, keeps casting a cold gaze over death, mortality, war, narrow nationalism and geopolitical border disturbances. Contradictions and chaos often visit her. But the creative forces outgrow them to write new history. India, walking on the high road of intellectual advancement with economic progress, shall be a equal partner in any global economic adventure. Her spiritualism will help to counter mortality, war, narrow nationalism, and open up vistas of a world without borders. It will thus help create 'One World and One Humanity'. India shall then turn truly ageless and towering like the great Himalayas. Then will start yet another cycle— like that of Khalil Gibran's "The Man" reminding us of the eternal truth:

> I heard the teachings of Confucius;
> I listened to Brahma's wisdom;
> I sat by Buddha under the tree of knowledge.
> Yet here I am, existing in ignorance
> And heresy.
>
> I gathered wisdom from quiet India.
> I probed the antiquity of Arabia.
> I heard all that can be heard,
> Yet, my heart is deaf and blind.
> I was here from the moment of the
> Beginning, and here I am still.
> And I shall remain here till the end
> Of the world, for there is no
> Ending to my grief-stricken being.